COMMON READING

COMMON READING

~

CRITICS, HISTORIANS, PUBLICS

Stefan Collini

OXFORD
UNIVERSITY PRESS

OXFORD
UNIVERSITY PRESS

Great Clarendon Street, Oxford OX2 6DP

Oxford University Press is a department of the University of Oxford.
It furthers the University's objective of excellence in research, scholarship,
and education by publishing worldwide in

Oxford New York

Auckland Cape Town Dar es Salaam Hong Kong Karachi
Kuala Lumpur Madrid Melbourne Mexico City Nairobi
New Delhi Shanghai Taipei Toronto

With offices in

Argentina Austria Brazil Chile Czech Republic France Greece
Guatemala Hungary Italy Japan Poland Portugal Singapore
South Korea Switzerland Thailand Turkey Ukraine Vietnam

Oxford is a registered trade mark of Oxford University Press
in the UK and in certain other countries

Published in the United States
by Oxford University Press Inc., New York

© Stefan Collini 2008

First published 2008

British Library Cataloguing in Publication Data

Data available

Library of Congress Cataloging-in-Publication Data

Collini, Stefan, 1947–
Common reading : critics, historians, publics / Stefan Collini.
p. cm.
Includes bibliographical references and index.
ISBN 978-0-19-929678-1 (acid-free paper) 1. Criticism—Great
Britain—History—20th century. 2. Great Britain—Intellectual
life—20th century. 3. English prose literature—20th century—History
and criticism. 4. Book reviewing—Great Britain—History—20th
century. 5. Literature—History and criticism—Theory, etc. 6. Books
and reading—Great Britain—History—20th century. I. Title.
PR63.C66 2008
801'.95—dc22
2007036880

Typeset by Newgen Imaging Systems (P) Ltd, Chennai, India
Printed in Great Britain
on acid-free paper by
Biddles Ltd, King's Lynn, Norfolk

ISBN 978-0-19-929678-1

1 3 5 7 9 10 8 6 4 2

To Ruth, for everything

CONTENTS

~

I *am* damned critical—for it's the only thing to be,
and all else is damned humbug.

(Henry James, Letter of 19 July 1909)

Not system but *commentary* is the legitimate form
through which truth is approached.

(Gershom Scholem, 'Revelation and Tradition')

Introduction

My title is intended to signal that this book deals with an activity that is both shared and everyday. The essays brought together here address some of the most familiar forms of writing about writing—not just those biographies, critical studies, and works of history for which we are all, more often than not, 'general readers', but also those articles and reviews that make up so much of our diet of regular literary journalism. Substantively, these essays explore aspects of the literary and intellectual culture of Britain from, roughly, the early twentieth century to the present. They focus chiefly on critics and historians who wrote about books and ideas for a non-specialist readership, and on the periodicals and other genres through which they attempted to reach that readership. Whether these figures also had claims to be thought of as novelists or poets, academics or journalists, they are principally considered here as essayists, reviewers, and contributors to general cultural and intellectual discussion—the role understood in the nineteenth century as that of 'the man of letters'. The mutations in that role across the course of the twentieth century, including the recurrent awarding (often with nostalgic or other polemical intent) of the title of 'the last of the men of letters', is one connecting theme, especially among the essays in Part I. Those essays are largely exercises in intellectual portraiture, attempts to characterize, evaluate, and situate their subjects. In Part II, the focus shifts more to the nature of the diverse publics for whom these figures wrote, and to the cultural traditions and institutional frameworks within which they operated. The essays in this second part employ some of the same literary-critical and historical modes to address broader themes, including the fate of 'general' periodicals, the history of reading, the role of criticism, changing conceptions of 'culture', the limitations of biography, and the functions of universities.

One of the reasons for using 'publics' in the plural is as a reminder that readerships are always segmented in various ways, including educational level, political sympathy, and specialized interest. In these terms, readers of the kinds of periodical in which earlier versions of most of these essays appeared probably make up only a small subset of what is rather cavalierly referred to as 'the educated reading public'. After all, these essays, it should be recognized, do presume a pretty developed interest in, and even some knowledge about, a certain range of books and ideas: reading critical essays about critical essayists is not everyone's idea of a good time. But the great thing about a genuine 'public'—as opposed to an audience limited to members of a profession, guild, party, or similar pre-determined group—is that it is in principle open to anyone.

The history of attempts to identify and reach such readerships is a theme running through nearly all these essays, one finding its most concrete expression in writers' relations with particular journals. This terrain has mostly been imagined as falling between, and constantly encroached upon by, journalism on one side and academia on the other. Cyril Connolly, the subject of the opening essay in this collection, characterized the first of these threats when announcing that he intended *Horizon*, the monthly periodical he edited throughout its ten-year existence in the 1940s, to be a refuge for those writers who wanted to escape 'the perpetual brightness, uniformity, brevity, and overproduction' demanded by journalistic writing. He hoped that a periodical conducted along more spacious lines would be able to welcome 'unpopular forms' and to encourage 'those contributions that can be reprinted'. Writing at the beginning of the twenty-first century as the editor of a very different kind of periodical, *New Left Review*, Perry Anderson (also the subject of an essay in this book) identified what now seemed a greater threat, 'the widespread migration' of potential contributors into 'institutions of higher learning' over recent years, bringing a decline in 'standards of writing'. Anderson went on to itemize the 'baneful effects' of academia in particularly unsparing terms: 'peer-group fixation, index-of-citations mania, gratuitous apparatuses, pretentious jargons, guild conceit'. Whether they might have concurred with these descriptions or not, the figures whose writing I discuss in this book mostly attempted to sail a course between the rocks of journalistic superficiality and academic unreadability.

Of course, both those stereotypes are, precisely, stereotypes, accentuating partial truths for polemical purposes. Good journalism, including literary journalism, is not necessarily superficial ('brightness' and 'over-production' are perhaps harder to avoid), just as the best academic work has the compelling readability of clear argument and unanswerable analysis of the evidence.

Even so, the idea that there is a desirable territory falling between those two dominant cultural forms has been constantly reimagined and restated in each generation. Writing that has attempted to fill that space not only provides much of the subject matter of this book; it also, as I have already hinted, represents the genre to which the book's constituent essays belong.

Many of these essays might be said to be about 'the literary life' rather than about literature itself. Although their primary focus is on bodies of writing, they are secondarily interested in authors' ways of living, their writing habits, their finances, as well as in their changing historical opportunities and constraints—available outlets, shifting markets, levels of cultural deference, and so on. I have also found myself attracted by the sheer variousness of the types of writing lumped together under the despairing label 'non-fiction prose': essays, reviews, critical studies, biographies, meditations, memoirs, histories, and so on. The unclassifiability of certain pieces of writing is part of their appeal, while the miscellaneousness of the *œuvre* of the 'general critic' is part of the challenge. Indeed, the labels 'critic' and 'historian' are often just terms of convenience rather than defining identities: it is not obvious that we should, for example, think of Edmund Wilson's *To the Finland Station* as the work of a 'critic' but E. H. Carr's *Dostoevsky* as the work of a 'historian'. Similarly, the role sometimes described as that of 'the journalist as man of letters' is not reducible to any one intellectual discipline or literary genre. The cultural standing of such figures comes, rather, from the power of their individual voice, from their capacity to identify overlooked truths, and from the accumulating successes of their earlier writings.

The essays in Part I, in particular, frequently brood on the shapes of individual careers. Perhaps it should be no surprise that for many of these figures the disputed, unstable boundary between academic and non-academic worlds was a preoccupation, sometimes a personal and troubling one, since few of them fall neatly into one category rather than the other. Actually, many of those who came to prominence in the first half of the twentieth century did largely sustain themselves as freelance writers—this is true, in various ways, of Cyril Connolly, V. S. Pritchett, Aldous Huxley, Rebecca West, Edmund Wilson, George Orwell, and Arthur Bryant (though brief stints at American universities occasionally supplemented the incomes of Pritchett, Huxley, and Wilson)—but thereafter some involvement with universities was nearly always part of the mix. Even so, Herbert Butterfield is the only member of the main cast to have had an orthodox, continuous academic career. Of the others, Empson mainly lived by university teaching in various countries, with gaps in between, but nothing about him was orthodox; Stephen Spender was primarily a writer and literary journalist, though one who occupied a professorial chair for a number of years; A. L. Rowse had a Fellowship at All Souls throughout his adult life but he essentially lived by his writing, plus occasional spells as a visiting teacher at American universities; E. H. Carr was by turns a diplomat, a professor, a leader-writer, a freelance, and a Senior Research Fellow at Trinity College, Cambridge; E. P. Thompson worked in adult education and as a freelance writer, apart from seven years at Warwick University; Perry Anderson has been a rare example of a modern independent intellectual, helped by a private income, though for many years now he has also held a half-time appointment in an American university; Roger Scruton had a regular academic career until about the age of 50, but has since been largely freelance. (The extent to which British literary and intellectual life has been subsidized, since at least the end of the Second World War, by American academia is another of the minor themes frequently touched on but not pursued in this book.)

It should be clear that an element of chance has helped determine the selection of writers included here—principally, the publication within the past six years of a biography or edition of selected works or letters—and no great significance should be attached to supposed 'omissions'. That is as true of the various women of letters who might be set alongside West in Part One (figures such as Rose Macaulay, Virginia Woolf, Edith Sitwell, Elizabeth Bowen, Iris Murdoch) as of the even larger number of historians, male and female, from Trevelyan onwards who made some kind of scholarly mark while also succeeding in addressing a wider public. The names just mentioned may also remind us how often the writers considered in this book came from socially advantaged backgrounds and belonged to what it has become common to term a 'cultural elite' (in practice, several overlapping elites of different kinds). Another of the secondary themes that crops up in more than one essay is the way in which such conditions may enable, as well as limit, good intellectual work. We are rightly aware of the coerciveness and exclusiveness fostered by groups that are both dominant and relatively homogeneous, but we do also need to recognize how shared assumptions, a common idiom, and a collective self-confidence can encourage sophisticated thinking and writing. The individualism of biography, the form in which these careers are mostly presented for our inspection, can obscure such questions, and several of the essays in Part II try to compensate for this bias.

In a characteristically ambitious and opaque phrase, Adorno declared that the essayist 'makes himself into an arena for intellectual experience, without unravelling it'. I'm not sure I know what this means, but there is something intuitively appealing about the idea that essays of this sort try to capture something of the 'intellectual experience' of reading, without dissolving the personal and temporal qualities of that experience into more systematic abstractions. At the same time, these are 'essays in criticism', and criticism suffers at present from the perception that it is a negative, ungenerous activity. Indeed, the business of noticing, characterizing, and estimating seems to be increasingly vulnerable to the accusation of condescension, involving an arrogation of (unmerited) superiority on the part of the critic. This reaction is even more pronounced when the writings under scrutiny are not works of so-called 'imaginative literature', or when it is a whole *œuvre* or career that is being assessed, or when the author in question is still alive—conditions that apply, severally and sometimes jointly, to all the essays in Part One. Length—or, rather, brevity—compounds the problem: the briskly summative can seem summarily dismissive. But length also relates to the question of publics: how much can the non-specialist be induced to read on these topics, how much to *finish*? The 6,000-word critical essay (the average length of these pieces) stands somewhere between the punchy opiniatedness of the newspaper column and the rigorous austerities of the scholarly article, without enjoying the ready legitimacy of either. For all its attractiveness, the genre can engender a certain resistance.

It will be evident by now that these are nearly all 'occasional' pieces in the sense that they were occasioned by the publication of a particular book or the timing of a particular anniversary or similar event. At the start of each chapter I have given details of the books or invitations which first prompted the writing of the main sections of that chapter, so that its focus should be evident to the reader at a glance. I hope that the selection, arrangement, and internal cross-referencing of these essays contribute to such unity as the book possesses. All of them have been revised since their first publication, many only lightly, a few more extensively, though I have not attempted to 'update' the references or allusions. In some places I have restored passages that had initially been omitted on grounds of length; in others I have deleted sentences or phrases whose appropriateness was limited to that of a 'review' in the strict sense; in a few instances I have preserved wording that had fallen victim to overconfident editorial intervention. In addition to this Introduction, three of the essays (Chapters 4, 10, and 12) have not previously appeared in any form, while two others (Chapters 21 and 22) are extended and reworked versions of shorter pieces. Publishing any book means giving hostages to fortune, but a book of essays exhibits special vulnerabilities, some of which I touch on when discussing such collections by members of my cast. I am well aware that this book contains assertions and judgements that would, in another setting, need to be argued through more thoroughly and buttressed by a fuller consideration of the relevant evidence. But essays, like aphorisms and other short forms, ask to be forgiven their excesses even as they take advantage of their licence to provoke.

By way of conclusion, I want to return to the point mentioned earlier about the self-reflexive relation between subject matter and form in these essays. In drawing attention to this relation (more evident in some of the book's contents than in others, it should be said), I realize I risk being misunderstood as trying to lay claim to a line of descent or, worse, as lamenting the passing of a genre and a role. Perhaps I should therefore declare that I do not understand myself to be doing any such thing. I do not write out of any nostalgia for the circumstances in which these authors worked nor do I attend to their achievements as a way of underwriting a jeremiad about the alleged sorry state of the present (especially since I do not endorse such cultural pessimism, as I have tried to make clear on other occasions). These essays explore aspects of the past and present of our common interests as reflective readers of critical writing and as members of a highly history-conscious literary culture. They have to earn their keep on their own terms, not on the back of some misplaced fantasy about re-creating the role of 'the man of letters' in the twenty-first century. And whether they do earn that keep will, in the end, depend upon whether readers find them of sufficient interest to keep reading.

PART I

WRITING LIVES

1

On not Getting on with it:
The Criticism of Cyril Connolly

I

When Cyril Connolly's *Enemies of Promise* was published in 1938, W. H. Auden sent its author an admiring letter:

As both Eliot and Edmund Wilson are Americans, I think *Enemies of Promise* is the best English book of criticism since the war, and more than Eliot or Wilson you really write about writing in the only way which is interesting to anyone except academics, as a real occupation like banking or fucking, with all its attendant boredom, excitement, and terror.

The word that catches the eye here is, of course, 'banking'. It is typical of Auden's off-hand daringness to suggest that the experience of writing might in some way measure up to the 'excitement and terror' of banking. Connolly no doubt appreciated both the compliment and the collusion, the acknowledgement from a fellow-writer that he had accurately characterized the 'real occupation' that they shared. In fact, Auden's comment had a wider application to Connolly's career as a whole, for what, above all, Connolly did was to 'write about writing'. That is, he wrote about the literary life as much as about literature; he wrote, with an empathy fed by constantly renewed experience, about the activity of writing, and, famously, about the much more common activity of not writing, the source of so much of the boredom and the terror. Perhaps no other author has written so much or so well about not writing. Drawing on the deep wells of his own disappointment and self-reproach, he turned himself into the laureate of literary sloth, the chronicler of time wasted, the learned anatomist of the obstacles to getting down to it.

Matthew Connolly (ed.), *The Selected Works of Cyril Connolly*, i. *The Modern Movement*, ii. *The Two Natures* (Picador, 2002).

Enemies of Promise itself is an inventory of the pitfalls that may all too easily prevent the writer from doing the one thing that matters, writing a book that will last. Several of the headings of this inventory have passed into the vocabulary of modern literary culture—'the pram in the hall', 'the charlock's shade'—as has the parable of the seduction of the promising young author, Walter Savage Shelleyblake, into the drudgery of regular reviewing. It is, not altogether paradoxically, the book of Connolly's that has lasted best. But for someone who turned habitual failure into a positive career move, Connolly actually wrote a great deal else as well. After coming down from Oxford in the mid-1920s, he largely existed as a freelance writer and reviewer; he edited the literary magazine *Horizon* from 1939 to 1950; and he was the lead reviewer on the *Sunday Times* (mostly in harness with Raymond Mortimer) from 1952 up until his death in 1973. He published one, not very successful, novel in the 1930s, *The Rock Pool*, one other unclassifiable prose work, *The Unquiet Grave*, in 1944, several volumes of collected essays and reviews, and a vast quantity of ephemeral literary journalism.

Considering the generic unclassifiability of so much of this *œuvre*, one is made to pause over Auden's praise of *Enemies of Promise* as 'the best book of criticism since the war'. The truth is that although Connolly is generally regarded as a literary critic, the greater part of his writing is not in any straightforward sense literary criticism. *Enemies of Promise* itself is hardly at all about particular works of literature. Its first part is more a diagnosis of a cultural situation, a temperature-taking enquiry into current literary fashions; its second section is the one mainly devoted to the dangers and disappointments of the literary life (the 'enemies' and the 'promise' of the title); and the third, entitled 'A Georgian Boyhood', is an avowedly autobiographical account, culminating in an extraordinary recreation of the literary atmosphere that helped form his sensibility during his last years at Eton. Much of his other writing shares this intriguing, mixed-mode character, always streaked with autobiography, overt or disguised. But surprisingly little of it is literary criticism in the purest sense of that term: the sustained analytical attention to the verbal texture of particular works of literature. Connolly thought of himself as a 'writer', usually as a failed writer; he was widely recognized as a 'critic', but in the broadest, most residual sense of that term: he was someone who wrote about books but could not be described by other, more specialized labels—he was neither a poet nor, it finally turned out, a novelist, but nor was he a scholar in any professional or accredited sense, though he was extraordinarily knowledgeable across a wide range of subjects. He made his mark by writing about other writers' writing and his own not writing. He has been variously described as 'one of the most influential literary critics in Britain' and as 'the last of the men of letters'. His most economical self-description was 'a hack'.

From this distance, therefore, one is bound to wonder about Auden's placing of him alongside Eliot and Wilson. Eliot's poetry was hugely important to Connolly, a formative literary experience: acting, as he often did, as spokesman for a generation, he described Eliot's early poetry as 'the great event of our youth'. But he does not in any obvious way seem to resemble or be comparable to Eliot the critic. It is not just that his writing is less feline, more exuberant (and much funnier), with none of Eliot's ecclesiastical hauteur. It is also that Connolly did not attempt the authoritative, indeed deliberately revisionist, critical reappraisal of earlier literary periods in the way that Eliot did with the Elizabethans and Metaphysicals. Connolly helped himself from the drinks cabinet of past authors when in the mood for some of his favourite tipple (Sir Thomas Browne, Rochester, Swift), but he was not interested in undertaking an elaborate expository criticism of their work, still less in rearranging the standard cartography of English literary history. His tastes were anyway far more cosmopolitan than that, and his critical attention was overwhelmingly focused on the Modernist generations after about 1880. One can perhaps more easily see him as having some of the qualities of an English Edmund Wilson in his range and not always predictable opinionatedness, but he had none of Wilson's political seriousness, his intellectual force, or his sheer, bull-like drive. No twentieth-century critic in English, academic or otherwise, has been able wholly to ignore the impact of Eliot's criticism, while Wilson turned himself into a three-star literary monument that, at the very least, *vaut le détour*. It is doubtful if anyone would now put Connolly in this exalted company.

Connolly's more natural place may seem to be alongside those other literary editors and reviewers who played influential parts in London literary life between the 1920s and 1960s, figures such as Desmond MacCarthy and V. S. Pritchett, Raymond Mortimer and Philip Toynbee, John Lehmann and Alan Ross. But these juxtapositions, while undeniably appropriate, also help to bring out a certain distinctiveness in Connolly. As a writer-critic, he seems a more considerable figure than any of them apart from Pritchett (whose novels and stories earned him a different kind of standing). It is hard to imagine a current mainstream publisher issuing a two-volume selected works of, say, Desmond MacCarthy, who first employed Connolly as a reviewer, or of Raymond Mortimer, with whom he shared the literary pages of the *Sunday Times* for so long. This may be attributable partly to the sheer quality of Connolly's writing, partly to the continuing life of at least two of his books (*Enemies of Promise* and *The Unquiet Grave*), and partly to the allure shed by his well-documented life. But it may also be that he has come to stand for a certain manner or ideal of writing for a so-called general audience.

Auden's slighting reference to 'academics' provides the key here, pointing to a recurring theme in Connolly's career. He constantly derided donnish dreariness, gloomily foreseeing that a 'long littleness of dons lies ahead of us' in that future when he and his contemporaries would be 'pushing up theses'. He was especially scornful of 'the chilly snows of Ben Leavis', a hostility heartily reciprocated in *Scrutiny*'s attacks on the 'flank-rubbing' herd of well-connected London literati. In practice, Connolly was constantly anxious not to be dismissed as a mere slapdash journalist by serious and learned scholars, constantly looking over his shoulder anticipating correction from those who had more qualifications and more time. But he needed his caricature of dons in the way many literary journalists did and still do, as a foil against which to set off and justify their own trade, compensating for its ephemerality and mere surface brightness by representing the alternative as an unlovely mixture of antiquarianism, envy, and constipation. Just as Connolly's undergraduate years at Oxford had been rather a come-down after the dizzying social and aesthetic pleasures of 'Pop' at Eton, so universities always figured in his writing as the natural habitat of pedantry and pinched provincialism by comparison to the stylishness and creative energy of great metropolitan cultural centres.

It is partly for this reason that Connolly has in recent years become the sort of figure whom trade publishers just love. He belonged to what can, in some lights, now seem like a glamorous social and literary elite; he knew everyone, went to every party, had affairs with many of the women (and married three of them), wrote long, gossipy, quotable letters. He figures prominently in memoirs and has been thoroughly biographized, at greatest length in Jeremy Lewis's admiring *Cyril Connolly: A Life*, published in 1997. Above all, he lends himself to nostalgic celebrations of 'the last of the men of letters', that allegedly extinct species with whom authors and broadsheet reviewers yearn to identify in ritualistic defiance of its supposed successors, the over-specialized academic and the over-commercialized celebrity. At the mere sound of his name, publishers fantasize about flocks of 'general readers' rising up like rooks from a field. As a consequence, Connolly may now be an overrated figure, but an underrated writer. The appearance of a new selection of his writings, edited by his son, Matthew Connolly (born when his father was 66: he wasn't indolent in every respect), provides an opportunity to take stock.

II

Questions of category and genre impose themselves from the outset. In his foreword to these volumes, William Boyd describes *The Unquiet Grave* as 'a perfect book for the young, would-be littérateur'. The notion of a 'would-be littérateur' is interesting in itself. It is not, after all, a common Careers Office listing. 'Littérateur' tends to be the label, not always flatteringly intended, given to someone who has put together a books-centred life while failing to get on with, or succeed in, a larger literary ambition. A 'would-be littérateur' sounds a bit like a trainee jack-of-all-trades or someone who aspires to be an understudy. Yet Boyd is right: *The Unquiet Grave*, like so much of Connolly's writing, *does* appeal to the 'young, would-be littérateur', to the kind of person (present to some degree in most reviewers and literary academics, no doubt) who is drawn to being part of the world of books and writing without being driven by some unstoppable talent or by having one big thing to say. Certainly, the 'young would-be littérateur' in all of us is flattered to be treated on terms of such intimacy by Connolly's prose; and the brevity of his preferred forms, at least when read singly, stops the experience from becoming boring or disillusioning. *The Unquiet Grave* itself has more the character of *pensées* than of table talk, but there is an unbuttoned, conversational quality to a lot of Connolly's writing that is seductive. There is still something attractive and mildly thrilling to have him saying from the opposite armchair, apropos the hackneyed question of 'the incontestably great masterpieces', 'I don't like most of the *Aeneid*' ('most of' signalling familiarity and considered judgement rather than mere subjective aversion).

Notoriously, Connolly announced in the first sentence of *The Unquiet Grave* that 'the true function of a writer is to produce a masterpiece and that no other task is of any consequence', and then dribbled his talent away in other tasks and the avoidance of tasks. The opening of *Enemies of Promise* similarly offers a moody meditation on the near-certainty of literary transience: here he declared the slightly more modest ambition 'to write a book that will hold good for ten years afterwards'. Even he had to acknowledge that the need for an introduction to a new edition in 1948 signalled an ambition more or less realized, and subsequent reissues, the most recent in 1996, demonstrate a continuing appeal, even if not everything in it can be said to 'hold good'. But, like almost anyone who writes for a living, he had to write too much, and he was acutely conscious that he spent most of his life carefully crafting sentences whose almost immediate destiny was the floor or the fireplace.

The *corvée* of regular reviewing produced some of his most mordant reflections. 'The reviewing of novels is the white man's grave of journalism;

it corresponds, in letters, to building bridges in some impossible tropical climate. The work is gruelling, unhealthy, and ill-paid, and for each scant clearing made wearily among the springing vegetation the jungle overnight encroaches twice as far.' A lot of his early years were spent hacking his way through the 'first-flowering blooms of Girtonia and Ballioli', and he knew all too well what it was to be 'tired with the feeling of obscure guilt that comes after a day spent in the thankless task of drowning other people's kittens'. So habitual had meeting the weekly deadline become by the end of his life that he joked that 'my funeral, should it fall on a Tuesday, will be remarkable for a hand holding an article thrusting itself out of my coffin'. A certain professional pride hovers behind this last remark, and the piece in which it appeared (on twenty years as the *Sunday Times*'s lead reviewer, not included in these volumes) suggested that he had made peace with his fate by then and recognized that it provided him with a necessary discipline.

It is only mildly paradoxical that the episode of literary journalism with which he is most closely identified, his ten-year editorship of *Horizon*, was in part inspired by the ambition 'to help free writers from journalism'. As I mentioned in the Introduction above, he aimed to make the magazine a refuge for those writers who wanted to escape 'the perpetual brightness, uniformity, brevity, and overproduction' demanded by journalistic work. 'These evils a monthly review can do something to alleviate by encouraging authors to write on subjects about which their feelings are deepest, by asking for thought and imagination instead of the overwhelming brightness by which so many of us are dazzled, and by affording them as much space as possible.' The more spacious and leisurely medium would enable him to welcome 'unpopular forms' and to encourage 'those contributions that can be reprinted'.

Horizon seems to have fulfilled these aims, at least in its early years, and it had a proud record of nurturing writers whose work might not otherwise have appeared during this period, as well as of making the latest work by foreign authors, especially French and American, available to a British readership. Of course, for Connolly himself the editorial treadmill became yet another way of dissipating his energies. He wrote a monthly 'Comment' for each issue (until he began to get bored with the whole enterprise), but these cannot be said to have lasted well. Connolly's editing of *Horizon* during the war years is often regarded as his finest hour, keeping alive the flame of culture when so much conspired to blow it out. But in some ways the case for the continuing value of the arts was almost too easy to make under those conditions, and Connolly's defiant manifestos (a couple of which are included here) have a preachy, self-satisfied feel to them. Some of his high-toned justifications in these years for the supreme importance of 'the artist' almost make one want to enrol in the ranks of the Philistines ('there are certain types of human beings who are especially equipped for the extension of human consciousness' and these form 'the aristocracy of a more perfect world', and so on). And, as the war was followed by years of even greater austerity and deprivation, Connolly's always hovering preciousness could too easily descend into simply snobbish nostalgia for the amenities of life among the comfortable classes before the war, constituting a kind of critical equivalent of *Brideshead Revisited*.

Writing in 1964 about editors of literary magazines (in a piece not reprinted here), Connolly pondered a familiar dualism between 'dynamic' and 'eclectic' editors. Dynamic editors were animated by a cause, and conducted their journals 'like a commando course where picked men are trained to assault the enemy position', whereas the eclectic editor 'is like an hotel proprietor whose rooms fill up every month with a different clientele'. Those in the first category figure more largely in literary history, though the pages they edited inevitably acquire a quaint and dated air, whereas the catholicity of the second group, though lacking the impact of a cause or a programme, may stand more chance of nourishing different forms of good writing. Connolly well knew which category he belonged to, but he showed that eclecticism does not mean an absence of discrimination. And he continued in this vein as a reviewer (when he was, so to say, the front porter at the hotel rather than the proprietor), delighted at the return of old regulars but equally willing to welcome interesting newcomers, genial on most occasions though also able to command a devastating raise of the eyebrow. As a reviewer, he served the 'occupation' of writing well by making readers feel that through it you meet a better class of person than through banking or fucking.

The nearest Connolly came to having a cause was his consistent championing of Modernism. In this respect, he certainly demonstrated that being a 'man of letters' did not at all entail being middlebrow, as some of his self-elected successors like to congratulate themselves on being. He took deep personal pleasure in some of the most difficult or experimental literary forms, especially in poetry, and his reviewing attempted to educate his readers up to the level of such writing rather than trying to drag the writers down to the supposed level of the available market. It captures something of Connolly's reviewing manner to say that he wrote more as a connoisseur than a critic. It is relevant that he was an ardent collector, especially of modern first editions; he once suggested that a memorial service should be held for him at Sotheby's with a 'sung bibliography'. He also seems to have been somewhat less interested in music than in literature and painting, which may partly have been because it's less collectable. All this meant that he could at times fall into being a mere book-bibber, lovingly compiling tasting-notes on literary vintages, but at the same time the mixture of greedy hedonism and romantic melancholy that suffused his prose prevented it from becoming too oracular. As he declared in a *New Statesman* piece in the mid-1930s: 'I am secretly a lyricist; the works to which I lose my heart are those that attempt, with a purity and a kind of dewy elegance, to portray the beauty of the moment, the gaiety and sadness, the fugitive distress of hedonism.' The 'fugitive distress of hedonism' beautifully captures the dominant mood of so much of his writing, just as 'a kind of dewy elegance' illustrates, alas, the bad habits inherited from late Aestheticism, hard though he strove to turn Pater-and-water into wine. But the indecisiveness that inevitably accompanied this mixture of greed and melancholy also prevented him from being too dogmatic. As he winningly put it in a 1941 draft: 'I believe in god the Either, god the Or, and god the Holy Both.'

Reading Connolly in anthologized bulk, one finds the celebrated account of his Eton years in the third section of *Enemies of Promise* still one of the most arresting things he ever wrote. We are not, the uninitiated should be warned, dealing here with 'education' as she is known in the age of A/S levels and 'after-school activities'. It is, rather, a lush threnody on a decadent civilization by a jaded Silver Age poet. The extraordinary scented richness of it still hits you as if stepping into one of the bigger greenhouses at Kew. Memoirs of public-school life of the period tend to dwell on sport, Christianity, drill, character, philistinism, and sport. Connolly's account of his time in 'Pop' (the select Eton society) is redolent, instead, of an old Mediterranean culture, pagan, languid, sensuous, pessimist. The masterpiece towards which literary effort was directed was the perfect epigram. Cultivation was cultivated ('By the time I left Eton I knew by heart something of the literature of five civilizations'), but swotting was not. Some of this is familiar from other periods, other sources, other schools; some of it is perhaps inherent in adolescence. But the really extravagant belatedness of it all, the sense of having riffled through the possibilities of several cultures ancient and modern, that characteristic regret of the Decadent that all one's most exquisite suffering was already over, plus a streak of wounded, vulnerable, honesty—this mix is Connolly's own. He was told at the time that he had known such triumphs at Eton that life thereafter could only be a disappointment. Here, art imitated life in a suitably perverse way; his writing *about* his time at Eton was such a triumph that his later work was bound to seem something of a let-down.

The Unquiet Grave, the other complete book included in this selection, now seems even more of an oddity than it did to many readers in the mid-1940s. It takes the form of a loosely connected series of meditations on love and loss, and on the unity of European culture, ending with 'an apology for the pursuit of happiness, an affirmation of the values of humanism'. It was published pseudonymously by 'Palinurus' (though its authorship was an open secret), and this classical persona plays a part in the book not altogether unlike that of Empedocles in Matthew Arnold's poem, irritably dissatisfied with his own achieved pessimism. Connolly liked to think of it as a modern attempt to extend the genre cultivated by Pascal, Rochester, and La Rochefoucauld. There is also some generic resemblance to Nietzsche's literary technique of provoking the reader out of received opinions by a calculated outrageousness that doesn't get bogged down in sustained argument, though the resemblance may be only superficial since German philosophical culture does not seem to have been part of Connolly's sensibility. The trouble is that epigrams in bulk are almost bound to feel cloying: the first few are arresting, but after 150 pages the mannered contrivance becomes tiresome.

For the most part, the occasional pieces included in these two volumes are reviews, the best of them from the *Sunday Times* in the 1950s and 1960s when Connolly was in his pomp (serving as reminders, if reminders be needed, that enthusiasm and discrimination reread much better than carping and distaste). But there is a generous leavening of other genres. Several of the later pieces included here, for example, are obituary tributes, a form that particularly suited his late manner. Like all collectors, he enjoyed ranking (the finest example of this, the best single that, and so on), and his summary assessments have a postprandial finality about them. But, as with his reviews, they are usually generous and not always predictable. He had a surprisingly high regard for Hemingway, for example, hardly aestheticism's most exquisite fruit. Conversely, he seems to have had little patience for Beckett's fiction, though one might have thought its late-Modernist experimentalism would have appealed to him. Again, one might not have predicted that he would admire Larkin, but he singled out 'MCMXIV' as a 'poem I would choose if asked to illustrate what poetry can do'. (This admiration was reciprocated, and Larkin wrote a surprisingly indulgent introduction to a reprint of *The Condemned Playground*, where he rightly noted that some of Connolly's best criticism 'took the form of hilarious literary romping'.)

Connolly was also a good travel writer, at least as long as the travel was in the Mediterranean, allowing local detail to loosen a flurry of literary scree and classical allusion. He wrote as the memorialist of a cultivated sensuousness, and moved seamlessly between meditations on the fall of civilizations and on the rise of soufflés; he loved writing about beautiful places, good meals, and golden hours. And, should the company be famous, the location exclusive, the wines rare, then so much the better. In this respect, a lot of his writing functioned as a kind of soft porn for the culturally aspirant: a Connolly essay gave aesthetic wannabees the illusion of insiderdom in the way *Hello!* magazine does for contemporary celebrity culture.

These volumes also include Connolly's most famous parodies: 'Where Engels Fears to Tread', on self-consciously left-wing writing in the 1930s; 'Told in Gath', a merciless satire on Aldous Huxley's disquisitive fictional manner; and 'Bond Strikes Camp', a genuinely funny take-off of his friend Ian Fleming's James Bond novels—Connolly's own susceptibility to brand snobbery was put to good effect here. Parody is, by definition, a very knowing literary genre, and Connolly liked to flaunt his knowingness ('that smarty-boots Connolly': Virginia Woolf). But it is a genre that can also testify to the presence of underused literary energy, Connolly's habitual condition. The parodist may have wit and inventiveness, a noticing eye and a responsive ear, but may not have anything of his own to say, and so is in danger of becoming simply a parasite, a tick who lives off others' tics. Connolly was, as usual, alert to all the dangers and utterly incapable of resisting the temptation.

A special historical interest attaches to 'Year Nine', a brief satire on a totalitarian future written in 1938, since it now seems uncannily anticipatory of many of the conceits of *Nineteen Eighty-Four* (one of Orwell's biographers, Michael Shelden, sees it as a possible source). The connection with Orwell was long-standing, of course—a contemporary at prep school and at Eton, Connolly published some of Orwell's best essays in *Horizon*. Matthew Connolly is right to observe that while Evelyn Waugh looms over much of the first volume of this edition, George Orwell is the most frequent point of reference in the second. (This also fits with one of Connolly's own little squibs of self-depreciation: 'At Eton with Orwell, at Oxford with Waugh,/He was nobody after and nothing before.') Orwell and Connolly seem to have remained on good terms even though some of their public statements suggested that they had got each other's number pretty accurately. For example, Orwell described *The Unquiet Grave* as 'a cry of despair from the rentier who feels that he has no right to exist', while Connolly observed of Orwell the essayist: 'he could not blow his nose without moralizing on conditions in the handkerchief industry.'

But the comparison with Orwell helps situate Connolly in another way. Connolly is, to start with the obvious, much the funnier writer, much more verbally inventive, able to concoct an altogether creamier prose (not difficult, it has to be said). But the parodies, in particular, reinforce the sense of undergraduate humour, calling attention to its own cleverness, aiming above all to make a circle of intimates laugh and admire. It is not just that there is no great political purpose animating his writing—it's all the better for that on the whole, certainly by comparison with some of his contemporaries in the 1930s and 1940s; it is rather the sense that some of his work has no greater goal than that of making a splash in the vivarium of literary London. Orwell's very different faults are by now all too familiar, but his writing was well served by the sense it always gave off of being about something more than itself. Orwell wanted the world to know how bad things were and how much worse they could yet become. It is clear that, as a writer, Connolly tired easily and even became bored with his own invention, whereas although Orwell also excelled at the briefer genres his performance in them did require a kind of stamina, the perseverance necessary to pare them down to the essentials. Still, it is wholly to Connolly's credit that he seems to have had a much better appreciation of Orwell's merits as a writer than Orwell did of Connolly's.

In his foreword, fellow Chelsea resident William Boyd concedes that there is no one work of Connolly's that can be regarded as 'unequivocally excellent or fully achieved', but he goes on to claim that nonetheless the whole body of his work and his life 'add up to something formidable'. I wonder. 'Formidable' seems a bit too, well, formidable for such an engaging but scrappily incomplete body of writing, and this judgement risks placing too much weight on the rackety, privileged life. Still, Connolly does seem worth reprinting in a way that some of his peers might not. Perhaps one of the secrets of those whose literary journalism bears rereading is that they were always more than literary journalists. In his later years, Connolly sometimes came perilously close to forfeiting this additional standing, the sense of speaking with the authority of achievement or of there being power in reserve. But at his best, he did manage to suggest that his first-hand knowledge of the excitement and terror of writing gave him a more than purely routine claim on the reader's attention. Sadly, one has to say that this 'edition' may not serve Connolly as well as might be hoped. No good is done to the cause of 'the man of letters' and 'the general reader' by associating those terms with high-handed or slipshod editing, failings largely avoided by Connolly the practised editor and obsessive proof-corrector.

Books made up of republished occasional pieces can make us think both better and worse of a writer whose work we more usually encounter in smaller servings. It can be revealing and sometimes impressive to see the same sensibility or intellectual power ranging across diverse subjects, but, as when going on a camping holiday with someone, we soon become oppressively aware of their hitherto unnoticed bad habits. Introducing a new edition of one of his collections in 1960, Connolly wrote: 'Do not despise the scrappiness of my book. I work best in scraps, and, besides, a little of me goes a long way.' After reading all the way through these two volumes, one has to say that both these judgements seem right.

2

Rolling it out:
V. S. Pritchett's Writing Life

I

It was all done with a pastry board and a bulldog clip. Sheets of paper were clipped to the board, the board rested on the arms of his chair, and the fountain pen began to cover the pages with a scrawl that barely hinted at intimations of legibility. Every day was much the same, weekday or week-end: a long morning at the board, lunch, a nap, errands, tea, and then back to the board; a drink or two before dinner, perhaps some more reading after, and then early bed in preparation for another day of turning the doughy ball of thought into light, crisp sentences. The secret of happiness, it has been said, is to develop habits whose repetition we find enjoyable and whose outcomes we find satisfying. For the greater part of his very long adult life, Victor Sawdon Pritchett seems to have been a happy man.

Pritchett's son, Oliver, later recalled that he and his sister grew up 'in a word factory'. 'The handwritten pages, covered in revisions, crossings out, second and third thoughts, and sideways writing in the margins, were given to my mother to type. They would be revised and typed again and again.' Transposing the usual location of domestic equipment, the Pritchetts lived out a kind of *Upstairs, Downstairs* version of the literary life: he, upstairs, rolling out the sentences on the pastry board; she, downstairs, pounding, turning the scrawl into copy for the printers, stopping only to prepare the traditional cooked lunch and substantial dinner that marked the end of the day's two shifts. Given Pritchett's reliance on his wife's unpaid labour, and indeed his rather traditional views of women's role more generally (of which more later), there seemed a momentary plausibility to a line in

Jeremy Treglown, *V. S. Pritchett: A Working Life* (Chatto, 2004).

the proof copy of Jeremy Treglown's biography, alas properly corrected in the published version, which had him setting the pastry board 'across the comfortable arms of his char'.

'Sooner or later, the great men turn out to be alike. They never stop working. They never lose a minute. It is very depressing.' Thus Pritchett, writing on Gibbon in 1941, in the essay that now stands at the head of his 1,300-page *Complete Essays*. He didn't really mean that it was depressing, of course: that's just the note of twinkly-eyed collusion with his readers' all-too human weaknesses that graces so many of his essays. Beneath the surface, a more strenuous moral is silently making itself felt, suggesting that this familiar fact is actually sobering or bracing, a reminder to Pritchett to keep himself up to the mark. The last essay in that volume, on Virginia Woolf, written over forty years later, observes almost as an aside: 'She worked harder than ever when she became famous, as gifted writers do—what else is there to do but write?' That rhetorical question may at first reading seem to strike a bleak note, as though all else had lost its savour, but in context it gestures more towards an inner imperative, that achieved condition of the writer, whether critic or novelist, in which experience is not fully possessed *as* experience until it has been cropped, shaped, and coloured. Pritchett wrote so well about authors as different as Gibbon and Woolf in part because he, too, knew the compulsions and desperations of that form of willing slavery that is the writer's life.

The credit for noticing the neat way in which these two remarks frame the collection of Pritchett's essays belongs to Jeremy Treglown, not to me. In a move that exemplifies the imaginative sympathy informing this biography, Treglown then juxtaposes a remark from one of Pritchett's revealing letters to his close friend Gerald Brenan. 'Pritchett knew that the virtues of industry could be illusory, especially for someone from his kind of background. "I realise what escapists we who rely on our own efforts are," he told Brenan. "Any effort, to us, is valid just because it is an effort".' The reach of this particular use of the first-person plural is interestingly hard to determine: addressed to Brenan, it may at first seem to embrace those who live by their pen, but questions of class are never far away in Pritchett's understanding of his own trajectory, suggesting that the pronoun mainly picks out those who, from humble beginnings, have made their own way in the world without the leg-up that in one form or another the comfortable classes provide for their offspring. The snares associated with the habit of hard work seem to have preoccupied Pritchett, for he returned to them in the second of his two volumes of autobiography, *Midnight Oil*, published in 1971, where he writes: 'There is always the danger that people who work hard become blinded by work itself and, by a paradox, lazy-minded.' Here, the very knowingness of the remark claims exemption for its author from his own generalization, while at the same time hinting that he has come close enough to this state to know whereof he speaks. For all his Stakhanovite habits, Pritchett clearly worked hard at not being merely hard-working.

All this makes Treglown's subtitle doubly apt: this biography is principally the story of Pritchett's career, but his life was, even by the standards of professional writers, unremittingly a life of work. Yet this may only bring into sharper relief the problem faced by the biographer of almost any writer: the activity whose products prompt posterity to take an interest in their creator is, by its nature, uneventful and largely unrecorded, perhaps unrecordable. Literary biography is mostly the story of what a writer did when he or she was not writing. Pritchett touched on this in his characteristically metaphorical way at one point in *Midnight Oil*: 'For a writer is, at the very least, two persons. He is the prosaic man at his desk and a sort of valet who dogs him and does the living. There is a time when he is all valet looking for a master, i.e. the writer he is hopefully pursuing.' Pritchett was here thinking of his much younger self, who set off for Paris with a patchy, truncated education and a series of unsatisfying jobs behind him and an intense, but still vague and wholly unrealized, aspiration to become 'a writer' in front of him. 'When, at 20, I got out of the train in the early spring of 1921 at the Gare du Nord, I was all valet.' As he demonstrated in that book and its predecessor, *A Cab at the Door* (1968), the memoir of the valet can be full of incident: he travels, has adventures, takes on bizarre jobs, falls in love, faces penury, and so on. Once the master is firmly in the saddle, however, there is less to report; there may be some record of who the valet had dinner with and even some of what was said, but the only surviving record of what happened at the long hours at the pastry board the next morning requires forms of attention more characteristic of the literary critic than the biographer.

It is one of the many merits of this perceptive biography that it contains a good deal of unobtrusive literary criticism. We are all too familiar with that kind of clunking literary biography that recounts, in tedious detail, a series of travels, parties, and affairs, merely pausing, when the date of publication of the various works is reached, for a synoptic content summary of the item in question, often treated as so much decodable biographical evidence (I return to this issue in Chapter 22, below). Treglown departs from this dispiriting model in several ways, while still fulfilling the biographer's contract by fully documenting the developing shape of his subject's life, and his critical alertness to the strengths and weaknesses of Pritchett as a writer is one of the most welcome of these departures. No less welcome is the book's comparative brevity, at least when seen alongside those great biographical pantechnicons that deliver every remaining stick of evidence no matter how trivial. And it seems right, after all, that a biography of Pritchett, acknowledged master of both the short story and the brief literary essay, should not be too long: Treglown gets through the almost ninety-seven years in just 250 pages without any sense of unseemly compression. His subject would surely have approved.

In this respect, the huge volume of *Complete Essays* that I mentioned earlier, along with its companion *The Complete Short Stories*, both published at the beginning of the 1990s, cannot help but give an inappropriate impression of monumentality, though neither compilation comes anywhere near to completeness. In practice, it is no easy task to try to compute the total of Pritchett's writing, and there seems to be no published bibliography. At a rough count of the books, and allowing for some duplication even while excluding 'collecteds' and 'selecteds' that reprint material already reprinted, there were five novels, at least ten books of stories, two volumes of memoirs, six travel books of various kinds, three literary biographies, and nine collections of essays and general literary criticism. Say, thirty-five books spread over some sixty years. But books were, if not exactly the icing on the cake, then the big display pieces of patisserie: most of his output can now be tracked down only in the rarely disturbed pages of old periodicals and newspapers, where the browsing researcher, eye suddenly arrested by a limpid phrase or still-fresh simile, glances to the end of the article or review and finds the once-familiar set of initials: 'VSP'. Treglown, with understandable proprietorial pride, claims that 'in his time' Pritchett was 'the most influential man of letters in the English speaking world'. That may be right—such claims are inherently unverifiable—though we would need to remember that his time coincided roughly with that of American candidates such as Edmund Wilson and Lionel Trilling, and special allowance might have to be made for the senses in which Cyril Connolly was 'influential' or George Orwell a 'man of letters'. But I would be surprised if any serious contender for that title between about 1930 and 1980 were more prolific than VSP.

II

Gore Vidal, always a master of understated hyperbole, praised Pritchett's criticism by saying 'it would be very nice for literature if he lived for ever'. Pritchett did his best: he was born in 1900 and matched the century year for year before dropping out with just three years to go. His sheer longevity can make him seem at once fustily remote and deceptively contemporary. He was born while Victoria was still queen, and he died little more than a month before Tony Blair became Prime Minister.

Pritchett's family bumped along on that uneasy late-Victorian border between the respectable artisans and the aspiring lower middle class. His father, a man with a limitless capacity for financial disaster, belonged to the Wellsian world of suburban shopkeepers and small businessmen. The 'cab at the door' in the title of the first volume of Pritchett's autobiography bespeaks not comfortable gentility, but the dawn flit to a new address to escape the bailiffs. Pritchett's father dominated not just his son's childhood (and his later account of it), but his literary imagination for years to come: the eponymous hero in *Mr Beluncle*, Pritchett's last and best-known novel, published in 1951, is largely a portrait of this extravagant, demanding, pathetically unrealistic man, whose life was increasingly subjugated to the teachings of Mrs Baker Eddy's Christian Science and the guiding messages that 'the Divine Mind' sent him at the numerous crises of his affairs. Pritchett's mother, from still humbler origins (the Sawdons, he later recorded, didn't have 'an aitch to their name'), suffered, complained, and was loyal. At various points in this rackety upbringing, young Victor caught snatches of education, including a brief spell at Alleyn's School in Dulwich, but money, or the lack of it, determined that he had to leave at 16 and start earning. He worked as a clerk in the leather trade near Bermondsey docks, read Ruskin and other staples of the self-improver of the period, and fantasized about girls. The ambition to be a writer was growing, however, and his taking the train to Paris that spring day in 1921 was a bid for freedom.

Not surprisingly, Pritchett figures as a frequently quoted witness in Jonathan Rose's recent book *The Intellectual Life of the British Working Classes* (discussed in Chapter 19, below), in part because he was so eloquent about his sense of being educationally deprived. Like other 'autodidacts' of his time (few of them, including Pritchett, entirely self-taught, of course), his reading was dominated by the established canon of classics and the middlebrow writers of the previous generation, such as George du Maurier and Hilaire Belloc. 'All my tastes were conventionally Victorian,' he despairingly recognized, 'I seemed irredeemably backward and lower class.' He knew nothing of the Modernist revolution taking place all around him in early 1920s Paris, and he records that later, when he did come across the work of figures such as Tristan Tzara, 'I was angry because he was smashing up a culture just as I was becoming acquainted with it'.

The 1920s were a difficult but exciting time for the young would-be author: a series of absurd jobs in Paris, work as a reporter for the *Christian Science Monitor* (through his father's connections), extensive travel in Ireland and Spain, an unhappy first marriage, and the usual accumulation of rejection slips. But by the end of the decade things were looking up, at least professionally: his first book, based on his travels in Spain, came out in 1928, his first novel, *Clare Drummer*, in 1929, his first volume of stories in 1930, he all the while doing what Connolly termed the usual *corvée* of reviewing new fiction for a variety of periodicals. In 1936 he remarried, this time happily and lastingly, and his life began to settle into its productive routine. His first real critical success came with the publication in 1937 of his subsequently much-anthologized short story 'Sense of Humour'. By then he was reviewing regularly for the *New Statesman*, going on to become that paper's star critic, in some years contributing over half its main literary articles, and eventually a director.

He later joked that it was the Second World War that turned him from a reviewer into a critic. New books were scarce, so Raymond Mortimer, the *Statesman*'s literary editor, set Pritchett to filling the 'Books in General' slot with essays on classic authors, French and Russian as well as English. Perhaps we tend now to romanticize the circumstances in which these essays were originally read, imagining people crouched in bomb shelters, or travelling in ill-lit trains, or receiving slightly tattered out-of-date copies on foreign postings, but some of these pieces do still seem marvellous examples of the genre—engaging without being chatty, informative without being didactic, creating the winning pretence that reader and critic are sharing their pleasure in familiar authors.

In the years after 1945, Pritchett developed into an established literary figure on both sides of the Atlantic, becoming a regular reviewer as well as fiction writer for the *New Yorker*, and, from its founding in 1963, contributing over 100 substantial pieces to the *New York Review of Books*. He was also invited to take up several visiting appointments on American campuses. All this made him prosperous. Treglown describes the life it bought at the beginning of the 1950s: 'The couple banked at Coutts, ate in good restaurants when they were in town and went to Harley Street when they needed medical treatment. Dorothy dressed well. Victor had his club, the Savile. Both children were soon sent to boarding-schools.' Given his lowly beginnings, VSP was understandably proud of his success, particularly proud that, once settled to his task, he was able to support himself and his family entirely on the proceeds of his writing. He relished recognition and honours of a more symbolic kind, too: he was made a CBE in 1968, a knight in 1975, a Companion of Honour in 1993. For the last couple of decades of his life, he was indisputably the Grand Old Man of Letters.

Since for the last sixty or seventy years of his life Pritchett did not really *do* much of public consequence except write, the focus of his biography, once we get beyond his childhood and *Wanderjahre*, is bound to be on, first, his domestic and emotional life, and, second, his career as a writer. Accounts of the later Pritchett always emphasize his close, passionate marriage and

his happy home life. Without coming at all close to prurience or sensationalism, Treglown profits from his access to letters and diaries to paint a more
complex, even troubling, portrait.

At the age of 23, Pritchett married Evelyn Vigors, the daughter of an
Anglo-Irish military family, apparently drawn as much by the charms of
exoticism and social class as by sexual attraction. To Pritchett, as Treglown drily notes, 'Evelyn represented everything that wasn't Bromley'
(where his parents had been living for some time, in one of the longer set-
tlements of their peripatetic life). After a few years, the marriage drifted
into sexless unhappiness, and they divorced in the early 1930s. By then he
had met Dorothy Roberts, fourteen years his junior, and with her he found
passionate love and sexual fulfilment. It was the beginning of a very long
marriage (she outlived him), but it was also for her the beginning of her job
in the word factory. Pritchett may have had more than his share of the necessary egoism of the writer, and perhaps he never quite acknowledged the
toll on his wife of the inequality in their lives and the amount of unpaid,
subordinate labour she contributed. In the 1940s and 1950s she was often
left alone with the children in their house in the country while Victor went
up to town, perhaps to the offices of the *New Statesman*, perhaps to his
club or to a literary dinner. When he was at home, one of her chief domestic
tasks was to ensure that he wasn't disturbed while he was working, which
was most of the time. Even when he discovered, rather belatedly, that his
wife had become an alcoholic, Pritchett seemed only to half-recognize the
part he had played in bringing this about. After the usual deceptions and
defeats, Dorothy managed to kick the habit, and thereafter her teetotal-
ism does not seem to have detracted too much from the jollity of their
social life (which became much more active and shared once they moved to
Regent's Park Terrace in north London in 1956). But, as his children recognized more readily than Pritchett himself, there were several years during
which they were a dysfunctional family. Pritchett's friend Al Alvarez said
of him that 'he was addicted to writing like some people are to the bottle', but Pritchett never seems to have grasped the dialectical relationship
between these two forms of addiction in his own household.

At one point, Treglown mildly observes that Pritchett was 'always a tra-
ditionalist in matters of gender', but it is surely not just the alerted sensitivity of a later age that now makes us wince at some of what he seemed to take
for granted. For example, at the height of Dorothy's alcoholism (obviously
a difficult time for him as for her), he wrote to her saying: 'I hate to see your
beauty being wasted in this ugliness, and my talents too. I have a responsibility to my gifts and you to your grace and attraction as a woman.' This
might be thought, by almost any standards, to be carrying 'traditionalism
in matters of gender' a little far.

It is less of a surprise to discover that even this famously happy marriage had to cope with the strains of both partners' extramarital affairs. While lecturing at Princeton in 1953–4, Pritchett began an affair with Barbara Kerr, a capable, vivacious American woman some dozen years younger than him. By his own confession, he enjoyed being in love (who doesn't?) and threw himself into the affair, which lasted intermittently, on both sides of the Atlantic, for several years. But as his life with Dorothy regained its equilibrium, Barbara came to represent a dangerously destabilizing force. Perhaps the endings of affairs are almost bound to produce unforgivable remarks, but for that reason it may be all the wiser to avoid committing them to paper. In December 1960, after they had not seen each other for some time, Kerr wrote from New York to ask if Pritchett would be visiting the States soon and if so whether they might get together, perhaps with Dorothy. Pritchett's curt reply seems brutal as a response to someone for whom he had professed passionate love only a short while before (and with whom he had even discussed the possibility of marriage): 'I have no notion of coming to New York', it concluded, 'and, of course (if you will reflect upon it for a moment) you will understand that it is impossible that you should meet Dorothy and me there or anywhere ever. I have no news that you would understand. Love, Victor.' I'm sure Treglown is right to quote this letter, as part of a frank and balanced portrait, but I can't help wishing that it hadn't survived—or, better still, that it should never have been written. (Treglown also records that over forty years later, and five years after Pritchett's death, Kerr's eyes filled with tears as she recalled it.) Actually, despite this appalling rebuff, Kerr must have persisted, or Pritchett relented, as their relationship briefly renewed itself three years later (when he was 62). In a notebook in the early days of the affair he had written: 'It came into my head this morning that the successful, happy adultery is not now often described.' Whether such descriptions were rarer then than before is hard to say, but one could be forgiven for feeling that his novelist's imagination might have prompted Pritchett to a few slightly more searching thoughts about what 'success' really means in this matter, and for whom.

The other central theme, Pritchett's career as a professional writer, raises no such troubling issues, though there are some interesting questions about its historical specificity. The preface to the selection of his essays published in 1985 under the title *A Man of Letters* contained a credo that was to become mildly celebrated:

If, as they say, I am a Man of Letters, I come, like my fellows, at the tail-end of a long and once esteemed tradition in English and American writing. We have no captive audience. We do not teach. We are rarely academics, though we owe a great debt to scholars. We earn our bread and butter by writing for the periodicals that have survived. If we have one foot in Grub Street we write to be readable and to engage the interest of what Virginia Woolf called 'the common reader'. We do not lay down the law, but we do make a stand for the reflective values of a humane culture. We care for the printed word in a world that nowadays is dominated by the camera and by scientific, technological, and sociological doctrine.

Actually, I'm not sure that this is one of the best examples of Pritchett's prose: the clauses about Grub Street seem awkwardly unbalanced and the last sentence surely tries to run together things that are too disparate— 'sociological doctrine', for example, is a part of 'the printed word' rather than some rival form. The pathos of being the last of a line may have had an obvious appeal for an 84-year old, but a couple of decades later we can still ask whether he was right about being the 'tail-end' of this tradition, and if so what were the causes of this profession's extinction.

The economics of the literary life is an endlessly fascinating subject, especially to writers, yet it is notoriously difficult to make comparisons between the conditions of authorship in different periods. The mere sums earned tell us very little abstracted from the realities of comparative purchasing power and associated questions of social status. Clearly, before post-war growth took hold and reshaped expectations for the bulk of the population, a reasonably successful literary journalist could live conspicuously well. At the end of the 1930s, when the Pritchetts' prosperity was only just beginning, they rented a large and handsome house in the Berkshire countryside for £1 a week; prices were depressed by the long agricultural depression, and many of the neighbouring rural labourers would have been on wages of not more than £80 a year. The hunger for reading matter widely remarked as a feature of the 1940s was good news for a productive author at the peak of his powers. For example, the second collection of Pritchett's literary essays, *The Living Novel*, published in 1946, earned him £650 within the year (roughly £20,000 at early twenty-first-century values), and that was, of course, in addition to the fees for their first periodical publication and any subsequent reprinting. By the mid-1940s he was receiving a retainer from the *New Statesman* as well as being paid for individual pieces, and Treglown records that Pritchett earned £1,500 a year from this paper alone (something over £40,000 similarly updated). In the 1940s and 1950s, his stories paid several times over, sold to magazines on both sides of the Atlantic, reprinted, anthologized, issued in book-club editions, and so on. In 1951, *Mr Beluncle*, his fifth and last novel, was a commercial as well as critical hit, quickly earning out its advance and then some. Buoyed by this success, the Pritchetts moved to an even grander house in the country in 1952.

But we also catch glimpses of how uncertain, even precarious, this prosperity could be, despite long hours at the pastry board. Nostalgists may be sobered to discover that even Pritchett could get into financial difficulties in the late 1950s, when he needed to repay the loan from the *New Statesman* that had enabled him to buy his house in Regent's Park Terrace. Some timely American commissions helped him out of this particular pickle by 1961, but, as Treglown observes, 'the experience was a harsh reminder of the realities of the freelance life'. Thereafter, he undertook an increasing amount of work for *Holiday*, a glossy American travel magazine that paid handsomely as well as subsidizing much of the Pritchetts' holidaying in later life. The books he made out of these commissions did not win universal critical acclaim.

In my view, the most telling evidence this biography contains about the fate of the tradition to which Pritchett assigned himself concerns his increasing reliance on the American market. Indeed, one may wonder whether any English writers have lived by their pen since 1945 without this being true of them. Several recent biographies suggest not. For at least three decades after the war, a particular cachet seems to have attached to leading British writers and academics in liberal circles in the USA, and the fees they could earn constituted a kind of cultural equivalent of the Marshall Plan, quite apart from that curious literary form of transhumance involved in spending a semester as a Distinguished Visiting Professor on some American campus. The Man of Letters may have ceased to be sustained by the British 'common reader' alone a good deal earlier than Pritchett allowed. Certainly by the 1960s, Pritchett himself, we learn, 'made significantly more of his income in the USA than in Britain'.

III

Pritchett is known, above all, as a writer of short stories, a form that suited his inclination to the episodic rather than the architectonic. This has led him to be dubbed 'the English Chekhov', but maybe he has to be thought of as a Chekhov who had absorbed Hemingway and looked forward to Pinter. That's not such an improbable or indigestible mix as it may at first seem. His stories are, of course, more domestic and less action driven than Hemingway's, but there is some of the same use of a deliberately spare prose to carry an occasionally too-heavy symbolist burden. Abstinence from any accompanying authorial commentary at times threatens to become a mannerism in itself. Still, no one could dispute that Pritchett had a wonderful ear for the baffling yet betraying inconsequentialities of actual speech, and if there is not usually any of the Pinterian menace, there is a fractured, banally proverbial quality to much of his dialogue that is more than just Elizabeth Bowen done in demotic.

I should like to be able to say, in the approved manner, that this biography has led me to 'reread' a good deal of Pritchett, but I have to confess that I have largely been reading him for the first time, culpably so in the case of the two memoirs and the selections of literary essays. Though not quite sharing the common admiration for the autobiographies, I have been struck by what a good critical essayist he could be at his best. His preferred mode was the general characterization rather than the minute examination of the texture of the writing, a kind of literary portraiture that was carried by his own writerly energy and richly metaphorical sensibility. One of his best-known set pieces in this vein must be his obituary tribute to Orwell as 'the wintry conscience of a generation' who 'had "gone native" in his own country', but we can see him achieving a somewhat similar effect by different means in his salute to E. M. Forster on the occasion of his eightieth birthday in 1962. Other, louder, writers may have tried to 'impose themselves', writes Pritchett, whereas 'Forster has interposed and influenced by a misleading slackness, by the refusal to speak in a public voice. This has given the personal a startling strength.'

These examples are taken from the literary equivalents of state occasions. For an instance of what he could do in more everyday critical circumstances, consider his meditation on Arnold Bennett's unyielding realism:

He catches the intolerable passing of time in our lives, a passing which blurs our distinctiveness and quietly establishes our anonymity; until our final impression of him is as a kind of estate agent's valuer walking with perfunctory step through the rooms of our lives, ticking his inventory and treating us as if we were long deceased. He cannot begin—and I think this is his inheritance from the French naturalists—until we are dead, until we and our furniture have become indistinguishable evidence. I find this very restful.

Writing about a passage in Bennett's *Clayhanger* in which Hilda Lessways is faced by ruin, he asks rhetorically: 'How do people face ruin? Variously, unexpectedly; they traipse, protected by conviction, through their melodramas.' This may seem casual to the point of offhandedness, but 'traipse' wonderfully suggests the prosaic, straggling, unnoticing way people get through the catastrophes of their lives.

Pritchett described himself at one point as 'travelling in literature'. He did this in several senses, most obviously reading as one who explores the geography of other writers' imaginations, but it is not too fanciful to think of him in the guise of that figure who crops up more than once in his stories, the commercial traveller, laying out his samples every week, pointing to the best features of each new 'line'. His range of goods was astonishing, embracing all the high (and some of the not so high) peaks of European as well as English and American literature from at least the eighteenth century onwards, reaching out to Garcia Marquez and Machado de Assis and on to *The Tale of Genji*, and saluting new talent such as Salman Rushdie and Ian McEwan. His own reflection on the extent of his literary travels was characteristic: 'I am appalled by the amount I have read.'

His two volumes of autobiography were among the most popular and successful of his books, especially *A Cab at the Door*, above all for its portrait of his father—Micawberish chancer, Kippsian shopman, Christian Science gull. The zest and comedy are appealing, but at times the effects can seem a little contrived. Pritchett's childhood is presented as taking place in a theatre of freaks and caricatured social types, the action a sequence of mishaps and ludicrousnesses, narrated with a chirpy, one might almost say Cockney, bounciness and a wilful lack of connecting causality. The abrupt transitions and improbable juxtapositions seem intended to convey the mad, Dickensian-grotesque, atmosphere in which he grew up and to heighten the comic effect, but they become a tic. The writing intimates that the world is a rum go yet full of interest. As it moves on it starts to suggest that if the world weren't so rum it wouldn't be so interesting, and this begins to slide imperceptibly into needing to *make* it rum in order to make it interesting.

At one point in *Midnight Oil*, Pritchett claims to have seen a reference to himself in a list kept by a BBC producer before the Second World War, where he was crisply pigeon-holed as 'Embittered, Left-wing intellectual'. This seems wrong on all counts. Pritchett never strikes one as embittered: he found the detail of the human comedy fascinating and diverting, and was for the most part rather pleased with life for having treated him generously. Nor was he an 'intellectual' in the now-dominant sense of that term: he played no public role, offered no direct commentary on the events and trends of the day, did not try to shape opinion on non-literary matters. And there must even be a question about how far he was, or remained, 'Left-wing', despite his long and close association with the *New Statesman*. His writing evinces an instinctive sympathy with the underdog and the downtrodden, it's true, but he tends to treat them as a series of individual bad-luck stories rather than the outcome of structural patterns. Treglown remarks, apropos an early article about Spain, that it was 'one of many in which Pritchett's pessimism comes close to conservatism', which may be right, though neither element ever took on the pretensions of a full-blown 'ism' in his case. He could write appealingly of 'the usual blindness to character endemic in the politically minded', but he could sometimes display that usual blindness to politics endemic in those minded to make character the measure of all things. By the 1950s and 1960s there is a bit of grumbling about Socialism, interpreting his experience of the increasing democratization of society and cultural life as a decline of standards brought on by ideology. But he did not go on to elaborate any general critique; he wasn't much drawn to general ideas of any kind. Deep down, he seems to have had something of the 'Tory-anarchist' temperament that expects most human enterprises to turn into fuck-ups sooner or later and does not altogether regret it. As he confessed in another context: 'I must say I enjoy things going wrong.'

'Enjoy' and 'enjoyment' are terms that occur with a much more than average frequency in Pritchett's prose, especially the overtly autobiographical writing. He is good about appetites, about what gives pleasure, but also about the sources of happiness, and maybe he found these things less far apart than traditional moralists would have them. He wrote as a man who enjoyed life, in the sense of finding it stimulating and interesting, but also as one who 'enjoyed life' in the sense of someone 'enjoying good health'—possessing it, being blessed with it, flourishing in it over a long period. As Treglown quietly but irrefutably demonstrates, more shadows had fallen across this life than the later Pritchett always acknowledged—perhaps more shadows than he had ever quite been aware of. But at the close, enjoyment remains the dominant note: Pritchett's continuing enjoyment of human pathos and foible; his concern, in both his criticism and his fiction, with the reader's enjoyment; and his own enjoyment of the life of a successful writer. He knew what he was about, in every sense, when he wrote the final sentence of *Midnight Oil*: 'I have done, given my circumstances and my character, what I have been able to do and I have enjoyed it.'

3

The Great Seer:
Aldous Huxley's Visions

Aldous Huxley's lack of connection with the world was remarkable. For a start, he couldn't see much of it, having been nearly blind after contracting a serious eye infection in his teens. Temperamentally, he coveted solitude and went to some lengths to find it. And then his chosen way of life almost seemed designed to prevent the world from impinging too closely. He lived abroad for almost his entire adult life, often in somewhat remote locations. True, he had a few miscellaneous jobs in the years immediately after coming down from Oxford, but from his late twenties onwards he was able to devote himself full-time to writing, an occupation premised on the achieved habit of regular solitariness. There was as much self-revelation as self-irony in a passing reference to his typewriter as 'the sole stay and comfort of my life'. As a form of relaxation, he liked to paint, despite his near blindness, but his stated reason is revealing: 'It's so nice to practise an art in which all the problems are internal to the art and where one doesn't have to bother about what goes on in the world at large.' It is questionable how far Huxley ever really bothered himself about 'what goes on in the world at large'.

This was true of matters both great and small. His wife reported (it doesn't seem to have been a complaint) that her husband had 'absolutely no wish to concern himself with practical matters. He doesn't want to talk about them or even to think about them.' His lack of connection with the world could make him seem emotionally cold or at the very least humanly thoughtless. For example, in 1956, barely a year after his wife had died, the 61-year-old Huxley remarried, but the first his son knew of

Nicholas Murray, *Aldous Huxley: An English Intellectual* (Little, Brown, 2002).

it was when he read the story in the newspapers. And the same was true of this leading social critic's engagement with contemporary culture. For long periods he didn't take a daily newspaper, and he rarely saw weekly and monthly news magazines. He lived in the United States for the last twenty-five years of his life, but explained to an interviewer towards the end of the 1950s, the decade that saw American life remade around the television, that he didn't own a set. He wrote several plays, but cheerfully confessed in 1945: 'I know nothing about the contemporary theatre, not having been to a play for years.' He became a celebrated and widely commented upon author, yet he never read reviews or criticism of his work. When in company, he talked—wonderfully, said some; at length, said everybody. In the late 1920s, Huxley spent a few days at an Italian spa. One of the others taking the waters was D. H. Lawrence's friend and publisher Pino Orioli, who later pithily recalled Huxley's mixture of physical inactivity and unstoppable talking: 'Aldous he sit and make remark.' That is indeed what Huxley did: he make remark, one way or the other; he not do much else.

The result of this single-mindedness was that he published over fifty books and an almost incalculable quantity of other writing, which earned him a worldwide audience. From the beginning, his books sold quite well, and after a while they sold very well indeed—Penguin reissued ten of them simultaneously in 1950. *Brave New World*, published in 1932, was to be one of the best-sellers of the century. Interviews, profiles, even full-length studies, proliferated during his lifetime. In the 1950s he was a celebrity; large crowds hung on his words wherever he went to lecture, which he did frequently. When he spoke at MIT in 1960 the traffic across the Charles River jammed, and extra police had to be summoned.

And yet now, some forty years after his death, it can be hard to recapture just what all the fuss was about. The whirligig of critical estimation has not been kind to his novels, the early Peacockian satires aside; the essays can easily seem mannered and vacuous; the prophecies have lost their edge, having become a familiar part of the currency of everyday punditry; and he is remembered for having turned into a kind of spiritual faddist, sampling drugs, Eastern mysticism, and health cures with an enthusiasm that could seem at once even-handed and wide-eyed.

In seeking to understand the sources of Huxley's once-great reputation, a good place to start is the volume of memorial tributes published in 1965, just two years after his death. Here the theme that recurs most frequently is the part played by his writings in liberating the intelligent young, freeing them from convention and orthodoxy, whether religious, sexual, or political. He acquired a reputation for being enormously clever and enormously knowledgeable: his speciality was Things in General. His writings recognized no disciplinary frontiers, ranging unclassifiably across ethics, literature, science, philosophy, and religion. 'The greatest humanist of our perplexed era' was Julian Huxley's understandably proud fraternal tribute. Perhaps Leonard Woolf came closer to something that was both characteristic of Huxley and in a way distinctive about him when he said simply: 'he was the uncompromising, unashamed intellectual.'

Huxley's life was recounted in two volumes in 1973–4 by Sybille Bedford, who had known him well and who enjoyed the privileges, as well as suffering the constraints, of being an 'authorized' biographer. Now Nicholas Murray has written the first full-length biography since Bedford's, drawing on a wider range of unpublished correspondence, freed from some of the reticences that shaped Bedford's account—especially, and predictably, about sex—and able to place his subject with an experienced biographer's touch (Murray has in recent years written well-received biographies of Matthew Arnold, Bruce Chatwin, and Andrew Marvell). In so far as a biography can have a theme, as opposed to a subject, it is in this case given by the subtitle. Huxley did indeed conform, as Leonard Woolf implied, to one stereotype of 'the intellectual': owlish, bookish, a polymath, ready with fluent opinions on all subjects, removed from the world, different from ordinary people, a bit weird. For a country in which that species is often popularly supposed not to breed, the life of this particular 'English intellectual' obviously has a general as well as individual interest.

II

Breeding may be the place to start, for Huxley was born into the intellectual purple: his father was the son of T. H. Huxley, 'Darwin's bulldog', while his mother was a niece of Matthew Arnold. His father, Leonard, was a schoolmaster at the time of Aldous's birth in 1894, becoming a few years later the editor of the *Cornhill*; the family name and his connections in literary journalism did his son's early career no harm. Young Huxley enjoyed the educational perquisites of his class: he went to Eton and Balliol. But disaster, or what would have been disaster for most people, struck in 1911 when an infection of the eyes turned nasty, leaving him more or less blind for the next eighteen months, and only very partially sighted for most of the rest of his life (among the many faddish enthusiasms he developed later was one for a system of eye exercises, from which he claimed great benefits, though it is not obvious that it really did him any lasting good). This condition further cut him off from his contemporaries as well as from the physical world. The usual boyish sports were clearly out (not much of a loss in his case, it seems), but so for a while was reading, at least until he learned Braille, one advantage of which, he claimed, was that it enabled him to read under the bedclothes after lights out. Still, better cut off than cut down, perhaps; his condition did mean that he escaped service in the First World War altogether.

It is often assumed, sometimes just on the strength of his name, that Huxley must have had a scientific or medical training, but that was far from the truth. At Oxford he read the recently established and rather ill-regarded subject of English Literature, and as an undergraduate and immediately afterwards he was very much the young literary dandy, publishing a slim volume of poems, helping to establish an avant-garde literary magazine, and meeting everyone who was anyone. A good deal of this meeting happened, inevitably, at Garsington, where, among the usual literary and political luminaries, he also met a pretty Belgian girl called Maria Nys, to whom he proposed on the main lawn. It seems to have been a close and happy marriage, aided by various sexual excursions on both their parts in the early years (Murray claims the revelation of Maria's bisexuality as one of his book's advances on previous accounts). She devoted herself to Huxley's needs, looking after all practical matters, including driving him (on their several trips across the United States by car, she entered her profession in hotel registers as 'chauffeuse').

At this stage of his life, Huxley did not have much by way of 'prospects', at least as future fathers-in-law tend to understand that notion. He tried both of the two options open to a well-connected young man of literary inclinations, schoolmastering and book reviewing, the latter mutating into short-lived editorial jobs on literary magazines such as John Middleton Murry's *Athenaeum* (and, more improbably, *House and Garden*). His first book of short stories was published in 1920 by Chatto and Windus, who remained his publishers for the rest of his life. *Crome Yellow*, the first of his 'novels of ideas', followed at the end of 1921, and on the strength of its success Chatto offered to bankroll him to produce two books a year for several years. This enabled him to give up his day job, and to move to Italy (and subsequently France), where the living was easy all the while the pound was strong. Thereafter, he never held a regular job again, never settled in England again, never did anything except write and make remark.

When the novels didn't come fast enough, he made up the numbers with books of stories, essays, and travel writing. Usually, however, they did come fast enough: *Crome Yellow* had been written in a summer; the 100,000 words of *Antic Hay* appear from Murray's account to have been written in little more than two months. There is a sense, of course, in which all he ever wrote were essays, in one disguise or another. In this respect, he was to describe himself fairly accurately to an American interviewer in the early 1950s:

By profession I am an essayist who sometimes writes novels and biographies, an unsystematic cogitator whose books represent a series of attempts to discover and develop artistic methods for expressing the general in the particular, the abstract through the concrete, the broadly historical and the deeply metaphysical and mystical within the special case, the localised scene, the personal adventure.

Within a decade he was an established man of letters: royalties from the English sales of his books totalled over £2,000 for the first time in 1930 (approximately £60,000 at early twenty-first-century prices). He was contracted to write syndicated columns for the Hearst papers in the USA, producing a very handy supplement to his income. Murray observes that 'these were the sorts of pieces that Huxley could throw off in his sleep', but that was the problem. He was cursed with a fatal fluency, and regular journalism exacerbated his condition. By the 1930s he was well advanced on his journey from witty young novelist to mellifluous sage. He was not unhappy at the development: 'I feel myself very much of a moralist.' D. H. Lawrence, with whom Huxley had an improbable friendship that did credit to them both, saw it coming when he first read the essays: he found them 'professorial', claiming to detect a continuity with the famous grandfather, 'that funny dry-mindedness and underneath social morality'.

Huxley's lack of connection with the world surely became more and more of a handicap as he increasingly took up the role of social critic, diagnosing the 'sickness' of man in modern society. In some moods he seemed to belong squarely among those fastidious critics of 'mass society' who flourished between the wars. There were certainly times when he wrote as though the Epsilons were at the gates. 'Universal education has created an immense class of what I may call the New Stupid.' And again: 'The gulf between the populace and those engaged in any intelligent occupation of whatever kind steadily widens. In twenty years time a man of science or a serious artist will need an interpreter in order to talk to a cinema proprietor or a member of his audience.' Characteristically, he does not seem to allow that the person engaged in an intelligent occupation might be a member of that audience. Or again, when deploring the 'hot smelly crowds' in the south of France in the early 1930s, he reflected: 'It's sad that all the things one believes in—such as democracy, economic equality etc.—shd turn out in practice to be so repulsively unpleasant.' It is surely telling that he can barely make the effort to itemize what he claims to believe in ('etc.'), yet his aversion grabs his prose by the neck ('repulsively unpleasant').

In 1933 he wrote to one correspondent: 'About 99.5% of the entire population of the planet are as stupid and philistine (tho' in different ways) as

the great masses of the English. The important thing, it seems to me, is
not to attack the 99.5%—except for exercise—but to try to see that the
0.5% survive, keep its [sic] quality up to the highest level, and, if possible,
dominates the rest.' Perhaps Huxley's prose never quite shook off some of
the mannerisms of the undergraduate-as-languid-aesthete, but this doesn't
seem to have been said *just* for effect. Certainly, the 'exercise' it refers to
is about the only kind one can ever imagine him taking. He predicted 'a
nightmare of total organization', though, apart from some sketchy ideas
about 'decentralization', he never really developed measures to combat
it. When in 1933 he attended a 'conference of intellectuals' to discuss the
'future of the European spirit', he was deeply bored, though it was hardly a
boring question in that of all years. Interestingly, the one figure he took to
was Julien Benda, perhaps registering that fundamental removal from the
world that, in different ways, they shared.

It should be said, on the other hand, that in the course of the 1930s Huxley was led by intellectual conviction to embrace pacifism, beyond question
a serious, if disputable, response to the state of Europe. He took an active
part in the Peace Pledge Movement, becoming Chairman of the wonderfully named 'Research and Thinking Committee' (his close friend Gerald
Heard was vice-chairman, which can't have helped since Heard was a one-
man Committee of Fuzzy Thinking). Huxley's root-and-branch approach
to contemporary problems struck a chord: his 'philosophico-psychologico-
sociological' book, unpromisingly entitled *Ends and Means: An Enquiry
into the Nature of Ideals and into the Methods Employed for their Realization*, sold 6,000 copies in the UK within three weeks. Murray suggests that
'it is not hard to see how Huxley became a favourite with liberal intellectuals . . . there was a sense of modernity and daring about his writing'. A 'sense
of modernity' seems strictly accurate: his books were good at staging what
might now be identified as 'the modernity effect', a skilful achievement
given that he was in so many ways an old-fashioned man of letters. But it
was just that combination that underwrote Huxley's cultural authority; he
seemed able to draw out the social implications of the latest advances in
science while making apposite references to the literature and thought of
several civilizations.

Huxley had a great talent for intellectual magpieism. He was mocked for
always having a volume of the *Encyclopaedia Britannica* with him when
he travelled (he even made a special carrying-case for it), and Bertrand
Russell joked that 'one could predict Huxley's subjects of conversation
provided that one knew which alphabetical section of the encyclopaedia he
happened to be reading at the time'. But his reading went deeper than that,
especially in areas such as the borderlands between psychology and the

biological sciences. He was given to intellectual enthusiasms. For example, in the late 1930s he read widely in linguistics, and lectured his brother about its importance: 'There is no hope of thinking and acting rationally about any of the major issues of life until we learn to understand the instrument we use to think about them.' This same infatuation with first principles could sometimes make his unworldliness seem almost culpable, as when he wrote: 'The persecution of the Jews in Germany is horrible in the extreme; but it is not by proclaiming the fact in a loud voice that this particular persecution will be stopped...'. It would be stopped only by changing 'the habits of thought, feeling, action and belief' that created such evils. That may be, but in the meantime? Latterly his approach to 'alleviating the misery of the world' became, if possible, still more indirect. As he told Mary Hutchinson in 1942: 'Of books I don't read much outside the field of mystical religion, which is what now interests me beyond anything else and in which, I believe, lies the sole hope of the world.' Similarly, in the 1940s he urged that we must cultivate 'the art of what may be called "goodness politics", as opposed to power politics....Society can never be greatly improved, until such time as most of its members choose to become theocentric saints.' Oh well, not long to wait then.

Huxley's emigration to Southern California in 1937 is usually taken as the symbolic point of transition between his earlier and later identities, but Murray sees more of a continuum in a career increasingly devoted to finding the sources of inner peace and enlightenment. These goals were more easily realized amid the stark beauties of the Mojave desert, where the Huxleys lived for much of the 1940s, than in the company of other expatriate Europeans in Los Angeles working in the film industry. And it is hard not to feel that something had gone awry with the career of the dazzling young writer of the 1920s when we find him spending his time in the studios doing 'treatments' on stories by lesser writers such as Charles Morgan. Huxley's multiple removal from the world is poignantly caught in the fact that, as Britain prepared itself for German invasion in the late summer of 1940, his name figured in the credits for the MGM version of *Pride and Prejudice*. His facility earned him a reasonable amount of employment in Hollywood, but it seems that the studio bosses got much more out of him than he did out of them. His later letters are full of references to unused scripts and unrealized projects. High on the list of the latter was the musical comedy version of *Brave New World*: the rights were sold, but, as Murray drily notes, 'the musical remains unmade'.

Huxley had long dabbled in 'alternative therapies'—he had been an early enthusiast for the Alexander technique, for example—and California was like a homecoming in this respect. At one point, he even arranged a meeting with L. Ron Hubbard to learn more about Dianetics, and this was later followed by visits to Parapsychology laboratories. When his friend Gerald Heard published an article on flying saucers, Huxley responded with ostentatious open-mindedness. Murray points out that Huxley read practically no contemporary American literature, but instead devoured books with such titles as *Human Personality and its Survival of Bodily Death*. Meeting him in the late 1940s, Robert Craft was not the last to be puzzled by 'the contrast between the searching, lucid, rational intelligence which was Huxley's most obvious characteristic and the most striking evidence of his Victorian inheritance, and the credulity with which he greeted (though he did not necessarily swallow whole) each new Southern Californian fad of mind and consciousness'. Another contemporary witness was Christopher Isherwood, who, after a meeting with Huxley, confided to his diary: 'He is still very much the prize-winning undergraduate, the nervous, fastidious, super-intellectual boy. Stupidity afflicts him like a nasty smell—and how eagerly he sucks at the dry teats of books!'

By the 1950s Huxley was putting some very different substances in his mouth. It was in the company of his psychiatrist friend Humphry Osmond (with whom he coined the word 'psychedelic') that what Murray calls 'the most famous English literary drug-taking since De Quincey took place'. His cult book *The Doors of Perception* recorded his experiences with mescalin and LSD, experiences that were later to earn him the ultimate accolade of a place in the collage that makes up the sleeve illustration for the Beatles' *Sergeant Pepper* album. This new enthusiasm threatened to open up an even greater gulf between Huxley and the everyday reality of the world around him, yet in fact the 1950s were also the height of his fame as a social critic and early prophet of environmental catastrophe. But his message itself had now become other-worldly: man was lost unless he renounced purely material goals, only 'spiritual enlightenment' could save the world, and so on. He had become a guru. It was an essential part of his role as a 'general intellectual', much admired by Murray, that Huxley should not be a specialist in any particular field, but it seems curious that the one thing he was always thought to speak about with special authority was the future.

I was slightly surprised to learn that 'throughout his life, Huxley's books sold more copies in Britain than in the United States'. It is not difficult to see how that would have been true of most of his earlier books on first publication, but the works of the 1950s on drug taking and mysticism seemed to find their most appreciative audience in the USA, and it is hard to imagine that anything could have matched the total American sales of *Brave New World* even before his death. Certainly the reception of his books in Britain became increasingly mixed later in his career. Reviewing *The Perennial*

Philosophy in 1945 (a book Huxley saw as collating the doctrines 'taught by every master of the spiritual life for the last three thousand years'), C. E. M Joad shrewdly noted: 'The trouble with Huxley is and always has been intellectual whole-hoggery. Ideas will go to his head.' Joad prescribed reading 'Aristotle on moderation', perhaps the philosopher's way of telling him that he should get out more. Huxley's last novel, *Island*, came out in 1962. It was supposed to be his 'good' utopia, to balance the bleak warnings of *Brave New World*. Among reviewers, Frank Kermode was notably unimpressed: 'Reviewers ought to watch their superlatives, but *Island*, it is reasonable to say, must be one of the worst novels ever written.'

Writing had provided the structure and rationale of every day of Huxley's adult life. Sybille Bedford, who stayed with the Huxleys for long stretches, calculated that 'he must have averaged 500 words a day, and that with very great regularity. Every day that Aldous was at home, every day he was not on a journey, he worked. He worked on Sundays. There was never any question of doing otherwise.' He wrote when he was on journeys, too, in hotel rooms, in cafés, naturally insulated from the people around him. And he evidently did not regard the approach of death (from cancer) as a reason to forgo his daily tryst with the blank page; quite the contrary. There is something both heroic and pitiful about his last days, as described by his doctor: 'He worked in his pyjamas and wrote sitting at a typewriter as long as possible. Then, when he felt too weak to sit up, he would lie in bed and write in large block letters on a yellow folio pad. If he felt too weak for writing he would dictate into a tape-recorder that stood by his bed.' In his final few days he completed a commissioned essay on 'Shakespeare and religion' (for *Show* magazine in New York, as it happened, but it didn't matter: the writing had become an end in itself). His last, dictated, letter was about the possibility of a stage adaptation of one of his novels. He had long been interested in the question of some form of life after bodily death, and one imagines he simply took for granted that the hereafter would consist of an eternity of writing. He died on the same day as President Kennedy.

Nicholas Murray regards Huxley as 'one of twentieth-century England's most distinguished writers, a constantly enquiring spirit, an intellectual presence with no parallel in the current literary scene, a "multiple amphibian" living in all the elements of art and science and perception that his omnivorous mind could gather into itself'. At times it is hard not to feel that it is the cultural *role* of the generalist that Murray, himself a freelance writer, most values and admires, rather than Huxley's actual performance in that role, for which he occasionally feels bound to apologize. But perhaps it is a bit too easy just to deplore the effects of increasing academic specialization. The danger, as this biography inadvertently illustrates, is that 'the generalist' has to write too much, on subjects about which he is radically underinformed, undisciplined by the bracing effect of belonging to a critical community. The deformations of professionalism in intellectual life have become an all-too-familiar theme, but it has to be said that some of Huxley's writings risk giving 'amateurism' a bad name.

For a final estimate that is both shrewd and generous, we may return to the 1965 memorial volume. 'He was one of the great culture-heroes of our youth,' Isaiah Berlin there acknowledged, recalling much similar testimony to Huxley's 'liberating' impact, especially in the inter-war years. But having gone on to meet his hero several times, Berlin also remarked 'a certain thinness in the even, steady flow of words to which we all listened so willingly and respectfully'. They listened willingly because Huxley had so much that was interesting to say on such a wide range of topics (after their final meeting Berlin found himself left with 'a degree of respect bordering on veneration'). At the same time, a certain thinness was always apparent, perhaps increasingly apparent (Berlin, for all his respect, concluded that Huxley's writings 'even at their best have something mechanical and derivative'). His reputation, both in his lifetime and more markedly since, has oscillated between versions of these two responses. But through all the vagaries of public estimation, as through the shifts in Huxley's styles and enthusiasms, the one undeviating constant, as this absorbing biography amply demonstrates, was 'the even, steady flow of words'.

4

Performance:
The Critical Authority of Rebecca West

I

'I doubt whether any such brilliant reviews were ever seen before; they certainly have not been seen since. She amused, she stung; but she held fast to her own standard of quality.' Probably no writer wishes to be remembered primarily as a reviewer. Rebecca West wrote in several genres—novels, stories, plays, biographical studies, histories, essays, travel writing, reportage—and of her various books it is her two-volume 'romantic ethnography' of Yugoslavia, *Black Lamb and Grey Falcon*, and perhaps her autobiographical novel *The Fountain Overflows*, that have commanded the most enduring attention (and were her own favourites). But her place, such as it is, in the literary and cultural history of twentieth-century Britain chiefly rests upon her prominence as the all-round 'woman of letters', and in her case this prominence was first achieved, as it was always most reliably sustained, by her reviews. The above quotation comes from Frank Swinnerton's *The Georgian Literary Scene* (1935), and he was referring particularly to the regular reviews West wrote for the *New Statesman* in the years immediately after the First World War. These were abundant as well as 'brilliant': for example, in the thirty-two months following April 1920 she wrote fifty-five of these 2000-word pieces, covering 136 novels altogether. This recalls Connolly's 'white man's grave of journalism' with a vengeance, yet it was the chief means by which she made both her living and her name. Just how she did this, so early and so successfully, is part of what makes her career so

Bonnie Kime Scott (ed.), *Selected Letters of Rebecca West* (Yale, 2000).

interesting. The main question it raises was that asked about another critic in the title of one of her subsequently anthologized review essays: 'What is Mr T. S. Eliot's authority as a critic?'

By the mid-1920s West was being hailed as 'the most brilliant literary critic of her sex now before the public'; 'Bernard Shaw in skirts' was, it seems, meant as high praise. When her book *The Meaning of Treason*, on 'Lord Haw Haw' (William Joyce) and other 'traitors', appeared in 1947, her face was put on the cover of *Time* magazine and she was hailed as 'indisputably the world's Number One woman writer'. From the mid-1920s till her death in 1983, in her ninety-first year, she lived the life of the literary celebrity, frequently in the public eye (as often for libel cases or controversial interviews as for her writing itself). The thread that held her disparate career together, in so far as anything did—the activity to which she returned whenever her star seemed to be waning or the inspiration for more substantial work dwindling—was reviewing. She published her last review just over seventy years after her first.

It must generally be true that any authors (barring the out-and-out best-sellers) who also do quite a lot of literary journalism will be likely to find many more readers for their reviews than for their books. In one sense, reviewers are endowed with a little temporary authority by the very nature of the exercise; they have been invited to sit in judgement and to deliver their findings to a public. In the course of the twentieth century, that public has more and more come to expect that the reviewer will possess some qualifications for the job, perhaps by knowing a lot about the subject matter under review, perhaps by having excelled in some relevant kind of other writing. But those reviewers who, over a career, consistently command the high-profile reviewing slots are usually thought to have achieved a personal standing as critics, which makes readers eager to hear their impressions of that week's new books. Several of the figures discussed in other essays in this book, such as Connolly, Wilson, and Pritchett, attained this standing as reviewers, and reading their reviews now one can see why. West is a more teasing case, and so, more insistently than with any of her peers and rivals, the question presses forward, demanding to be asked: 'What was Rebecca West's authority as a critic?'

In various ways, West cuts a rather exceptional figure when considered in the company of the other writers discussed in this book. I have already touched on the most obvious mark of her distinctiveness, her sex, but she stands out in other ways, too. She is, to begin with, the only one who began her career as a literary journalist before 1914. E. H. Carr, her exact contemporary (b. 1892), was still an undergraduate when war broke out, as was Aldous Huxley, a year her junior, and even Edmund Wilson, with whom she has some things in common, did not start to submit articles to national periodicals till 1919, when he was 24. But West published in the *Freewoman* just before her nineteenth birthday, and in the next couple of years she worked for the paper and left it, wrote for its successor (the *New Freewoman*), and became a regular columnist and reviewer for the *Clarion*. Before she was 25 she had reviewed for several national newspapers, appeared in American periodicals, and published a critical study of Henry James. The fact that she was still writing book reviews at the beginning of the 1980s may easily lead us to forget how successful a journalistic career she had already had long before those who came to be regarded as her peers had received their first rejection slips.

This professional precocity points to another contrast: West had no higher education to speak of, apart from an unsatisfactory year at the Academy of Dramatic Art in London (later RADA). Out of necessity as well as inclination, she was earning a living sooner than her 'well-educated' male contemporaries. Of the fifteen figures discussed in Part I of this book, eleven went to Oxford or Cambridge (plus Wilson to Princeton). Orwell had no higher education, but had, of course, been at Eton. Only Sir Victor Pritchett had less formal education than Dame Rebecca West (and, like him, she complained: 'I have always felt the lack of a University education as a real handicap').

She was also somewhat unusual in doing so much work as a general reporter as opposed to as a literary journalist *pur sang*. She went on assignments for newspapers, was called upon to 'cover' major events, travelled to interview politicians and other non-literary people. When in 1947 Beaverbrook's *Evening Standard* announced that she would henceforth be writing regularly for the paper, it billed her as 'The Greatest Journalist of Our Time'. Orwell, it is true, was also a working journalist for much of his life, though perhaps rarely a 'reporter'; among more recent figures, Susan Sontag or Christopher Hitchens might suggest possible parallels. But, in general, the leading men of letters were writers first and journalists only by occasional avocation. For the most part, it has to be said, West was chosen for her assignments because she was already an author, even a 'personality'; but she nonetheless probably wrote more pieces that appeared on pages other than the books pages of newspapers and magazines than most literary figures of comparable stature.

In the final decade of her life, and even more in the couple of decades following her death, she was celebrated by academic scholars eager to identify women who, it was argued, had powerfully rendered the experience of being a woman and who had made their mark despite the hostility or neglect of a male establishment. West was always a slightly awkward recruit

for this cause, despite her practical feminism and early support for female
enfranchisment. During her lifetime she had been far from neglected; if
anything, she excelled in the arts of gaining attention and constructing
a successful professional identity. She frequently earned more from her
writing than most of her male contemporaries. The problem facing those
wishing to 'retrieve' West at the end of the twentieth century was not that
she had been condemned to obscurity or 'marginality' during her life, but,
rather, that the critical reputation of her work had not worn well since her
death. And that work was not easily accommodated by the prevailing academic catgeories, since it was evident even to her supporters that she would
rank as only a relatively minor novelist, while the various forms of non-
fiction prose to which she devoted most of her literary energies fell between
the disciplinary stools of history, literature, politics, and so on. Moreover,
she clearly had no desire for her work to be corralled into the category of
'women's writing'. She was well aware that being a woman had complicated her career, but she did not want to be judged by different standards
from those male writers with whom she had always competed so fearlessly.
Rather than benefiting from any special posthumous dispensation or being
treated as a representative of any 'oppressed' or 'suppressed' group, she
wanted her writing to have its own authority. So, the questions remain:
how did she acquire that authority and in what did it consist?

II

Cicely Fairfield (she later preferred 'Cicily') was born in London in 1892.
Her father, after a variety of unsatisfactory careers as soldier, journalist,
and entrepreneur, in effect left the family home when she was 9, and died
five years later. Her mother took the three daughters back to Edinburgh,
where she had grown up, and where Cicely completed her schooling at
George Watson's Ladies' College. Already ambitious and combative (and
a supporter of the suffragettes), she enrolled at the Academy of Dramatic
Art in London when she was 18, but left after three terms. Contact with
the intellectual and feminist circles around Dora Marsden led to her writing book reviews for the *Freewoman*, a little magazine of advanced views
launched in November 1911. To pacify her mother's genteel anxieties, she
adopted a pseudonym early in 1912, taking the name of the female character in Ibsen's *Rosmersholm*.

   For a successful author all of whose work appears under a single pseudonym, questions of identity become teasing. Cicely Fairfield started to
sign letters even to friends as 'Rebecca', just as Eric Blair came to write to,
and be known by, many of his friends as 'George'. And the question could

be even more complicated for a married woman in conventional circles: when the author of *Middlemarch* died, she was known as 'Mrs J. W. Cross'. After her marriage in 1930, Cicily Fairfield was formally 'Mrs Henry Andrews'; she chose to sign some of her letters, even to other writers, 'Cicily Andrews'; she was referred to almost universally, though not by her family, as 'Rebecca West'; the *ODNB* knows her as 'Andrews [*née* Fairfield], Dame Cicily Isabel [*pseud.* Rebecca West]'.

'Rebecca West' wasted no time in establishing her characteristic reviewing style. Here she is, just 19, laying into Mrs Humphry Ward, the *grande dame* of English letters in the early years of the century:

> Even her deficiencies are of value to the student. For instance, at first sight it seems merely a very damning proof of the worthlessness of Mrs Ward's writing that she should have written her two most pretentious works, *Robert Elsmere* and *The Case of Richard Meynell*, about a national movement which could not exist, but a movement which she describes as sweeping over the country and turning the hearts of Englishmen to flame... For an example of her complete lack of sense, let us turn to *Daphne* [the novel under review].

Some literary editors always regard this sort of thing as 'good value', especially if it issues in a little controversy. The modern academic editor of a collection of West's early literary journalism says that 'taking on Mrs Humphry Ward in 1912 was brave and foolhardy for a young woman with literary aspirations', but it seems more likely it was a shrewd and timely thing to have done: Mrs Ward was an increasingly spent force, with her best novels far behind her and a general acknowledgement that her political and literary allegiances were becoming somewhat passé. It probably did the young reviewer's career more good than harm to take a few free potshots of this kind.

As that passage suggests, West deployed a calculated outspokenness to arrest the reader's attention. Reading a run of her early reviews, one sees her striving to achieve an eye-catching strikingness in her opening sentences, usually staying just the right side of cheap Chestertonian paradox. 'Writers on the subject of August Strindberg have hitherto omitted to mention that he could not write'; or 'Mr J. M. Kennedy [a leading Nietzschean of the day] is a bishop manqué'; or 'Mr Wells's mannerisms are more infuriating than ever in *Marriage*' (the review that led to their ten-year affair). The son she had with the already married H. G. Wells grew up, and himself became an author, as 'Anthony West'; having as a last name a pseudonym adopted for the purposes of literary journalism may have been especially appropriate for a child who was, indirectly, the outcome of a book review.

Robert Blatchford, editor of the Socialist weekly the *Clarion*, admired West's early reviews in the *Freewoman*, especially savouring her 'handling of the battle-axe and scalping knife', and recruited her to be a regular contributor while she was still only 19. During the First World War she started writing book reviews for the *Daily News* and theatre reviews for the *Evening Standard*, as well as contributing to the recently founded *New Republic*. Thereafter there were few major newspapers or literary periodicals in Britain (and, increasingly, in the USA) for which she did not write at some point. Some of her longer tenures began with her 'Notes on Novelists' series for the *New Statesman* from 1921 and her regular reviews for the *New York Herald Tribune* from 1926. 1927 finds her writing triumphantly to one correspondent about an 'incredible arrangement' with *T. P.'s Weekly* 'by which I write whenever I like on whatever I like for vast sums'. At the same time she was regularly contributing to *Time and Tide* and *John O'London's Weekly*, as well as doing a series for Beaverbrook's *Express* in the form of 'Open Letters to Celebrities'. Later she enjoyed extended stints for the *New Yorker* under Ross from 1940, and for the *Sunday Telegraph* for the final decades of her long life (it was for this paper that she wrote her last review). Returning to that encomium from the 1920s quoted earlier ('the most brilliant literary critic of her sex now before the public'), it is clear that across this long writing life there was a close, sustaining relationship between being 'brilliant' and being 'before the public'. Just what kind of 'literary critic' she was remains harder to pin down.

In 1928 she brought together several of the review essays she had written for the *Herald Tribune*, prefacing them with a 200-page piece on the nature of art entitled 'The Strange Necessity', the title she gave to the whole volume. This was her bid for intellectual standing as a critic. She instructed Jonathan Cape that the book should be 'treated as a *technical, highbrow* book, reviewable really as a *book on psychology*'. She confided to another correspondent: 'I think it is the best thing I have ever done', but perhaps many writers hold this conviction about whatever is the most recent of their offspring.

The title piece is a curious performance—and it is very much a performance—circling around Joyce's *Ulysses*, interjecting details of a day she spent shopping in Paris, moving with equal confidence between Proust and Pavlov. It can be seen as yet another attempt to address the venerable question 'why does art matter?'. Her high-toned answer is, at bottom, a familiar one. Works of art such as Joyce's create 'beauty, beauty of the sort whose recognition is an experience as real as the most intense personal experiences we can have, which gives a sense of reassurance, of exultant confidence in the universe, which no personal experience can give'. Whatever its merits as a piece of aesthetic theorizing, the essay, and even more the pieces in the second half of the book, are more interesting as examples of her critical voice and as affording us glimpses of the cultural foundations of her critical authority.

The most frequently cited piece in the collection, entitled 'Uncle Bennett' (written in 1926), begins: 'All our youth they hung about the houses of our minds like Uncles, the Big Four: H. G. Wells, George Bernard Shaw, John Galsworthy and Arnold Bennett. They had the generosity, the charm, the loquacity of visiting uncles.' She then goes on to put each in his place, mixing high praise with wounding mockery of his literary foibles (for example, inventing a comic pastiche of Wells to represent those 'passages where his prose suddenly loses its firmness and begins to shake like blancmange', or saying of Shaw: 'when he talks about science he makes a noise like a Los Angeles Yogi'). The bulk of the essay is devoted to Bennett, ostensibly reviewing his political novel *Lord Raingo* but in practice attempting to pin down his particular gifts as a novelist, above all his gift for capturing the dignity of the ordinary ('Like Wordsworth, he has triumphed over the habitual; he has not let it disguise the particle of beauty from him'). If her praise sometimes seems a little overheated, her criticisms can be swingeingly dismissive. Several of Bennett's works are dispatched as 'mere runnings of the pen'; the most recent of his plays 'set a whole London theatre whimpering with boredom'; and so on. The extended conceit of the 'uncles' starts to wear thin before the end, but it allows her to camp up her criticism as that twitting of her seniors customarily permitted to an outrageously outspoken but affectionate 'niece'.

Reading 'Uncle Bennett' now, it is hard not to recall a much more celebrated attempt to identify the limitations of the leading Edwardian novelists, Bennett in particular, that was written only a year before West's: Virginia Woolf's 'Mr Bennett and Mrs Brown'. For Woolf, too, invents examples of how Wells, Galsworthy, and Bennett (she does not deal with Shaw) might handle an imaginary topic—in her case 'Mrs Brown', the little old lady seated on the other side of the railway carriage, representing the eternal subject of fiction. Both West and Woolf imagine something similar for Galsworthy, concentrating on how his plots attempt to reveal the injustice embedded in the social system. What they propose for Wells, though cast in different forms, is recognizably similar, emphasizing his exuberant inventiveness and para-scientific imagination. But although there are predictable common elements in their hypothetical or representative work by Bennett, they diverge when it comes to the significance each attaches to his meticulous realism. West finds it inadequate to the higher spheres of heroism and emotion: 'Mr Bennett can never work happily on a character which is not socially and personally mediocre.' Woolf, more pointedly, wonders whether, with all his concentration on the material and social circumstances of life, Bennett ever really enters into the interiority of *any* character: 'He is trying to hypnotize us into the belief that, because he has made a house, there must be a person living there.' Woolf's essay is much more of a manifesto, a statement by a rival about how fiction was now to be practised, a validation of Modernist experimentation. But there is also a difference in the register of the two pieces and the implied audience in each case. West is addressing *le grand public*, grabbing its attention, shamelessly pulling out the *vox humana*, and sending her readers home with the warming thought that, for all Bennett's limitations, 'he remains an artist'. Woolf's more fastidious and discriminating intelligence addresses itself to a more thoughtful audience, one already drawn to but puzzled by the works of Joyce and Eliot. (Woolf's essay began life as a paper to the Heretics at Cambridge and was published only posthumously, though its gist, especially the characterization of the three 'Edwardian' novelists, was contained in the essay 'Modern Fiction', which was actually published in 1925.)

Although West was ten years younger than Woolf, the style of her criticism more generally seems closer to the summative, post-prandial manner favoured by the 'literary uncles' themselves than does Woolf's teasing *pointillisme*. West's essays rarely contain much quotation or extended analysis of particular passages, of the kind that Eliot and Empson, and later the New Critics, were to make fashionable. Instead, there is broad-brush literary portraiture accompanied by a would-be winning mixture of whimsicality and slash-and-burn destruction. The writing is intensely metaphorical, leaving even her better insights looking a little too self-conscious and showy. In criticizing one of Bennett's books, for example, she writes that it contains 'an antithesis between a society woman and a prostitute, which is as wooden and made for a purpose as a clothes-horse'. In complaining about the brute salience of sadness and death in Thomas Hardy's poetry, she writes: 'Really, the thing is prodigious. One of Mr Hardy's ancestors must have married a weeping willow.' This is quite amusing in its way, but its studied pertness and the echo of a Wildean drawing-room epigram require too much collusive indulgence from the reader. We may remember the phrase, but we learn nothing about Hardy.

For the most part, West prefers to rhapsodize rather than to argue, as her prose works itself up into a frenzy of 'fine writing' that claims the critical authority of an exquisite personal cultivation.

The greatness of Proust! One cannot exaggerate it. Like the greatest, he draws one out of the house of one's life into his house. Shakespeare performed such abductions mercilessly. Making one's father less real than King Lear, his old lips turning back like a wolf's from his toothless gums while his dying flesh cursed live mating flesh and he talks of the small gilded fly; and the wench that broke one's heart less real than Cleopatra, proving curiously that all love is not divine. The memory, the poet's memory, experiencing and re-experiencing, has such power over one's mere personal life, that one has merely lived. Even so, one finds oneself seated in the great salon of Marcel Proust's mind, witnessing events which are more clarified than those of life, which clarify life.

As we pause for breath, we may find it hard to repress the sceptical thought that this doesn't, in the end, amount to saying very much. Or, rather, it tries to claim too much, it sets the bar too high and gives no guidance to those who do not find themselves spontaneously joining in the spring-heeled vaulting.

Of the 'literary uncles' who responded to *The Strange Necessity*, Shaw was benign; Wells did not care for her tactics but resignedly noted 'You win—as far as you are read'; and Arnold Bennett, reviewing the book from his regular pulpit in the *Evening Standard*, pointed to the recurrent weakness of her writing: 'She must, at all costs, "perform". She must be odd.' The comments of both Wells and Bennett have wider application to West's criticism: her tactics, the very forcefulness of her metaphors and the highly coloured quality of her characterizations, draw attention to themselves rather than directing attention to properties of the work under review. Perhaps younger reviewers striving to get noticed and to make a mark are particularly prone to such tactics; in West they became habitual, almost compulsive. Even her last reviews written in her eighties still had what the literary editor at the *Sunday Telegraph* nicely termed her 'unmistakable pounce'. Such characteristics were, of course, functional as far as appealing to the readers of the broadsheet press in the mid-twentieth century was concerned, and West was certainly widely read. Perhaps even now readers will continue to divide on whether she mostly stayed on the right side of the line that separates 'being readable' from 'performing'.

III

There are literary critics who, even when writing on non-literary subjects, do so unmistakably *as* critics. Leavis would be an obvious example writing in one critical style; Pritchett, working in a different idiom, another. Rebecca West does not really fall into this category. *Black Lamb and Grey Falcon* is the most celebrated of her 'non-literary' books, and alongside it one could place, among others, her biographical study of St Augustine (1933) or her controversial account of wartime traitors and spies, *The Meaning of Treason* (1947; in a revised edition, 1964). In bookshop terms, her works of this kind were as likely to be found under 'Politics', History', 'Philosophy', or 'Current Affairs'; they are not in any obvious sense the work of a literary critic. Unlike critical essays and reviews, the persuasiveness of such works depended to a great extent upon the research and specialized knowledge that lay behind them (though both the attractiveness of her writing and her larger reputation also came into play). Even *Black Lamb*, which mixes autobiography and travel writing with its accounts of Yugoslav history, politics, and landscape, stood or fell by whether it had, in the broadest sense, got its facts right. For some readers, its passionately pro-Serbian partisanship meant that its analysis simply could not be trusted. West's first biographer, Victoria Glendinning, an admirer of her writing in general, offered this sympathetic but telling description of the book: '*Black Lamb and Grey Falcon* is a great work of romantic art constructed over a framework of research and scholarship. Judged by the stiff criteria of this framework, it is excessive, unbalanced, sometimes wrong.' Getting things 'wrong'—or at least being accused of doing so; she defended herself vigorously—became something of a motif of the second half of West's writing life, as politics and current affairs absorbed more and more of her literary energy. A. J. P. Taylor was not alone in finding her 'a strange mixture of penetration and wrong-headedness'.

In the 1930s, her political sympathies were broadly on the Left: she applauded the New Deal in the United States, she supported the Republican cause in Spain, she even attended the 1936 conference of the International Association of Writers for the Defence of Culture. But her vitalist leanings made her susceptible to the appeal of the more elemental political emotions, especially an idealistic form of patriotism. Nigel Dennis (a regular reviewer for the *Sunday Telegraph* alongside West in later years) saw *Black Lamb* as displaying the quest of 'the frustrated Western intellectual for a Nirvana of vitality and self-expression'. After the war she became vehemently anti-Communist, and her largely sympathetic accounts of the McCarthyite 'witch-hunts' in the USA provoked a chorus of condemnation from liberal opinion in both Britain and the United States. She came to regard 'treachery' as the cardinal political sin. Her writing on topical subjects undeniably had a passion and verbal power unusual in everyday journalism. But it was also a high-risk style. She was involved in more than one libel action during her later decades as she chanced her arm on subjects ranging from Communist 'spies' to the politics of apartheid in South Africa.

Her letters give us some insight into how these various styles of writing formed part of a single sensibility—as well as, incidentally, illustrating the very considerable comfort in which a successful author could live in the middle decades of the twentieth century. She and her husband had a staff of seven at the eighteenth-century country house in Buckinghamshire that they bought in 1940 (financed largely by her earnings, she claimed, though her husband's inheritance must have given them a comfortable cushion). Even the peak of wartime austerity did not pinch too hard, since indoors she still kept a cook, a housemaid, a parlourmaid, and a live-in secretary. As 'farmers', they were allowed enough petrol to keep running the Rolls. She sold the house after Henry's death in 1968, but continued to live in some style in a large flat in Knightsbridge. Her energy for work remained remarkable into her eighties.

She wrote a lot of letters, well over 10,000 during her life by most estimates. As one might by now expect, she could be a lively correspondent, although the forcefulness that both made and marred her criticism also gives some of her letters a ranting quality. Too often they contained long tirades, frequently about Wells or Anthony (with whom she had a complex, explosive relationship involving several highly publicized spats). Sometimes, these tirades were addressed to correspondents who might have thought of themselves as quite uninvolved in the lives of any of the principals. Her 1929 letter to Bertrand Russell, whom she hardly knew, asking him to become Anthony's guardian, to save him from Wells, verges on the crazed.

Perhaps inevitably, Bonnie Kime Scott's edition of *Selected Letters of Rebecca West* leans towards her later career, when she was not always to be seen at her best. For example, she suffered the uncomfortable fate of the long-lived writer in the twentieth century of surviving to read the first academic studies of her work. She was not pleased, and all the old forcefulness was mobilized. A long letter in 1978 to Alan Maclean who was her friend as well as publisher (at Macmillans) documents her grievances against an American scholar who had written a monograph on her work (Harold Orel, *The Literary Achievement of Rebecca West*, which does not seem to have been published until 1986). As one reads the letter, one begins to feel that he may have got some things right and that the 84-year-old author is not always the best judge of her earlier work. 'He represents me as being uneducated and as acquiring knowledge on the subjects which I write about only when I begin the actual writing.' Rebecca West was not 'uneducated' and she read assiduously in some of the topics she wrote about, but too many well-informed readers found too many mistakes in too much of her writing for this charge to be entirely dismissed. Orel emphasized her professional career as a reporter and the speed at which she wrote, implying, she thought, that her work was 'scamped and hasty'. Her defence was that she had written so much as a reporter in her early life because 'I badly needed the money' and that she 'wrote at the speed common among reporters sixty-five years ago when I learned my craft'.

She certainly had remarkable facility: by her own account she 'often had only thirty-six hours between receiving the book and handing in her article'. A diary entry in 1950 records that she wrote a 3,000-word article about the atom spy Klaus Fuchs for the *Evening Standard* in 2 hours 25 minutes. That, as it turned out, was too fast: at the time she had conceded that in this case she had made 'a bad slip', and that more generally 'I'm inaccurate'. In 1960 she reported for the *Sunday Times* on the trial of ANC members in South Africa: her critical account of the judge's conduct of the trial was challenged, and the paper had to settle out of court, publishing an apology and a correction, though West herself refused to acknowledge her mistake. The *Sunday Times* did not employ her again. Her account of the tangled politics of Yugoslavia at the beginning of the Second World War came in for a good deal of scholarly criticism, and she seems to have been particularly culpable in the picture she painted of Prince Paul's pro-Nazi sympathies. In this case her error was demonstrated beyond question by later writers, but when she republished the book in 1982 she did not alter a word of her account. Another of her letters complaining about Orel's book noted some of his criticisms of *Black Lamb*, and then snorted: 'The rebuke is made with a superb air of academic authority', something that always galled but also threatened her. Overall, the 'American professor's' general characterization of her weaknesses was not without foundation.

A minor theme that recurs in her later letters is the malign influence on English literature of T. S. Eliot. She nourished her antipathy to and resentment of Eliot, reviving it with a sprinkling of scorn whenever it seemed in danger of wilting. The neglect suffered by some minor writer is explained by the fact that 'the influence of T. S Eliot has been to make people distrust writers who have any substance to their work'; the personal and semi-fictional form she had adopted in 'The Strange Necessity', on the model of French authors, had been 'killed stone dead since by T. S. Eliot'; in her lifetime literature had been fatally damaged by 'T. S. Eliot preaching that you must not have three-quarters of an idea to every ten pages'; and so on. After having dinner with the ailing Eliot and his second wife in 1962 she concluded triumphantly: 'I do not see anything in this man but the charlatan I have always seen.'

Most remarkable of all is a letter from 1973 rehearsing bitter grievances about how her own work had always been derided or neglected: 'I have forced my way into recognition of a sort, but I am treated as a witch, somebody to be shunned' (this from one of the best-paid serious authors of her time, who had been made a CBE in 1949, a DBE in 1959, awarded the Benson medal of the Royal Society of Literature in 1966, made a member of the American Academy of Arts and Sciences, along with a clutch of honorary degrees and fellowships and such like). But according to West, her personal circumstances had been so unfavourable that 'It is a

wonder I have written any books at all'. And then comes this extraordinary paragraph:

> I was also handicapped because you are right, I do care above all for reality. What
> chance did that give me in a world dominated by Eliot, who did not care for reality,
> who only cared to give out passes that certified the holder to be respectful to reality.
> I couldn't bear him or his work. The dominant factor in him was ambition, which
> is the enemy of reality—ambitious people don't wait to be classified by reality. The
> cultural England he made seems to me like that cynical building, is it Centre Point
> or High Point, which looms against the sky and should be sheltering the homeless
> and shelters no one. I don't feel that anybody in English literature has cared for
> reality since Yeats.

Eliot undeniably exercised considerable influence over literary life in England from the 1920s through the 1950s, but the pent-up resentment and
personal hostility in this paragraph seem, to put it mildly, under-explained
by this fact alone. It is sometimes said that people reveal most about themselves when they impute motive to others, and West's concentration on
ambition as Eliot's driving force may say at least as much about her as
about him. And what she resents above all about his success, I suspect, is
the way even his slightest review essays laid claim to a critical authority
that exacted a certain deference from his readers, thereby bolstering his
reputation and reinforcing his authority on future occasions.

Seen through the optic of these later letters, her 1932 essay mentioned
earlier, 'What is Mr T. S. Eliot's authority as a critic?', though only a relatively
brief review, becomes one of the key texts of West's career, revealing of
her intense preoccupation with this theme. Anyone reviewing Eliot's
Selected Essays might have remarked the increasingly pontifical strain
in his criticism; anyone might have detected a certain emptiness in his
repeated invocation of 'tradition'; and anyone might have challenged the air
of casual omniscience that characterizes his critical tone. West goes further,
deploring the use of 'tradition' as a stick with which to beat writing that
Eliot regards as undisciplined or self-indulgent—writing that West thought
likely to possess the essential spark of creativity. She detects the presence
of a dead hand, at once condescending and throttling, and so she bites it.
She exempts from her general criticism those topics on which Eliot has been
(in her rather limiting term) 'industrious'—the essays on Elizabethan and
Jacobean dramatists where he exhibited what appeared to be a genuinely
scholarly command. But in his other essays she is galled above all by that
'air of authority', 'the sober and seemly quality of [his] balanced sentences',
that serve as a mere cover for judgements that are too often 'flippant',
'superficial', and 'patronising'. (She doesn't address the question of how
far his poetry helped earn him his standing as a critic.) By contrast: 'It is a

relief to turn to writers who care not a fig for claiming authority, but who humbly perform the kind of task of discovery and analysis that continues the tradition of English literature.' If she sounds almost proto-Leavisian here it may be because she is just about to go on to praise D. H. Lawrence. But she is also fighting for *Lebensraum* for herself: she felt that she had to 'perform', albeit far from 'humbly', if she was not to be disregarded by a literary culture that took its tone from Eliot.

In their exactness and austerity as well as in their off-handed decisiveness, Eliot's critical essays now seem recognizably more modern than West's, but this may partly be explained by the fact that he was writing for a more select audience. Eliot intuitively understood the fragmentation of the reading public of which Modernism was both a symptom and a cause. Given the proliferation of so-called critics in various popular publications, Eliot sought to provide a cultivated public with a model of intellectually serious criticism. His 'authority' came in part from the sureness with which he hit the right note for the more discriminating readers of, say, the *Athenaeum* or the *Times Literary Supplement* rather than pleasing the broader publics reached by, say, the *Daily Telegraph* or the *Herald Tribune*. West cast her bread more widely, out of inclination, opportunity, and need. Initially, she had nothing to fall back on other than the quality of her writing, the tangible presence of her own literary personality: amusing, lively, unafraid, adept with the battleaxe and scalping knife. In time, her authority came from being 'Rebecca West', the well-known writer, but also from the continuing vivacity of her reviewing. Her complaint about being 'shunned like a witch' displayed more than the usual dose of author's paranoia, but perhaps she was not altogether wrong to sense that she did not command the unreserved esteem of the most influential of her fellow-critics. Meanwhile, Eliot, damn his eyes!, uttered a series of grave platitudes and was treated with an almost reverential seriousness. Really, the thing is prodigious.

V

Virginia Woolf's pen-portraits in her diaries and letters of people whom she met were not always kind or free from snobbery, but they were usually perceptive about something. Here is her report, to her sister Vanessa, after her first meeting with West at a lunch in 1928: 'Rebecca was much the most interesting, though as hard as nails, very distrustful, and no beauty. She is a cross between a charwoman and a gipsy, but as tenacious as a terrier, with flashing eyes, very shabby, rather dirty nails, immense vitality; bad taste, suspicious of intellectuals, and great intelligence.' Not surprisingly, Woolf and West never became intimates, even after West's eulogistic review of

Orlando. The term that might most have piqued West had she known of this assessment is 'shabby', since she was passionate about beautiful clothes and accessories, spending a great deal of time and money on them (Woolf was surely more vulnerable to the charge of shabbiness where clothes were concerned). But in other respects this seems spot on. The hardness, tenacity, and vitality emerge forcefully (no other word will do) from biographies of her and are abundantly illustrated in her letters. Most intriguing is the juxtaposition of 'suspicious of intellectuals' with 'great intelligence': it is a far from unfamiliar pairing in British culture, but it does also point to something particularly characteristic of West. She could be very resistant to any claims to cultural authority, certainly to any that might challenge or override her own. And she was temperamentally antipathetic to the kind of 'de-vitalised abstraction' that she (like D. H. Lawrence, about whom she wrote with flashing sympathy) associated with 'intellectuals'. As Bonnie Kime Scott notes in her edition of the letters: 'West favours whatever sustains the life force'—not something always associated with those who get called 'intellectuals'.

Yet West was, arguably, an intellectual figure of some standing in twentieth-century Britain—or, putting it more cautiously, a figure of some standing who wrote about intellectual topics among others, and her unclassifiable, all-rounderish literary identity was part of what sustained that prominence. There are quite a few candidates for the title of 'the last of the men of letters'; as I argue elsewhere, the logic of such claims is recursive, and each generation finds ways to revive the label. Nonetheless, part of the interest of Rebecca West's various performances surely comes from the fact that in her time there were few candidates who could so plausibly be regarded as 'the last of the women of letters'.

5

Man of Letters as Hero:
The Energy of Edmund Wilson

I

Edmund Wilson has become an object of fantasy. A lot of desire is currently invested in him as the representative of a cherished role: the critic-as-generalist, the man of letters as cultural critic, or what in the last decade or more it has become common in the United States to call 'the public intellectual'. Fantasies are, by definition, about the not-present, and all these notions are deployed to express a sense of absence or loss, a form of keening for a vanished world. Now, it is said, we have only specialists, experts who address other experts, uninterested in and unintelligible to those outside the walls; but then wide-ranging, readable critics addressed their fellow Common Readers on equal terms (quite when 'then' was turns out, as we shall see, to be tricky to pin down). Cultural controversies fuelled by some version of this fantasy promote the need for icons, and this is what has led so many parts to be scripted for Wilson—the modern Dr Johnson, the American Sainte-Beuve, the Man who Read Everything, the last of the men of letters.

There is even something about the surviving pictures of Wilson that uncannily colludes with this process: the stubby, solid figure, with its big head and staring eyes, as though Evelyn Waugh had been reincarnated as a Roundhead; the dark three-piece suit, an interposing formality signalling that ceremony is a proper thing to stand on; the shadowed, book-lined interiors in which he sits, robed and ready to pass judgement. It is all too easy to see him as the Sidney Greenstreet of literature, holding court in a private room across from Rick's Bar.

Lewis M. Dabney, *Edmund Wilson: A Life in Literature* (Farrar, Straus, 2005).

In addition, these nostalgic celebrations of Wilson make him out to be one of those figures to whom, when History was thinking of coming to a turning point, it made sure an invitation was sent. He was at the Western Front during the First World War, in Manhattan in the Jazz Age, on the picket line during the Great Depression, in the Soviet Union just before the news of Stalin's butchery started to become widely known. Although his relations with the Zeitgeist soured in the second half of his career, the invitations kept coming. He managed to be in place to write one of the first reports on the state of Europe at the end of the Second World War; to be on hand for the discovery of the Dead Sea Scrolls; to champion Native American peoples being driven off their ancestral lands in upstate New York, where he had a house; to be a slightly reluctant literary adornment to Camelot during the Kennedy era; to take a highly visible stand against the Vietnam War; and so on. As his journals and letters make clear, he knew everybody (and the very fact that he kept such discursive journals and wrote such copious letters contributes to his iconic standing). As he liked to tell it, he caught the springtime of Modernism and the autumn of Culture. Part of the fantasy he has come to embody is the yearning for a period when it seemed easier to be at the heart of things.

Even while still alive, Wilson had become a semi-mythical figure in American letters (writing about him always tends to grandly archaic phrases such as 'American letters'). He played up to people's expectations, mischievously combining the parts of *doyen* and bad boy. He really does seem to have detested what he identified as the academic spirit, but he also knew that he had already become a stick with which other people could beat whatever it was they didn't like about universities and academic literary criticism. His late squib against the professors, *The Fruits of the MLA* (1968), was not just an idiosyncratic contribution to what has become the rather tiresome ritual of MLA-bashing in the American press; it was also a calculated deployment of his considerable cultural standing to stoke the ever-smouldering fires of middlebrow prejudice.

Over the last two decades or more, certainly since the publication of Russell Jacoby's *The Last Intellectuals: American Culture in the Age of Academe* in 1987, there has been a minor boom in polemical recensions of recent American intellectual history, each of which has attempted to pinpoint when the old-style 'public intellectual' was finally supplanted by the modern 'academic expert' (it has been part of the crudity of this literature to assume that these are mutually exclusive categories). The so-called New York Intellectuals of the 1940s and 1950s, who were in effect the referent of Jacoby's title, feature in practically every round-up of suspects—figures such as Clement Greenberg, Philip Rahv, Lionel Trilling. But outdoing them all in his credentials for the title role is Wilson, the freelance writer who never held a regular academic position and who, it is claimed, wrote authoritatively on questions of literature, culture, and politics, matters that are now parcelled out among half a dozen non-communicating university departments. These narratives are nearly all to a greater or lesser extent unhistorical, condensing into a single, dramatic turnaround complex developments that have been taking place for well over a century and that anyway do not all point in the same direction; but each retelling of this overworked story only magnifies the symbolic importance of 'Edmund Wilson', the locus of unmanageable amounts of longing and regret. And just as, during his lifetime, Wilson came to be a considerable presence for critics and literary journalists in Britain, admired if also sometimes feared, so, since his death, has his centrality to this story of decline made him a constant point of reference in comparable debates in this country. Among the several reasons for including an essay on Wilson in this book despite his nationality is the frequency with which he figures, in Britain no less than in the United States, as the favoured embodiment of what has been lost.

There is also a subtler kind of anachronism at work in these broad-brush accounts since Wilson did not belong to the generation before the Fall, the generation supposedly furnishing the examples of the now-lost 'critic as intellectual', those emblematic figures such as Trilling or Irving Howe who assumed their cultural inheritance in the 1940s and 1950s. Wilson, born in 1895, was in some ways a belated Edwardian who came into his own in the 1920s. It underlines his remoteness to recall that he had already graduated from Princeton before America entered the First World War. His masters, as he himself acknowledged, were H. L. Mencken and George Bernard Shaw. Even the most ideologically liquored-up combatant in the culture wars of recent decades might blanch at taking them as models. The sobering fact is that, by the time 'the last intellectuals' were in their pomp, it was already too late for anyone else plausibly to set about trying to be another Edmund Wilson. All this means that it is hard to get a clear sight of Wilson just now, something that the sheer volume and variousness of his writing anyway make difficult.

II

Wilson came from fairly typical comfortably-off, East-coast Protestant professional stock of the Progressive era, and enjoyed the advantages of private schooling and Princeton when the latter was still partly a drinking club for young Southern gentlemen. He attributed his own widened social sympathies to his service as a private in the US medical corps in France in 1917–18, though in later life the manners and attachments of his class were what struck younger observers. It had been clear from his schooldays that he wanted to write. What now seems striking is the confidence with which he set out not just to write, but to have an all-round literary career. It wasn't, as with some aspiring writers, that he had a novel in him that just wouldn't let him get on with living until it had transferred itself to the page; nor was it, as with some others, that the impulse to write poetry kept overtaking him and reminding him that he was not put on earth for lesser tasks. Wilson, it is true, did want to write both novels and poems, but from remarkably early on he seems to have had the more middle-aged aspiration to become a 'man of letters'. After he had completed his war service, he set about realizing this aspiration in the approved manner: in the summer of 1919 (when he was 24) he moved to Greenwich Village and set up his writing table. 'He wrote steadily and, not letting rejection slips unnerve or discourage him, made a list of magazines and systematically circulated everything he'd written.' He 'wrote steadily' for the rest of his life.

That 'list of magazines' was as important symbolically as it was practically. The story of Wilson's life as a writer can be organized around his relations with literary periodicals; this has the advantage of reminding us of the intimate relations between his writing and particular readerships, specified in social and cultural terms, and of the constraining imperatives of that relation, imperatives that his present-day admirers might be likely to find pretty uncongenial. In his 1943 essay 'Thoughts on Being Bibliographed', on the occasion of Princeton library attempting to draw up an annotated bibliography of his writing to date (something that jolted Wilson into a moody piece of stocktaking), he deliberately distanced himself from the paraphernalia of scholarship. 'This list... is the record of a journalist,' he declared, explaining that by this label 'I mean that I have made my living mainly by writing in periodicals'. He went on:

To write what you are interested in writing and to succeed in getting editors to pay for it, is a feat that may require pretty close calculation and a good deal of ingenuity. You have to learn to load solid matter into notices of ephemeral happenings, you have to develop a resourcefulness at pursuing a line of thought through pieces on miscellaneous and more or less fortuitous subjects, and you have to acquire a technique of slipping over on the routine of editors the deeper independent work which their over-anxious intentness on the fashions of the month or the week have conditioned them automatically to reject, as the machines that make motor parts automatically reject outsizes.

Among those he was pleased to think of as his predecessors, he particularly admired Poe for getting journals to publish revised versions of some of his essays, 'scoring the triumph of thus making them pay him for the gratuitous

labor of rewriting demanded by his artistic conscience'. 'My own strategy', he confided, 'has usually been, first, to get books for review or reporting assigments to cover on subjects in which I happened to be interested; then, later, to use the scattered articles for writing general studies of these subjects; then, finally, to bring out a book in which groups of these essays were revised and combined.' As a compositional method, this pattern may have served Wilson well, but that wasn't the chief point: getting paid more than once for essentially the same words was the thing.

Of course, he was attempting *épater les professeurs* on this occasion, so he deliberately played down the amount of preliminary reading that went into his review essays. In a piece from the mid-1930s, he had set out a more daunting prescription for the practice of his trade. The 'reviewer critic', he declared, 'should be more or less familiar, or be ready to familiarize himself, with the past work of every important writer he deals with and be able to write about an author's new book in the light of his general development and intention. He should also be able to see the author in relation to the national literature as a whole and the national literature in relation to other literatures.' The really surprising thing is how close Wilson seems to have come to following this prescription himself; the fact that he did not need much sleep was not the least of his attributes as a critic.

The first of the magazines on which he found regular employment was the monthly *Vanity Fair*, 'the most successful of the "smart" magazines of the 1920s', with a circulation that reached 80,000. Wilson had already submitted some pieces to it when, in 1920, following a sudden turnover of the magazine's staff, his undergraduate journalism experience helped him land the post of managing editor. Jeffrey Meyers (in his 1995 biography of Wilson) describes the *Vanity Fair* of that period as 'a cross between today's *Esquire*, *Paris Review*, and *New Yorker*'; Wilson was not one of those who cultivated aesthetic purity by working for impoverished avant-garde 'little magazines'. After a while he gave up the *Vanity Fair* job and tried supporting himself and his new wife as a freelance writer: as a result, he was in his fifties before he enjoyed anything approaching financial security.

Part of what, in retrospect, seems distinctive about Wilson's literary journalism in the inter-war years comes from the fact that, although he largely wrote for mainstream publications, he constantly attempted to introduce his readers to the newest and most experimental writing. Famously, he reviewed both *Ulysses* and *The Waste Land* on publication, the former in the *New Republic*. Wilson wrote for that journal throughout the inter-war years, contributing over 350 articles and reviews; from 1925 to 1931 he was, in all but name, its literary editor and resident lead reviewer (he later described himself as the magazine's 'cultural man-of-all-work'). During those years the magazine, with a circulation of about 30,000, was the leading progressive weekly; the nearest British analogue may have been the *Nation and Athenaeum* (which was in turn merged with the *New Statesman* in 1931). In other words, it was primarily a political journal with a 'back half' where the literary editor was allowed considerable latitude. Even so, Wilson's markedly Left-wing politics of the early 1930s caused some strains within the editorial board, and the paper's strong support for the allied cause in 1939–40 was the final straw for Wilson, an old-style principled isolationist who saw no reason for the great democratic republic to get involved in corrupt Europe's quarrels. He broke with the *New Republic* then and never wrote for it again.

Already by 1952, Lionel Trilling, exhibiting the kind of nostalgia that seems inseparable from this topic, lamented that 'we have nothing in our intellectual life today like the *New Republic* of that time, no periodical generally accepted by the intellectual class, serving both politics and literature on the assumption that politics and literature naturally live in lively interconnection'. It is questionable whether, even in its heyday, the *New Republic* was 'generally accepted by the intellectual class'; such periodicals almost always seem more central in retrospect than they did at the time. But Trilling was surely right to go on to observe that Wilson benefited not just from the standing of this particular periodical, but from the very regularity of his contributions:

The authority with which he could speak by right of function as well as by right of talent; the frequency with which, as a matter of duty, his work appeared; the continuity of his writing over a considerable time—these circumstances were of great benefit to him. He was not in the situation of the merely occasional reviewer or essayist, who, if he has anything to say, is likely to say too much and to say it too hard in order to establish his identity and his authority, and this editorial situation of Wilson's had, I think, a decisive effect on his style.

One can certainly see signs of this intimacy with his readers in Wilson's articles from these years. Halfway through a piece on T. S. Eliot's *For Lancelot Andrewes*, for example, he can break in on his own prose and say: 'I was writing last week on John Dos Passos...', and then go on to make a comparison between the two authors' respective forms of revulsion from industrial society.

Describing himself as 'a concision fetishist', Wilson recommended that the literary journalist should steer a path between two available styles: 'the impressionistic criticism of the day before yesterday' and the 'sort of literary scholasticism that limits itself to putting things into categories'. This required a constant responsiveness sustained by deep wells of intellectual energy. Part of Wilson's subsequent standing, and much of his status as a fantasy object, is due to the stamina he displayed in fulfilling his regular reviewing duties. The sheer miscellaneousness of what he covered has its own romance. But this role also fosters its characteristic failings, all too observable in the work of resident reviewers in contemporary broadsheets—superficiality, overconfident judgements, self-importance, puffing—and Wilson was not as exempt from these as it might please his admirers to think. Nonetheless, this platform made him a person of consequence in literary New York. Though scarcely more than 30, he was already being teasingly referred to as 'the Great Wilson'. Lionel Trilling recalled that when he had first met the 34-year-old Wilson at the offices of the *New Republic* 'he seemed in his own person, and young as he was, to propose and to realise the idea of the literary life'. It has been part of Wilson's enduring appeal that, aside from the merits of any particular work, he can be taken to have realized 'the idea of the literary life'.

In 1929 he added another important element to this profile by publishing a semi-autobiographical novel, *I Thought of Daisy*, a book Lewis M. Dabney forthrightly describes as 'a commercial disaster'. (Wilson apparently liked to tell the story of how, when a woman said to him that she had bought and enjoyed the book, he replied: 'Oh, it was you who bought it', but variants of that self-protective *mot* are surely familiar from the biographies of several subsequently popular writers.) The first book that won him any lasting recognition came in 1931 with *Axel's Castle*, in which he introduced to a relatively uninstructed readership the difficult, sometimes forbidding, work of several of those figures who were coming to be recognized as the leading European Modernists, such as Proust, Eliot, and Joyce. The literature on Wilson repeats various slightly different versions of his remark that (as Dabney reports it) he 'was never happier than when telling people about a work they were unfamiliar with in a language they didn't know'. This is certainly something that Wilson was very good at, but *Axel's Castle*, in particular, exhibits the simplifying, didactic voice encouraged by this role. 'To persons already familiar with the field, my explanations in this first chapter will seem rudimentary,' he begins, with understandable defensiveness, for the tone of the exposition is introductory in the extreme ('Romanticism, as everyone has heard, was a revolt of the individual', and so on). Even in the best chapters, such as that on Eliot, there is a disconcerting mix of expository levels. It is impressive to see the author of such a book responding appreciatively and perceptively to *Ash Wednesday*, which appeared only as he was writing. Yet the Eliot chapter begins with a brief account of the work of the French Symbolists, Tristan Corbière and Jules Laforgue, containing little more than anecdotal character sketches, including sentences such as this:

In Paris, he [Corbière] slept all day and spent the nights in the cafés or at his verses, greeting at dawn the Paris harlots as they emerged from the station house or the hotel with the same half-harsh, half-tender fellow-feeling for the exile from conventional society which, when he was at home in his native Brittany, caused him to flee the house of his family and seek the company of the customs-men and sailors—living skeleton and invalid as he was, performing prodigies of courage and endurance in the navigation of a little cutter which he sailed by preference in the worst possible weather.

Quite apart from the fact that there is precious little sign of the 'concision fetishist' here, this is surely a case of an author underestimating his readers, or at least succumbing to a publisher's misguided notion of how the pill of literary criticism needs to be sugared.

Not that the book contains much 'literary criticism' in the form in which the generations after Empson and the New Critics came to understand that activity. Wilson didn't for the most part dwell on the mechanics of the writing under discussion; instead, there is a quantity of thematic summary with the passages quoted being treated in a relaxed, 'look at this' kind of way rather than providing the occasion for any special attentiveness or set-piece pirouetting. He sounded more like a genuinely if idiosyncratically learned tour guide, able to give his party the sense that he was in some way on the inside track yet uncorrupted by official or merely academic orthodoxies.

When in 1948 the American critic Stanley Hyman published *The Armed Vision*, his survey of modern criticism, he began with a chapter on Wilson that was omitted from later editions of the book, perhaps because its tone was offensively dismissive. Hyman focused on Wilson's role as a popularizer and what he called an 'introductory critic', observing that 'the introductory critic suffers the handicap…that his value decreases in direct proportion to the literacy of his audience and its familiarity with the work he is discussing, until it becomes almost nil for the relatively informed reader'. This may have been exaggerated as well as condescending, but it does highlight a difficulty for those who think today's literary professors should write like Wilson. The best reviewer-critics often manage to cloak the didactic in the conversational, something at which Wilson was adept, but there was also more than a dash of the village explainer in him, and—as was said of Ezra Pound, another with this trait—that was all right if one were a village and not if not.

III

As far as the art of turning journalism into successful books was concerned, the end of the 1930s marked something of a golden period for Wilson. In 1938 he published *The Triple Thinkers*, 'ten essays on literary subjects', later enlarged to twelve, and including some of his best known, such as his surprising disquisition on A. E. Housman as a classical scholar or his influential meditation on 'The Ambiguity of Henry James'. 1940 saw the publication of *To the Finland Station: A Study in the Writing and Acting of History*, his account of the revolutionary tradition from Michelet through Marx and up to the Bolsheviks. This may look like the one among his works that was wholly conceived and written as a book, though in fact most of its chapters had first been contracted to the *New Republic*. And then in the following year came *The Wound and the Bow*, the collection that contains his most widely read essay, 'Dickens: The Two Scrooges', which was itself a reworking of two earlier pieces that had appeared in the *Atlantic Monthly* and the *New Republic*.

It was a sign of Wilson's growing reputation by the late 1930s that the *Atlantic Monthly* paid him special rates for several of the pieces that went to make up *The Wound and the Bow*. But the freelance life remained precarious, even for someone who seems in retrospect to have been such a successful practitioner of it. The early 1940s found him at something of a turning point: he was in his own mid-forties, in debt and with no prospect of a regular income; his third marriage (to the writer, Mary McCarthy) was becoming bumpy; and his country was heavily committed to a war he opposed. It is interesting to learn from Dabney that 'Wilson sometimes dreamed of an organ of American literature like the *Nouvelle Revue Française*', and that in 1942 he even went so far as to propose to Harold Ross, editor of the *New Yorker*, that such a journal should be established with Wilson as editor. A similar inspiration had lain behind the establishment of the *Criterion* in London twenty years earlier with T. S. Eliot as editor, and Wilson clearly hankered after a pulpit that would possess undisputed literary authority in even the most intellectually serious quarters. The income from such a position would have been handy, too: in 1941 Wilson had to borrow money for the deposit on the old house at Wellfleet on Cape Cod that was to be his principal home for the rest of his life.

The upturn in his fortunes came in 1943 when Harold Ross offered him what seemed initially an attractive platform: the post of weekly book-reviewer on the *New Yorker*. Again, there has been a good deal of subsequent idealizing of his performance in this role. In practice, this was a very different berth from the one he had enjoyed at the *New Republic*. Sustained by glossy advertising, the *New Yorker* largely catered for a chic, moneyed, and metropolitan readership; during the period of Wilson's association with the magazine, its pages were cultivated and literary in a rather self-conscious way. Before long, Wilson came to find the atmosphere at the magazine a little staid and apolitical—Meyers is, for once, more informative than Dabney on this episode. Wilson did not welcome the interventionist editing of his pieces; it is heartening to find that even a writer of his stature had to plead with his editor not to 'take out the semi-colons' in his copy. After doing the weekly book review for several years, he found the task irksome and moved on in the late 1940s to an arrangement that suited him better, still writing frequently but at greater length and on a more miscellaneous range of topics, not so tied to the tread-mill of that season's catalogues. Both his erudition in some of these pieces and the magazine's indulgence of it still seem remarkable; it was in the pages of the *New Yorker* in 1955, for example, that he published the first version of what became his book on the interpretation of the Dead Sea Scrolls. (Dabney quotes Malcolm Cowley saying that one followed the *New Yorker* 'to see what in God's name he would be doing next'.) At the same time, his reviewing was becoming crustier; he now seemed keener to express his irritation at books he did not like than eager to introduce new readers to those he did.

As Wilson's reputation grew, so the opportunites for transmuting jour-nalism into books increased; by the time his journals started to appear at the end of his life, some passages had done several tours of duty in only slightly revised forms. Even so, the first book of his that was immediately a commercial success was his novel (in practice a collection of related stories) *Memoirs of Hecate County*, published in 1946 when he was 51. This was briefly a best-seller, clocking up sales of 50,000 in four months—chiefly, it seems, because of its allegedly scandalous sexual explicitness. His mother's death in 1951 further improved his financial position (in 1969 he also inherited the family house in Talcottville, in upstate New York, which was to be the inspiration for his last book, *Upstate*). His relations with publishers took an altogether more favourable turn at about this time. Roger Straus, at the recently formed house of Farrar, Straus, and Giroux, was an admirer, and in 1950 he brought out a collection of Wilson's pieces from the 1940s called *Classics and Commercials*, followed two years later by *The Shores of Light*, subtitled *A Literary Chronicle of the Twenties and Thirties*. These two lucrative bits of recycling consolidated Wilson's repu-tation rather than, as can sometimes happen, damaging it: the quality and variety of his essays drew admiring notices (*Shores of Light* remains, in my view, the best of his collections). Meanwhile, Jason Epstein had launched his Anchor paperback imprint and reissued several of Wilson's earlier books: *To the Finland Station*, in particular, sold much better in this format in the 1950s and 1960s than in the decade following its original publication. All this allowed him to feel, as he confessed in 1954, 'a little, for the first time in my life, as if I were a real success'.

Thereafter, references to him as 'the dean of American letters' became commonplace, a standing reinforced by his large study of American literature of the Civil War period, *Patriotic Gore*, which came out in 1962 and which, unlike his earlier critical studies, was an immediate success. (Those of us who can only goggle at Wilson's productivity may find some small encouragment in the fact that he had signed the contract for this book fifteen years earlier.) President Kennedy tried to quiz the author about his recently published book at a dinner in the White House, but Wilson was not to be drawn into a glib summary of a work on which he had laboured so long. 'I suppose I'll have to buy it,' sighed Kennedy; 'I'm afraid so,' returned the unyielding author. He refused an invitation to the Lyndon Johnson White House because of his opposition to the war in Vietnam. To his journal he confided the thought that a law should be passed forbidding Texans to be president (ah, if only...). In 1972 he supported McGovern, but died before the election. Though in his later years he was insistently an American patriot, he toed no party line. Robert Penn Warren, reviewing *Patriotic Gore* for *Commentary*, was surely right to say that what most moved Wilson was 'some courageous manifestation of the old virtues', regardless of political affiliation. Once, when he was asked why he was so anti-British, he replied simply: 'The American revolution'. Long after it had ceased to be fashionable, he remained an old-style Abe Lincoln-admiring, man's-last-best-hope-believing, republican citizen.

If one thinks about his near-contemporaries in Britain, it is tempting to try to see Wilson as a blend of George Orwell, V. S. Pritchett, and Isaiah Berlin (three writers around whom a fair bit of nostalgic commentary has also clustered). But even that alluring amalgam doesn't altogether catch him, and one element it doesn't represent is the impression he gave even from quite early on of being a survivor from a previous age of civilization. As his career progressed, this became a matter for comment. 'There is indeed something very appealing in Wilson's old-fashioned, undoctrinaire voracity for print,' remarked Lionel Trilling in reviewing *Shores of Light*, and it is indicative of the pitfalls awaiting contemporary nostalgia that Trilling should already see this as 'old-fashioned' in 1952. Wilson himself liked to play the dinosaur. As early as 1943 he was lamenting that 'we are left now with very little journalism of the literary and liberal kind that flourished just after the last war', and consequently he saw himself as 'the distant inhabitant of another intellectual world', belonging to 'a kind of professional group...now becoming extinct'. This mood was intensified in his last years as, holed up in the eighteenth-century family house in Talcottville, the blinds closed as protection against the light, the Scotch open as protection against the dark, he brooded on his affinities with his stern, upright ancestors. 'Nobler country here, which, I think, has made nobler people. It is a part of the whole moral foundation of my life.'

IV

One of the ways in which the recent idealizing of Wilson veils the historical reality is that it turns him into altogether too equable and too civilized a critic, something of a cross between the urbanity of Trilling and the thoughtfulness of Kermode without the sharper, engaged qualities of either. But the actual Wilson was a darker, more troubled soul; less likeable, and even in some sense less intelligible, than the figure celebrated in so many admiring eulogies, and certainly more tangled, more blocked, than his clear, commanding prose usually reveals. Isaiah Berlin, a fairly close friend in Wilson's later years, thought him by nature 'disharmonious', 'an uncomfortable man'. Mary McCarthy, who knew a bit about inner conflicts, recalled: 'He was two people. One is this humanistic Princetonian critic and the other is a sort of minotaur, really, with his terror and pathos.' Dabney doesn't altogether scant this side of Wilson, though he may be thought to play it down. But, reading between the lines of people's recollections published elsewhere (Wilson's was the kind of presence that prompted others to record their impressions), one can see that he wasn't just daunting; he could be frightening, and this was surely something to do with the fierceness of his passions, the suggestion that even physical violence might not be altogether out of the question on occasion. Obviously, it is tempting to apply the Philoctetan story to Wilson himself, to find the wound that enabled him to draw the bow 'that never missed its mark'. Whatever the merits of the various attempts to do this (Dabney is admirably restrained in his psychological speculations), one effect of keeping the racked, unsocialized side of Wilson in view is to make his writing seem more hard won and less imitable. It is not only too late for anyone now to try to be Wilson; it's not obvious that it was ever such an easy or attractive part to slip into.

There is one respect, it must be said, in which this thoughtful biography does provide support for contemporary nostalgia for Wilson as representative of a world we have lost. The evidence really does suggest that drinks just aren't what they used to be: nowadays they're mostly lower in alcohol and a hell of a lot less frequent. Dabney reckons that Wilson was 'the only well-known literary alcoholic of his generation whose work was not compromised by his drinking'. But it seems at least as true to say that his drinking wasn't compromised by his work, either. He really could put it away, quarts of the stuff: gin and whisky for the most part, various bootleg substitutes when necessary, all kinds of fashionable cocktails when available, and anything that was going when the cocktails ran out. In the 1920s one of his contemporaries teased him about getting by 'upon a diet of Proust and grain alcohol', but the truth was that by then he had his dependence on Proust well under control. Reminiscences of Wilson always include drink. For example, Harry Levin remembered him, when delivering a lecture at Harvard in the late 1930s (he was a poor and nervous lecturer), 'fortifying himself from a pint of whiskey behind a screen at the side of the stage, not knowing he was visible in silhouette'. Jason Epstein recalled meeting Wilson for the first time at the Princeton club in New York; the great man asked the bartender for 'a half-dozen martinis'. 'They were those small martinis that in those days you got in academic clubs of that sort. But even so, half a dozen, and they were all for him.' His attempts at abstemiousness contain telling and often comic detail. In the mid-1930s the poet Louise Bogan reported after a visit to Wilson that 'out of a desire for work and sobriety' he now bought gin 'only one bottle at a time'. When in his last years his declining health forced him to cut back, he was confined to 'a pint a day' (and we're not talking beer).

Of course, in the years when Wilson was forming his habits, there was a lot of it about. He spent a fair bit of his time in the company of those who, as one party-lover put it, were 'making the best of the last twenty-four hours of capitalism'. His friend Scott Fitzgerald tried periodically giving up the booze, but, apparently, 'his "on the wagon" could mean any number of things, including drinking lots of beer'. Wilson reflected in one of his later journals: 'I am a man of the twenties. I am still expecting something exciting: drinks, animated conversation, gaiety, brilliant writing, uninhibited exchange of ideas.' First things first. Elena Mumm Thornton, his fourth wife, thought 'Edmund just about never wrote when drunk', but this must only have been true of the years she knew him (during which she did manage to get him to cut down for longish stretches): given how much he wrote and how much he drank, the sums just wouldn't add up for the earlier period. It's astonishing that he lived to be 77 and published (depending on how one counts) over thirty books in addition to his quantities of uncollected journalism.

Wilson was good at final paragraphs, and the juxtaposition of two from his best-known books may serve as an epitaph, since they frame two ideals to which he gave lasting allegiance. The first passage comes from the ending of *Axel's Castle*, where Wilson saluted his chosen authors for the way 'they have revealed to the imagination a new flexibility and freedom', adding:

And though we are aware in them of things that are dying—the whole belles-lettristic tradition of Renaissance culture perhaps, compelled to specialise more and more, more and more driven in on itself, as industrialism and democratic education have come to press it closer and closer—they none the less break down the walls of the present and wake us to the hope and exaltation of the untried, unsuspected possibilities of human thought and art.

The second passage concludes his portrait of Oliver Wendell Holmes at the end of *Patriotic Gore*; these sentences are tellingly quoted by Dabney to round off his deftly sympathetic account of that wilful, lumpy book. Wilson judged that Justice Holmes knew exactly what he was doing when, dying childless, he left his estate to the United States rather than to some more conventional good cause.

He had fought for the Union; he had mastered its laws; he had served in its highest court through a period of three decades. The American Constitution was, as he came to declare, an experiment—what was to come of our democratic society it was impossible for a philosopher to tell—but he had taken responsibility for its working, he had subsisted and achieved his fame through his tenure of the place it had given him; and he returned to the treasury of the Union the little that he had to leave.

But life has a way of being less shapely than art. The Augustan element in Wilson would no doubt have liked to deliver itself of a few graceful, enduring last words to an admiring (and recording) audience; the reality was more mundane, but perhaps no less appropriate for that. On the last morning of his life, his heart and various other organs failing, Wilson managed to get himself out of bed and into the chair at his writing table, feebly miming, from some mixture of will and habit, the activity that had defined his life. The nurse who was looking after him at home asked if he would like a bath or breakfast first. He replied: 'Breakfast'.

6

Plain Speaking:
The Lives of George Orwell

25 June 2003 saw the centenary of the birth of the failed Hertfordshire gro-cer E. A. Blair. He moved into The Stores, Wallington, a small village near Baldock, at the beginning of April 1936. The front room of this tiny cottage had once served as a general store for the village, though it had gone out of business some time before. Blair had no previous experience as a grocer, but he had worked in a bookshop—'I suppose it isn't more complicated than a bookshop'—so he and his wife reopened the shop, and by June they had achieved the modest turnover of between 30 and 35s a week. But he was clearly not a career grocer, and in December he decided to abandon the busi-ness, if only temporarily, and travel to Spain. His Aunt Nellie was installed at The Stores in his stead, but she was even less of a grocer than her nephew, and the shop closed once more. Blair and his wife returned after seven months to live in the cottage again, but decided against trying to revive the shop. They were anyway still regarded in the village as a rum pair. When the vicar made his rounds, he was rather alarmed to discover that the former shop-keeper had been away fighting on the Republican side in the Spanish Civil War, since the English newspapers carried stories about its troops destroying churches and executing priests, though he seemed somewhat reassured when told that they were Catholic churches. In fact, the villagers might even have experienced a small spasm of pride had they known that, when Wallington's contribution to the war against Franco had arrived at the Lenin barracks in

D.J. Taylor, *Orwell: The Life* (Chatto, 2003).
Gordon Bowker, *George Orwell* (Little, Brown, 2003).

Barcelona at the end of December 1936 to enlist in the militia of the Partido Obrero de Unificación Marxista, he had enrolled as 'Eric Blair, grocer'.

By that stage of his life, when he was 33, Blair had several occupations from which he could have chosen his self-description: policeman, *plongeur*, schoolmaster, bookshop assistant, author. He could also have chosen to use another name, as he had done more than once in the past. When living as a tramp for a few months in 1929-30 he had been known as 'P. S. Burton'. When in 1932 he came to publish his first book, a semi-fictionalized account of these experiences, he suggested three further possible pseudonyms, including 'Kenneth Miles' and 'H. Lewis Allways'. The world owes a debt of thanks to his publisher, Victor Gollancz, for the firmness of his preference among these options: one cannot help thinking that the centenary of the birth of 'H. Lewis Allways' would have been bound to be a rather muted affair. But by the time the tall, prematurely gaunt Englishman was signing up in the courtyard of the Lenin Barracks, there was really only one identity that mattered: he was already 'George Orwell, writer'.

At that point he had been only marginally more successful as a writer than as a grocer, but the chancy way in which that particular pen name was settled on seems astonishing when one considers the extraordinary fact that, simply as a *name*, it may now be better known around the world than that of any other serious twentieth-century writer. And it figures in that very short list of names that have achieved adjectival immortality: 'Orwellian' phrases are up there with 'Dickensian' alleyways and 'Proustian' moments, possibly ahead of 'Kafkaesque' nightmares. 'Catch-22' may be a term used by millions who could not name Joseph Heller; few cannot name the creator of 'Big Brother is watching you' and 'Some animals are more equal than others'. Orwell's long, sad face has become a commodity for poster and T-shirt designers, on a par with bushy Marx and shadowy Che. Similarly, as John Rodden has pointed out, '1984 is surely the only number that has become a cliché'. No one seems to be certain how many copies of Orwell's books have been sold around the world: the figure of 'over 40 million' is frequently repeated for the combined sales of *Animal Farm* and *Nineteen Eighty-Four* alone. And rising. Some observers predicted that the end of the Cold War would see a lessening of Orwell's 'relevance' and hence his fame. Publishers' catalogues clearly indicate otherwise. New 'editions' of Orwell's books keep appearing, with new(ish) introductions by leading literary and political figures such as Malcolm Bradbury, Thomas Pynchon, Christopher Hitchens, and Michael Foot.

With the approach of his centenary, publicity departments and literary editors have gone into overdrive: one would need to have been living in the seclusion of a 1930s Hertfordshire village not to have noticed the proliferation

of Orwelliana in the media recently. One of the most striking features of
these slightly ritualistic celebrations is the high degree of self-identification
on the part of those in the media who write about Orwell, especially political journalists. And the job description he is supposed to have laid down for
them always features the same roll-call of virtues: honesty, bravery, clarity,
independence, outspokenness, and so on. One may criticize him for various
failings, but one had better end with a high-toned peroration about 'common decency', 'writer's craft', and 'speaking truth to power' if one is not to
be suspected of fellow-travelling, literary snobbery, or *trahison des clercs*.

Writing the life of a man who has become such a culturally sensitive
icon would be difficult enough in any circumstances, but the biographer of
Orwell has to face two additional complexities. The first is that Orwell's
writing grounded the moral status of its claims in the supposed authenticity
of personal experience. As a result, the relation between the 'experience'
invoked in the writing and the historical evidence for its occurrence, or
otherwise, will come under special scrutiny and be thought by some to be
specially consequential (did he actually shoot the elephant and did he actually see the hanging?). The second problem is that the 'identity' of the subject of the biography is more vexed than usual. Most of what we think we
know about Eric Blair is extrapolated from our familiarity with the literary
persona of 'George Orwell'. Because so much of that writing is apparently
autobiographical and documentary, it is fatally easy to set aside our usual
critical scruples about conflating author with narrator or central character.
Moreover, Eric Blair did not just write under the name of 'George Orwell':
as I remarked in discussing the comparable case of 'Rebecca West', he grad-
ually came to live out that identity, using the name in private correspondence, being addressed as 'George' by those who knew him only in later life,
and so on. It is expressive of the special complexities involved, in his case,
in teasing out the relations between literary persona and historical person
that each biographer has a not insignificant choice to make about the name
by which to refer to his subject at any given point in the life.

II

In the will that Orwell made shortly before he died (in January 1950),
he stipulated that no biography of him should be written. Such an inter-
diction is pretty much always doomed: only a writer who has become of
sufficient interest to a wide public to make the prospect of a biography
likely would feel any need to call for such a ban, in which case it will usually be in someone else's interest to disregard it. Three months before he
died, the fast-sinking Orwell married the much younger Sonia Brownell;

the ceremony, such as it was, took place in his hospital room, the groom propped up in bed wearing a smoking jacket for the occasion in place of his dressing gown. Sonia soon revealed herself to be a true member of that fierce and protective species, the literary widow, and used her role as literary executrix to try to prevent any biography. When in the late 1960s two young American scholars were attempting to piece together the story of Orwell's early years, she refused to give them permission to quote copyright material: nonetheless, Peter Stansky and William Abrahams's *The Unknown Orwell*, published in 1972, marked the first serious attempt to go beyond the unreliable tissue of memoir and anecdotage that had accumulated since Orwell's death.

At this point, Sonia (who had curiously mirrored her late husband's development by increasingly styling herself 'Sonia Orwell' rather than by her legal name 'Sonia Blair') decided that the best means to prevent unsatisfactory accounts of Orwell's life from gaining authority might be to commission a satisfactory one. She eventually chose Bernard Crick, then Professor of Politics at Birkbeck College, London, and gave him unrestricted access to all papers and biographical materials. She also, necessarily, gave him complete freedom to frame his own interpretation, but was then horrified, reading the proofs of the completed book, to find that she detested Crick's sceptical, analytical approach, and tried, unavailingly, to prevent publication at the last moment. She died shortly before the book appeared in 1980.

Crick's *George Orwell: A Life* was not only the first full account, but it was also an exceptionally fine book that stood out from the usual run of cradle-to-grave literary biographies in several ways. There was no question but that Crick greatly admired Orwell as a political writer: he even, perhaps a little hyperbolically, suggested that *Nineteen Eighty-Four* could in its own way stand comparison with 'the masterpiece of English political philosophy', Hobbes's *Leviathan*. But although appreciative of Orwell's achievements as a writer, Crick was tough-mindedly agnostic about the status of some of the 'evidence' for the life of this much-mythologized figure, and, what was more unusual still, he took the reader behind the scenes to examine the machinery, as it were, by which the illusion of the narrative of a life is produced. Crick also understood the politics and political theories of the period much better than literary biographers normally do, and gave these issues their due prominence.

Crick's book was both stylish and passionate, but his commitment to 'showing the working' may have constituted too much of an alienation effect for some readers, importing a manner that was thought to belong rather to a seminar on problems of evidence and interpretation. Inevitably, other writers and other publishers have since been persuaded that there must be a market for more conventional, less analytical, narratives of the life of 'Orwell the man', a phrase usually interpreted as guaranteeing a more thorough, or more speculative, snoop around the subject's sex life. Michael Shelden's *Orwell: The Authorized Biography* was the first in the field in 1991, 'authorized' in the sense that it had been written with the full support of the agent who had become the literary executor of Orwell's estate, and this was followed in 2000 by Jeffrey Meyers's *George Orwell: Wintry Conscience of a Generation* (the subtitle taken from the much-cited obituary piece by V. S. Pritchett). All the while, Peter Davison was engaged in his massive labour of producing the magnificent twenty-volume *Complete Works of George Orwell*, the final volumes of which came out in 1998, Davison's scholarly and relatively brief *George Orwell: A Literary Life* having been published two years earlier.

Orwell's life is thus not exactly uncharted territory, but the arrival of his centenary was obviously too good a marketing opportunity to pass up, so now we have two new, fat biographies, one by D. J. Taylor, novelist, critic, reviewer, and biographer of Thackeray, writing from the perspective of the worldly man of letters, and one by Gordon Bowker, writing as a professional biographer with lives of Malcolm Lowry and Lawrence Durrell to his account. Predictably, the advance publicity and, rather more carefully, the authors' own introductions, make claims about the 'wealth of new material' they have uncovered, and about how their 'strikingly human portrait' or 'fully realized account' supersedes existing biographies. So, how much new material is there, how much difference does it make, and which biography should one be recommended to read?

III

It should first be said that Taylor and Bowker have each interpreted their brief somewhat differently. The character of Bowker's book will be familiar to anyone who reads much contemporary literary biography. It is immensely detailed, maintains a brisk narrative line, and appears to be based on extremely assiduous research. It veers at times towards the chronicle, with its juxtaposition of not obviously related doings and happenings, while at the same time allowing itself a fair amount of speculation about motives and personality. Taylor, too, gives us the usual kinds of information in a broadly chronological sequence, but his book contains more (and better) literary criticism, more ruminative assessment, and less detail. Its greater writerly ambition is also signalled by the presence of short inter-chapters on arresting topics such as 'Orwell's face', 'Orwell's things', 'Orwell's paranoia', and so on. Taylor appears to have been a rather less diligent researcher than Bowker, except in the matter of interviewing people who knew Orwell, but the more distinctive character of his book may be thought to have lessened the obligation to try to ferret out new material.

The fact of the matter is that the vaunted 'new evidence' constitutes a tiny proportion of the content of both books. Bowker has certainly tracked down some new sources or pieces of information, though the use made of one or two of these remains a touch conjectural. Thus, for example, he makes much of the claim that Orwell's 'early Catholic education has not previously been uncovered'. This refers to the fact that from the ages of 5 to 8 Orwell attended a local convent school near his parents' home in Henley-on-Thames. Previous biographers have referred to it as run by Anglican nuns; Bowker indicates that local records show it to have been run by recently exiled French Ursulines. We know nothing about Orwell's experiences there, in marked contrast to his time at St Cyprian's, his prep school, upon which he and the several other subsequently famous writers who went there were to confer an unlooked-for literary immortality. Bowker speculates that Orwell's 'Catholic education' may have been the source of the notorious anti-Catholicism of his later writings, though Orwell's attitudes seem perfectly intelligible within the economy of his other adult beliefs and purposes. The paragraph about the convent school is reduced to using 'probably' in successive sentences. A similar air of damp squibishness hangs over the other much-hyped revelations, with one exception.

The one exception to the insubstantiality or insignificance of the new 'discoveries' is also a good example of how Bowker has been more energetic and persevering in his research than Taylor. In addressing the controversy over the revelation a decade or so ago that late in his life Orwell supplied the Information Research Department of the British Foreign Office with comments on writers who may have had Communist connections, Taylor reflects that criticism of Orwell's behaviour here 'is perhaps to ignore the NKVD file on Orwell himself, which exists somewhere in the vast mass of pre-*glasnost* Russian archives'. Bowker, characteristically, has consulted at least part of this file: in Barcelona Orwell was indeed reported on by agents working, indirectly, for the Kremlin, especially by a young Englishman called David Crook whom Orwell briefly befriended. Even here, however, the evidence does not add much, except possibly to strengthen Orwell's justification for his so-called paranoia about the activities of 'Stalinists'. Mainly, the finding increases one's sense that in 1937 half the foreign population of Barcelona seems to have been spying on the other half in a low-grade, '*x* has been seen having lunch with *y*; they may be sexually involved' sort of way.

Both biographers, but Taylor especially, base their claims to be drawing on new material largely on the fact of having interviewed people who knew Orwell. These interviews have yielded a few intriguing glimpses of his idiosyncrasies, but neither biographer seems particularly concerned about the evidential status of these memories. The recall of octogenarians for events that happened over half a century ago can be very sharp, but one might want some corroborative evidence of another kind in any given case, or some sense of the informant's track record in recollections of this sort, before rushing to conclude that we must adjust our understanding of 'Orwell's temper' or 'Orwell's attitude to women'.

This last topic is, of course, vital to the goal of getting a biography reviewed in the broadsheets and displayed at the front of bookshops. Bowker claims to have made significant discoveries about Orwell's sexuality, but he hasn't really: he has simply identified one or two more women with whom Orwell may have had an affair. We are no nearer knowing what his sexual life was actually like, and trying to list the name of every woman Orwell may have been to bed with risks turning into a prurient form of trainspotting. More important, much of the so-called evidence is frankly conjectural. This is strikingly the case with Bowker's account of Orwell's time in Burma. Thirty years ago, Stansky and Abrahams rehearsed the necessarily indirect evidence for the claim that Orwell visited the brothels of Rangoon, but Bowker works this up into the fact of Orwell's 'illicit habit'. 'The simple act of handing over money and enjoying a beautiful woman without having to perform the delicate preliminaries...must have been a revelation to such a sexual innocent.' The point is clinched by quoting Orwell's jingly little poem: 'When I was young and had no sense/In far off Mandalay/I lost my heart to a Burmese girl/As lovely as the day.' Comments Bowker: 'She might haggle, but once he had paid her he could treat a girl just as he pleased,' and so on. One begins to wonder just whose fantasies are actually in play here, quite apart from the lumberingly reductive reading of a five-finger exercise in Kiplingesque versifying.

The tone of the divorce-court private detective hovers over several of Bowker's attempts to uncover this 'secret' life. The scrappy, inconclusive evidence of Orwell's relations with the wife of a colleague is said by Bowker to 'suggest something more intimate than mere friendship' (what sad, cliched innuendoes 'intimate' and 'mere' are here). Orwell may indeed have had some more sexual relationships than were previously known about. Let's hope so, since it hadn't previously seemed to be a particularly rich or rewarding side of his life. We already knew that he could be awkward and inconsiderate with women; so he could with men. Like most serious writers, he was obsessive and self-absorbed, and the writing always came first. Bowker claims to be uncovering the 'contradictions' in Orwell's personality, such as that he was 'a champion of human decency yet a secret philanderer'. This is tired and suburban stuff. 'Philanderer' is an idiot term anyway, but worse is the implication that a person who has a variety of sexual experiences is thereby debarred from speaking up for 'human decency'.

Bowker wants to go still further: his index entry for 'George Orwell' has a large sub-entry headed 'misogyny and sadism'. Most of these passages turn out on inspection to be based on Orwell's own later reflections in his published essays about the mixture of impulses in his (or any complex) personality. These usually amount to little more than such stylized provocations as 'normal healthy children enjoy explosions', and anyway we are again back in the quicksand of the extent to which the literary persona of 'George Orwell' provides reliable evidence about the personality of Eric Blair. For example, in the course of elaborating a general sociological observation in a later piece of journalism, Orwell made figurative use of his having cut a wasp in half when a child; this then provides the basis for Bowker's references to Orwell's 'childhood cruelties—wasps cut in half', and so on (the unwarranted plural suggesting something positively habitual). Other instances of alleged 'sadism' amount to little more than freely expressed aggression towards those Orwell had good reason to hate. It is hard to see that his describing himself as 'thoroughly pleased' by the news of the death of Mussolini's air force chief who had been responsible for bombing the Abyssinians is evidence for 'the sadistic side of his nature'. But having decided early on that the (ambiguous and patchy) evidence firmly establishes the existence of 'Orwell's sadistic streak', Bowker then repeatedly invokes this in describing or explaining later episodes.

None of the entries, incidentally, even purports to provide direct evidence of Orwell's 'misogyny'. The one page on which this is discussed observes, rightly, that he sometimes did not treat women well; there was certainly much that was not admirable in his attitudes towards women, if the later testimony of some women who knew him is anything to go by. This is enough for Bowker: 'Orwell's anti-feminism... probably stems from early childhood.' Liberal use of 'probably' in a biography is always a bad sign, but worse is the tendency to reify one possible description of a piece of behaviour into an explanatory character trait.

An instance of this, and a good example of the different styles of what are for the moment the three leading contenders among Orwell biographies, comes when Orwell, on his way to Spain in December 1936, stopped off in Paris and went to visit Henry Miller. Bowker writes:

En route to Miller's studio, he had a violent altercation with a taxi driver, and ended up threatening to smash his face in. Later he felt ashamed of how he had behaved and could hardly bring himself to write about it. Again the sadist had broken through and again he felt guilt-stricken.

Taylor recounts the story thus:

The Paris stay was memorable for one other episode—another of those guilt-ridden encounters which Orwell later set down for the benefit of his *Tribune* readers— when a mix-up over addresses found him hiring a taxi to carry him a distance of a few hundred yards. The taxi-driver was incensed, and the ensuing row ended with both men screaming abuse at each other. Furious at the time, Orwell later came to appreciate the view that the man had taken of him: simply another moneyed foreigner traversing the Paris boulevards while 500 miles away the class struggle was in full swing.

The differences are clear enough, especially in Taylor's much better presentation of the *class* significance the episode had for Orwell. In addition, his reference to *Tribune* alerts the reader to the source of this story, a piece that Orwell wrote almost eight years after the event in question.

Turning back to Crick, we find the episode presented in a way that is more illuminating still:

Visiting Miller he was upset by an absurd quarrel with a taxi-driver who got aggressive and abusive on being asked by Orwell, in innocence and ignorance, to drive him a very short distance and then presented with a large bank-note which he could not change. Orwell reminisced that he must have appeared to the taxi-driver as 'a symbol of the idle, patronizing foreign tourists who had done their best to turn France into something midway between a museum and a brothel'. He was to contrast this incident to what happened when he boarded the train for Spain that night, virtually a troop-train full of tired Czech, German and French volunteers, and to the following morning when 'as we crawled across southern France, every peasant working in the fields turned round, stood solemnly upright and gave the anti-Fascist salute'. He concluded that the motives of the 'polyglot army... of the peasants with raised fists... my own motive in going to Spain, and the motive of the old taxi-driver in insulting me, were at the bottom all the same', all part of 'the wave of revolutionary feeling'. Writing in 1944, he may have predated his own revolutionary feelings as distinct from a fierce commitment to the defence of the republic.

The source of so much 'biographical evidence' in Orwell's own writing could hardly be better illustrated. The incident with the taxi-driver may or may not have happened as Orwell described, but its place in the piece of writing that is the only 'evidence' for its having happened is entirely conditioned by Orwell's political purpose. Crick's treatment is much superior even to Taylor's, partly because he actually quotes more of Orwell's own words, partly because he brings out the political moral that, as so often, Orwell used such stories to illustrate, and partly because of his proper scepticism about the reliability of an account written several years later.

The question of which biography the reader should now be recommended to read obviously depends in part on who the reader is and what he or she wants from a life of Orwell. Specialist scholars, trying to corroborate an interpretation or check a source, will need to consult each of the available biographies; although Crick will remain indispensable, the greater detail in Bowker may occasionally be helpful, if used carefully. For the knowledge-able admirer of Orwell's writings, wanting an integrated critical portrait, Crick again provides the benchmark, but Taylor's is by some margin the best of the rest; he has a good ear for the tones of Orwell's prose and is particularly shrewd about the weaknesses as well as the strengths of the fiction. And for the kind of 'general reader' who is alleged to be in search of 'the man behind the name'? Well, such readers may find themselves most comfortable with Bowker, whose book belongs to the dominant style of contemporary literary biography, managing to sustain a page-turning narrative pace while bringing together a great deal of detail. They may be most intrigued by Taylor, whose literary voice is good company and whose writerly inventiveness is refreshing. But perhaps this category of reader, too, should be urged to go back to Crick as providing the best estimate of the kind of writer and thinker Orwell was, as well as conveying some of the complexities involved in reconstructing this particular life from the self-mythologizing writings and miscellaneous materials that have happened to survive it. It is true that a certain amount of material has come to light since Crick wrote his biography, and this would need to be incorporated into any full account (the last updated edition of his book came out in 1992). But no subsequent biography has been so adept at doing justice to both parts of Orwell's description of himself as 'a political writer'. Let grocers bury their fellow-grocers: to do justice to Orwell, a biographer needs to have thought a lot about writing and a lot about politics and a lot about the relations between them. Taylor comes reasonably close starting from one side, Crick still closer from the other.

IV

Centenaries over-stimulate piety. The truth is that Orwell was a writer of very variable quality. He was not for the most part an outstandingly gifted novelist; he could be a reductive, anti-intellectual, over-insistent polemicist and journalist. But he did write several really fine essays and an impressive number of trenchant, outspoken articles; he also wrote some hard-to-classify pieces of social reportage that retain their power and readability. Above all, he wrote two books whose actual merits it is now almost impossible (and perhaps almost irrelevant) to gauge: they have been adopted as emblematic expressions of the twentieth century's nightmares about political power. In consequence, he is one of the few writers who may have become more important as a symbol than for what he actually wrote. He has come to stand for one conception of the intellectual in its idealized form, for truth against falsehood, courage against orthodoxy, decency against corruption. The story of how Eric Arthur Blair, old Etonian, former imperial policeman, and failed grocer became 'George Orwell', icon of a century's anxieties about the relation between truth and politics, remains an intriguing and moving one, however well or ill the biographers do their job.

But in a sense 21 January 1950 marked the end only of the first act of that still-continuing drama. We need to turn to John Rodden's excellent *The Politics of Literary Reputation: The Making and Claiming of 'St George' Orwell*, published in 1989, for the extraordinary facts of 'George Orwell's' posthumous career, a career that knew appropriations and distortions that we have come almost wearily to describe as 'Orwellian'. And the story is not yet over: signs of the need to invoke, and in many cases to identify with, some simulacrum of an 'Orwell' are all around us, and not just in Britain. Part of Orwell's achievement was to have created the sense that we *need* for there to have been someone like him.

But like *whom*? The Eric Arthur Blair whose remains were buried in an Oxfordshire churchyard over fifty years ago and whose life these biographies attempt to reconstruct is only part of the story, arguably not the most important part. The 'George Orwell' whose name appears on the cover of the twenty-volume collected works and who exists only as the author of those volumes is much more important, though even so he is not the whole story. For that, we would have to venture where no biographer or even most critics would dare to tread, though Rodden has pointed the way: we would have to go to the 'Orwell' of schoolchildren first glimpsing the magic of allegory by reading about dictatorial pigs; to the 'Orwell' of writing classes eagerly trying to imitate the (subtle effect of the) plain style; to the 'Orwell' of those who read *Nineteen Eighty-Four* as science fiction, those who remember only its neologisms, and those who know what it is about without ever having read it; to the 'Orwell' of the producers and the heritage merchants lazily recycling images of essential Englishness; to the 'Orwell' of columnists and leader-writers across the world reaching for a clichéd alternative to the clichés of their particular political culture; to the

'Orwell' of countless lectures, articles, and books by scholars yearning to be writers and by writers ambitious to be more than writers; to the 'Orwell' of moralists anxious to make decency not seem a feeble virtue; to the 'Orwell' of those angry at the injustice and cruelty of man to man who admire and are grateful for the power of his sympathetic observation of the life of the poor; to the 'Orwell' of the persecuted everywhere who find in his name hope and encouragement.

For other purposes, we must make do with biographies and the nuggets of 'information' they contain. Both these new lives add some eye-catching details to the broadly familiar picture. For example, from Taylor I learn that when in 1940 Orwell joined the Local Defence Volunteers, later better known as the Home Guard, his unit's main duty consisted of 'defending' the St John's Wood telephone exchange. And from Bowker I learn that Orwell's company commander in this *Dad's Army* farce was a grocer.

7

Believing in Oneself:
The Career of Stephen Spender

I

When Stephen Spender's son Matthew was 10 years old, he caught his hand in a car door. 'The event', writes John Sutherland, 'recalled other tragedies in the boy's little life; the running over, for example, of his dog Bobby—a "rather lugubrious looking spaniel" and a present from his godmother, Edith Sitwell. Six-year-old Matthew had been disappointed by the hound's demise not being reported in the obituary columns of next day's *Times*.'

This cute narrative bagatelle turns out to epitomize something both about Spender and about the problems of writing his biography. To begin with, the past tense of 'recalled' indicates that it is not Sutherland who is thus reminded of the earlier incident. The passage, a rather spare endnote informs us, draws on an entry in Spender's journals: the one accident 're-called' the other to Spender, who took a certain pride in his elder child's grave precocity. So Sutherland's version is written in what one might call the biographer's equivalent of free indirect style; only the description of the dog is given as a quotation (I'm not quite sure why; I suppose there *may* be spaniels who don't look lugubrious). However, when one pursues the incident to its source in the published version of Spender's journals, one finds none of the detail of the earlier accident, merely a mention that the car-door incident 'brought to mind so many past episodes—his dog being run over, his canary being eaten by the cat in front of his eyes'. One has to infer from Sutherland's general practice that the detail of the earlier accident must come from material in the Spender archive, 'currently administered by the

John Sutherland, *Stephen Spender: The Authorized Biography* (Viking, 2004).
Stephen Spender, *New Collected Poems*, (ed.) Michael Brett (Faber, 2004).

author's estate', perhaps from an unpublished section of the journals, perhaps from correspondence, perhaps from some other reminiscence. But this
in turn starts to make one wonder how much the 'source' was a writerly
composition intended for the public eye in the first place. Was it Spender
père who added the identification of his son's famous godparent as donor
of the dog, and if so, to whom was the account addressed, implicitly or explicitly?

This passage seems to me (though not, I can only assume, to Sutherland)
emblematic of two central characteristics of Spender that are bound to affect
the writing of his life. The first, unwittingly reproduced in miniature in this
episode, is Spender's own unspoken certainty that happenings that bulked
large in his emotional life were of public interest. The paternal egotism
lurking behind such stories of infant precocity here takes a cultural form
that was central to Spender's own habitual confidence or self-importance.
And the second is that Spender was, as he sometimes acknowledged,
a constant autobiographer. In *World within World*, his first formal
autobiography, published when he was only 42, he contrasted himself with
those of his poetical peers whom he saw as responding to the world or to
imperatives of their craft: 'As for me, I was an autobiographer restlessly
searching for forms in which to express the stages of my development. '
This passage, like much of Spender, is surely more egotistical than it knows:
that each successive stage of his 'development' should interest *him* is hardly
surprising, but there is always this same assurance that the world, too,
needed to be kept up to date.

These two characteristics taken together put the biographer in a tricky
position. The life has already, in one sense, been written (and rewritten);
much of the surviving material has been fashioned for just this purpose.
How much should the biographer be challenging this account, pointing to discrepancies with other items in the historical record? And how
far is he to take over his subject's own conviction about his claim on the
attentions of the world? At the very least, such a subject may seem to call
for a rather sceptical eye, treating the behaviour and the assumptions it
expressed as material for analysis, even as symptoms, perhaps requiring a
certain amount of historical distancing or sociological 'placing', perhaps
even a dash of mildly deconstructive literary criticism (Spender, like most
autobiographers, tended to betray at least as much as he declared).

Writing as an 'authorized' biographer makes the position trickier still.
The label inevitably calls up suggestions of a Faustian pact. After all,
biographers nose after 'papers' with a zeal that makes sniffer-dogs seem
like easily distracted wasters. Whoever controls the literary estate, often
a surviving spouse, can offer to gratify this lust in a way nobody else can,

and in return for this largesse demands—nothing at all, no restrictions, no unduly favourable account, no finger on the scale. For the eager biographer, such luck must seem almost too good to be true. And there is the added advantage that there is an authoritative source to hand against whose memory the details of far-off events and confused motives can be checked and errors of fact and interpretation thereby corrected.

Sutherland has been fortunate in this way, as he handsomely acknowledges. Natasha Spender, the poet's second wife, gave him 'unfettered access to her husband's literary and personal papers'; she also 'contributed, often in the spirit of a co-author, to the writing of the work', as well as 'point[ing] out errors of fact, scholarship, interpretation or emphasis which I have gladly corrected'. In addition, several godparents have stood at the font to oversee this biography's entrance to the world. Apart from help from Spender's family and friends, we are told that the typescript was read by Frank Kermode, Stuart Hampshire, Richard Wollheim, and Karl Miller, a formidable jury who, at the very least, seem likely to have ensured that a satisfactory analysis of the *Encounter* imbroglio would be given.

Faced with such difficulties and such good fortune, John Sutherland has coped very dexterously indeed. His own narrative voice is excellent company throughout, relaxed and accessible in his explanations, crisp and no-nonsense in his judgements, with a good eye for enlivening anecdotes. And he writes with sympathy for his subject: his aim, as he fairly declares, has been 'to convey the admiration I have come to feel for him, the more I have learned about his remarkable life and his distinguished body of literary work'. Spender has apparently been traduced, or at least very unsympathetically treated, in previous unauthorized biographies, and this full but still pacey account sets out to right the balance. If one is already disposed to find Spender interesting and if one enjoys the contemporary genre of detailed literary biography (the sort in which one can expect to find the name of the writer's son's dead dog), this book can be enthusiastically recommended.

And yet, the Case of the Squashed Pooch can still make one a bit uneasy. Quite whose voice are we hearing in such passages? The hint of a light ironic coating to the account of the 6-year-old's reaction to 'the hound's demise' may be an expression of paternal fondness, or it may rather come from the biographer, collusive but also smiling, perhaps more alive than I am allowing to a family style of presuming a claim on public attention. I have deliberately chosen a trivial example with which to illustrate what is a recurring characteristic of this biography, but the relation of Sutherland's narrative to its sources and a consequent uncertainty about just who is speaking can, as we shall see, complicate our response when weightier matters are at issue.

II

Although *Stephen Spender: The Authorized Biography* is not overtly argumentative, Sutherland is exercised by what he regards as a puzzle: why in his lifetime did Spender, here presented as a transparently likeable and gifted man, come in for so much hostile criticism? 'Few poets of the twentieth century have been more attacked: less for his poetry than for what it is supposed "Stephen Spender" stands for as a poet.' Sutherland, following Spender's own complaints, singles out 'Leavisites' as the chief culprits. Leavis himself could, it is true, be a world-class sniper and caviller, but when, having read this biography, one returns to some of his celebrated pronunciamentos about Spender, it is impossible not to recognize, amidst a good deal of exaggeration and unfairness, the aptness of some of his main criticisms. 'Keynes, Spender and Currency Values', published in *Scrutiny* in 1951, provides a good example. Having launched an interesting riff on the theme 'the autobiographical bent is not a sign of creative power, but the reverse', and having detected a want of 'literary intelligence' in specimen passages of Spender's work—'the flatness of the writing', 'the bent for cliché and ineptitude'—Leavis asked the pertinent question: 'How, then, comes the question, did Mr Spender, with such disadvantages, achieve such confidence in himself as a poet, a critic, and an intellectual? Or how (to put it another way) did he achieve recognition as such, so that for years now he has been an established value, and a major British Council export?'

Leavis found a text for his sermon readily to hand in the recently published *World within World*. There, Spender confesses (he rather cultivated confession as a mode) that from early in his life he wanted fame and saw poetry as a more promising route than politics, in contrast to his political journalist father: 'But although I wanted a truer fame, I cannot deny that I have never been free from a thirst for publicity very like that of my father. Even today it disgusts me to read a newspaper in which there is no mention of my name.' 'Frankness' was supposed to be Spender's long suit, and one might read an element of endearing hyperbole or self-parody into this last sentence, but someone setting out to provide his critics with an easy target could hardly have bettered this, and Leavis, much derided then as now for the 'puritanism' of his judgements, was surely right that the praise lavished on the very young poet had not exactly helped to curb the self-advertising, self-indulgent strain in his writing.

Certainly, success came early and came hot. His contributions to *Oxford Poetry* (1929, when he was 20) were singled out for praise by metropolitan reviewers. 'During his second year [at Oxford] Stephen began to form contacts in the London literary world. Commissions and contracts would follow.' His success had the fatal consequence that he was treated as a person whose views were of general significance: he published his first piece of criticism in the *Spectator* in August 1929 on, portentously, 'Problems of the Poet and the Public'. Then T. S. Eliot published four of the 21-year-old Spender's poems in the *Criterion*, bestowing the imprimatur that really counted at the time. Predictably, hosannas of praise greeted his slim volume *Poems 1933*, published, of course, by Faber—'an unmistakable declaration of genius', 'another Shelley speaks in these lines', and so on.

Spender himself was not bashful about building on this success. As Harold Nicolson, who also helped his career on, observed: 'He is absolutely determined to become a leading writer.' Being a 'leading writer', not merely a writer, mattered enormously to the young Spender, and this role required more than just writing. The success of his 1933 collection meant, as he recorded, that he soon began 'to lead a literary-social life of luncheons, teas, and weekends at country houses'. 'He had already', Sutherland tells us, 'begun the routine of fast reviewing (five pieces for the *Criterion* alone in autumn and winter 1932).' 'Even at this embryonic stage of his career,' Sutherland continues, 'he provoked intense envy and malice in fellow-writers to whom his own feelings were entirely benign'. Gosh, that seems jolly unfair: can't a fellow be given a leg-up now and then without other chaps getting all shirty? The sense that Sutherland is being a bit *too* collusive with Spender's calculated innocence is inescapable at moments like this: are any intensely ambitious young writer's feelings about his or her peers *'entirely* benign'? Spender played his part in keeping the balloon in the air, too. For example, in 1936 his first wedding provided an occasion to stage his persona as man of letters about town: 'During the reception a courier arrived with a set of proofs which the groom absented himself for a few minutes to correct for immediate return.'

'Meanwhile, Europe was moving inexorably towards cataclysm,' as Sutherland puts it in an uncharacteristically clunky narrative transition. The outbreak of the Second World War coincided with the end of Spender's twenties: during the previous decade, his enthusiasms and the world's fate had seemed to move to the same rhythm in a way that would never quite be sustained thereafter. Opening his account of the next decade, Sutherland hits the authentic Spenderian note: 'Most importantly for Stephen Spender, the 1940s were the end of the 1930s.' He had a rather anti-climactic war, serving in the Fire Service in north London until 1944, when he was recruited to the Political Intelligence Department of the Foreign Office (which had the great advantage that he could once again 'lunch in town'). Like many of those who were at the time called, not always flatteringly, 'intellectuals', Spender had an undentable assurance about presenting his own current preoccupation as the inevitable next step in world history. In 1951 he held forth in his habitually large and confident terms (in a passage not quoted by Sutherland) on the theme of 'the English intellectuals and the world of today': 'What has happened is that the 1940s were an almost total failure,' the years from 1938 to 1950 were 'simply a gap in my development', and so on.

Perhaps inevitably, the second half of this biography becomes a bit of a travelogue as Spender flies hither and yon as a British Council lecturer and all-purpose cultural envoy. He obviously enjoyed being made much of and he liked a good junket. A trip to Japan with Angus Wilson was particularly rewarding in this respect. At one striptease club, as Wilson recorded, 'when word went round that we were Spender and Wilson—every single person in the place asked for our autograph' (including some who wanted them written on paper, presumably). Mainly, Spender went to America, where from 1947 onwards he held a series of visiting appointments at a wide range of universities and colleges, not always of the very first rank. He was completely frank about the chief incentive: 'America means money.' But it also meant more time to himself to write than he had when at home, and it was on these trips that he formed some close friendships with men much younger than himself, which he evidently needed. Spender liked America and America liked him. In 1965 he was made Poetry Consultant at the Library of Congress (a kind of annual Poet Laureate), the only foreign citizen to have held the post.

Ironically, this honour came at a period in his life when he was publishing hardly any new poetry. When in 1971 he finally brought out a new volume, his first for twenty-two years, many of the periodicals ignored it. (Sutherland cites a somewhat severe review of it in the TLS, still in those days anonymous, as being by Anthony Thwaite; interestingly, if one turns to the recently compiled online index of TLS contributors, one finds this is one of the very few items whose authorship is not identified, either because the reviewer 'wishes to remain anonymous or is not yet identified'.) The truth, though a painful one for Spender, was that once the 1930s were over he cut a larger figure as an 'ambassador for literature in general' than as a practising poet. Between a brief spell at UNESCO in the mid-1940s and helping to found Index on Censorship in the 1970s, Spender lent his increasingly prestigious name to various cultural good causes. He also spent five years as a professor in the English department at University College London, where the young Sutherland was briefly his colleague. This episode is fondly described in terms that may be a little more redolent of Lucky Jim than the deeply metropolitan Spender would have cared to acknowledge. Or that the commissars of the contemporary assessment culture would wish to condone, come to that; paperwork was, shall we say, not his *forte*, but he did what mattered well enough. More teaching in America followed, more honours (the Queen's Medal for Poetry in 1971, a knighthood in 1983), and more autobiographical books, including his *Journals* and a revised, reordered version of his *Collected Poems, 1928–85* (this volume has now been superseded by Stephen Spender, *New Collected Poems*, edited by Michael Brett, which restores earlier versions and preserves chronological sequence). Stephen Spender died in 1995, aged 86.

III

So much is known about Spender not just because he told us so much but also because he knew everyone who was anyone, and many people recorded their impressions of him. Indeed, one cannot help thinking that after any meeting among the inter-war literati there must always have been a bit of a stampede as they rushed home to describe the occasion for posterity. Following one such meeting, for example, Virginia Woolf duly noted her impression of the tall young man: 'A loose-jointed mind, misty, clouded, suffusive.' This doesn't seem too wide of the mark, especially if one thinks that a certain loose-jointedness may be a merit in a poet's mind. Auden called him 'a parody Parsifal', and Louis MacNeice drily spoke of his 'redeeming the world by introspection'. In almost all these accounts, his good looks feature prominently ('the Rupert Brooke of the Depression'), as do his celebrated innocence and others' doubts about its authenticity. Reviewing *World within World*, Cyril Connolly discerned a distinction between Spender I ('an inspired simpleton, a great big silly goose, a holy Russian idiot') and Spender II ('shrewd, ambitious, aggressive and ruthless'). Several observers played with some variation on Spender as one of Dostoyevky's 'Holy Fools', but he wasn't foolishly holy or wholly foolish. As Sutherland emphasizes, he did a great deal of service for good causes and was kind to many individuals, though even in this favourable portrait an unpushy egotism comes through, a blithe assumption of entitlement. He was possessed of a curious capacity to be at once unthinking and *bien pensant*—but perhaps that's not really so unusual. We are not here told who coined the wonderful nickname 'Stainless Splendour', but evidently one of the endearing things about Spender was that he could turn such wit on himself, as when, in his address at Connolly's memorial, he imagined his late friend introducing him: 'And now, Bishop Spender will say a few words.'

Sutherland's biography is excellent at conveying Spender's own sense of himself, but a more analytical register would be needed to attempt to explain, in terms other than those of simple envy and malice, the hostility he frequently provoked. The convenience for Spender himself of his fabled 'innocence' was obviously in play in some cases, and a certain class condescension that he could give off may have helped provoke some of the reactions to him. For example, responding to Hugh David's unauthorized 1992 biography, which criticized him for being, among other things, a snob, Spender wrote: 'The (so called) biography is amazingly spiteful and vicious: and vulgar: written in the tone of voice of a skivvy... there really is an underclass of people who envy and hate us all.' Sometimes it may have been the taken-for-grantedness of some of his grander social connections, something that comes out here in passing details, such as the time Spender and his son drove up to Edinburgh, 'staying overnight with the Devonshires at Chatsworth', or the period in 1968 when he was in Paris to write a book on the students' revolt: 'And every evening, after spending the day with the young rebels, Spender would return to the apartment of his friends the Rothschilds, whose guest he was.' When Spender was offered a knighthood in 1983 by a Right-wing government still puffed up by its success in the Falklands, he hesitated, but again Sutherland's chosen voice makes it hard to know whether it is he or Spender who appears to be endorsing at face value the reason given for finally accepting: 'It was a club his friends thought he ought to belong to—as they (Isaiah, Stuart, "K" [Kenneth Clark], Noël, Freddy) did.'

Part of the difficulty of saying anything even halfway critical of Spender is similar to the difficulty of raising even the mildest reservations about the genre of contemporary literary biography: one risks being cast as some latter-day Leavisite puritan, sourly begrudging worldly success in the first case and offended by unstrenuous readerly pleasures in the second. But there surely can be something troubling about this genre's apparent imperative that the reader must not be reminded of the patchiness and unreliability of much of the evidence that underwrites the smooth narrative flow, especially in a case like this where the subject himself has already rewritten many of the sources. That is why the difficulty of establishing whose voice we are hearing in some passages is important. More detailed references would certainly help, but Sutherland was presumably constrained by the prejudice against this that is so widespread among trade publishers, though it is hard to see why they think that having decent endnotes that would enable any quotation or piece of information to be tracked to its source will deter the 'general reader'.

Spender's sexuality can, it is assumed, be guaranteed to interest 'scholarly' as well as 'general' readers, plus those who swing both ways. Sutherland's no-nonsense briskness is salutary here, though again there is occasionally a slightly unsettling sense that more probing questions are not being asked.

Spender's sexual life in his early twenties was relatively straightforward: he had Auden and Isherwood to keep him up to the mark, and there were the last moments of Weimar freedoms to be enjoyed in Germany. As Isherwood pithily put it: 'Berlin meant boys.' In a much later interview, Spender could recall the time with a kind of serene condescension that bordered on self-parody: 'Sex with the working class of course had political connotations. It was a way in which people with left-wing sympathies could feel they were really getting in contact with the working class.' Sutherland immediately adds: 'The conjunction is immortalized in the first line of one of Stephen's 1931 poems, "Oh young men, Oh young comrades".' When one turns to the poem itself, however, it doesn't seem obvious that it's particularly about 'working-class' young men. The comrades in question are urged not 'to stay in those houses/your fathers built' but to get out more: 'It is too late to stay in great houses where the ghosts are prisoned/-those ladies like flies perfect in amber/those financiers like fossils of bones in coal.' As in a lot of the early poems, there is a strong vitalist strain that celebrates release, togetherness, bodies, and sunshine, but it's not clear that this added up to much of a political programme, even of the 'bugger a boy for Socialism' variety.

Perhaps Sutherland is to be congratulated on bucking the fashionable trend by not telling us anything much about Spender's sex life after his marriage to Natasha in 1941, from which date, we are left to assume, his sexual tastes were heterosexual and monogamous, though buttressed by a few crushes, doubtless platonic, on young men whom he met on his frequent solitary travels. This is a bit disappointing, really, since one might have assumed that this biography was going to confirm Spender as someone who had managed, in a grown-up and relatively open way, to combine a happy marriage with a good deal of sexual self-expression outside it. Just occasionally, the disquieting effect of Sutherland's ventriloquism comes in here, too. As a parallel to the vignette about the Squashed Pooch, one might cite the Case of Connolly's Cock. Spender and Connolly were visiting Spain together in 1957: 'As he lay in the bath in their shared apartment in Madrid, Stephen reflexively glanced at his friend's genitalia. "Hot stuff, eh?" Cyril chortled.' What dangles most noticeably here is the pronoun (who is in the bath?), though there is also the question of what 'reflex' was at work. As far as one can deduce from the irritatingly exiguous reference system, this passage must be based on Spender's unpublished journal of the period (it doesn't seem to appear in the published version). One question is whether the adverb was present in Spender's original—'I reflexively glanced at my friend's genitalia'?—in which case it (the adverb) seems curiously limp and not quite to be trusted. It is hard to tell if anything much was in play either in the original incident (assuming it actually took place) or in Spender's recording of it: was this just the compulsive writer, perhaps garnering material for a future portrait of his mildly celebrated friend, or was there any sense in which Cyril was torpedoing Stephen's boats?

IV

One episode in the last fifty years of Spender's life (years that are otherwise dispatched rather more briskly than his childhood and youth) is given such disproportionately detailed treatment in this biography that one senses a stronger than usual urge to set the record straight. It centres on the much-debated question of whether Spender can really have been, as he always claimed, unaware that *Encounter* was indirectly funded by the CIA and by British Intelligence. Spender had become co-editor of the magazine in 1953; despite constant rumours that the foundations that subsidized it, largely via the Congress for Cultural Freedom (CCF), were actually front organizations for American and British intelligence agencies as part of the 'cultural war' against Communism, he remained in post until 1967, when the cover was finally and comprehensively blown, at which point he, eventually, resigned. This is an episode on which a good deal of new information has become widely available in recent years. Frank Kermode, who was in effect Spender's locum for the last two years (during which Spender was mostly away in the United States), gave a characteristically rueful account of their shared deception in his memoir, *Not Entitled*, in 1996. Since then, Frances Stonor Saunders has published her controversial study, *Who Paid the Piper? The CIA and the Cultural Cold War* (1999), based on extensive research in official and unofficial archives on both sides of the Atlantic, while the role of MI6 has been touched upon in Stephen Dorril's *MI6: Fifty Years of Special Operations* (2000).

Sutherland cites these sources while also drawing upon other correspondence and reminiscences to tell the story more from Spender's own point of view. Estimations of Spender's conduct in this affair will, it is a pretty safe bet, continue to differ, and there may, anyway, be further revelations still to come (for example, Melvin Lasky, Spender's American co-editor, who did know about the source of the funds, died in May 2004 without, up to that point, having given the world his version of events). But in the light of this biography, it may be worth standing back and asking what is really at issue in this matter.

Interviewed by Stonor Saunders shortly before his death, Spender offered a comparison (not quoted by Sutherland) that may, or may not, have been more revealing than he intended. He acknowledged that people had been telling him about the alleged CIA funding for years: 'But it was as with the people who come and tell you that your wife is unfaithful to you. Then you ask her yourself, and if she denies it, you are satisfied with it.' Well, maybe, but what is actually taking place at such a moment? There may, after all, be various explanations for why the husband is 'satisfied' with his wife's denial. Perhaps it is because he takes the very fact of that denial as a reassurance about her overriding commitment to their marriage whatever the facts of infidelity may be. Or he may be so in love with his wife that he simply can't see the evidence clearly, or so appalled at the possibility that he is wilfully blind, and so on. But, if Spender's proposed parallel applies in any of these ways, it suggests a remarkably deep commitment to the magazine, a strikingly strong desire that their joint life should continue uninterrupted. And perhaps it suggests that we are not talking about 'knowing' or 'not knowing' the facts in any straightforward cognitive sense.

After all, with *Encounter*, the rumours of adultery began almost before the marriage, and they then increased throughout the next fourteen years. Spender had already lent his name to the anti-Soviet cause in the previous few years—for example, by contributing to the 1950 volume *The God that Failed*, a series of personal testaments by writers who had once been drawn to Communism. It is now clear that American and British intelligence agencies were involved in the very conception of this project, but characteristically Spender, as Sutherland records, 'was unaware of the political machinations behind the book'. This was to be the pattern. In 1951–2 (in an episode not discussed by Sutherland) Spender was closely involved in manœuvres within the British branch of the CCF to oust Michael Goodwin, editor of *Twentieth Century*, the periodical that had already been covertly subsidized by the Americans to provide an alternative platform in Britain to the 'pro-Soviet' *New Statesman*. Stonor Saunders, whose book tells the story of CCF funding in greatest detail, concludes of this episode: 'For somebody who was consistently characterised as a watery, silly soul, Spender displayed a gritty determination to get what he wanted out of this situation.'

Eventually, the CCF managed to set up a new journal to serve its purposes, and Spender and Irving Kristol became *Encounter*'s founding co-editors. 'From first to last,' writes Sutherland, 'Spender knew nothing of the CCF's covert political connections with the CIA.' Quite what 'knew' means is one question here; quite when 'last' was may be another. Within a few months of its launch, Spender was complaining to Michael Josselson, the CCF link man who was also a CIA agent, about the 'political' half of the paper. 'It is very generally thought here that I am in some way obliged to publish certain tendentious material.' (As Sutherland reveals, politically sensitive articles were in fact always cleared with Josselson: 'He was, on the

whole, light-handed. But the touch was always there.') Spender said that
from the start he was viewed as 'an American stooge' by his British friends,
which was 'naturally very painful to me'. But this in itself cannot have been
wholly a surprise to him. Stonor Saunders quotes a letter he wrote to Josselson when T. S. Eliot, scarcely a left-wing firebrand, declined to contribute
to the new magazine since it was so 'obviously published under American
auspices': 'The point is that Eliot here states the kind of reputation we have
to try and live down of being a magazine disguising American propaganda
under a veneer of British culture.' This does sound just a little like saying:
'I must henceforth behave in a way that will give people no grounds for
saying my wife is having an affair.'

Spender's salary was in effect paid by the Information Research Department of the Foreign Office, laundered through the British branch of the
CCF. According to Stonor Saunders, Monty Woodhouse, the British
intelligence official in charge of the project, assumed Spender knew that.
Spender didn't. But things looked increasingly suspicious to others. Sutherland recounts how, at a party in 1961, 'Stephen had become so infuriated
by [William Empson's] aspersions against *Encounter*'s American backers
that he threw a glass of wine at him' (Empson cheerfully remarked that another drink stain on his clothes would hardly show). Was this uncharacteristic violence the expression of anxiety? Was she having an affair after all?

In the eyes of American liberal intellectuals, such as Robert Silvers,
Encounter had 'one obvious defect. It was inherently uncritical of the
American situation.' For the most part, it dealt gently, if at all, with topics
such as race and Vietnam. When in 1963 Conor Cruise O'Brien published
the first of his allegations that the journal had been 'consistently designed
to support the policy of the United States government', subsequent versions
of which allegations were eventually to help precipitate the *dénouement*,
he did not have access to any secret information but based his argument
largely on the magazine's contents. When, also in 1963, Spender raised the
possibility of leaving his editorial position to take up a teaching post in the
States, the 'CCF management' showed just how keen they were to keep
his name on the masthead. As Sutherland records, a 'charm offensive was
launched. The Spenders were made much of, in Geneva and Paris. They
were "suddenly" invited, in early July, to join Junkie Fleischmann on his
yacht.' (Julius Fleischmann was the multi-millionaire head of the Farfield
Foundation, one of the conduits for money to *Encounter*.) Sutherland gives
no source for 'suddenly', so we don't know who, if anyone, thought this largesse suspicious. The Spenders accepted the invitation.

After all, it could be said that Spender still had no firm evidence incompatible with the official line that funding came from various American

charitable foundations, channelled through the CCF, and that a certain tenderness for the United States as 'the leader of the free world' was not discreditable in itself. But rumours increased that the link was more direct than this. As another American liberal, Jason Epstein, later recalled (as quoted by Stonor Saunders): 'By the middle of the sixties anybody who didn't know it was a fool. *Everybody* knew.' Of course, that's easy to say once the adultery has been admitted. However, in this case Epstein did say it at the time, directly to Spender: 'Stephen, I think this whole outfit is being paid for by the Central Intelligence Agency, and you haven't been told, and you should find out right now what's going on.' Spender duly enquired of the relevant official and was given the usual categorical assurances that there was nothing in the rumour. He believed no adultery had taken place; it was all the work of malicious tongues. Spender was lied to, all along the line (as was Kermode when he became involved from 1965). And he believed it all along the line.

Some of the continuing fascination of this story may be evident even from this brief and necessarily highly selective summary. It is, for example, striking that the success of the magazine as a general cultural periodical mattered so much to the CIA. They clearly believed that it did help to win 'the war of minds'. And it is striking, too, how crucial to this success they thought it was to have Spender on the masthead: Sutherland's characterization of him, in another context, as 'England's best known, and most highly regarded, man of letters in America' may come into play here. But, equally, there is the question of why continuing as editor mattered so much to Spender, especially given that it provoked this constant stream of critical gossip. He, too, set a high value on having a successful 'journal of ideas'. He also enjoyed the patronage it gave him, and, not to be discounted, he needed the money. He was, after all, otherwise a freelance, and one who struggled to finance an expensive way of life, with children in private schools, much travel and socializing, an extravagant car, and so on. But other kinds of insecurity may have been in play as well. *Encounter*, Spender liked to say, was the only steady job of any kind he had ever been offered in Britain. As his widow recalls, he was drawn to the USA partly because there 'he was *appreciated*, not subjected to incessant Leavisite sniping and denigration'. A lot was at stake, and the evidence was not, until the end, ever conclusive. And perhaps some of that political innocence that so infuriated the less sympathetic Spender-watchers in the 1930s never left him. The deceived husband, it has become almost a cliché to say, wants both to know and not to know.

In any event, whatever one's analysis of the whole tangled business, Sutherland's exposition of its final act is masterly and absorbing. In places, a lingering uncertainty about who is speaking remains, but this account must now be required reading even for those who think they already know a good deal about this episode. And Sutherland's conclusion may stand both as the epitaph Spender would have wished for himself and as an emblem of the biographer's loyalty to his subject: Spender, he judges, was 'honourable to the end'.

8

Smacking:
The Letters of William Empson

I

'Personally I am attracted by the notion of a hearty indifference to one's own and other people's feelings, when a fragment of the truth is in question...' We normally think of letters as a medium more hospitable to considerations about feelings, one's own and other people's, than most of the more public or impersonal genres. But in making this feisty declaration, the literary critic William Empson was being true to his nature as a correspondent as well as a controversialist. Indeed, for Empson (at least as represented by this sumptuous Selected Letters) these two roles were frequently hard to distinguish.

This is not just because many of his letters take up literary-critical disputes with friends and colleagues, turning them into opponents for the duration of the (often remarkably long) wrangling epistle some must have been taken aback to receive. The overlap also works in, as it were, the other direction: wrangling was a form of sociability for the sociable but sometimes rather isolated Empson. As he put it in an early essay (quoted in John Haffenden's deft introduction): 'Our whole mental life is based on being social animals. Of course the man may quarrel with his company when he gets it, and feel pleased about that, but what he chiefly needed was the company.' Empson was apparently good company in person, especially if one had a robust capacity to absorb large quantities of alcohol (he regarded a good party as 'one of the keenest pleasures in life'), but it clearly took robustness of other kinds to sustain any kind of friendship with him through

John Haffenden (ed.), *Selected Letters of William Empson* (Oxford University Press, 2006).

letters. It was a characteristic touch of off-hand realism, in the passage just quoted, to throw in 'and feel pleased about that'. But it was self-knowledge, too: Empson did appear to relish the quarrelling, and this starts to raise questions about his persuasiveness not just as a correspondent, but more generally as a critic.

Empson famously characterized a lot of what went on in writing as 'argufying', which he glossed as 'the kind of arguing we do in ordinary life, usually to get our own way; I do not mean nagging by it, but just a not specially dignified sort of arguing'. He was attractively alert to the combative aspects of this activity: 'Argufying is not only mental; it also feels muscular. Saying "therefore" is like giving the reader a bang on the nose.' There is, one way and another, quite a lot of pugilism in Empson's writing. He liked his prose pieces to have 'a bang at the end', and someone else's nose was often as handy a place as any for these to land. As an undergraduate literary magazine editor, even before he had fatefully changed from Mathematics to English, he welcomed a contribution that would disagree with the views of his future supervisor partly because 'it would be rather a smack at Richards'. One of his best-known bits of fraternal joshing in poetry is entitled 'Just a Smack at Auden'. In wrangling about the Elizabethan theatre he is pleased to note that he lands a good few 'whacks at Wickham' (Glynne Wickham's was the nose in question). His most frequent punchbag was his typewriter. 'I smack this out in a state of moderate beer', he declares in a letter to Charles Madge, ostensibly to soften the force of some awesomely frank criticism of the latter's typescript. 'I am smacking out my silly Inaugural on the typewriter,' he announces almost two decades later, again turning to the colloquial register to undercut the inherent pomposity and absurdity, as it pleased him to make out, of such professorial pronouncements.

He liked his antagonists to fight back: that made them better company, for the most part. Like the hard-riding, hard-drinking squires from whom he descended (and whom he still in some ways resembled), he admired 'spirit'. He sought a further reference on a student he had turned down for graduate work largely because 'the fighting reply of Mr Trotter to my letter of rejection has made me think better of him'. Deploring the apolitical character of Anglo-American literary criticism on his return to Britain in 1952 after five years in China, he mocked the new academic decorum: 'I hope there isn't a new rule in the game, so that politics mustn't be mentioned when one is playing literary criticism; that would sound to me like funk.' There are quite a few moments when Empson can sound like a character out of *Tom Brown's Schooldays*: it takes all the fun out of the game if you can't kick your opponents or they don't kick back.

Even those who wrote in his praise come in for a spot of biffing. One correspondent is thanked, after five pages of vigorous correction, for his 'sympathy and sensitivity' towards Empson's poetry, 'apart from the appalling effects of your being systematically deluded at the taxpayer's expense'. The American critic Roger Sale, having sent Empson a copy of his *Modern Heroism*, still one of the most appreciative and even moving appraisals of Empson's criticism, was greeted with: 'You will not be surprised if I try to answer your attacks on me rather than return thanks for your praise.' Sale may or may not have been surprised, but he surely had the right to be a tad disappointed. Even Christopher Ricks, Empson's most brilliant champion and already by 1971 a friend, came in for a public wigging, followed up by the kind of letter that only Empson could think compatible with the 'affection' he professed for the younger man ('your answer ... is worse than the review, because it seems incapable of understanding the matter'). For the most part, this volume gives only Empson's side of any correspondence, but Haffenden's tactful editing extends to the occasional inclusion in extended headnotes of relevant passages from incoming letters, and in this case he prints Ricks's concluding letter in full, an impressively dignified and stout-hearted vindication in which both sorrow and anger have their due place and through which affection is not allowed to become a victim of the shrapnel.

For the most part, Empson seemed only half aware of just how offensive he was being, and only half to care. Even when he did care, he would keep gnawing at the bone. T. S. Eliot, as publisher of his poetry, was the recipient of a breathtakingly sharp complaint about his failure to promote Empson's last book of verse. Clearly ruffled, Eliot replied that Empson's was 'the most insulting letter which I have ever received', and rather pompously requested Empson only to communicate with him via a third party in future. Empson, 'shocked by your reply, which I had no idea that I deserved', hastens to make amends, but even as he offers his hand it clenches in the old reflex ('I was simply complaining that you had let the thing get into a muddle'; 'it seems to me quite obvious that you are an enormously better poet than I am; but it is very bad for a great writer to refuse to be treated like other people', and so on). At least in this case the exchange was brief and the practical matter soon resolved. Where 'a fragment of the truth' was in question, in some literary-critical dispute, the later Empson's desire not to let go of his point could verge on the obsessive, and one or two of the recipients might be forgiven for feeling that it was hard to determine where his much-celebrated 'bracing sanity' ended and the green ink began.

And this is where this divertingly rich hoard of Empson prose starts to raise doubts, not about his brilliance as a critic, which could never be in question, but about his persuasiveness. (Haffenden has by now rendered so many services to Empson's posthumous reputation, editing several of his unfinished works as well as writing the biography, that it almost goes without saying that this edition is authoritative, impeccable, and very usable.) Haffenden rightly observes that Empson 'loved the disarming kick of informality' in his prose, but reading him in bulk one begins to wonder whether it really does 'disarm'. It is true that it seems to puncture any tendency to pomposity on his own part, but it can, in context, simultaneously have the opposite effect: by staking a claim to see through all forms of cant and to have a securer hold on the fundamentals of life, it puts everyone else in their place. Patrician demotic, one of Empson's favoured registers, can be an attractively deflationary mode, but it can also be condescending or superior in the way it pooh-poohs the earnest pettinesses with which we mostly prop ourselves up. When this was combined with that 'hearty indifference to other people's feelings' that this otherwise warm-hearted man allowed himself once he unsheathed his sword, he became as likely to provoke resistance as agreement. One cannot help wondering whether the critic who exhibited an unparalleled sensitivity to nuances of tone in literature can have been entirely unaware of the effect of some of his own preferred tones.

This becomes more of an issue in his later letters, as indeed it did in his later published criticism, notoriously so in the case of his unrelentingly forensic indictment of Christianity in *Milton's God*, published in 1961. In the 1930s, Empson's writing, both public and private, seemed more marked by a sunny acceptingness, a placid accommodation to life and its rum goings-on, which provided a winning accompaniment to his dazzling critical solos. This strain seems less in evidence by the 1950s and 1960s; he becomes less winning and more concerned to win.

It should be said that this picture may partly be an optical illusion created by the nature of the book under review, and this for three reasons. First, this volume, substantial though it is, contains only a selection of the surviving letters, and for understandable reasons the emphasis has clearly been placed on letters that continue or elucidate Empson's critical engagements. One assumes there are more personal letters where the sheer attractiveness and charm of his company are more in evidence. There is, for example, very little here about his colourful wife, Hetta ('a tall blonde Boer'), and that mostly off-hand ('Hetta likes Mongols', accounting for her absence in the interior of China). There are no letters to Alice Stewart, perhaps one of the closest companions of his last three decades. Second, because this selection is appearing, a little oddly, between what one assumes will be the two volumes of Haffenden's hugely thorough biography (the first instalment,

Among the Mandarins, which covers the years up to 1940, was published in 2005), we at the moment know a lot more about the younger than the older Empson, and this weight of biographical detail inevitably draws us into sympathizing with his plights and making allowances for his mistakes, whereas the later letters do not yet benefit from this process. And third, the distribution of the letters selected for inclusion tilts the picture heavily towards the latter years. Over half of this volume is devoted to letters from the 1960s and 1970s (from his mid-fifties to his mid-seventies), and these do not appear to have been the years when his writing was at its most engaging or his biography at its most intriguing.

There are some wonderful letters from the 1930s, largely though not exhaustively quoted in the first volume of Haffenden's biography, but there are disappointingly few from the 1940s, the key decade that saw the brilliant, itinerant young critic marry, become a father, and take up the civic burdens of patriotism, as well as finishing the most substantial statement of Empsonian criticism, *The Structure of Complex Words*, which was finally published in 1951. Following his return from his second stint in China, Empson became Professor of English at Sheffield in 1953, with the more or less inevitable result that there is a higher quotient of dreariness and exasperation in his correspondence from then on. There are still delicious and stirring things in his later letters, but there is an understandable decline in the quality of amused chirpiness that breaks through even the most impersonal of the earlier ones. The biffing starts to seem more relentless than playful. Bystanders might well have thought it the better part of valour not to take him on in the correspondence columns of the literary periodicals.

II

One reason why so little strain is involved in treating many of Empson's letters as extensions of his literary criticism is because as a critic he always wrote with a sense of his audience and where he had got to in an extended conversation with them. This, rather than any scientist 'methodology', governed his critical conduct: 'It is a delusion for the critic to think he can cover a subject completely; he is always talking to an audience who know quite a lot but may not know the small extra thing he is saying, and a later audience may always disagree.' He liked to maintain that he wrote for 'the ordinary tolerably informed reader', and although in the post-war years there was an element of bluff about this (he must have known that his contributions to *Essays in Criticism* or the *Kenyon Review* were mostly, though not exclusively, being read by other critics and scholars), it still constituted an admirable regulative ideal for the purposes of avoiding obscurity and clique-speak.

It is hardly surprising that two of the most trenchant letters included here (and trenchancy was not a quality in short supply in Empson's correspondence) directly addressed the question of the relation between critic and publics. The first is the 1937 letter to Charles Madge already referred to, where he argues vigorously that 'the point about writing as plainly as you can is that you are testing your ideas against somebody who is not a specialist and just knows about life in general'. The second is a bristling reply to Boris Ford in 1959 on the question of what kinds of day-job writers should have and, in particular, whether trying to remain some kind of freelance was better than becoming an academic. Empson conceded this might be the case with poets (although as he modestly reflected: 'Minor poets such as myself need not I think regard it as very dreadful to stop writing poetry in middle age'), but the case was different with literary criticism.

This has become a much more powerful and interesting tool since about 1900, and many of the able literary young want to go in for it. They can I think certainly do it quite as well while employed as dons, though they should be warned against insisting they must be Professors, a capacity in which they are liable to get heavy extra chores... I do not know how a literary critic could be in such close contact with the existing audience reaction anywhere else; he certainly won't do it by writing journalism in obedience to the hunch of an editor... You must remember that, if a young critic makes the great renunciation, saying 'It is beneath me to read all these horrid essays', the next thing he will have to do is turn out a lot of shockingly coarse hackwork, which really is beneath him and will remain permanently in print to shame his later years. A university job does at least mean that you are free to print in a decently considered manner.

That tone of 'sturdy good sense', which Empson so prized in others, is again prominent here, applied to a topic close to home. It is a pity—indeed, it may be thought a spiteful whim of that kind of sadistic God against whom Empson constantly inveighed—that his death in 1984 deprived us of the surely succulent delights of reading Empson on the Research Assessment Exercise.

Nonetheless, despite his lively sense of addressing an audience in both public and private forms of writing, Empson's manner could be counterproductive, again especially in his later years. 'Some of the recent reviews of my work have wondered why I am so *facetious*, making it impossible to take what I say seriously,' he lamented to his younger colleague, Roma Gill, in 1979. His revealing defence was that 'I can't bear to print a thing till I can read it over without feeling bored; if it feels boring, that proves it is wrong'. Boredom may have been a larger existential problem for Empson, as for many mathematicians; he may partly have been impelled into

his characteristic focus on ambiguity in his early career because this simply made literature more interesting. But here it is a matter of not finding
his *own* writing boring, and as a defence it rings rather hollow. He clearly
registers that his recent writing, at least, is not achieving its intended effect,
and he has more than an inkling of how his own tone contributes to this
failure. Yet there's a shrug of *je m'en foutisme* about his response: the whole
activity would just become unbearably tiresome if he had to give up his
favourite forms of intellectual self-stimulation, even though he knows these
do not help gain acceptance for what he writes.

Another aspect of Empson's somewhat chequered relations with his readers comes to light when we consider how far and in what ways he chose
to play any kind of public role. There was, of course, a kind of politics
involved in continuing to try to write for a non-specialized readership, and
his sustained campaign against what he saw as the bizarre and barbaric
superstitions of Christianity went well beyond the usual confines of literary
criticism. Yet in comparison to several of his relevant contemporaries, he
largely abstained from the role of the commentator on society and politics.
We get some insight into the intellectual and temperamental complexities at
work in this unusual mix in a letter from July 1940. Empson believed it was
his duty to get back to Britain to help in whatever way he could in the fight
against Hitler (he was to spend most of the war organizing BBC broadcasting to China), but he wrote in some agitation to one correspondent asking
that he not publish the preceding letter in which Empson had set out his
sense of obligation. 'It's all right for me to say "this is the proper place to be"
in a private letter, where I am talking about myself, but as soon as I have it
published I am obviously hinting about other people, and I want to avoid
that.' (He may well have been thinking of high-profile literary expatriates
such as Isherwood and Auden, whom he had visited in New York on his way
back to Britain.) He went on: 'This anxiety not to tell anybody what to do
or what they ought to have done isn't altogether a good thing no doubt, the
"flight from leadership", but in the present case it's surely only right.' This
union of a strong sense of personal obligation with an unwillingness to tell
others what they ought to do suggests that strain in Empson that seemed to
owe more to the clipped Englishness of his forebears than to the habitual behaviour of the literary intellectuals among whom he mostly moved.

But this did not mean that Empson was apolitical or lacking in partisan
convictions. It is interesting to find him, in a letter to Ricks thanking him
for his contribution to the Festschrift for Empson, emphasizing this as a difference between them: 'I had already thought it a gap, a limitation in your
mind that you cannot imagine a man taking a real interest in public affairs'
(this in a letter of 'thanks', remember). Empson did take such an interest,

but the interest was often expressed a little obliquely, as it was in his poetry in the late 1930s warning about 'the gathering storm' (a title he half-joked, half-believed, Churchill pinched from him). When asked, he declared his opposition to America's war in Vietnam in forthright terms, though by and large he didn't use his cultural standing to write about such matters in the general press. One index of his sound political instincts was the way he got *Encounter's* number from the start; as he remarked in 1967: 'Ever since *Encounter* was founded, I have noticed that its political contributors have great difficulty in opening their mouths without a lie hopping out.' (It was, presumably, his frank expression of this conviction to Stephen Spender that provoked the dousing referred to in Chapter 7.) He was, without question, serious about his politics, but he preferred to keep the expression of his seriousness largely private and in a minor key. 'I generally do the first day of the Aldermaston march,' he informed Robert Lowell in 1962, 'as it is through nice country with a few spectators, and the Anglican parson of a parish along the route has been tending to crack up under it.' Empson genuinely wanted to ban the bomb, but it pleased him to give the impression that it was the chance to tread on the toes of a parson that really made him put his walking-boots on.

The letters included here certainly enrich our sense of the relation between these particular political commitments and his broader cultural loyalties. To begin with, the mathematically trained Empson had a feel for the achievements of science that may not have been exceptional in inter-war Cambridge, but that has since been unusual among literary critics. As he wrote to one correspondent in 1947, referring to the discoveries of Einstein and Eddington: 'A critic who cuts himself off from the only fertile part of the contemporary mind is I think unlikely to understand what good work feels like when it is new, and as far as my own work is concerned anyway I am sure I have always found the worldview of the scientists much more stimulating and usable than that of any "literary influence".' In his letters he can be unbuttoned about the partisan implications of such sympathies. In the mid-1960s he declared: 'I think that the Enlightenment is the only hope for civilisation, and that the crawling insinuations against it mainly introduced by T. S. Eliot poison our whole intellectual life.' And, in his public response to Roger Sale, published in the *Hudson Review* in 1967, he pronounced: 'The Whig Interpretation of History is the correct one, and it is remarkable that the book given that title offers no single reason to think otherwise, being merely a fashion report of some High Table giggles. Anything I print about the past, ignorant as I know myself to be, is intended as real truth about the past which I think worth fighting over.' This is not, I think, just a smack at Butterfield (on whom, see Chapter 11 below): Empson retained a wider optimism than was fashionable among the literary elite of the day that science, secularism, liberty, and the social-democratic state were advancing on a common front. As he insisted in 1973, against any interpretation that would assimilate him to literary-critical fashions he had never shared: 'I don't believe, and never have believed, that a social and literary "dissociation of sensibility" ever occurred; I don't even believe that everything is getting worse.' With that knack he displayed in his later letters for snatching defeat from the jaws of victory, at least as far as persuasion of the uncommitted was concerned, he went on: 'Evidently the split is believed to have occurred soon after the Reformation, so the belief is best explained as R. C. propaganda.'

In general, though, his sturdy liberal convictions made him a telling critic of all forms of cultural pessimism. For example, in a letter from the mid-1960s he characterized the American critic Allen Tate as a follower of the Eliot fashion:

and the fashion seems to me a nasty one, which I hope will soon die. It expresses contempt for the modern world on aesthetic grounds, explaining that the speaker would have been a cultured aristocrat in earlier times... A young man with the generosity of mind which comes from energy, and feeling a power to join in, would not despise the actual triumphs of the human mind and spirit which he found bursting out all around him. Surely it is time a generation grew up which isn't all the time crying 'Boo-hoo, I can't afford to keep a butler any longer'.

Empson never lost the class confidence that was second nature to a bohemian Wykehamist of gentry stock, but perhaps that made it easier for him to see through the social fantasies that partly fuelled such cultural pessimism. Though 'the generosity of mind that comes from energy' may have declined in him a little as the years went by, he never wavered in the democratic conviction that things were, on balance, getting better for most people and that that was what mattered.

One thing that, in his view, was all too obviously *not* getting better was the study and teaching of English Literature in Britain and the United States, and from the 1950s onwards his correspondence takes constant potshots at what he saw as its over-professionalized and over-methodized fatuities. Much of his spleen is directed against the 'anti-intentionalist' doctrine of the second-generation New Critics, an orthodoxy that attempted to deny the legitimacy in literary interpretation of 'a process which all persons not insane are using in all their social experience'. The institutionalized divorce between the study of literature and all the other activities of human life was at the root of the problem. As he remarked after taking part in the Kenyon College summer school, one of the temples of the New Criticism in the 1950s, 'we are as concentrated on our profession as a conference of dentists practically'. There are occasional signs of confidence about the future of

literary criticism—'with periodic sanitary efforts it can probably be got
to continue in a sturdy, placid way, as is needed'—and several of the letters show him wielding the scrubbing-brush to some purpose. But at other
moments the excess of his tirades against 'the greasy lies' and 'fetid marsh-
gas' seems grumpily counter-productive. In his reply to Roger Sale cited
earlier, he did at least acknowledge that Sale had praised him 'for what
I would most hope to be praised for, that is, for being large-minded and
resisting the sordidity of modern Eng. Lit.'.

Appropriately, one of the last letters included here is to Haffenden himself, who, in 1982, was proposing to write Empson's biography (a reminder
of how many years he has devoted to his task). Perhaps surprisingly, the
potential subject was encouraging, even keen: 'If you show that my work
takes a coherent position, and is not just a series of pointless cooked-up
shocks, you will be doing me a great service.' But the more predictable dep-
recating impulse soon kicks in. He fears, from the synopsis Haffenden has
sent, that 'my colleagues would find the account too saintly and inflated'.
'*Total* consistency is a good deal to say of anyone; and my *public life* has
consisted mainly of getting comfortable seats to observe the great events of
our time.' This, as Haffenden's first volume has already made clear, considerably understates the privations Empson endured in the 1930s, above all in
China during the Japanese invasion, while the full account of his war years
in London and of his adventures in Peking during the Communist revolution and its immediate aftermath is yet to come. But the remark indirectly
underlines the point about his not having much of a 'public role' in the sense
that, say, Eliot or Leavis, or even Raymond Williams or Richard Hoggart,
did as literary critics who were also social critics.

III

In textbook surveys, Empson still tends to figure as the star performer
of the whizz-bang school of criticism, the verbal fireworks of what, after
Richards, was termed 'Practical Criticism' in Britain, with the 'New Criticism' as its close American relative. Empson displayed immense virtuosity
in minute close reading, especially in *Seven Types of Ambiguity* (published
when he was 24), but his critical practice more generally went far beyond
such techniques and was governed by his sturdy hold of human fundamentals and his relentless drive for clarity, even when dealing with the most
delicate literary effects. This selection of his letters amplifies and illustrates
the ways in which he maintained a steady focus on 'sense': his claims about
the 'plain sense' of a disputed passage often rested on attributions of 'good
sense' to the author and on invocations of 'common sense' among readers.
In clumsier hands, such moves can be just a kind of philistinism, a bluff

refusal to reconsider premises or to acknowledge irreconcilable points of view. There was perhaps a dash of this in Empson's later years as he became increasingly exasperated by the various methodological fashions in literary studies, but in his early and middle decades these emphases expressed an uncowed acknowledgement of the relation of language to ordinary (and extraordinary) social experience. Once the critic lost a hold on this, Empson believed, he became (as he said of the over-professionalized analytical philosopher) 'an almost insanely specialized type of acrobat'.

A further reason Empson so hated the various moralizing and politicizing orthodoxies that dominated academic Eng. Lit. in his later years was because they encouraged in students 'a craving to scold'. Empson had admirably little of this urge. Controverting factual or intellectual error was one thing: there was a lot of it about and, as we have seen, he rather enjoyed laying about him with the Sword of Truth. But he displays very little desire to judge people or try to make them like himself, or like any one model. As he wrote to his methodologically over-zealous graduate student Philip Hobsbaum in 1966: 'It seems to me that the chief function of imaginative literature is to make you realise that other people are very various, many of them quite different from you, with different "systems of value" as well; and the effect of almost any Orthodoxy is to hide this, and pretend that everybody *ought* to be like Homer or Dr Leavis.' Dealing with Empson himself evidently called for no little tolerance from others, partly because of the occasional fallout from his taste for copious drink, domestic squalor, and a rather unconventional style of fulfilling his professional duties. But he in his turn seems to have been profoundly, instinctively tolerant where different ways of life were concerned. What he hated was cant and hypocrisy, and daft intellectual systems that had lost touch with the reality of human experience, that 'vast facade of imbecility' that, in his view, protected so much academic writing from saying anything important. Thus, even when he fails to persuade, he still retains, as these letters vividly remind us, a wonderful, unnerving power to take the wind out of professorial sails.

For one of the great things about Empson is that he remained open to the magnificence of the world while being properly severe on the idiot things said about it by people in the grip of some schoolroom crotchet. 'It is petulant snootiness to say "The world is not good enough for me"; the world is glorious beyond all telling and far too good for any of us.' And he can put us in our places in more local ways, too. 'Congratulations on your splendid piece in the *TLS*,' he wrote to Ricks in the late 1970s about an essay on Geoffrey Hill, adding his trademark bang at the end: 'the dismal old paper does not deserve it.'

9

Disappointment:
A. L. Rowse in his Diaries

I

One cannot help feeling that A. L. Rowse's life went badly wrong some-where. It is not just that his later writings became a byword for crankiness and venom, but rather that this was merely the most visible expression of a bad and rapidly worsening case of egocentrism. Once his symptoms were well developed, no form of tribute or appreciation from the outside world could ever be sufficient, so to his native touchiness were added the unlovely qualities of resentment and jealousy at others' success. His notorious delusion that he had identified the 'Dark Lady' of Shakespeare's sonnets, first announced in 1973, became emblematic of the failings exhibited in the later stages of his career as a whole—a high-handed way with the evidence, disdain for the work of other scholars, vituperative responses to criticism, unshakeable belief in his own genius. When he reached the conventional retiring age of 65, Rowse had already published thirty books. By the time of his death twenty-nine years later in 1997, he had published, astonishingly, a further forty-seven volumes of one kind and another. It might have been better if he hadn't.

His younger friend Richard Ollard understandably took a more indul-gent view in his fair-minded biography of Rowse, *A Man of Contradictions* (1999), but even he had to wince his way through much of his subject's later career. That biography was based on unrestricted access to the hoard of documents and memorabilia Rowse, always mindful of posterity, had pre-served, above all on the diaries that he kept throughout his adult life. These

Richard Ollard (ed.), *The Diaries of A. L. Rowse* (Allen Lane, 2003).

diaries existed in more than one state: Rowse often made rough notes to be written up more fully later; much of this material was then transformed into typescript in subsequent years; and thereafter Rowse returned to it, obsessively correcting and improving. What we are given in the present volume is Ollard's own selection from this accumulated ego-bank, tactfully spliced and annotated, covering the mid-1920s to the late 1960s, though in practice heavily concentrated in the 1950s and 1960s.

The volume contains many of the usual ingredients that connoisseurs of this genre seem to hunger for—country-house lunch parties, post-prandial *bons mots*, gossip, barbs, and that general air of lifting the veil on the Great, the Good, and the Ugly. But they possess a deeper interest than that on at least two counts. First, they do, almost despite themselves, illuminate where and how Rowse's life went wrong. And second, they give the historian a rare chance to study the slow, inner formation of a kind of reactionary sensibility that played such a large part in twentieth-century British culture. On both counts, the diaries demonstrate the impossibility of neatly separating what is individual and private from what is common and public.

One way to bring out both the puzzlingness and the representativeness of Rowse's career is to reflect that, had he died in 1938, as he might well have done (he had to be operated on for long-undiagnosed duodenal ulcers), he would have taken his place alongside those other promising left-wing intellectuals whose lives were cut short in Spain or in the war, and who are now remembered in some quarters as constituting Britain's 'lost intelligentsia'.

Born in 1903 into the just respectable ranks of the Cornish working class, Rowse followed the trajectory laid out for the bookish boy by the highly selective education system of the time, culminating in a First in History at Oxford in 1925 and election to All Souls in the same year. '*That* was much the greatest event in my life,' he reflected thirty years later. (Sadly, he may have been right.) His early historiographical masters were Marx and Tawney. The diaries reveal that when in 1926 he received his first cheque for tutorial teaching, he 'went out and bought exultingly Tawney's long-awaited *Religion and the Rise of Capitalism*', and then spent most of the ensuing weekend 'reading Tawney with excitement'. But in Rowse's apprentice years, in the late 1920s and into the 1930s, Marx trumped Tawney, who was held to be insufficiently 'materialist' in not recognizing that economic interests, rather than moral values, ultimately drove history.

The iconoclastic young historian, profiting from the connections opened up to him by All Souls, is soon to be found living what he described as 'this university cum writing cum margin-of-politics life'. Thus, for example, in 1931 we see him preparing a radio talk on Marx, writing reviews of books by Bernard Shaw and G. D. H. Cole for the smart weeklies, giving two courses of lectures at the LSE, and all the while researching hard in the British Museum and the Public Record Office. Nor was his involvement with politics merely theoretical: he stood, unsuccessfully, as the Labour candidate for Penryn in the elections of 1931 and 1935, the model of the local scholarship boy who returns to help fight for a better life for the class from which he has risen. Though he was already delving into the archives of the Tudor period, most of his publications during these years were intended as contributions to contemporary political debate, notably *Politics and the Younger Generation* in 1931 and *Mr Keynes and the Labour Movement*, which argued, promptly and perceptively in 1936, that the political logic of Keynes's *General Theory* aligned him with the Labour Party not the Liberals.

But even at this stage of his life, Rowse was also driven by very different, and sometimes downright contradictory, urges and loyalties. From an early age, it was the past, the English past and more especially the local Cornish past, that most stirred his imagination: he grew up nostalgic for worlds he knew only through books. He was a published poet and liked to think of himself as a 'man of letters'. In practice, his acquired literary culture was essentially pre-Modernist; his tastes were formed by the Romantic and Victorian canon disseminated to earnest seekers after self-improvement in the early years of the century. A diary entry in 1929 finds him reading Arnold's *Thyrsis*: 'This was so touching, I found myself crying over the end of it, reading it aloud.' The rest of the evening 'I dawdled away at the piano and looking into books, Carlyle, Browning and Cobbett'. In other ways, too, many of the main elements in that social aesthetic summarized as 'Englishness' already had possession of him—love of medieval churches, hatred of creeping suburbia, a deep susceptibility to grand country houses and the way of life they represented, while from his first sight of it Oxford's beauty exerted a hold over him it never lost despite his later quarrels with the place ('heaven but a prison').

Writing about English intellectuals in the middle decades of the twentieth century, some commentators have speculated that a nascent 'oppositional intelligentsia' was forming in the 1930s, only to be 'coopted' by various kinds of public service in the Second World War, resulting in the establishment of a more 'integrated' and complacent intellectual class, happy to go on celebrating Albion's rich distinctiveness. Although the terms of this now-familiar analysis invite challenge at almost every point, it is easy to see how Rowse could be taken to provide a confirming example. But the complex interplay of private and public at work in Rowse during these years cannot easily be subsumed into such a monocausal narrative. As with several of his contemporaries—Orwell, dissimilar in so many other ways, comes to mind—a deep cultural conservatism that easily tipped over into anti-intellectualism accompanied the more overt forms of radicalism even in the pre-war years. Perhaps the much-vaunted 1930s intellectual was anyway quite often a belated Edwardian man of letters caught up in the bewildering era of totalitarian politics. In Rowse's case, antipathy to appeasement bulked larger in his political affiliation than antipathy to capitalism. Someone so shaped by an essentially late-nineteenth-century sense of England's greatness was always going to find the post-1945 world a disappointment, though it is intriguing to find that Rowse did not actually resign his membership of the Labour Party until Suez. So the war, in many ways a turning point in his life, did not in any simple sense turn him from a Blum into a blimp.

In fact, the 1940s and early 1950s now look to have been the most fruitful and fulfilled phase of Rowse's career; it may be revealing of one of the functions served by journal keeping that his diaries are at their thinnest in these years. He made his name with the publication of *Tudor Cornwall* in 1941 and *A Cornish Childhood* the following year. His patriotic *The Spirit of English History* chimed with the mood of the war years, selling well, and a decade of achievement was capped by the appearance of *The England of Elizabeth* in 1950, the first of what was to be a trilogy on Elizabethan England—according to some critics the last really serious works of history that he ever published. Rowse's ill health debarred him from military service, but his romantic historical imagination thrilled to the drama of 1940; he aspired to be the equivalent in the literary sphere of his great hero, Churchill, in the world of action, invoking the roll-call of England's glories in order to stiffen the sinews in defence of ancient liberties, and much more in that vein of resurgent Whiggism. At the same time, his personal life went through a rare sunny spell. In what Ollard calls Rowse's 'last and greatest affair of the heart', he conceived a passionate attachment to Norman Scarfe, when the latter was still a sixth-former, and for some years tried to nurture the younger man's development with a mixture of desire and paternalism. More prosaically, he had a period as Sub-Warden of All Souls, in effect running the college for a while, and he apparently discharged the role honourably enough.

The event that marked the end of this relatively happy period, at least symbolically and perhaps causally too, was the election for the Wardenship of All Souls in 1952. A great deal has now been written about this relatively insignificant piece of clubland manœuvring, partly because such anecdote-generating figures as Isaiah Berlin and John Sparrow were at the heart of it. Rowse, against his first and better judgement, let himself be persuaded into becoming a candidate, and then lost (to Sparrow). Although there was a sense in which Rowse always needed and even courted rejection (as he occasionally half-acknowledged), this was a wounding rebuff from an institution in which he had invested so much intense emotion, and he withdrew in a huff. For several years he divided his time between the beautiful eighteenth-century house in Cornwall that he leased for the rest of his life and what Ollard nicely calls his 'annual transhumance to America', converting his reputation into dollars in a series of visiting professorships. 'At sixty, England has had enough of me,' he declared a few years later. There was a peculiar truth in this syntactically wonky but characteristically egocentric assertion. His intellectual (and, for long stretches, social) isolation intensified: from now on, his books became more popular, more controversial, and, above all, more frequent.

II

With the passing years, habitual self-absorption slid into damaging solipsism. Fatal to both the historian and the social commentator alike was the way in which his aversion to the society around him became complete and therefore indiscriminate. His imaginative immersion in the past now became wilful and vengeful. 'I hate the guts of the modern world, everything about it, even its good points. I am furious that things have gone this way.' Always the disappointed lover, Rowse raged that the 'England' he had lusted after had been wantonly destroyed by the barbarians, 'the inhabitants of the fuck-hutches in millions' who have been given a new prosperity but 'who don't know what to do to spend it'.

An early sign of Rowse's disconnection from the reality of life (as well as abandonment of his earlier social radicalism) was his absurd railing against income tax. He took this sense of outrage to practical lengths that even his sympathetic biographer admits amounted to tax evasion (and that had finally to be settled by a massive payment to the Inland Revenue). 'They' were stealing the fruits of 'his' labour, and for what? To pay for 'the upkeep of the Idiot People's children, their perambulators crowding the pavement wherever one goes', or else for 'the slackers of the Slacker State'. There was only one political destination to which such bile could lead. As early as 1967 he is to be found contrasting England's degeneration with what De Gaulle had achieved for France: 'It shows what *can* be done with will, determination, thrift, hárd work, hard-fistedness, no illusions about one-self or anybody else—all the values I believe in, totally disregarded in deca-dent, declining Britain.' Here, ominously, was the voice of England waiting for Thatcher to happen. It was only a matter of time before he indulged in an admiring elaboration of the parallel between the Iron Lady and Good

Queen Bess. The sensibility nurtured by the nostalgic 'Englishness' of the inter-war years, faced with a world it didn't understand, turned rancid.

Despite this sharply downward spiral, these diaries are at their richest in the 1950s and 1960s, partly because Rowse had by then moved even further in the direction of the reworked and polished entry, sometimes given its fullest, most finished form long after the events recorded. He is manifestly mindful of posterity indeed by this point; from now on, it is the set-piece accounts rather than the incidental details that stand out.

Thus, short essays on the spirit of place weave themselves around visits to D. H. Lawrence's birthplace at Eastwood in Nottingham, to Elizabeth Bowen at Bowenscourt, to Evelyn Waugh's home at Combe Florey after the writer's death, and a lovingly detailed record of a day visiting his great hero, Churchill, recently out of office for the final time. One of the more moving portraits issues from two visits he paid to the very elderly G. M. Trevelyan, to whom Rowse looked up as a historian who reached a wide public by telling the national story in readable prose. That was not all they shared: 'Trevelyan hates the modern world—more completely and consistently than any of us; for he hates modern science and the world it has made.' But then there comes one of those perceptive comments that remind us of the talents that were going to seed in the ranting, self-indulgent curmudgeon Rowse was becoming. 'His whole attitude to history springs from the *general* point of view of a member of the old governing class, whose judgements came from proximity to government rather than from the specialist outlook of the historian. Therein lies its advantage, though creaking a bit.' It seems somehow to Rowse's credit that he can see this and still keep some critical distance from it. By the time of his second visit, in 1959, the 83-year-old Trevelyan could no longer see to read or write, and solaced himself by reciting poetry from memory, treating Rowse to several stanzas of Meredith's 'Love in the Valley', which he declared to be 'the most beautiful poem of them all'. Two late-Victorian bookmen strolling in the grounds of a country house, a brief moment of unclouded success in Rowse's determined attempts to put the historical clock back.

As in the best of his historical works, what comes through most strikingly in this volume is Rowse's observant responsiveness to the relation of landscape to architecture, refracted through the prism of history. Even some of the run-of-the-mill connecting narrative passages exhibit this quality, as when he goes to visit his friend and fellow popular historian Arthur Bryant (the subject of the following chapter):

On a golden autumn day we motored through the blue Dorset landscape, past Creech Manor—classic front of cream stone looking up against the last sweep of hill before Kimmeridge bay—up and up and then a long swoop down upon

Smedmore, demure, bow-fronted, blue-painted, very virginal and lovely, waiting at the end of the road beyond which there is no further.

But this entry also touches on one of the diaries' most recurrent themes, his yearning not just to own a beautiful old country house, but to have inherited one. This desire receives its most naked statement on the occasion of a visit to G. M. Trevelyan's older brother, Sir Charles Trevelyan, at Wallington, the family home in Northumberland: 'This room gave me the feeling how fascinating it would be to belong to a family like that, rich in interest, intelligence, history—instead of belonging to no-one at all. All very well to create everything for oneself, but better to *belong*. I belong nowhere.' Visits to Chastleton, Boconnoc, and other historic houses stir the same yearning: 'The place made an extraordinary impact on my mind; for the next twenty-four hours I could think of nothing else'; and again: 'Just what I should like to have inherited.'

That visit to Bryant's country house came as part of a friendship that would have seemed highly improbable in the 1930s, when the two men were far apart politically as well as in background. Indeed, in the mid-1930s, Rowse might have seemed the very embodiment of the '*New Statesman*-reading Left-wing intellectual' whom Bryant so abhorred, and the fact that Bryant became a vocal advocate of the policy of appeasement that Rowse detested only made any intimacy between them seem even less likely. But they were brought together by their response to the war, and particularly by the rightwards migration of Rowse's political identity for which the war was part cause, part occasion. They came to share an ardent, romantic patriotism—Bryant's *The Years of Endurance* (1942) was dedicated to Rowse as an expression of their 'common devotion to the English past'—which in time was buttressed by a sense of their common distance from professional academic history, a loathing of rancorous left-wing intellectuals, and an insatiable snobbery.

Nonetheless, for all that they had in common, they were very different characters, and the differences help explain their contrasting public standings. Rowse, manifestly the cleverer man, confided to his diary after a visit to his friend in the 1950s in which they had had a violent disagreement about which politicians were most responsible for Britain's vulnerability in 1939: 'Actually, I think him on the purely intellectual plane second-rate—in spite of his gifts, which are different.' Bryant may have had a narrower range of talents, but in putting them to use he was not inhibited by self-division. Rowse was much the more riven figure, with many more sharp edges: he was conscious of his unfavoured background and, having moved from the Left to the Right of the political spectrum in middle life, had a more complex public as well as personal history to come to terms with. Bryant was more at one with the identity that inheritance, chance, and achievement had delivered, more able to throw his considerable energies into his work and his networking without any of Rowse's resentments or angularity—characteristics that attracted some particularly barbed comments from Rowse, who yearned for comparable social and official recognition yet despised many of the arts by which it was obtained.

In reviewing Rowse's *The Spirit of English History* in 1943, Richard Ollard nicely caught some of these differences when he observed that the book 'does not quite glow with the Christmas-card cheerfulness of his friend Sir Arthur Bryant'. That may be seen as a virtue on Rowse's part: Christmas cards do not usually furnish the most probing analyses of the scenes they depict. But it may also point to one source of Bryant's greater popular success. Olde England, Yuletide logs burning the year round, apple-cheeked children gambolling in traditional games, boards groaning under roasts and puddings: Bryant's vision of the English past was a relentlessly cosy one. No one ever thought of Rowse as cosy.

Unfortunately, far too much of the diary is given over to the rehearsal of his grievances, an activity in which Rowse could give a masterclass to even the most accomplished whinger. In 1956 he hears that A. J. P. Taylor has been asked to give the Ford Lectures in Oxford: 'They have never asked me.' Then begins his formulaic ranting against the usual roll-call of those Rowse cast as his rivals: he was simply obsessed with the undeserved success enjoyed by Taylor among historians and by Cyril Connolly among men of letters. In 1969 he vents his resentment that his recent book *The Cornish in America* hasn't been reviewed in the weeklies or the Sundays, explaining this to himself as only what one should expect in a 'sick and diseased society' where 'the centre of the sickness is the Leftist, liberal establishment'. But again he can console himself with the thought that that establishment 'is still unrepresentative of the country: wherever I have been this autumn, Preston, Stroud, Eastbourne, Newton Abbot, I have had enthusiastic reception and response. The London establishment regards me as an enemy.' It is hard to know which parallel from the culture of the time to draw: he veers between being Leavis minus the moral seriousness and Tony Hancock ('Oh yes, I was *big* in Newton Abbot'); the Angry Middle-Aged Man; Look Back in Pique.

There are occasional glimpses of Rowse's positively Trollopian rate of composition in his later years. In 1955 he records writing the 180,000-word *The Early Churchills* in five months. An entry the following year shows how: 'a tremendous spate of work, writing all day up to midnight, managing 5,000 words' of *The Later Churchills*. This is impressive in its way, but it also explains a lot. Even the sympathetic Ollard had to acknowledge the weaknesses of these volumes—'tub-thumping rhetoric, banality', 'slipshod scholarship', 'slackness of writing', 'sheer carelessness'. 'The prose ranges from a nudging woman's magazine style to the clear, dignified but lively English the author naturally commands when he stops to think'. But from this point on, Rowse stopped less and less. The pitfalls of writing 'popular history' receive a graphic illustration in the later career of the scholar capable of writing *Tudor Cornwall*.

Indeed, read in bulk, the diaries suggest that writing was Rowse's downfall in the way drink is for others. He wrote all morning, and sometimes had to retire to bed in the afternoon to sleep it off. He wrote heavily before dinner, and sometimes for long after, concluding with a stiff shot of his diary as a nightcap. Even during a bout of heavy writing on one of his books, he would tipple at reviews (a tell-tale sign); he was a compulsive letter-writer, knocking back slugs of correspondence when in bare hotel rooms; and if nothing else was available, he resorted to making notes for future full-length diary entries, the bedrock of addiction, the British Sherry of the hardened writer. It hardly comes as a surprise to learn that he was a teetotaller: he didn't need it.

III

Thinking back from later years to the point at the end of the 1930s when he had almost died, Rowse thought that an appropriate label for his biography up to that point might be 'An Arrested Life'. These diaries make one feel it would not be a bad title for an account of the whole ninety-four years. Though Ollard, biographer of Pepys, likes to suggest the parallel, as a diarist Rowse is no Pepys. There is not enough unselfconsciousness, not enough incidental detail, not enough interest in other people; too much artifice and polish, too much self-importance, and above all too much resentment and bitterness. But Ollard had a point in calling his biography *A Man of Contradictions*. One could find in these diaries a quotation with which to contradict almost every characterization of Rowse I have given here. It is part of what makes him simultaneously interesting and repellent. Much of the pathos—and it is a life whose dominant note now seems to be pathos—comes from the fact that he was half-aware of this uneasy combination.

These contradictory elements, clashing like tectonic plates beneath the apparent orderliness of Rowse's daily round, suddenly throw up one quite extraordinary diary entry, a piece of sustained self-analysis and inadvertent self-revelation that does bear comparison with the great diarists. The year is 1959, the unlikely setting is his small functional bedroom in the University Club in Madison, Wisconsin, where Rowse is spending four months as a visiting professor. A Friday evening in February, his week's teaching over and with it his small amount of unavoidable human contact, he settles down to commune with his diary as he looks forward to the solitude of the weekend. The long entry that issued from this unpromising occasion (occupying nine printed pages here) ranges over his life, his character, his longings and disappointments. It has something of a diva's set-piece soliloquy, veering between lament, self-justification, and true heart-searching; by turns combative, complacent, and racked by a keening for lost chances of happiness.

The entry moves towards what looks as though it is going to be its climax after only a few paragraphs.

I think then that this practically solipsistic way of life I have worked out, the isolation and the insulation, moving out of people's reach, in the margin between one and the other, not sharing in people's lives, except superficially as a visitor, a spectator—sad and the less fulfilled as it is, for it has little stimulus or inspiration from outside, no immersion and no love—is nevertheless, in the circumstances, the best line of defence, and even way of life in the world we have inherited.

But down below the tectonic plates rumble away, disturbing this too-easily achieved settlement. He starts to complain, again, about how he has never 'received any *real* encouragement to my work or any real lift from circumstances. Except for the heroic, thrilling years of the war and tension and love: for a moment only, books and essays like *The English Spirit* and *The Spirit of English History* were in tune with the public mood.' At this point he peels off for a familiar resentful riff on his exclusion from the cultural establishment, 'the envies and enmities with which I am dogged—*New Statesman*, even *Spectator* (for nothing that I have done to them), BBC Third Programme, the Left Intellectuals, the academics, Oxford—a wall of misestimation surrounds me, in line with nothing, no party or body of opinion.' And then of course the soothing balm that all such 'excluded' authors can apply: 'It is a wonder that the *public* responds as it does,' his popularity a poke in the eye to his detractors.

Having brought that line of reflection to a partial resolution, he swerves off in another direction, one that is particularly revealing of the interplay between individual sensibility and larger cultural shifts:

I grew up with intense pride in England and her past, inspired by it, a strong motive always to do my best. It was an unquestioned assumption, the air one breathed, that England and the Empire were the greatest thing in the world. I came to maturity in a world where that has vanished at a touch. As a child, I grew up on the fringe, at the park-gate, shut out of the way of life of the gentry. Theirs was the life I always meant to share. When, by my own efforts, I arrived at the point of commanding such a life for myself, it was undermined or broken down.

Sweeping cultural pessimism and a sense of personal tragedy sustain each other here. Rowse believes himself to be registering 'really the end of a civilization', and he has no interest in its modern successor. 'I do not care what follows the world that was already vanishing when I glimpsed it through the park-gates: that was the only civilization I care for, though it was never mine and I did not belong to it. But it was what was in keeping with my innermost nature.'

One is still lingering over the image of the child, separating himself in fantasy from the graceless world of his birth, pressing his nose to the park gate through which can be glimpsed the whole beauty and charm of English history (or at least one powerful, selective, version thereof), when he moves off into another, more public form of regret at worlds lost. He looks back enviously to writers of the previous generation such as Shaw, Wells, Maugham, and Bertrand Russell. They were paid attention to, and 'handsomely remunerated' (he cannot restrain his usual screech at the evils of income tax at this point). 'Everywhere they were made much of: they were the leading writers of the world's leading people'. No such luck for him, a jobbing lecturer holed up in a mid-West town, a cultivated Greek now retained to divert the philistine young Romans. 'The question becomes, then, how to live one's life in such a civilization. The answer is—*to live it as an inner exile*... One becomes a constant watcher from outside, for which state all my life has been a preparation.' Only after having reached this fresh resolution of the recurring motifs, having communed with himself across nearly 4,000 words, does he finally lay down his pen. Or perhaps it was simply time for his solitary dinner in the university cafeteria.

10

Believing in England:
Arthur Bryant, Historian as Man of Letters

I

'His works gave more pleasure to more people than those of any other historian past or present.' Perhaps remarks made in the course of a Thanksgiving Service in Westminster Abbey should not have to bear very much scrutiny, though in this case the address—given by Lord Blake, Provost of Queen's College Oxford and a leading Conservative historian, as part of a 'Service of Thanksgiving for the Life and Work of Sir Arthur Bryant', who had died two months earlier in January 1985—was subsequently published in *England*, the journal of the Royal Society of St George. It is hard to know how one could go about trying to decide the truth of Blake's claim: it carefully does not suggest that Bryant had more readers than any other historian, something that could in principle be quantified though in practice estimated only in the most speculative terms. Its insistence on the 'pleasure' Bryant's works gave makes the claim both polemical and unfalsifiable. Even so, one immediately begins to wonder whether, among Bryant's near-contemporaries, Trevelyan's possibly no-less numerous readers may not have taken a comparable delight in their reading, and, reaching further back, whether readers of Gibbon and Macaulay may not, over a much longer period, have notched up a higher score on the felicific calculus (not to mention the readers of some of the classical historians over more than two millennia). But by making his claim in this form, Blake was positioning Bryant in a particular kind of cultural role, forestalling unsympathetic questions about the rigour of his method or

Julia Stapleton, *Sir Arthur Bryant: National History in Twentieth-Century Britain* (Lexington Books, 2005).

the originality and significance of his findings. Bryant's histories gave pleasure to the many: he was to be judged as a writer—the historian as man of letters.

To have been judged in these terms would, of course, have been congenial to Bryant, who prided himself on fulfilling the modern equivalent of Macaulay's ambition that his *History of England* should 'supersede the last fashionable novel on the tables of young ladies' (though Bryant's readership does not seem to have been notably young or female). But at the same time, Bryant also hankered after, and to some extent achieved, a different role, one amply filled by Macaulay—that of the figure who, in addition to intellectual or literary distinction, plays a prominent part in his country's public life, is an influential political voice, and is generally regarded as a personage of consequence. These roles can be complementary in certain respects, but they can also be in tension with each other, especially where the price of political influence includes toeing a partisan or ideological line. The legerdemain at the heart of Bryant's long career depended on his being able to present what was in fact a deeply Tory interpretation of English history and society as though it were an unproblematically inclusive and celebratory national story.

Bryant is also of interest, especially in the context of the other essays in this book, as a case study in the shifting relations between reputations and publics in twentieth-century Britain. In his most traditional guise, 'the man of letters' had addressed, or aspired to address, a general, educated but non-specialist, readership. With the self-conscious professionalization of history taking place chiefly, though not exclusively, in the universities in the late nineteenth and early twentieth centuries, it became more and more difficult for a writer simultaneously to appeal to the successors of such readers while retaining the professional esteem of the leading scholars in any given field. (One of the remarkable things about G. M. Trevelyan's career is the way in which, having spent a couple of decades as a freelance historian enjoying considerable literary success, he could still be regarded as an appropriate appointment as Regius Professor of History at Cambridge in 1925—though at the time considerations other than pure scholarly standing affected appointments to Regius chairs, which were in effect in the gift of the Prime Minister of the day.) For those at the most popular end of the spectrum this hardly mattered: Arthur Mee needed no imprimatur from the experts for his popular illustrated narratives, and even figures such as Belloc and Chesterton could frankly cater to a readership that valued sectarian passion and novelistic colour above the drier scholarly virtues. But they were writers for whom history was only one among the several genres they cultivated, and not the primary one for either of them.

By contrast, when Bryant embarked on his first substantial historical work, he had no such general literary reputation, indeed practically no public reputation at all. He felt it was important that his work should not be disparaged or dismissed by professional historians; he laboured over his three-volume life of Pepys in the 1930s with at least one eye on the response from the specialist seventeenth-century historians. But thereafter not only did he become more confident in, even belligerent about, the standing of his work in its own terms; the various reading publics also became increasingly segmented, with separate arrangements and expectations coming to govern marketing, reviewing, and so on. It was not so much that the academic historians found fault with Bryant's later books, though they occasionally did; it was rather that they ignored them, much as academic literary critics were coming to ignore popular 'middlebrow' fiction.

Bryant aided this process where the reception of his own work was concerned by his explicit identification with a 'middlebrow' readership, something that underscores the extent to which his identity as a writer was fixed in terms that had particular resonance in the inter-war years. Bryant was a proud combatant in the 'battle of the brows' that was so much discussed in this period, presenting himself as a gentrified, Tory version of J. B. Priestley in his hostility to 'highbrow intellectuals'. In practice, 'Bloomsbury' (by then a composite term of cultural abuse, not restricted to the original members of the set of that name) and 'university historians' were far apart in their membership, idiom, and concerns, but Bryant, fighting a war on both fronts, often conflated them as equally removed from the natural patriotism and healthy moral instincts of 'the ordinary Englishman' for whom he professed to write. The tendentious avoidance of the category of 'class' was part of the implicit Toryism of Bryant's self-cast role as a 'national historian', but the partial evidence available suggests that in his later years, at least, his own readership became increasingly confined to the more genteel, or would-be genteel, sections of the conservative middle class.

There is a strong temptation for a modern scholar and critic to write Bryant off as a mere popularizer, a colourful drum-and-trumpet chronicler who provided light reading and patriotic uplift for an instinctively nostalgic suburban or colonial readership, but whose work does not merit any closer examination. Julia Stapleton has resisted that temptation admirably: *Sir Arthur Bryant and National History in Twentieth-Century Britain* is a thorough, careful, and sympathetic exploration of Bryant's entire career that never condescends to him, but instead quietly and patiently explicates his extensive *œuvre*, setting it in the context of the intellectual and political life of mid-twentieth-century Britain. (I should declare an interest at this point: many years ago, I was Stapleton's Ph.D. supervisor.) Ultimately, she is, for my taste, a little too indulgent towards Bryant, not just to his rabidly right-wing and at times Fascist-sympathizing politics, but also to the intellectually flaccid, overwritten character of his work as a whole. But my response is, in this case, the more conventional one; it is a great merit of Stapleton's more charitable reconstruction that it does not take the academic valuation of Bryant for granted, trying instead to bring out what was involved in upholding 'a conception of knowledge as primarily an instrument of cultural uplift and national unity at a clear "middlebrow" level'. This enables her also to demonstrate just how successful Bryant was at squaring the various circles referred to above, at least in the 1940s and 1950s, his real heyday, as his huge sales were matched by public standing and official recognition, allowing him to become both an ornament of the Tory party and a national possession.

Such a careful study of Bryant is worth having on its own account, but it is all the more welcome for the fact that, prior to this book, the only extended scholarly engagement with Bryant's career was the chapter in Andrew Roberts's *Eminent Churchillians*. This amounted to a sustained exercise in denigration. The pious encomiums bestowed on Bryant on the occasion of his eightieth birthday, Roberts gleefully recorded, could not survive the evidence subsequently made available by the opening of archives that had come about with the expiry of the fifty-year rule. Far from being the doyen of national history, justly lauded from all parts of the establishment, and 'far from being the patriot he so long and loudly procaimed himself, Bryant was in fact a Nazi sympathiser and Fascist fellow-traveller, who only narrowly escaped internment as a potential traitor in 1940. He was also, incidentally, a supreme toady, fraudulent scholar, and humbug.' Roberts's whole chapter is unrelentingly hostile in its treatment of Bryant, mocking his 'glutinous style', declaring his reputation as a historian and scholar to be 'largely undeserved', describing him as the 'Uriah Heep of historical writing', and so on. Although overstated and, as Stapleton quietly demonstrates, not always supported by a more careful examination of the evidence, there are grains of truth in many of these charges, and even her far more charitable portrait has to accommodate the fact that, as she fairly acknowledges, Bryant was 'a relentless networker across the British establishment' and 'a master of the art of obsequiousness'. But against the major charges of his having been a Fascist fellow-traveller and fraudulent scholar, Stapleton's unhurried, detailed reconstruction of the key episodes in Bryant's career, while it does not completely exonerate him, brings a greater, and more interesting, complexity to the story.

II

Bryant literally began his life surrounded by expressions of what were to become the central themes of his work: monarchical pomp, military ceremony, the great monuments of English history. His father was chief clerk to the Prince of Wales, so Bryant was born, in 1899, on the Sandringham estate. When his employer succeeded to the throne two years later, Bryant's father moved into the royal secretariat, living within the precincts of Buckingham Palace. Bryant was immensely proud of these royal associations, but his father remained essentially an employee rather than a courtier, and everything about the son's early environment encouraged the snobbery and social climbing that were to be so conspicuous a part of his adult life. He was sent to Harrow, and then briefly saw service in the Royal Flying Corps at the end of the First World War. At the beginning of 1919, he went up to Queen's College, Oxford, to read History, taking the short course (five-term) degree permitted to those who had fought in the war. Bryant was already beginning to diverge from the pattern common among those who went on to become leading members of the literary and intellectual elites: he didn't much enjoy Oxford and didn't distinguish himself there. He had begun to develop what Stapleton describes as 'a deep-seated antipathy towards the academic profession as a thorn in the side of England's inherited culture', while his ready responsiveness to the military and imperial glories of English history also put him markedly at odds with fashionable opinion among the young in the 1920s. It may have been a sign of things to come that his first publication was in *Punch*.

Although his father was to be knighted for services to the royal family in 1920, the young Bryant had to make his own way in the world, with no expectation of inherited wealth. A form of Tory-paternalist social conscience seems to have led him into adult education, first at the College of Arts and Technology in Cambridge (in whose founding Ruskin had played a part), and then as a lecturer for the Oxford University Extension Delegacy. At the same time, he qualified for the Bar, chiefly with an eye to pursuing a political career. In 1924 he had improved his prospects by marrying the daughter of a baronet. His good connections within the Tory party led to his becoming educational adviser to the party's Bonar Law College at Ashridge in Hertfordshire, an institution that was intended to counter the perceived appeal of progressive ideas among the young. The short book that Bryant published in 1929 on *The Spirit of Conservatism* was meant to serve a similar purpose, though Bryant typically tried to play down its obvious party-political character by insisting that it was 'an attempt to express in simple language the meaning of Conservatism, not so much as a political creed, but as an emotion inherent

in our race'. His enthusiasm for the national past at its most colourful found
expression in the late 1920s in his role as a pageant organizer, culminating
in the Greenwich Pageant of 1933, an extravagant celebration of England's
military and naval history that was attended 'by the Queen and the Prince of
Wales as well as the entire Cabinet on the first night'.

Bryant entered his thirties with only modest achievements to his name
thus far and no very clear sense of direction to his career. He aspired to be
adopted as a Tory candidate for Parliament, but he knew he could not really
afford to pursue that ambition. He had qualified for the Bar, but with little
enthusiasm and no desire to practise. Lecturing to adult education classes
yielded him a certain satisfaction, but it was never going to be the route
to fame and fortune. And then came the major turning-point of his life.
He had for some time been transcribing some seventeenth-century papers
that had come into his possession through his wife's family, and a friend,
impressed by the powers of imagination and reconstruction that Bryant
displayed in this task, suggested to Longmans (for whom he was a reader)
that Bryant be commissioned to write a new biography of Charles II. That
monarch had usually received rather unsympathetic treatment at the hands
of orthodox Whiggish historians, and Bryant set out to provide a far more
favourable account in which the monarchy, not Parliament, constituted the
animating heartbeat of national history. After initially following the usual
chronological progression, Bryant was advised by the American historian
Wallace Notestein to ditch the chapters on Charles's early life and to begin
the book with a dramatic account of his escape following his final military
defeat in 1651. Throughout the book, he drew less upon the official documents or later accounts and more upon vivid first-hand reports in letters,
diaries, and other personal papers from the period.

The immediate success of *King Charles* II, published by Longman in 1931,
took the publishers by surprise; it went through seven impressions within
eighteen months, selling 27,000 copies and being made a 'choice' of the
Book Society. Stapleton emphasizes its repudiation of the established Whig
story of the seventeenth century, though more elemental qualities surely
explained its popularity—its use of details of everyday life, its extravagant
evocative prose (the *ODNB* entry on Bryant, by Richard Griffiths, remarks
'the rather sentimental, mannered tone, which was to be a constant in his
output'), its romanticism, and above all the fact that its subject was both
colourful and royal. The heady experience of literary success spurred Bryant into the career of popular historian, though he did not actually resign
his University Extension post until 1936. In 1932 he accepted an invitation
from Cambridge University Press to write the life of Samuel Pepys, a task
for which much of the material had been gathered by two earlier scholars

who had died without completing it. In the event, Bryant's biography ran to three volumes (he never completed a projected fourth), and this enterprise consumed much of his writing energy through the 1930s, with the volumes being published between 1933 and 1938. He hoped that a work of such detailed research, appearing from a scholarly publisher, would establish his credentials as a serious historian. Though sales were not spectacular, they were certainly impressive by normal CUP standards: by 1948 the three volumes together had sold just over 30,000.

From 1936 onwards Bryant lived entirely by his writing, and lived well. Most freelances end up doing a great deal of reviewing and miscellaneous literary journalism; Bryant was unusual in concentrating his energies on his books, as well as in making so much money from them. He did, it is true, a fair amount of journalism over his long writing life, especially on the subject of the monarchy, but compared to his peers he did relatively little reviewing or essay writing. There was, however, one great exception to his general abstention from regular journalism. When G. K. Chesterton died in 1936, the *Illustrated London News* was faced with finding a replacement to write the 'Our Notebook' column that GKC had writen since 1905. Bryant jumped at the invitation; early exposure to the *ILN* had nourished his attachment to the Empire, and Chesterton had been one of his literary heroes. He continued to write the column until his death forty-nine years later (it appeared weekly until 1971, and thereafter monthly). Continuity was a notable feature of the *ILN* in several respects, not just its increasingly dated appearance and style, but above all the fact that it had the same editor, Bruce Ingram, from 1900 until 1963.

The *ILN* was a special kind of publication, as much an institution as a periodical by this point. It had pioneered illustration in the nineteenth century, but as it was overtaken technologically by other publications it subsided into a comfortable middle age, more concerned to promote the glories of Britain's imperial and military achievements than to break the news, strongly upholding a traditional, hierarchical, rural, sepia-tinted Englishness. In its pomp in the mid-Victorian period, when it had a near monopoly on illustrated news, it sold 200,000 copies each week, though circulation had fallen to around half that number by the 1930s. Its readership appears to have included a particularly high proportion of expatriates and descendants of colonial settlers, attracted by its nostalgic picture of an unchanging 'old country' (Stapleton notes that the preponderance of advertisements for luxury goods in its later years suggested an increasingly well-heeled readership as well). Pamela Street, Bryant's one-time secretary and, later, biographer, recalled that during the Second World War it was 'regarded by the authorities as our principal export journal'. Looking back during his long tenure of the 'Our Notebook' column, Bryant observed with tangible pride: 'The page itself has continued, in one form or another, for over a hundred years and is the oldest column in British or, so far as I know, global journalism.' The column normally ran to between 1,200 and 1,500 words: it therefore required Bryant to write over 65,000 words a year, alongside his thirty-five books. By the time it ceased to keep its weekly rhythm, he had already written over two million words for it.

In the late 1930s, Bryant used his *ILN* pulpit to promote the case not just for appeasement but for a more generally sympathetic view of the new Germany. In addition to believing that the Versailles settlement had been harsh and unjust, he also admired the work of 'national regeneration' being carried out by the Nazis, while having reservations about some of the extremer expressions of its anti-semitism. Across Europe, including Britain, it was the Left, Bryant believed, that represented the real threat, and he was sympathetic to anything that enabled people to take pride in the traditional values of their *patria* and to resist the fashionable fallacies of Modernism. In the course of 1939 he elaborated these sentiments in a book, entitled *Unfinished Victory*. The outbreak of war just as he was completing the writing led him to add a preface acknowledging the new situation, but in pressing ahead with publication he perhaps underestimated the dramatic difference that hostilities made to the reception of his case. The book, which appeared in January 1940, was savaged by reviewers. Bryant was shaken, but not deflected from his view that a negotiated peace with Germany was still desirable; indeed, he seems to have been involved in a semi-official initiative aimed at securing such a peace in early 1940. Stapleton has an exemplary analysis of Bryant's tergiversations in 1939–40: his behaviour undeniably had its shabby aspects, and his indulgence of the basic Nazi argument about the threat posed by the Jews was simply shameful, but she convincingly shows that he is not rightly described as a 'Fascist fellow-traveller'—at least, not quite.

Ironically for a historian who positively throbbed with excitement at the thought of moments of 'national crisis', and one who thrilled to the rhetoric of patriotism at its most swelling and belligerent, Bryant came perilously close to missing his finest hour altogether. Only in the late spring or even early summer of 1940 does he seem to have realized that he was backing the wrong horse; not only was there not going to be a negotiated peace, but his concern to defend the reputation of Baldwin and Chamberlain had made him resistant to Churchill's claims. Roberts does seem to have been right in suggesting that Bryant's links with the 'Union and Reconstruction' movement, promoting a sympathetic account of Nazi economic ideals, raised the question of whether he should be interned in the round-ups of known

Fascist sympathizers following the fall of France. Dunkirk and the prospect of invasion stirred his blood and gave him the opportunity to make amends. Clichés about the English being at their best when their backs were to the wall had an irresistible appeal to Bryant: here was a moment when 'national character' could come into its own. *English Saga (1840–1940)*, which was published at the beginning of December 1940, was still suffused with the hostility to laissez-faire capitalism that had underlain his attraction to the policies of National Socialism, but this was now transmuted into a meditation on the eternal qualities of the true Englishman, beyond the reach of the 'rationalists and economists'. The English character prized independence, courage, and fairness. This was what we were fighting for; this was what would see us through, as it had seen us through at previous crises in our history (Bryant always made free with the first-person plural).

Not surprisingly, this was a popular message at the end of 1940, and *English Saga* was the beginning of Bryant's period of great success as a 'national historian' (coincidentally or not, it was also the first book he published with Collins, who remained his publishers for the rest of his life). It was made a Book Society 'choice' and sold 28,000 copies within its first year, with a renewed boost following its adoption in the World Books series in 1943. Much greater success came with the first two volumes of his trilogy, *The Years of Endurance, 1793–1802* (1942) and *Years of Victory, 1802–1812* (1944)—which, after an uncharacteristic delay, were followed by *The Age of Elegance, 1812–1822* in 1950. These made much of the parallel between the present and England's plight (and eventual victory) during the Napoleonic wars; they were Bryant's major contribution to the war effort. Collins later calculated that these three volumes, taken together, had sold over 814,000 copies by 1974. Only Trevelyan can really stand comparison here: in his *History and National Life* (2002), Peter Mandler describes Trevelyan's *English Social History* as 'probably the best-selling history book of the twentieth century'. It notched up 100,000 copies in its first year, over 500,000 in its first decade. Churchill's *The Second World War* outstripped even those figures, but that work was as much self-justifying memoir as history, and was anyway not wholly written by Churchill himself. The latter's four-volume *History of the English-Speaking Peoples* (largely drafted in the late 1930s but completed and published in the late 1950s) might provide a fairer comparison—though it was even more reliant on his team of assistants—and it, for understandable reasons, handsomely outsold both Trevelyan and Bryant in the United States.

Bryant's popularity continued into the 1950s, albeit with some hiccups. The first volume of his projected history of England from earliest times, *Makers of the Realm* (1953), also sold well: over 30,000 in the first month, going on to sell over 200,000 when adopted as a World Books choice not long after. Even in 1963, the second volume, *The Age of Chivalry*, did scarcely less well. As one reviewer of this work observed, not perhaps altogether without irony: 'Sir Arthur Bryant always approaches the past from the point of view that to be English is to belong to the best club in history. The century he has reached in this second round of "The Story of England" gives him much scope for turning on the genial heat of patriotism.' The 'genial heat of patriotism' glowed through his work to the end.

Meanwhile, in the mid-1950s Bryant constructed a history of the Second World War around his selections from the diaries of Field-Marshal Lord Alanbrooke, wartime Chief of the Imperial General Staff. This enjoyed something of a *succès de scandale* on account of its criticism of Churchill's handling of the war: the first volume, *The Turn of the Tide, 1939–43* (1957), sold 75,000 copies in the home market alone in the first four months, and the second, *Triumph in the West, 1943–46* (1959), did almost as well. But none of Bryant's later books matched the success of his 1940s trilogy: *Protestant Island* (1967), for example, sold only 10,000 copies in three months, including the Christmas peak period, and his short biography of Nelson (1970) did even less well; *The Elizabethan Deliverance* (1980) may have been a book too far, with notably disappointing sales. By now, even A. L. Rowse, hitherto one of his most vigorous champions, was flagging: 'In the 1970s [Bryant] turned out a number of his patriotic little books, not all of which I have read.' And yet, surprising to the end, Bryant managed something of a comeback with the last book published in his lifetime, the first volume of a projected *History of Britain and the British People*, which briefly earned a place in the best-seller charts in 1984. Overall, however, it is clear that his audience diminished in his later years; Stapleton suggests that it also became socially more homogeneous, as the autodidact tradition (discussed in Chapter 19 below) dried up and as more potential readers now entered higher education, reading a different kind of history. His career on the *Illustrated London News* was marked by a similar decline. The 'Our Notebook' column was relegated from its flagship position in the late 1960s, at a time when the *ILN* itself was declining in popularity: by 1963 its circulation was down to 73,000, falling to around 50,000 at the time of Bryant's death.

Nonetheless, his success overall remains remarkable: Collins reckoned that their total sales of his titles exceeded two million copies, and he certainly managed to finance a handsome style of life on the proceeds, for some years dividing his time between a town house in Knightsbridge and a series of historic piles in the country, each furnished in appropriate period style. Already by the late 1940s he had become that indefinable entity, 'a national figure'. In 1946 he was asked to assist the king in the preparation of his Christmas message; he was also asked to write the official naval history of the war, a project he finally had to abandon; and, inevitably, he served on a vast number of boards and committees, including a spell as President of the English Association. His success also brought him the honours he craved (the fact that he was a relentless networker, an assiduous clubman, and a consumate Tory insider did him no harm where gongs were concerned). He was made a CBE in 1949, knighted in 1954, made a Companion of Honour in 1967. Sir Arthur Bryant died in 1985, leaving an estate valued at £780,000.

III

Bryant's career can be seen as a response both to the professionalization and specialization of history in the early twentieth century and to the growth of a self-consciously 'middlebrow' culture in the 1920s and 1930s. This middlebrow culture, like the autodidact tradition with which it partly overlaps but should not be confused, was defiantly old-fashioned in its literary and intellectual tastes. Neither academic austerity nor Modernist experiment appealed to it: colourful narrative, unabashed sentimentalism, and assertive patriotism did. *King Charles* II was published two years after Namier had supposedly inaugurated a new historiographical orthodoxy, but Bryant owed his success to his ability to please a taste formed on models written at least half a century earlier.

Disputes about the soundness or otherwise of Bryant's 'scholarship' are not really to the point here: for some of his books he manifestly did a lot of first-hand research, both in archives and in the obscurer published documents of a period. What his books did not provide was any analysis of the nature and representativeness of these sources, nor any sustained engagement with the state of historical scholarship on any topic. Moreover, the terms of his history did not weigh factors in explanation; instead, his books tended to be a combination of three levels : vignettes, narratives, panoramas. 'England' is often the main actor; 'national character' is its alter ego, much called upon in moments of 'crisis', which prove to be very frequent. The retelling of such moments is conducted in a high register: 'honour', 'courage', 'nobility', 'destiny' play the leading parts. Landscape, costumes, and artefacts are lavishly described; battles are dwelled on in loving detail (Bryant's histories contain a lot of battles). In the late nineteenth century, J. R. Green had achieved considerable success with his *A Short History of the English People* while deliberately eschewing what he christened 'drum and trumpet' history. For Bryant, war was *the* great national theme; he was proud of his standing among senior officers, who were among his most devoted readers, and he wrote more than one regimental history.

It is always difficult to illustrate a historian's style with brief extracts, which cannot capture the architecture, the narrative pace, the set-piece tableaux. But two brief passages may at least begin to suggest both the appeal and the limitations of Bryant's prose. The first comes from his debut work, *King Charles II*:

Through France, England drew at this moment a deep draught from those eternal waters which have their spring in ancient Greece and Rome, and from which she has drunk at every great era in her existence. The calm, the balance and beauty of the eighteenth century is Charles's legacy to his people.

The second is from *English Saga*:

As a result of long and unbroken Christian usage, it became native to the English to live and work in a society in which moral responsibility existed. And when England broke with the Catholic past—partly out of a critical sense of its human imperfections—she still cherished the old ideal of a nation dedicated to the task of breeding just and gentle men. All that was best in Puritanism was an attempt to re-state it. Without justice and charity there can be no England. That is the historic and eternal English vision.

Uplift is one common characteristic of these passages, complacency another. Those whose stomach was not turned by the cloying rhetoric presumably drew a kind of sustenance from them, a comforting sense of much being right with the world, especially their bit of it. One word common to both passages, it may also be worth noting, is 'eternal', a curious term for a historian, of all people, to place so much emphasis on.

Two of Bryant's contemporaries among historians offered contrasting but illuminating assessments of his qualities. Although in his diaries A. L. Rowse could at times be waspish about Bryant, as about everyone else, he did recognize his friend's genuine gifts. Reviewing *The Age of Elegance* ('puffing' might be a more accurate verb), he asked rhetorically 'what are his [Bryant's] gifts as a historian?', and answered in terms that tell us a lot about the source of Bryant's popular success:

He has an extraordinary gift for historical landscape, so that his scenes live intensely in the mind; then there is the love of every sort of humanity, particularly the fighting man... Suffusing the whole book is the poetry, the poignant sense of the past, the feeling: how can one be a historian without these? He loves the past—a better recipe for understanding it than the superciliousness of the uncreative... He is not a dry philosophical historian—though his reflections are often as much to the point as theirs; he is a descriptive narrative writer, with something of Dickens and again of Rowlandson in him—the humanity, the humour and the poetry.

Rowse, typically, cannot help turning a characterization into a polemic, but this may nonetheless be the best version of the case for Bryant and his style of history, a case in which the terms 'love' and 'humanity' are recurrent and central.

The other assessment is by Herbert Butterfield, who gave *The Age of Elegance* a notably fair-minded review in the *TLS* in 1950 (published anonymously, of course), praising where praise could be given (the narrative, the colour), and only gently noting 'certain shortcomings in the technical and analytical side of the historian's task'. Butterfield chiefly used the review to expatiate on the desirability of combining what had become separated as popular and academic history—that is, history as an 'attempt to "resurrect" a bygone age', and a 'more analytical kind of history' that looked for causes, explanations, comparisons. He considered Bryant the heir of 'the literary historians of the nineteenth century', one who followed their emphases 'to the point of caricature'. 'They made great play with the setting and the narratives of battles, and they developed the panoramic and pictorial treatment of social history.' Bryant, Butterfield acknowledged, was good at the first of these, but not at the second. 'This is too much the mere pageantry of history, and the vast panoramas are too amorphous, too lacking in structure.' Bryant was too prone to treat his idiosyncratic literary and memoir sources as representative, too prone to treat the unusual as typical. Butterfield similarly found Bryant's handling of his major characters lacking in analytical depth, 'but if some minor figure merely crosses the stage for a moment, so that a purely pictorial treatment is entirely adequate to the case', then Bryant was in his element.

Butterfield may have been willing to take the *problem* of this kind of writing seriously because it related to his own concerns about the relations between 'technical' and 'general' history (discussed in the following chapter). Most academic historians, however, did not give Bryant's work any extended attention, especially in his later years: they recognized that Bryant (and, again, especially the later Bryant) was not writing for them. As Stapleton fairly acknowledges: 'Bryant signally failed to make an impact at higher literary and cultural levels.' But this then raises some interesting questions about the relations between his style of history, his cultural standing, and his role as a commentator on contemporary affairs.

One of the recurring themes of Bryant's commentaries, above all in his *ILN* column, was the claim that an 'intellectual elite' was attempting to undermine 'ordinary people's' inherited religious and moral beliefs in order to impose a 'progressive agenda' that was alien to English traditions. This is, needless to say, a familiar aspect of reactionary rhetoric, not just in England and not only in this period. A reductive binarism continually surfaces in his prose on this theme: such (conservative) beliefs were natural and timeless, whereas his opponents' (radical) beliefs were the programmatic outcomes of 'system' and 'theory'. In a similar style, he tended to present his favoured (Tory) policies as 'national' and non-partisan, his opponents' as sectarian and divisive. This is, as I say, a deeply familiar pattern, and would not be of any great interest in itself had Bryant not occupied such a pivotal role in identifying the very genre of popular history with such an anti-intellectual and conservative stance. Such history told 'the national story', which in turn revealed adherence to these traditional values to be the core of patriotism. Conservative beliefs were English beliefs, and the continued flourishing of England depended upon their continued vitality.

Bryant's wilful elision of the differences among various supposed 'elites' underwrote this tendentious account of national identity. For example, he treated the Left Book Club and 'Bloomsbury' as two faces of the same beast, just as he ran together the failings alleged to be characteristic of 'intellectuals', 'dons', 'highbrows', 'secularists', 'progressives', '*New Statesman* readers', and so on. Though he was in reality the consummate metropolitan insider, Bryant always positioned himself as outside all elites, an 'unfashionable' voice standing up for the values of the 'good ordinary Englishman'. (Unlike Trevelyan and Rowse, as Stapleton shrewdly notes, Bryant was hostile to the secularism of educated opinion, which he traced back to 'the endowed university dons and the dividend-supported men of higher education of the British bourgeoisie during the late Victorian and Edwardian eras'.) In a characteristic twist, Bryant blamed the 'progressive elite' for all the ills of 'modernity', even when these could more plausibly be seen as the outcomes of the Tory party's promotion of capitalism. England, he railed, was becoming 'an ugly wilderness of screeching cars and jerry-built houses'; it was becoming—to take the great symbolic bugbear of inter-war cultural commentators—one big Peacehaven.

It is no surprise to learn that Stanley Baldwin was his political hero in the 1930s, and in a retirement tribute he praised the Tory leader for the way he won the sympathy of ordinary working-class voters, thus causing 'bitter mortification to the intellectuals who had thought to find themselves the unchallenged leaders of the toiling masses whose real character they so little understood'. His polemics on behalf of the National Book Association and of Ashridge College (both engines of Tory propaganda for all their avowals of non-partisanship) played variations on the same tune. The NBA, unlike the Left Book Club, would have 'no prejudicial axe to grind', but would simply present 'the facts' to ordinary men and women of 'sane outlook', so as to counteract the distortion of those facts by a small body of 'denationalised intellectuals' in furtherance of their 'revolutionary purposes'.

Defending the right of Ashridge to adult education funding despite its de facto party-political character, he complained that 'a comparatively small group of Socialist intellectuals are obtaining a monopoly of the machine of adult education (which the country supports with vast sums of money) in order to propagate a philosophy of life which has a political implication from start to finish'. Here as elsewhere in his political writings, the exaggerations ('monopoly', 'vast', and so on) contribute to the slightly paranoid effect. Richard Crossman was surely right to say of the Bryant of the 1930s that he 'lulls the reader into a belief in breezy superiority to partisan politics and then slips in unawares...snippets of Fascist propaganda'.

IV

For a fuller sense of where Bryant fits into the wider conservative sensibility evident among several leading historians and cultural commentators in the middle of the twentieth century, we need to restore him to the company of such friends and peers as Trevelyan, Rowse, and Ernest Barker (discussed as a group in Stapleton's previous book, *Political Intellectuals and Public Identities in Britain since 1850* (2001)). Two aspects of this broader sensibility call for comment here. The first is the cosy, archaic picture of 'England' informing these figures' exhortations about 'national identity'. This is, needless to say, familiar from many other sources, but in writers explicitly attempting to promote an active attachment to the *patria* it inevitably draws attention to itself. Predictably, their image of Deep England always turns out to be rural rather than urban or—more offensive still to the sensibilities of the well-housed metropolitan country-lover—suburban. No less predictably, the modern world is figured as an agent of destruction, corrupting the Edenic purity of a not very exactly located past. What is more interesting but also, especially given this last point, more problematic is their confident retailing of the second-hand truisms of a broken-down Whiggism, especially the complacent celebration of England's unique gift for combining liberty and political stability, an achievement ultimately grounded in those hackneyed features of the 'national character', the native preference for practical good sense over the abstract symmetries of 'theory' and 'doctrine'. Bryant fully shared this sensibility for all his early departures from the classical form of the Whig interpretation.

In this respect, the centrality of the 1930s and, especially, the 1940s to Stapleton's account is easy to understand. The threat of totalitarianism and the demands of national survival did promise to give a version of the Whig story a renewed relevance: never having sacrificed to false gods, the sceptr'd isle was liberty's natural champion. As we shall see in the following chapter,

Herbert Butterfield, in pre-war years the scourge of the teleological simpli-
cities of 'the Whig interpretation of history', came to find a pretty Whiggish
comfort in his 1944 examination of *The Englishman and his History* ('who
amongst us would exchange the long line of amiable or prudent statesmen
in English history for all those masterful and awe-inspiring geniuses who
have imposed themselves on France and Germany in modern times?').
George Orwell's mutation into something of a tub-thumping patriot in the
early years of the war involved a comparable (and comparably selective)
celebration of 'the English character', and the huge sales of Trevelyan's
English Social History were part of this larger story. Gazing on thatched
hamlets nestling in the folds of grassy downs, hearing the drone of German
bombers overhead, stirred to thoughts of Agincourt and Trafalgar as well
as of 1688 and 1832, it was easy to feel that in staving off the Hun one
was defending civilization, liberal principles, and Olde England all in one.
This surely gave added force to the hostile, in some cases almost hysterical,
reaction to the Labour government of 1945–51: had the shades of Burke
and Macaulay been invoked, had the sinews been stiffened and the blood
summoned, just so that the commissars of a levelling egalitarianism could
tax away one's birthright and one's servants?

The second broad area in which some readers may want to draw different
conclusions from Stapleton's material concerns those figures whom she sees as
examples of 'the "non-intellectual" intellectual'. The awkwardness of the label
may seem apt in some cases, but perhaps too kind in others, where the more
downright 'anti-intellectual' seems called for. Their irritable, unenquiring
dismissal of (other) 'intellectuals' asks to be treated as a symptom, an inner
conflict or neurosis disguising itself as a willed complacency. Of course, the
complex resonances of the term 'intellectuals' itself in twentieth-century British usage come into play here, but, even so, the sweeping dismissiveness of
these views suggests a deeper need for easy certainties. Something curious is
going on when 'political intellectuals' habitually express themselves in a style
that might almost have been designed to curb critical thinking rather than to
enable it. Four quotations may help bring out the force of these points.

As the political theorist Ernest Barker moved further to the Right in the
1930s and 1940s, he became uncomfortable with aspects of his Liberal
inheritance. As he confided in a 1938 letter to Bryant:

I am bothered today by the abstract intellectualism of those with whom I used to
associate, and by the conventional lip service to phrases in my old party—the Liberal
party. I admire more and more the practical wisdom of the good ordinary Englishman,
facing the facts and 'feeling' the right way through them—as a good Englishman feels
his way through a new countryside. This means that I am getting nearer and nearer to
you. It is a late change—at the age of 64. But I am glad that it is coming.

Setting aside other sceptical responses, one might wonder how Barker saw his own activities in terms of this rather minimalist hiker's guide to the galaxy: writing books with titles such as *Principles of Social and Political Theory*, as Barker did a few years later, might seem closer to 'abstract intellectualism' than to 'feeling' one's way through the facts. Of course, in such books Barker wanted to recommend a pragmatic, 'non-ideological' approach to politics (as those frightened by the overdue reforms of the Labour government of 1945 usually did), but he was here caught in the toils of the contradiction inseparable from the role of this kind of conservative intellectual—namely, to be making the case, in general and abstract terms, for not being guided by cases made in general and abstract terms.

We catch a different aspect of this vernacular idiom in a letter from Bryant to Trevelyan in 1937: 'For years past, a rootless intelligentsia (to use, as S[tanley] B[aldwin] once said, a very ugly word for a very ugly thing) have been undermining the English tradition, which for some reason they loathe; in adult education, in the provincial universities, above all in the printed word.' No doubt, the stylish *Spectator*ly way to respond to this is to murmur something about its scarcely mattering what goes on in the *provincial* universities, my dear. But charges of 'undermining a national tradition' have all too often been part of an attempt to clamp down on the work of critical intellectuals, and of course the possible rationality of the criticism is pre-emptively discounted by Bryant's *faux-naif* 'which for some reason they loathe'. Moreover, it is hard not to remember the ways in which 'rootless intelligentsia' was used in Europe at the time; this is another of the places where what Stapleton mildly refers to as 'Bryant's evident attraction to Nazism' can seem more sinister than she quite allows.

My third example raises a different kind of reservation. On receiving his copy of Bryant's *The Years of Victory* in 1944, Trevelyan responded by noting that he, Bryant, and Rowse held 'somewhat the same view of history and how it should be written. We are, of course, not all agreeing on all points in the past, though all are in love with England which is the essential.' One can allow that it might have seemed a bit more 'essential' in 1944 than at some other times, but even so one cannot help wondering whether this throwaway comment did not signal a potentially damaging limitation. Notoriously, being in love is to be in a condition that might now be termed 'epistemologically challenged'. To make this the *essential* requirement, especially when also pronouncing on 'how history should be written', looks as though it builds a severe restriction into the historian's public, educative role. Trevelyan and Bryant (and, for a while at least, Rowse) certainly did reach a large non-specialist readership, but, writing as England's suitors, they may have done that public no favours by in effect making military victory and social harmony the central (and unproblematically compatible) features of 'Our Island Story'.

The sentiments expressed by Barker, Bryant, and Trevelyan come together in Rowse's characteristically more unbuttoned prose. Writing to Bryant in 1942, Rowse tried to express their shared convictions as follows:

(1) A deep devotion to the historic past of our country and one both [sic] inspired by its glories and achievements.

(2) We both loathe the abstract intellectualism of Left intellectuals, whether Liberal or Socialist—the mentality of the *New Statesman* par excellence— what more appalling?

In Rowse's letter, these two convictions are presented as not simply compatible but pretty much entailed by each other. But should they be? The 'historic past' of this particular country, like most others, presumably, can yield at least as much ammunition for the Left as for the Right (rather more, some of us might say), and there is no good reason why the form taken by one's 'deep devotion' might not be a proper pride in the country's *intellectual* achievements. In fact, one is bound to wonder what it was about 'intellectualism' that this group were all so frightened of. Its Leftness, one is tempted to reply, and that was, in the context of the cultural clichés of the 1930s and 1940s, clearly part of the answer. But one can't help thinking there's a psychological form of denial at work here, too, an uneasy (at times peevish) resistance to the unresting, boundless task of thought itself. Although they all banged on about how uniquely tolerant and open to different ideas and ways of life England had always been, in practice they seemed scared stiff of any idea that didn't come already dressed in tweeds and brogues.

Pondering the elements of Bryant's success as a writer of 'national history', one finds that the contribution made to his popularity by this combination of celebratory patriotism and un- or anti-intellectualism comes into clearer focus, as does its period-specific quality. The extended cultural impact of the Second World War was crucial, as was the stage reached in the segmentation of reading publics. These conditions enabled Bryant to pull off an otherwise unlikely literary achievement: the figure whom Britain's cultural and political establishment had gathered to honour in Westminster Abbey in the 1980s had sustained into the 1950s a relation with a public defined in the 1920s and 1930s while writing in the manner and with the confidence of an Edwardian man of letters who in turn was striving to emulate the achievements of Victorian historians.

11

Believing in History:
Herbert Butterfield, Christian and Whig

I

Do you speak Whiggish? The most recent edition of the *Oxford English Dictionary* does not, it appears, at least not fluently. The original *OED*, compiled in the late nineteenth and early twentieth centuries, contained full entries for 'Whig' and its adjectival derivatives, denoting that grouping or tradition that had been one of the two main contending forces in British political life from the late seventeenth to at least the mid-nineteenth century. The dictionary wisely refrained from attempting to specify in any detail what this tradition's informing principles were, beyond a certain attachment to liberty, parliamentary government, and the Protestant succession to the English throne; the general bearing of the term was suggested by the observation that in political life it had largely been superseded by 'Liberal', though it could still be used occasionally 'to express adherence to moderate or antiquated Liberal principles'. The illustrative quotations reinforced this emphasis: 'The term Whig', opined Lord John Russell in the 1850s, 'has the convenience of expressing in one syllable what Conservative Liberal expresses in seven.'

The entry ranged widely over the (mainly pejorative) extensions of the core use, including such delights, now lost, as 'Whiglings' and 'Whigissimi', but all these terms and their accompanying definitions were dependent upon the central political sense. It was not until the *Supplement* to the *OED* published in the mid-1980s that the phrase 'Whig historian' made a separate appearance, defined as 'a historian who interprets history as the continuing and inevitable victory of progress over reaction'. As so

C. T. McIntire, *Herbert Butterfield: Historian as Dissenter* (Yale University Press, 2004).

often with this magnificent but frustrating compilation, there appeared to be some tension between this encompassing definition and the illustrative examples. Should one simply conclude that 'Whiggish history' was history informed by Whig principles in the political sense, as suggested by quotations referring to Macaulay and G. M. Trevelyan (and as the dictionary's own internal system of cross-referencing implied), or did 'Whiggish history' have a larger sense applicable to *any* account of the past that appeared to be selected and arranged so as to lead up to and confer legitimacy on the present, as in a quotation from 1975 warning against the 'whiggish perspectives' that tended to infect the writing of labour history and women's history? Clearly, it was not being suggested that toilers in these latter fields had been extolling parliamentary government and the Protestant succession, though the entry was still being offered as a further example of the original political definition. As is indicated by this and similar quotations (including one, I am disconcerted to find, by my younger self), the term expanded at some point to embrace historical accounts of 'continuing and inevitable' progress in *any* desirable direction, rather than simply the direction implied in the original political sense.

The clue, albeit a rather gnomic one, to the relation between these senses (still not discriminated as such) is given by the inclusion of a quotation from 1931: 'The truth is that there is a tendency for all history to veer over into whig history.' That sentence is taken from the introduction to Herbert Butterfield's *The Whig Interpretation of History*, one of those 'classics' that are now more referred to than read. Its title, together with the generalized sense of (lower-case) 'whig history', may have entered the language, but beyond having a vague awareness that whiggish history is, in the terms used by another historical classic of the same vintage, a Bad Thing, many of us might struggle to state Butterfield's argument any more precisely, and certainly very few people outside a small circle of professional historians could confidently recall what else Butterfield wrote, and how—or indeed whether—his other work consorted with his strictures on the whig interpretation of history.

When we return to the book itself, a slim volume of 132 small pages, our uncertainties are likely to increase rather than diminish. It is a stylish but oddly elusive work in which proper names are strikingly rare. E. H. Carr was being only slightly unfair when, in *What is History?*, published thirty years later, he mocked Butterfield for attacking the Whig interpretation of history without naming 'a single Whig except Fox, who was no historian, or a single historian save Acton, who was no Whig'. This quip points to a larger unsteadiness about the object of Butterfield's criticism, an unsteadiness that was to be reproduced as a tension running throughout his career.

In the narrow or literal sense, the 'Whig interpretation of history' (usually so capitalized, though not by Butterfield) refers to an account of English history. It is an account that celebrates the unbroken continuity of representative institutions and the legal protection of individual freedom, an account that identifies a deep political wisdom in the English, expressed above all through the wise moderation of those statesmen who adapted to changing circumstances without falling into either rigid reaction or unbridled revolution. The origins of this account are traced to the middle of the seventeenth century as parliamentary lawyers attempted to formulate their case against the encroachments of the royal prerogative, arguing for the 'restoration' of supposedly ancient liberties rather than pressing the claims in the present of either abstract principle or mere expediency. By the nineteenth century, this account, generalized and suitably buffed up to accommodate Reform Acts and the like, became the dominant narrative of English history, versions of which could be found in Macaulay, Stubbs, Freeman, and on into the twentieth century in the writings of such latter-day Whig historians as Trevelyan and, less obviously, Churchill.

Butterfield, as we have seen, did not name these, or any other, celebrated exemplars of Whig history. Instead, his attack turns out to be directed rather at the informing assumptions to be found in popular and outline histories. 'It is perhaps a tragedy', he writes, or overwrites, 'that the important work of abridging history is so often left to writers of text-books and professional manufacturers of commercial literature.' In such passages he appears to be primarily concerned with the kind of historical framework imbibed and half-forgotten by non-historians. 'Perhaps all history books', he remarks with similar loftiness, 'hold a danger for those who do not know a great deal of history already.'

Yet at other moments in the book he appears to be preoccupied with a dilemma facing professional historians. He extols detailed research or what he calls 'technical history' as the antidote to the elisions and superficialities of narrative or synoptic history, but at the same time he doubts that such archivally grounded research leads to any fundamental change in the accepted framework. The inconvenient findings of technical history tend to be set on one side as 'exceptions', and 'these exceptions are lost indeed in that combined process of organisation and abridgement by which we reach our general survey of general history'. So in the broadest terms it is the problem of 'the relations between historical research and what is known as general history' that stirs him, and in issuing his warning against 'an unexamined habit of mind into which we fall when we treat of history on the broad scale', his use of the first-person plural indicates a predicament he shares. This, and not the prevalence of Protestant and progressive allegiances, nor even, quite, the failing of writing about the past 'with direct and perpetual reference to the present', is what lies behind the remark quoted in the *OED* about the 'tendency for all history to veer over into whig history'.

But we are then left with a double uncertainty at the end of *The Whig Interpretation of History*. First, is Butterfield actually repudiating the broadly Whig story of the growth of English liberties, and if so what if anything is he suggesting should replace it? The book does not seem to be advocating any kind of 'Tory' interpretation, whatever that might look like. It is surely the smugness and the anachronism pervading popular forms of Whig history that arouse his ire, not their emphasis on the growth of English liberty and stability. This is well illustrated from his discussion of the relation between the Reformation and the establishment of religious toleration in England: what Butterfield repudiates is any slack claim that toleration was part of the intrinsic superiority of Protestantism or was the goal aimed at by the reformers themselves. Instead, he depicts the slow evolution of toleration as the by-product of the otherwise uncheckable zeal of Catholics and Protestants alike in the sixteenth and seventeenth centuries, a lesson in the working of the law of unintended conseqences. More generally, he appears to be urging what in another vocabulary might be called a more dialectical account of history, one in which conflict and discontinuity constitute the norm and outcomes are rarely the result of deliberate agency.

Secondly, does Butterfield's extended sense of 'whiggish history' apply only to a certain kind of present-minded, triumphalist or teleological narrative, or is it an unavoidable feature of large-scale synoptic history in general? He hints at the latter view when he writes: 'The whig interpretation of history is not merely the property of whigs and it is much more subtle than mental bias; it lies in a trick of organisation, an unexamined habit of mind that any historian may fall into.' This almost reduces it to a general difficulty of exposition—what he calls in his Preface 'an aspect of the psychology of historians'—where it is not clear how the difficulty is to be overcome short of refusing to draw the findings of 'technical history' into any larger picture. Yet he seemed to be unwilling to abandon the ambition to write 'general history', and was evidently not content to leave it to those 'professional manufacturers of commercial literature'.

The Whig Interpretation of History itself does not explicitly confront these difficulties, and its mix of rhetorical indignation and studied elusiveness does not help to resolve them. The book has no conclusion; the last chapter deviates into some unprofitable jousting with Acton over the role of moral judgements in the writing of history, ending with a highly coloured passage in which History is personified first as 'a harlot and a hireling' who 'best serves those who suspect her most', and then as 'an old reprobate, whose tricks and juggleries are things to be guarded against'. The 30-year-old Butterfield was already good at sounding as wearily wise as the most wrinkled, seen-it-all, sage. This tone no doubt contributed to the book's later authority, but apart from setting traps for future students of what was coming to be called 'Historiography', it also left unclear what kind of history its author could now go on to write.

These issues only become more puzzling as we broaden our view to take in two further facts about Butterfield's career. First, we find that thirteen years after his assault on the Whig interpretation he published another little book, called *The Englishman and his History*, which waxed lyrical about the intimate and animating relationship between the English and their past (his friendship in the 1930s with Michael Oakeshott may have played a part here): 'Let us praise as a living thing the continuity of our history, and praise the whigs who taught us that we must nurse this blessing—reconciling continuity with change, discovering mediations between past and present, and showing what can be achieved by man's reconciling mind.' Stirred by the 'deliverance' of 1940 and by Churchill's 'great speeches' of that year, he here sounds to be belting out a familiar patriotic tune from a score marked 'Whiggissimo'. The contradiction between this and his most celebrated work seems so glaring that it has been called (in allusion to German scholars' attempts to reconcile the apparently conflicting positions of Adam Smith's two great books) *Das Herbert Butterfield Problem*. The problem is only made more intractable when one realizes that although the heightened emotions of wartime may have contributed to the rousing register in which Butterfield wrote in 1944, these views were in fact repeated, in tones that were not significantly cooler, at other times, too. Thus, for example, in his brief study of Napoleon, published in 1939, he had written: 'Liberty comes to the world from English traditions, not from French theories,' and in a series of lectures delivered in Toronto in 1952 he declared that the story of liberty was 'the basic theme of English history'.

Second, we discover that although Butterfield wrote a great deal in the later stages of his career, it is hard to see that much of it could be counted either as 'technical history' or as 'general history', as he understood those terms. Most of his later publications were revised lectures and collected essays, many of them given over to meta-historical musings on the nature of 'historical-mindedness'. Moreover, in his few more sustained publications he was either defending an interpretation of eighteenth-century English politics that gave a central place to the struggles between popular liberties and royal power or he was writing brisk surveys with titles such as *The Origins of Modern Science, 1300–1800*. We seem to be driven to the vexing conclusion that not only was Butterfield a Whig historian in the full political sense of the term, but he also committed a fair bit of whiggish history in the extended sense as well.

If we attempt to resolve these apparent contradictions by turning to the other works by which Butterfield is, or at least was, known among historians, the picture becomes more complicated still. Much the most successful of his books in terms of sales, one that brought him a substantial readership in the USA in particular, was *Christianity and History*, which appeared to make all forms of merely secular history secondary when viewed from the perspective of a personal faith in the Incarnation and the Resurrection. He helped establish important areas of intellectual history with his books on the Scientific Revolution and on historiography, yet he used state occasions, such as his inaugural lecture as Regius Professor of History at Cambridge, delivered in 1964, to reaffirm the primacy of political and diplomatic history. Similarly, he was influential in promoting the study of international relations as a scholarly discipline, even though the antidote he recommended to what he saw as the naivety of liberal optimism was a reminder of the existence of Original Sin, not something easily convertible into a 'research programme' for professionalizing academics. And finally, in his chosen field of eighteenth-century English political history he was the tireless critic of Namier and the Namierites for their reduction of politics to the prosopography of the governing factions at Westminster, to the neglect of political ideology or popular participation, yet his own chief institutional legacy was the group of historians often referred to as 'the Peterhouse Tories', such as Maurice Cowling or John Vincent, who aggressively promoted a conception of the primacy of 'high politics' that accorded little role either to ideas or to wider social forces. For all these reasons, Butterfield's is an exceptionally difficult career to make sense of or give a shape to.

II

C. T. McIntire's *Herbert Butterfield: Historian as Dissenter* provides some assistance in this task, albeit indirectly. The book is not a full biography, but nor is it a purely critical study: for the most part, it is a detailed exposition of Butterfield's writings set within a loosely biographical frame. It has clearly been a very long time in the making: McIntire draws on interviews he conducted with Butterfield in the 1970s, as well as with colleagues and pupils in the ensuing decades. He also draws extensively on the voluminous collection of Butterfield's personal papers and unpublished writings now held in Cambridge University Library, as well as on other archival

sources. All this adds to the usefulness of the book, though I have to say
that its learning is rather heavily worn and McIntire's punctilious stations-
of-the-cross summaries of every aspect of Butterfield's numerous writings
does not make for exciting reading. But the picture it discloses, sometimes
despite itself, is an intriguing one.

Herbert Butterfield was born, in 1900, into the respectable, deferential stratum of the working class in a small mill village between Halifax
and Keighley in West Yorkshire, on the fringe of the northern heartland of
industrial Britain. His father had worked his way up from the mill floor to
a supervisory role as clerk in the mill-owner's office, an ambiguous social
position that was dependent on the owner's personal favour while attracting
suspicion from the men whose work he now helped control. Herbert followed
the route of the bright scholarship boy through the local grammar school and
on to Peterhouse, Cambridge, in 1919. Exhibiting a practical commitment
to continuity that would have done credit to the most Whiggish of Whig
politicians, he remained at Peterhouse until his death sixty years later. But
this did not signal either lack of ambition or lack of success: Butterfield was
appointed to the chair of Modern History in 1944; he was elected Master
of Peterhouse in 1955, serving a turn as Vice-Chancellor of the university
from 1959 to 1961; he progressed to the Regius professorship in 1963; he was
elected a Fellow of the British Academy in 1965, was knighted on his retirement in 1968, and was the recipient of thirteen honorary degrees.

McIntire's chosen method allows us few glimpses of the private man
behind this impeccably successful public career. One can only speculate
about the strains of adaptation as the shy young man with a Yorkshire
accent who still served as a lay preacher at Methodist chapels in the fens
found himself thrown into the pomp and snobberies of college life in inter-
war Cambridge. Butterfield remained a practising Methodist, though at
some point he ceased to preach, and was also a lifelong teetotaller, rather
ostentatiously sipping ginger beer at college feasts. He made a conventional
and apparently happy marriage, to the daughter of a Methodist minister.
The couple had three sons, the elder two of whom went to Peterhouse.
When the second son committed suicide while a student, his father maintained a stoic demeanour in public. What seems to have been one of the
closest relationships in his life from his mid-forties onwards was with Eve
Bogle, a woman of similar age who acted as his ill-paid private secretary and
personal research assistant, even accompanying him on trips to the archives.
McIntire gives no indication that he believes the relationship was anything
other than professional. Bogle was clearly devoted to Butterfield, but at
least part of the ground of the connection may have been suggested by her
later remark: 'He introduced me to the historical Jesus.' (An acquaintance

in Cambridge remembers Butterfield's response to hearing that one of their married colleagues had run off with another woman as 'Good for him'; his mischievous taste for saying the unexpected and shocking may, of course, have been in play here.)

McIntire does not attempt to probe the recesses of Butterfield's character, though at least some of the surviving biographical evidence asks to be read in terms of what another son of the Yorkshire working class, Richard Hoggart, wrote about 'the scholarship boy', who goes on to lead an 'apparently normal life, but never without an underlying sense of some unease'. Butterfield worked ferociously hard all his life, driven by who knows what mixture of ambition, duty, and anxiety, and he displayed a marked hunger for the conventional badges of success. We are told that he 'delighted in the knighthood probably more than any other of the honours he ever received'. Sitting proudly in his new study on taking possession of the Master's Lodge at Peterhouse, he confided to Eve Bogle: 'If I die tonight, I shall have been Master of my college.'

Butterfield's professional ascent can, whiggishly, be made to appear steady and inevitable, but in fact there was a dramatic lurch in the late 1940s. The careers of few intellectual figures, especially historians, can have turned so decisively on a single month as Butterfield's did in October 1949.

In the mid-1940s, he attempted to bring his detailed but scattered research on the politics of the reign of George III to some sort of fruition, finally sending a bulky typescript to G. Bell and Sons (who had published *The Whig Interpretation*) in early 1948. We lesser mortals who have endured frustrating delays by publishers may take some perverse comfort from the fact that Butterfield's script languished on the publisher's desk and did not appear until over eighteen months later—and that at a time when the usual gap between submission and publication was much shorter than has now become the norm. Meanwhile, Butterfield's ambition in the 1930s to make his European history lectures cover the development of 'European civilization', not just politics and diplomacy, had led him to take an interest in the history of science. After the war, he played a leading part in moves within Cambridge to promote the study of this new field, and especially to keep it under the control of the historians and philosophers rather than the natural scientists. As part of this initiative, he agreed to give a course of lectures in the first half of 1948 (at noon on Saturdays, then still a recognized teaching time). He revised these lectures over the summer and in August sent this, shorter and more shapely, script off, also to Bell, but again nothing happened quickly.

The problems of the post-war world as well as the intellectual and spiritual needs of students who had been in uniform were making life in

Cambridge less inward-looking in the late 1940s than at some other times in its history. As part of this ferment, the Faculty of Divinity sponsored additional lecture series on topics of contemporary interest (again at noon on Saturdays), and Butterfield agreed to lecture on 'Christianity and History' in the autumn of 1948. Locally, they became an intellectual event of some note: 'several hundred students and dons crowded' the lecture hall, according to McIntire. The following spring, the BBC invited him to repeat the lectures on the Third Programme, where they were also a great success. He sent the revised typescript of these lectures to Bell at the beginning of the summer of 1949. Whether it was Butterfield's recent public prominence that now stirred Bell to swifter action, or whether the firm had all along been planning a major publishing coup (surely an implausible, as well as rather whiggish, explanation), they now hurried all three books into print, so that October 1949 saw the simultaneous publication of *George III, Lord North and the People, 1779–1780*; *The Origins of Modern Science, 1300–1800*; and *Christianity and History*. The third of these attracted more attention than the other two put together, but it was the impressive conjunction across such disparate topics that gave Butterfield's reputation a decisive boost.

An incidental by-product of his newly heightened visibility was the republication of *The Whig Interpretation of History* in the early 1950s in both Britain and the USA. 'The extraordinary impact and international reach' of this book, McIntire points out, 'dates from the early 1950s, not from the early 1930s'. This timing meant that the book was more and more regarded as a contribution to the expanding academic field of 'the philosophy of history', and Butterfield's target was often thought to correspond to those kinds of determinist theories that Karl Popper was attacking at about this time, especially in *The Poverty of Historicism*. That association and the enthusiastic reception in Europe and the United States of the 'Providentialist' message of *Christianity and History* (which was translated into several languages) briefly promoted Butterfield to the status of a leading intellectual in Cold War culture, even though he ventured little direct commentary on contemporary political developments.

The curve of Butterfield's career can be charted from McIntire's impressively detailed bibliography of his published writings (there is also a long list of unpublished items). Publications falling in the first forty-five years of his life occupy just under a single page, but it then takes seven pages to list the vast output of his remaining three decades. This may be a not uncommon ratio as people become more successful, and one also has to allow for his transition from teaching fellow to professor, but the wider acclaim that greeted his triple whammy of October 1949 transformed his life. Thereafter, he received a constant flow of invitations to speak, a large proportion of which he seems to have accepted (McIntire calculates that there were some years in the 1950s when Butterfield delivered over fifteen invited lectures, on top of all his other duties). His radio talks—this was the heyday of the Third Programme—brought him still wider audiences, leading McIntire to speak, with forgivable hyperbole, of 'his status as a public celebrity'. But the costs of celebrity include superficiality and repetitiveness: Butterfield's lectures became windier, his examples tireder, his books thinner. Although he published some twenty-two books, only two measured up to the standards of what he called 'technical history': his 1929 study of Napoleon and the peace negotiations of 1806–8 (the book that constituted his guild qualification as an academic historian), and the 1949 book on the politics of 1779–80. Significantly, both deal with a very short period, not much more than a matter of months; the problems intrinsic to writing extended history seem to have had a sharply personal force for him.

Perhaps the most poignant pages in McIntire's study occur, improbably, in the bibliography, which includes a section entirely devoted to works Butterfield 'proposed, planned, or agreed to write or edit, but did not complete or, in some cases, begin'. It is an unnervingly long list. Any scholar, especially one who gave as much time as Butterfield did to university administration, may be likely to leave some such testimony to thwarted literary aspirations, but even so the length of the list suggests deeper intellectual inhibitions. Pride of place must go to his projected life of Charles James Fox, a project for which he collected, even hoarded, material for almost forty years. Trevelyan had generously lent the younger historian his family's collection of Fox papers; after Butterfield had kept them for twenty years without producing, Trevelyan finally insisted they be transferred to the British Museum. In 1939 Butterfield signed a contract to write *The Concise Cambridge Modern History*: more than twenty years later he spoke of this as 'a large volume hardly half finished', and although CUP continued to nag him gently about it at intervals during the 1960s, it was never completed. Even where his loyalties were most strongly engaged, Butterfield had a bad record as a non-finisher. The diplomatic historian Howard Temperley had been his patron and model in the early stages of his career, and after Temperley's death Butterfield promised his widow that he would write a book-length memoir of his former teacher. The promise was given in 1946; he took receipt of a large collection of Temperley's papers, and began collecting further material. When Temperley's son enquired about progress in the early 1960s, Butterfield had to confess that the papers were still in his basement, largely untouched. Eventually they had to be returned and the biography was never completed. In 1965 he gave the Gifford Lectures on 'The History of Historiography', but decided against following the usual convention of swift publication. For several years thereafter he laboured to expand his script into a publishable book, reading widely about the development of 'historical-mindedness' among the ancient civilizations of the Near East; the book never appeared. It would surely have been no surprise, when Butterfield came to present himself at the Pearly Gates, had St Peter confronted him with a consolidated breach-of-contract suit from the Publishers' Association.

I suspect that the tensions within Butterfield's commitment to 'general history' played a key part in this repeated pattern of self-frustration. He took the term 'general history' from Ranke, for whom it connoted something more ambitious than merely a piece of extended or synoptic narrative. As Butterfield pointed out in the inaugural set of Wiles Lectures in Belfast, published in 1955 as *Man on his Past: The Study of the History of Historical Scholarship*, Ranke (contrary to his later reputation as a blinkered archive hound) did not repudiate the eighteenth-century ideal of 'universal history': 'he simply claimed that it should be in the hands of historians rather than philosophers. Both he and his predecessors seem to have assumed that, if the historian himself does not undertake the task, some H. G. Wells will carry it out, and will acquire undue power over the minds of men.' The use of the anachronistic example is telling: Butterfield is projecting the particular form of his own preoccupation onto Ranke. Disparaging references to Wells's enormously popular *Outline of History*, first published in 1920, recur in Butterfield's writing. We are back with those 'professional manufacturers of commercial literature' he had inveighed against in 1931.

The problem was an acute one for Butterfield because, unlike most of his highly professionalized colleagues and successors, he was not willing to abandon the ambitions of 'general history' understood in these large terms. One of the main reasons he resisted the introduction of numerous optional courses into the Cambridge history syllabus was that he clung to the honourable ideal of history as a form of moral education for a non-specialized governing elite rather than as a training for future historians, and for this purpose he thought it a duty of the university history lecturer to provide a coherent interpretative account that ranged across different countries and several centuries. It is revealing in this respect that he emphasized in *Man on his Past* that he was not writing as a specialist in the subfield of 'history of historiography', but from the perspective of the general historian interested in many other things alongside historiography.

Because the role of the general historian is so important, and because the decisions that we make in our capacity as general historians are liable to be the most far-reaching of all—because, also, we cannot even escape having a general history which in a certain sense must preside over the works of multiple specialists and coordinate them with one another—it would be a serious matter either to neglect the training or to overlook the function of the general historian.

This, he added, had been a central concern for both Ranke and Acton, naming the chosen predecessors to whom he returned most frequently throughout his career.

It was this aspiration to chart nothing less than the rise and fall of whole 'civilizations' that had first led him to take an interest in the history of science in the 1930s. By the time he published the fruits of this thinking in 1949, he had come to believe that he had identified the key transformation in modern history. The notion that the late-sixteenth and seventeenth centuries had seen a 'Scientific Revolution' did not originate with Butterfield (Alexander Koyré, for one, was well ahead of him here), but his little book did more than almost any other to give the idea general currency. In the introduction to that book he spelled out the implications of this shift of focus for the received historical categories: 'it reduces the Renaissance and Reformation to the rank of mere episodes, mere internal displacements within, the system of medieval Christendom.' The Scientific Revolution 'looms so large as the real origin both of the modern world and of the modern mentality that our customary periodisation of European history has become an anachronism and an encumbrance.' By the time of his Wiles lectures six years later, he had broadened the perspective still further:

I should like to cry from the housetops that the publication of Newton's *Principia* in 1687 is a turning-point in history for peoples to whom the Renaissance and Reformation can hardly mean anything at all—peoples amongst whom the battle of Waterloo would hardly be calculated to produce an echo. And, before the Scientific Revolution, the great event in our history—the big new thing which made more difference to the world than even the fall of Rome—was surely the victory of Christianity in the civilisation that surrounded the Mediterranean Sea.

'General history' didn't come much more general than this.

Butterfield's energy as a historian was both stirred and dissipated by the tension between his strong desire to find large patterns in history—even, it could sometimes appear, to identify one overall direction—and his no less strong but much more corrosive urge to dismantle all received accounts, to be sceptical of all overarching narratives. It was the tension, one might say, between Butterfield the programmatically Whig historian and Butterfield the nominalist critic of whiggish history. These two inclinations roughly correspond to the two extremes of his published *œuvre*: sweeping but gnomic second-order ruminations about the nature of history, on the one hand, against minutely detailed monographic researches, on the other. The increasing part played by Providence in his thinking can be seen as one rather desperate attempt to overcome this tension: Providence often seems to be little more than the law of unintended consequences in Christian dress. In this way he could indulge his taste for demonstrating how human purposes were constantly frustrated or productive of ironic outcomes without having to present history as just one damn thing after another.

III

'Historians', Butterfield declared in his Wiles lectures, 'cannot have too great flexibility of mind'. But perhaps they can. For all the appeal of that sentiment, and for all the suggestiveness of Butterfield's own diverse and, in their way, impressive writings, he may not have had quite enough of that combination of confidence, pragmatism, and monomania essential to writing, to *completing*, major works of history. And perhaps this was allied to his counter-suggestibility and cultivated disengagement: although he was, by any measure, a serious historian and, beneath the layers of self-protection, a serious man, it may be that his apparent lack of interest in and commitment to the task of understanding the contemporary world (he regarded reading a newspaper as a 'boring duty') lent some excess of intellectual fastidiousness to his attempts to write genuinely explanatory history on any large scale. Butterfield had made his name mainly on the strength of his adroitness at turning the received wisdom on its head; for the most part he was less successful at replacing it with some alternative account. The reasons why he left behind no major piece of fully realized historical writing were partly contingent and circumstantial (no one working in a modern university can fail to sympathize), but partly the result of this self-inhibiting mixture of scepticism and ambition.

The fact that *Christianity and History*, the book that brought Butterfield most acclaim in his lifetime, is now largely neglected while the slighter and more negative *Whig Interpretation* still has some currency probably says as much about the chaster protocols of contemporary professionalism as about the diminished place of religion in national life more generally. Butterfield frequently wrote and spoke as a committed Christian, even calling for a more 'insurgent' type of Christianity from his lecture audience in 1949. In this connection, it is worth remarking the strikingly visible presence of active Christianity in the higher reaches of the Cambridge History Faculty during this period. The sequence of Regius Professors makes the point. Butterfield's immediate predecessor (who held the chair from 1954), Dom David Knowles, was a Benedictine monk whose speciality was medieval monasticism, while his successor (who held the chair till 1983) was the Revd Owen Chadwick, an ordained priest and former school and college chaplain who wrote extensively about the role of the church in modern history. This is another indication that though Butterfield may, from an ecclesiastical point of view, have been a Dissenter, this did not during this period really make him a 'dissenter' in any larger social sense.

Butterfield concluded *Christianity and History* with the injunction: 'Hold to Christ, and for the rest be totally uncommitted.' Perhaps it's because I find both parts of this credo more or less equally unappealing that it seems to me to offer something of a key to understanding his role in mid-twentieth-century British culture. His was a respected, influential, and (at least from the late 1940s to the late 1960s) often-heard voice, yet it is peculiarly hard to discern the effects of his influence in public debate beyond the encouragement of an obstructive scepticism about the possibility of rational agency in politics and society. Urging the wise statesman to 'work with Providence' just sounds like the historian trying to pull rank because he is on first-name terms with Hindsight.

None of this, we may feel, gets us very far in trying to identify Butterfield's own politics, for this is where he was at his most elusive. As a young man, he seems to have inherited his father's allegiance to Asquithian Liberalism, but after the First World War this became a notorious dead end, and in his adult life Butterfield professed to have no party-political affiliations. In keeping with this declared political agnosticism, he rarely voted; when the anomalous university franchise left him with three votes in the 1945 election, he is said to have cast one vote for each of three main parties. In one sense, his ringing endorsement of 'the English political tradition' in *The Englishman and his History*, a tradition distinguished by its eirenic encompassing of all sensible points of view, effectively ruled out political commitment, since that could be viewed only as a lapse into sectarianism. Butterfield, it appears, did not demur when his position was described as 'New Whig', but here, one might say, the term 'New Whig' has the convenience of expressing in two syllables what 'apolitical conservative' expresses in nine.

That would, however, be far too pat as a characterization of his stance across his entire career, not least because his mercurial intellect was prone, especially in his younger days, to try out various positions for effect without fully adopting them as his own. Such temporary affinities were usually founded on negation, on the way they enabled him to discredit some larger orthodoxy. An example of this is provided by one of his most interesting early essays, a somewhat neglected piece entitled 'History and the Marxian Method', which appeared in *Scrutiny* in 1933. His appraisal of the Marxist approach to history (then coming into vogue among his pupils in Cambridge) was more positive than one might at first expect, but

I suspect this was because he found a way to construe it as an ally in his own campaign against outdated historical assumptions. Marxism, he argued, attempts to go beyond that concentration on the doings of governments and statesmen that 'is particularly our habit when we are dealing with general surveys of modern history', and instead offers 'a profound structural analysis of a whole society'. He praised Marxists for recognizing that historical change is powered by the 'clash of wills' understood as a series of 'contradictions', and then, revealingly, went on to propose that in this respect 'the antithesis to Marxism... is the kind of history which hankers after some logical development, and sees men moving step by step towards some expanding purpose, freedom broadening down from precedent to precedent'. The terms of this contrast are doubly revealing. First, there is the very fact of taking Marxism as the antithesis of this kind of developmental or teleological history, since dialectical materialism, in the form chiefly familiar to English readers between the wars, might more obviously have seemed a prime illustration of just such a view. And second, there is the way in which the last phrase in that passage—'freedom broadening down from precedent to precedent'—is offered as though it were a mere synonym for or expansion of the preceding clause when in fact it is only one particular example of such a developmental account. But for Butterfield in the early 1930s there was a particularly intimate connection, amounting almost to interchangeability, between history understood as a story, any story, of progressive development, and English history interpreted in terms of the progressive expansion of liberty.

The piece also throws light on his attack on the Whig interpretation in another way. Occasionally visible in the essay is Butterfield's belief that although the world has changed dramatically since the nineteenth century, the dominant ways of thinking had not been adjusted to keep pace with these changes, with the result that there is now a 'discrepancy between our mentality and the contemporary situation', a discrepancy that has led to the tragic mistakes of the generation before his. (It seems, from other evidence, that he had the policies crystallized in the Treaty of Versailles in mind rather than the outbreak of the First World War itself; identifying this concern also points to a certain continuity with the aggressively 'realist' emphasis of his later attacks on the damaging consequences of a misplaced liberal self-righteousness in foreign relations.) In particular, 'our historical theory seems determined not to catch up' with the new reality: his generation were still 'starting where the old history-books had started'. This is where Marxism becomes an ally: 'I do not think we can deny that the Marxist has put his finger on the fundamental fallacies of that history which the average Englishman holds in his head.' His *Scrutiny* essay thus hints

at the political concern that had, indirectly, animated his assault on the
Whig interpretation: because the traditional story of the growth of English
liberty inherited from the nineteenth century was too complacent, too
individualist, and too rationalist, it constituted a fatal handicap in trying
to deal with the very different situation of the world since 1914.

IV

Butterfield always insisted that it was no part of his case to try to replace
the Whig interpretation with a Tory one, but he did, perhaps despite himself, end up giving aid and comfort to the Tory cause. Those who are principally stirred by their irritation with what they see as fashionable liberal and
progressive pieties, rather than concentrating on the states of the world that
those views aspire to remedy, are always likely to end up in a kind of clotted,
generalized grumpiness that becomes, in practice, hard to distinguish
from simple conservatism. Butterfield clearly cherished a sense of his own
mischievousness, a light-footed provokingness that couldn't be easily labelled
or pigeon-holed in political or intellectual terms. But this, in those who are
rather heavier of foot, can encourage that kind of intellectual nihilism that
issues in know-nothing conservatism. Partly through his sceptical teaching,
partly through a series of appointments he presided over at his college, he
came to be thought of as a progenitor of the so-called Peterhouse Tory school
mentioned earlier, though he did not share their leaning towards a form of
reactionary populism nor their combative delight in sheer bloodiness. It is
wholly appropriate that, by his teaching and example, Butterfield, subtle
celebrant of the play of unintended consequences, should have been held to
have produced 'disciples' whom he would have been unwilling to lead.

In the mid-1930s, the young J. H. Plumb felt lost as a research student in
Cambridge, largely neglected by Trevelyan, his aloof and shy supervisor. He
found stimulus and affirmation in long talks with Butterfield, eleven years
his senior, but his later recollection of these intense exchanges pinpointed
both the attraction and limitation of Butterfield as a historical mind. 'I loved
yet distrusted Butterfield's impish qualities, his almost electric versatility
at times daunted me but his major principles—the deep belief in the role
of Providence (Christian of course) in human history—left me, in the end,
bored as well as disbelieving.' Butterfield, Plumb had come to realize, exaggerated any position he took up 'in order to provoke the inevitable outburst,
for deep down he loved to shock, to be contrary'. This sharp judgement on
Butterfield in his mid-thirties may have incorporated a little hindsight, but
it does seem right about the central tension in his temperament, and right,
too, about at least one major part of his legacy.

For 'bored as well as disbelieving' is just how one comes to feel in the end about the so-called Peterhouse Tories whom Butterfield spawned, only half-deliberately. The intention to provoke becomes too transparent, too merely tiresome: the *raison d'être* of history seems to be limited to turning any moderately popular or, still worse, liberal notion on its head. Intellectual nihilism becomes boring in the end because it just seems like an expression of unresolved adolescence. Moreover, in practice it is tied to a substantive conservatism: all attempts at serious analytical explanation are derided, leaving force and established mores in possession. When this is conjoined, as it was in Butterfield's case and, in different ways, in some of the Peterhouse historians, with an insistence on the all-powerful but ever-inscrutable ways of God in history, it is bound to look like trying to have the best of both worlds—all the debating-club benefits of the negative forms of cleverness allied to the smugness that comes from always having a hand full of trumps. Butterfield the polemicist, Butterfield the challenging but corrosive supervisor, Butterfield the deeply conservative Master of his college cannot altogether escape responsibility for having enabled this unlovely combination of qualities to become a noisy presence, if perhaps not a real force, in the land from the 1960s to the 1980s.

Even at this distance, one can still experience some of the attractiveness of Butterfield's 'almost electric versatility', and this helps to explain how he could also have inspired pupils who went on to become serious and original intellectual historians in the next generation, such as Duncan Forbes and J. G. A. Pocock. He saw the importance of the history of science so much earlier than most historians of his formation, just as he saw that the history of historiography was too significant and rich a field to be left to political historians pursuing their professional genealogy as a retirement hobby. It was also to his credit that he refused to let British and European history be confined to wholly separate boxes and that he publicly stood out against the Namierite interpretation of the eighteenth century when that school was in its heyday. And although *The Whig Interpretation of History* is, as a book, a patchy and contradictory affair, its identification of that perspectival error which is constitutive of so much celebratory and teleological history is of permanent value. But, for all his talents and the diversity of his achievements, the more one reads of Butterfield's later pronouncements—the murky invocations of 'Providence', the complacent celebration of 'the English political tradition', the constant preaching about the limitations of human reason and human agency, the endlessly relaid each-way bet on 'technical history' as the corrective of all over-confident generalizations and 'general history' as the antidote to disabling specialization—the more, alas, one starts to become 'bored as well as disbelieving'. Butterfield certainly wasn't, as at moments it seemed he aspired to be, 'the English Ranke'. Perhaps he came closer to being 'the Methodist Acton'. It is an intriguingly contradictory identity, of course, but at least it is one that allows for the coexistence of a frequently indulged taste for moralizing on the past with a soberingly long list of uncompleted projects in the present.

12

The Intellectual as Realist:
The Puzzling Career of E. H. Carr

I

The career of E. H. Carr presents us with so many paradoxes that we might almost be forgiven for believing that he was created by a counter-suggestible divinity for the express purpose of calling some of our most familiar categories into question. The puzzles begin with his place in twentieth-century British culture. He probably did as much as any other single figure to shape reflective assumptions in the second half of the century about the nature of historical knowledge, especially among sixth-formers and university students, yet he had not been educated as a historian nor did he ever hold an appointment as a teacher of the subject. He was the principal British founder of what was to become the dominant 'realist' school in the study of international relations, yet in the latter part of his long and productive life he disparaged the discipline and kept his distance from it. Throughout the Cold War, he courted intellectual and political isolation by championing the achievements of the Russian Revolution and the Soviet Union, yet he was largely untouched by Marxist theory.

There are comparable paradoxes in the manner in which he occupied his various roles. Some of his most-noticed writing took the form of leading articles for the acknowledged voice of Establishment opinion in the middle of the century, *The Times*, of which he was assistant editor from 1941 to 1946, yet his contributions were regularly denounced by ruling politicians

E. H. Carr, *From Napoleon to Stalin and Other Essays*, with Introduction by Jonathan Haslam (Palgrave, 2003 [1st pub. 1980]).

E. H. Carr, *What Is History?*, with a new Introduction by Richard J. Evans (Palgrave, 2001 [1st pub. 1961]).

and administrators alike, who saw them as dangerously subversive of national policy. In the 1960s and 1970s he was hailed as something of a lost leader of the intellectual Left, yet he was dismissive of the 'abstract analysis of Marxist texts' he saw characterizing the *New Left Review* of the period, preferring to publish his own views in the far more mainstream *Times Literary Supplement*. Carr was a forceful writer with both a talent and a taste for polemic, yet much of his most influential writing was published anonymously (albeit his authorship was often widely known or suspected).

There was also a paradoxical quality to many of his characteristic views and intellectual sensibilities. He vigorously spoke up for progress, against all forms of conservatism and nostalgia, yet he was in no way a liberal. His major work, the fourteen-volume *History of Soviet Russia*, was devoted to one of the greatest upheavals in modern history, the deliberate remaking of a whole society in accordance with an elaborate ideology, yet his own inclinations as a historian were to concentrate on the legal and adminis-trative procedures of governments and to play down the role of ideas. He was scathing about the provincialism of British intellectuals, yet Edmund Wilson was not alone in finding his writings marred by a 'never intermit-ting British chill'. He deliberately courted controversy, yet he shunned publicity and was by habit and temperament something of a recluse. And finally, he was someone who, shortly after his death in 1982, had the rare distinction of being violently denounced in both of the two leading organs of intellectual and literary opinion, the *Times Literary Supplement* and the *London Review of Books*, yet thereafter his name seemed to slip from view with dramatic suddenness. He rarely appears in surveys of leading twentieth-century British intellectuals or even of that century's outstand-ing historians, though he might seem to have better credentials for these titles than several of those to whom they are more readily applied.

Sheer contingency played a larger part in determining the contours of Carr's career than is true for many writers, but if any consistent or unifying theme is to be located among these baffling tensions, then it must be found, at least from that point in the late 1930s when he can be said to have found his own voice, in his unwavering commitment to what he understood as 'realism'. And in the case of this deeply contentious man, such an under-standing found habitual expression in criticizing and dismissing those he deemed guilty of various kinds of 'illusion'. In the 1930s, he principally took issue with those liberal idealists who had deluded themselves that the Treaty of Versailles should be based on the twin foundations of German guilt and the rights of small nations rather than on efforts to assure the long-term security of Europe through a recognition of the realities of the large power blocs. Thereafter, he evinced a similar exasperation with those who could not see that laissez-faire capitalism had failed and needed to be superseded by planned economies. He gave short shrift to those who did not recognize the extraordinary achievements of the Soviet Union in transforming itself in a relatively brief period from a backward peasant economy into one of the two leading industrial giants, and he was particularly impatient with those who did not acknowledge the fact that the war in Europe had largely been won thanks to the Red Army. In the 1950s and 1960s, he could barely contain his disdain for those who refused to recognize the reality that Britain was no longer a major power and Europe no longer the centre of world history. And in his dealings with a variety of opponents, he complained of their failure to see that, although technological and economic advances may have dealt roughly with some of the cherished idols of the nostalgic and comfortably-off intellectuals of the West, the welfare of the mass of mankind had benefited immeasurably and that *that* was what mattered in drawing up the balance sheet of progress.

In every sphere, Carr insisted that the realities of power be acknowledged (or indeed, according to his critics, celebrated). This may seem simply the essential entrance qualification for anyone setting up as a commentator on world affairs, but the central question about Carr's career has to be whether this unwavering commitment, always accompanied by an eagerness to expose the irresponsible illusions of ideologues and idealists alike, did not in the end become a limitation. A degree of insensitivity to the play of ideas may be characteristic of officials of any stripe, just as a rather-too-pleased-with-itself hard-headedness may be typical of political historians: Carr had a share of both these identities, and this inheritance, when combined with an almost solipsistic absorption in his own projects, expressed itself in a perspective of considerable power and penetration, but one that, in the ultimate paradox, may not have been best suited to taking the measure of the ideas-driven century he lived in and wrote about.

II

The contingencies that helped shape Carr's career illuminate both some of the possible modes of being an intellectual in mid-twentieth-century Britain and some of the ways in which the older role of the man of letters metamorphosed into more specialized and even professionalized identities. Seen in these terms, the inaugurating moment came in December 1928, when Carr was already 36 years old. Up to that point, his life had followed a pattern familiar among the cleverer sons of the educated and professional classes at the turn of the century. A First in Classics at Cambridge had been followed by a temporary wartime appointment attached to the Foreign

Office, including a spell at the Versailles Peace Conference in 1919. In the early 1920s, Carr allowed himself to drift into what looked as though it was going to be a permanent career in the diplomatic service, specializing in relations with the powers in Eastern Europe and the Baltic states. His longest posting was at Riga between 1925 and 1929, but he was bored by embassy life, and having learned Russian he formed the desire to write about Russian literature. It was while on leave in London in December 1928 that he met V. S. Pritchett, then just beginning a regular reviewing stint on the *Spectator*, and this gave him the opening he craved: the first of Carr's reviews for that paper appeared in March 1929. Initially, Carr struggled to get any recognition for his longer literary efforts: his biography of Dostoevsky, the earliest of his several books on nineteenth-century Russian figures written in the course of the 1930s, was turned down by various publishers before being accepted by Unwin in 1931. His first real success came with the appearance in 1933 of *The Romantic Exiles*, a group portrait of Herzen, Bakunin, and the generation of the 1840s. Thereafter, he was to be found writing fairly frequent articles and reviews in publications such as the *Fortnightly Review* and the *Spectator*, the former of which, at least, was a pale shadow of its great nineteenth-century self and hardly an influential organ of opinion in the 1930s. Given the delicacies involved in commenting upon contemporary international affairs while still working for the Foreign Office, he published several of these pieces under the *pen name* 'John Hallett', a portent of a career in literary journalism that was to be, to an extent unusual by this date, often carried on under the cover of anonymity or pseudonymity.

This was particularly the case with his contributions to the *Times Literary Supplement* (which extended the practice of anonymous reviewing until 1974). It is only with the recent compilation of the *TLS* contributors' index, covering the period from its foundation in 1902 until 1974, that the quite remarkable scale of Carr's writing for the paper has become fully apparent (it was known that he had been a frequent contributor, even during the years of ostensible anonymity). When his friend Stanley Morison became editor in 1945, Carr enjoyed favoured status among contributors and reviewed most of the leading books on Russia and international affairs more generally. He maintained this position under Morison's successor, Alan Pryce-Jones, editor until 1959; Derwent May's history of the *TLS*, *Critical Times*, reveals that for many years Carr was paid a retainer by the paper. In the half-century following his first review in 1930, he contributed several hundred reviews and articles, mostly on international affairs and Russian history; when his letters to the editor and other lesser items are added in, he turns out to have made more than 900 contributions in total.

All the while he was trying to build up his literary career in the early
1930s, Carr continued his rather undemanding role at the Foreign Office
in London, but in 1936 he successfully applied for the Woodrow Wilson
Chair of International Politics at Aberystwyth. (This was one of the several
points at which his career intersected with that of Herbert Butterfield, who
was a candidate for the same chair; in 1944 their roles were to be reversed,
Butterfield getting the Chair of Modern History at Cambridge over Carr.)
The Wilson professorship was not a conventional academic chair: it had
been established in 1918 with the express purpose of furthering the study
of international relations so as to 'promote peace between nations', and it
was expected that the holder would travel a good deal and keep abreast of
current political developments. This liberty suited Carr, who thus assumed
an academic identity for the first time at the age of 44. Even then, it was
only a very partial identity: he continued to live in Surrey, commuting to
Aberystwyth each week in term to deliver his lectures, and he continued to
write in the general periodicals and to do an increasing amount of political
journalism as well.

In the mid- and late-1930s, Carr was most prominent as an advocate
of appeasement. He believed that the 1919 settlement had been need-
lessly punitive towards Germany, and that it was in the interests of the
balance of power in Europe that Germany be encouraged to reassert its
national claims. At a time when there were few professors whose brief
was to concern themselves with current politics at all, the holder of the
Wilson chair commanded more attention than might be the case today. As
Carr's biographer puts it, without irony or any risk of bathos: 'The appointment to Aberystwyth had given Carr a prominent platform from which to
pronounce on world politics.' During his tenure, he wrote several books
on international affairs, the best known being *The Twenty Years' Crisis
1919–1939*, first published in 1939, a 'realist' account of the conduct of
international relations and an indictment of the misguided liberal idealism
that resulted in an ineffectual League of Nations. In its opening pages,
Carr elaborated an extended contrast between the perspectives of two
ideal types, that of 'the bureaucrat' and that of 'the intellectual', scarcely
disguising his disdain for the delusions of the latter. (Once again, a writer
who would, on most measures, soon come to figure among Britain's leading
intellectuals sharply distanced himself from membership of the category.)
He had intended to entitle the book 'Utopia and Reality' before his publisher
persuaded him to change it, and it is clear that 'intellectuals' correspond to
the 'utopian' half of the pairing. Blame for the catastrophe of 1914 and
for the disasters that followed in the inter-war years was placed at the door
of the idealistic liberal. Liberals ('liberals', 'utopians', and 'intellectuals'

were near synonyms for Carr at this point) simply did not understand the nature of power: this was to become his abiding message.

The approach of war in 1939 discredited the case for appeasement, but it also provided Carr with a new role. He had written occasional pieces for *The Times* since 1937 and had got to know the deputy editor, Robin Barrington-Ward, who had a high opinion of his talents, and who was to replace Geoffrey Dawson as editor in 1941. In the course of 1940 Carr began writing leaders for the paper, officially becoming assistant editor (a post that involved some administrative responsibility as well as writing) in 1941. From this position, he immediately began to campaign for what he saw as the two faces of a successful policy of reconstruction to follow the war: a recognition of the reality of Soviet power in Europe and a recognition of the need for collectivist planning at home. 'The European house cannot be put in order unless we put our own house in order first.' (Carr had a taste for political 'order', something that did not always recommend his views to liberal critics.) The role of a leader-writer on *The Times* was, at least up until the transformation of that paper in the 1960s, a curious one, and this was at the root of one of the more paradoxical features of Carr's career. *The Times* was still seen, especially abroad, as a semi-official organ, close to the government of the day, uniquely well-informed, concerned not to take a 'sectarian' or idiosyncratic political line. Leading articles were, of course, always anonymous, and so, although they provided an exceptionally influential channel for the expression of ideas, particularly where impact on the world's political and administrative elites was concerned, they were doubly impersonal: they were not the opinions of a named individual and they were not the expression of a partisan or campaigning newspaper (as leaders might be in a paper such as, for example, the *Manchester Guardian*). But in Carr's case, his authorship of certain leading articles became widely known, especially because they tended, even after having been toned down first by Geoffrey Dawson and then by Barrington-Ward, to be more critical of government policy than the paper usually allowed itself to be. Carr's name thus acquired considerable currency in official and political circles without his ever once appearing as the author of the pieces that attracted this attention.

Throughout his period as assistant editor at *The Times*, Carr continued to hold his chair. As he explained himself to Ifor Evans, the Principal at Aberystwyth, he intended to return to his post after the end of the war, but he could not bear to be sidelined in merely academic activity during it.

It would be...intolerable to sit in pure academic seclusion writing long-term stuff: indeed I've never believed that, even in peace, anything useful can be written on politics by anyone wholly isolated from current realities...Hence I need something which gives me (i) the necessary contact with day-to-day affairs (ii) the sense that I am making some sort of contribution to the war—or at any rate to the peace (iii) a platform, other than the long-range one of book-writing, for getting some of my ideas across. *The Times* at [the] present moment comes nearer than anything else I've discovered to fulfilling these conditions.

This is a revealing *cri de cœur*. To 'get across' his ideas about politics he needs a 'platform' and, equally indispensable, contact with current 'realities'. Since the ideas were seen by many as emphatically 'left-wing' and Carr's as a distinctive and indeed idiosyncratic voice, the conclusion that there was no more appropriate platform for this activity than the impersonal organ of the political Establishment indicates something of the paradoxical quality I mentioned earlier. Yet, viewed under another description, there was nothing in the least puzzling about Carr finding such a berth in Print ing House Square: after all, he wrote in the approved mandarin style (a First in Classics or History from Cambridge or Oxford had long been the chief vocational training undergone by *Times* leader-writers); he was a Foreign Office insider; he tended to equate public life with politics and politics with government policy, especially foreign policy; he had little truck with 'ideology' and always used 'sound', 'practical', and, above all, 'realistic' as strongly positive terms—as one goes on, Carr comes to seem almost the perfect recruit for the peculiar institution that was *The Times* in the first half of the twentieth century.

But while his formation may have corresponded to that of a familiar social type, his views did not, especially his views about Soviet Russia. The war had opened Carr's eyes to the strength of Russia and hence to the great achievements in modernization that had been made under the Soviets. Moreover, he believed that the Russian model had wider significance: laissez-faire capitalism had failed, the modern era was to be the era of the planned economy. Such views were hardly unknown in Britain during the war, of course, but Carr exploited the prominent cultural position of *The Times*'s leader columns to express them in vigorous terms. A notable early example was his long leading article on 'The Two Scourges' published on 5 December 1940. (This piece was also notable for the fact that 10,000 reprints of it were sold and demand for the paper shot up in its wake.) The scourges in question were war and unemployment: the first was henceforth to be avoided by a new international order based on a realistic acknowledgement of the interests of the dominant powers, the second by adapting to the peacetime economy many of the measures of central planning and control that were willingly accepted in the circumstances of war. The air of hardheaded briskness, and lack of 'sentimental' consideration for small nations and civil liberties alike, were characteristic of Carr's political writing.

In the course of the war, Carr's leaders became something of a *cause célèbre*. It is hard to know what Tom Jones, leading Whitehall fixer of the period, meant when, in his telegram to the Principal at Aberystwyth justifying Carr's continuing secondment, he declared: 'Professor Carr on *The Times* is worth several generals in the field,' but this was scarcely a common view in official circles. In 1942 the Foreign Office even went so far as to minute the opinion that 'HMG are definitely opposed to the policy advocated by Professor Carr in *The Times*'. But the Foreign Office was not the only government department. As his biographer, Jonathan Haslam, puts it: 'Had he restricted his pen to foreign affairs, Carr's influence would have been considerably less. But it was the fact that he advocated radical social reform at home in conjunction with an assertively pro-Soviet stance abroad—both of which found a strong echo among the general public— that made him such a force to be reckoned with and such an object of fury to Whitehall.' And not just Whitehall. For example, a leader on 'Security in Europe' in March 1943 provoked criticism from several quarters. The Polish ambassador to Britain was predictably infuriated by the article's argument, which seemed to involve the possible sacrifice of Polish interests to the maintenance of the balance of power; he emphasized that he knew who had written it 'and knew what Carr's idea of Eastern Europe was, but it was not the idea of the Poles'.

At one point Carr was even denounced in the House of Lords (by Viscount Elibank): 'Professor Carr is indeed an active danger to this country and its future in the position which he holds, and if we were so foolish as to be guided by his views, we should certainly lose the peace and all our sacrifices would be in vain.' But he also took a lot of stick from what might be regarded as the opposite flank: Orwell, in one of his rants about 'the general Russophile feeling of the intelligentsia', sneered that 'all the appeasers, e.g. Professor E. H. Carr, have switched their allegiance from Hitler to Stalin'. Churchill himself was infuriated by leading articles by Carr that were severely critical of the policy that led British troops to be engaged on the anti-Communist side in what was in effect a brief Greek civil war in 1945, and the tone of official feeling towards *The Times* at this point is captured in the diary entry of Sir Alexander Cadogan, Permanent Under-Secretary at the Foreign Office: 'I hope someone will tie Barrington-Ward and Ted Carr together and throw them into the Thames.' By the end of 1945, the situation had become yet more extraordinary, since the Foreign Office felt that even normally critical liberal papers were supportive of the broad lines of the government's policy, but 'the one weak patch in our position are the leader columns of *The Times*, where Professor Carr...continues to sabotage the policy of the Labour Government and of its predecessors on all matters where Russia and the Eastern bloc are concerned'. It is hard to know whether to be more struck by Carr's expressing such provokingly heterodox views from such an unimpeachably Establishment platform, or by the evident importance that all parties attributed to the peculiar literary genre of the leading article.

Despite the repeated charges of his critics, Carr was not in fact ideologically pro-Soviet, at least not in the way that many on the Left in Britain were at the time; he was, instead, in favour of recognizing the geo-political interests of *Russia* and acknowledging the determining part that the Russian state would necessarily play in the post-war world. But by the same token, he tended to underestimate the role of ideology in determining *Soviet* policy, just as he had in the case of Nazi Germany in the late 1930s. His devotion to *Realpolitik* thus turned out to be in this respect *un*realistic, a failure accurately to register the actual moving forces in world affairs. Nor is it obvious that his views were in any conventional sense those of 'the Left'. He was impatient with the strain of anti-industrial nostalgia that constituted a defining feature of British socialism; he evinced little sympathy for oppressed minorities of any kind; he was indifferent to the claims of small nations or other ethnic groups. He was critical of most forms of conservatism as obstacles to progress, yet he was neither a liberal nor a utopian. Even his largely sympathetic biographer speaks of Carr's 'ruthless philosophy' in international affairs and his 'deference for power' generally.

It was in the autumn of 1944, with the Red Army, victorious the previous year in the decisive battle of Stalingrad, approaching the outskirts of Warsaw, that Carr formed the idea of writing a large-scale history of the momentous social and economic experiment that lay behind these military successes. In the event, the scale of the enterprise outgrew even his ambitious plans: the first volume, part one of *The Bolshevik Revolution 1917–1923*, appeared in 1950; the last instalment, the third part of *Foundations of a Planned Economy, Volume Three*, taking the story up to 1929, appeared in 1977 when its author was 85. Thirty-three years; fourteen volumes (two of them partially co-authored); 6,553 pages: Carr was fortunate to have been such a striking instantiation of one of his own pet themes, the increased longevity that came with the industrial progress of the nineteenth and twentieth centuries.

Initially, however, the decision to embark on a *History of Soviet Russia* complicated his career prospects rather than improving them. Carr left his position at *The Times* in 1946, though he continued to write for it for some years thereafter, and he resigned his Aberystwyth chair for personal reasons in 1947. At the age of 55, just embarking on a second marriage, he had no secure income and sought to make a living entirely by his writing.

But with the intensification of the Cold War, he found that he risked becoming *persona non grata* in some circles. An internal BBC memo by the *Listener's Digest* editor, who was unwilling to publish the text of some of Carr's radio broadcasts, put the general case: 'Carr has proved himself so often a very dangerous seller of opinion, and very often prejudiced opinions of only local or temporary significance at that,—in the disguise of facts and apparently purely academic or final historical judgements.' He twice failed to be elected to Oxford's Montague Burton Chair of International Relations in the 1940s; he was vetoed for a chair in Russian studies at the School of East European and Slavonic Studies in London for being too 'pro-Soviet'; and he was in effect blackballed for a Senior Research Fellowship at King's College, Cambridge, on account of his 'support of the Stalin regime'. But as his biographer fairly records: 'For every individual trying to hold him back, Carr invariably found support elsewhere.' A short-term teaching post at Balliol College, Oxford, was followed in 1955 by election to a Senior Research Fellowship at Trinity College, Cambridge, a comfortable berth that allowed him to devote his energies over the next two decades or more to the completion of his *magnum opus*.

There has been no shortage of scholarly discussion of the strengths and weaknesses of Carr's *History of Soviet Russia*; I have nothing of value to contribute to that debate. But I would observe, as others have noted in more detail, that not only is the whole conception of the work expressive of Carr's general intellectual sensibilities—for example, in the early volumes he typically saw Lenin more as a state-builder than as a revolutionary—but also that a characteristic, if subdued, polemic underwrote his more notorious judgements. As his narrative inched into the mid-1920s, he came to believe that 'agriculture was the crucial problem of the Russian Revolution'. Setting his face against conventional opinion in the West, he maintained that collectivization had been a success, at least in terms of increasing production and feeding the population; his recognition of the human costs of this process seemed to some of his critics little better than perfunctory. This may have been one of those places where his habitual counter-suggestibility was particularly unhelpful; he suspected that the concern among Western intellectuals for the fate of the peasant was simply part of a wider nostalgia for a simpler rural past. 'The peasant is the spoilt child of Western historians.' However large the grain of truth in that provocative assertion, it seemed to most observers to be outweighed a hundred times over by the blood-soaked fact that the peasant was certainly not the spoilt child of Stalinist commissars.

Essentially moral criticisms of this kind lay at the heart of the two posthumous assaults on Carr's reputation mentioned earlier. Reservations had, of course, been expressed by fellow-specialists along the way: even his friend Isaac Deutscher, the biographer of Trotsky, had remarked in reviewing the third volume of his *History* that Carr was sometimes 'carried away by his sound respect for Realpolitik and his contempt for illusion'. But as time went on, the number of Carr's friends seemed to shrink while that of his enemies increased; part of the sadness of his biography lies in the fact that his undeniable gifts seemed better suited to creating the latter rather than the former. In addition, as Derwent May reports: 'In the universities there was a good deal of annoyance that Carr got all the books on Russia to review for the *Lit Supp.*' Nonetheless, when the storm finally broke, its ferocity was striking. Within a couple of months of his death, Norman Stone, a historian of Russia and Eastern Europe who held pronounced if unorthodox right-wing views (and who was, perhaps not coincidentally, also a Fellow of Trinity at the time), indulged in a swingeing exercise in character assassination in the *London Review of Books*, depicting Carr as cowardly and morally evasive. A few months later, Leo Labedz, a noted Cold War polemicist and stalwart of *Encounter*, took the opportunity provided by the appearance of *The Twilight of Comintern*, Carr's brisker survey of the years following the period covered by his detailed *History*, to launch a damning critique of his whole œuvre in the *Times Literary Supplement*. 'Intellectual love of power', 'blinkered pedantry', 'moral indifference': Labedz zestfully lived up to his reputation as an anti-Communist hatchet man. Correspondents wrote in to say that they found 'this exercise in posthumous denigration offensive', but, as usual in such cases, the sweeping allegations received far more attention that did the judicious corrections. There was some irony in the fact—as well, perhaps, as some satisfaction for the many authors who had over the years suffered at the hands of Carr the (mostly anonymous) reviewer—that this savage assault had been launched in the pages of the journal to which Carr had been such a voluminous contributor for over half a century.

III

Carr's absorption in his *History* during the thirty years after he left *The Times* helps to account for his diminished visibility in British intellectual life during these decades. 'Playing to the gallery', as Haslam puts it, 'simply did not interest him. The BBC were forever phoning, only to be told that he was unavailable for comment. Scholarship was all that counted.' But this is plainly not the whole story, since even during this period Carr continued to engage in various controversies. The best known of these concerned, first, the justification of Soviet policy, especially the forced collectivization of agriculture in the 1930s, and, second, the character and purpose of historiography. But underlying and surrounding these two prominent topics, there was a recurrent motif to the engagements of Carr's later decades that has not, I believe, been properly recognized: over and over again, he took issue with what he saw as the conservatism and pessimism of intellectuals in the West, especially in Britain. In doing so, he revealed a certain unclarity or tension in his conception of intellectuals and, more significantly, a betraying unsteadiness about where he placed himself within this vexed category.

The roots of this difficulty can be traced back at least as far as *The Twenty Years' Crisis*. In the contrast elaborated in its opening pages between the 'intellectuals' and the 'bureaucrats', the former are held to be inherently utopian, marked by their 'failure to understand existing reality'. The latter, by contrast, are characterized by their 'empirical' approach to political problems, and so seem to earn the author's endorsement from the very outset of the analysis. But he does also note that 'the bureaucrat... is bound up with the existing order, the maintenance of tradition, and the acceptance of precedent as the "safe" criterion of action'. He also goes on to draw the obvious contrast in terms of political affiliation: 'The intellectual, the man of theory, will gravitate towards the Left just as naturally as the bureaucrat, the man of practice, will gravitate towards the Right.' As with most writers who set up a pair of binary ideal types, Carr, by implication, transcends his own categories, though in general his evaluative language suggests considerably greater respect for the bureaucrat than for the intellectual (and also appears to give the former the more impressive pedigree: 'It is worth remarking that both Machiavelli and Bacon were bureaucrats'). But in at least two ways, the terms of this contrast (in a book that was frequently reprinted during Carr's lifetime) created pitfalls for his subsequent identity: after all, he was outspokenly antagonistic to those he regarded as defending 'the existing order' and he saw himself as occupying a position on 'the Left', albeit of an idiosyncratic kind. Yet Carr, the apostle of realism, cannot have been willing to place himself among those he was here calling 'the intellectuals'.

Similar difficulties of self-inclusion crop up in *What Is History?*, the book that grew out of his Trevelyan lectures, especially in its last chapter. Here (it is an aspect of the book that is often overlooked) Carr allowed himself a purely local reference. He upbraided the Cambridge History Faculty for the narrowness and Anglocentrism of its teaching, a criticism he evidently felt all the freer to make for the fact that he, though a distinguished historian living in Cambridge, did not hold an appointment in that faculty himself. But he made clear that he thought the intellectual parochialism he was pointing to was in fact 'typical of most other British universities and of British intellectuals in general in the middle years of the twentieth century'; extending the charge still further, he added: 'it sometimes looks as if we, by our inability or unwillingness to understand, were isolating ourselves from what is really going on in the world.'

The use of the first-person plural seemed initially to point to a national community and Carr's membership of it, and yet, as the argument developed, it became apparent that he saw himself as speaking from an offshore vantage point, at least in intellectual terms. 'What is *really* going on in the world': this was Carr's frequently played trump. He cast himself as the bringer of news to his audience in Cambridge's Mill Lane lecture rooms, news from outside a syllabus still largely confined to European and, above all, British history. More broadly, he appeared to be exempting himself from the failings ascribed to 'British intellectuals in general'. He diagnosed 'the current wave of pessimism and ultra conservatism', grounded in a 'paralysing nostalgia', as the debilitating ailment of the 'middle-class intellectual', against whom Carr implicitly aligned himself with 'the man in the street' who intuitively recognized the benefits of progress. On Carr's showing, intellectuals seem even more prone to herd behaviour than do other groups in the population. (It is interesting to note that in a broadly sympathetic assessment of Karl Mannheim, written several years earlier, he dismissed the idea of the 'unconnected intellectual' and displayed his scorn for 'the belief that intellectuals were better equipped than any other section of society to resist the ideological or the economic pressures of the current orthodoxy'.)

Carr's correspondence suggests that his choice of subject for his Trevelyan lectures was partly guided by a desire to challenge the liberal understanding of history made fashionable in the 1950s by Karl Popper, Isaiah Berlin, and others. But in his concluding lecture, he broadened the assault to include other 'voices of the 1950s' who contributed to what he saw as a prevailing conservatism, such as Michael Oakeshott, Hugh Trevor-Roper, and Lewis Namier. Namier was in some ways the odd one out in this list, not just because of Carr's considerable admiration for him, but also because of an intellectual or temperamental affinity between the two men, and this highlights from another angle Carr's ambivalence about his own position. He regarded Namier as 'the greatest British historian to emerge on the academic scene since the First World War'. Namier understood power: for Carr, this was the highest accolade. And Namier, like Carr, was hostile to those he categorized as 'moralists' rather than 'historians', those who rushed to pass judgement (judgement was, of course, not exactly absent from the writings of either of them). Namier's great strength, Carr maintained, came from his non-British background: he had 'no roots in nineteenth-century liberalism, and suffered from no nostalgic regrets for it'. (Carr, as he always acknowledged, did have such roots—and so, by implication, was prey to such nostalgia?) By choice, Namier returned to a period before ideas and revolutions had attempted to remake the world: he returned to the stable society of the governing classes in eighteenth-century England. In so far as Namier did write about revolution, Carr noted, he chose not one of the great turning points of European history, but the failed revolution of 1848. In Namier's hands, what this demonstrated was that 'the intrusion of ideas into the serious business of politics is futile and dangerous; Namier rubbed in the moral by calling this humiliating failure "the revolution of the intellectuals"'. And so he did, though Carr may seem a little too ready to endorse the sneer in Namier's label here, as though it were self-evident that 'intellectuals' would make a mess of 'the serious business of politics'. This is certainly a conclusion several generations of readers have taken from *The Twenty Years' Crisis*.

And yet as Carr moves into his peroration over a hundred pages later, he shifts the emphasis. Now, Namier's 'exaltation of practical reason over idealistic theorizing' is damned as 'of course, the hallmark of conservatism'. Namier is indicted alongside the other 'voices of the 1950s' for encouraging a 'waning of faith in reason among the intellectuals and the political thinkers of the English-speaking world'. Now, 'when our political and economic pundits prescribe, they have nothing to offer us but the warning to mistrust radical and far-reaching ideas, to shun anything that savours of revolution'. Carr explicitly repudiates this pessimism and this distrust of 'far-reaching ideas'. He embraces radical change—'I remain an optimist'—and fears that 'this country' will relapse into 'some nostalgic backwater'. The shifts in Carr's tone and self-positioning may fall some way short of logical contradiction, but they surely betray a not wholly harmonized set of animosities. He is not one of the 'intellectuals', chronically unable to recognize the operation of power in the world, yet nor is he one of the critics of intellectuals, scorning all ideas for far-reaching change. He is not one of those commentators who have never shaken off the impress of nineteenth-century liberalism, yet he often recalls his susceptibility to the charms of pre-1914 Britain. He is not one of 'our pundits', yet he made tireless efforts to 'get his ideas across', principally to the local, British audience. There is a recurring ambivalence in Carr about whether he really belongs to any of the categories he discusses.

Carr was neither the first nor the last intellectual given to bolstering his sense of purpose by characterizing himself as an 'outsider', but as usual such a label grossly simplified a complex relation to his own society and its institutions of cultural power. As we have seen, the period of his greatest estrangement from those institutions may have been in the first decade or so of the Cold War, but even here Archie Brown's later assessment seems shrewd: Carr, he noted, 'was far from being an outsider vis-à-vis the British Establishment even in the late 1940s and early 1950s. He had, on the contrary, positions of influence as head of the Russian Studies Committee of the Royal Institute of International Affairs (Chatham House) and as a regular, anonymous reviewer of works on the Soviet Union for the *Times Literary Supplement*.' Someone who, when in need of a job during this period, was first edged into a Tutorship at Balliol (though 60 was a somewhat unusual age at which to take up such a post) and then provided with the security of a Senior Research Fellowship at Trinity, can scarcely be thought of as ill connected.

And yet in some respects he did stand at an oblique angle to aspects of his own society, and his career did not really conform to any of the conventional patterns of success. This is not the least of the ways in which he can be contrasted with Herbert Butterfield, a figure with whom he seemed destined to collide. (In his Trevelyan lectures he could not resist twitting Butterfield for the apparent inconsistency between the scepticism of *The Whig Interpretation of History* and the enthusiasm of *The Englishman and his History*, while good-humouredly disclaiming any intention of wishing to 'confront Professor Butterfield drunk with Professor Butterfield sober'; the quip relied on the fact, widely known in Cambridge, that Butterfield was an ostentatious teetotaler.) Their respective relations to the emerging discipline of International Relations in Britain is indicative of Carr's curious position. It was Butterfield's long-held ambition that the history of diplomacy, especially that sustaining the balance of power in eighteenth-century Europe, should inform the study, and indeed the practice, of contemporary statecraft. In mounting this case, Butterfield was wont to describe 'moralists' as 'specialists in wishful thinking'—a phrase which the discipline's historian has described as being drawn 'from Carr's realist language game'. Yet Butterfield never acknowledged the extent of his affinity with Carr's thinking in this area. *The Twenty Years' Crisis* is the one British work that is regularly placed alongside the founding American texts of the 'Realist' approach to the subject, though what developed as the distinctively 'British school of International Relations' shaped its identity largely via a critique of Carr. Hedley Bull—one of the leading figures in that school, along with Butterfield and Martin Wight—later insisted that Carr's 'realism' was 'blind to the "reality" that there are certain interests and values which are held in common by all states'. The discipline in Britain developed out of a rejection of Carr in other ways, too: the British Committee on the

Theory of International Politics met in Cambridge three times a year from 1958 under Butterfield's chairmanship (and under Wight's from 1966), but, even though Carr was probably the most famous writer in the field then living in Cambridge, he was never invited to attend.

One incidentally revealing source for Carr's sense of his own role is his 1972 review in the *TLS* of a memoir of James Headlam-Morley and his involvement at the Versailles peace conference. Carr, a close colleague of Headlam-Morley at Versailles and thereafter at the Foreign Office, took the opportunity to read a lesson on the innocence of the pre-1914 generation (he was almost thirty years younger than his former colleague). He took the memoir to display 'the standpoint of the generation of liberal intellectuals which flowered before 1914 and enjoyed a brief Indian Summer in the 1920s'. Headlam-Morley 'was an able and altogether admirable representative of a powerful group in the life and thought of the period, the ripples of whose influence can still be felt from time to time. Yet the total collapse of the Paris peace settlement in the space of twenty years spelt the bankruptcy of everything they had stood for.' This restated one of the defining perspectives of Carr's life: it was the lack of a 'realist' analysis that had led these liberal idealists to Armageddon, and even after 1919 they still failed to understand how the world had changed, not least as a consequence of the Russian Revolution. And yet, even as he makes this familiar point, Carr's own ambivalence peeps through. Headlam-Morley 'lived and flourished in what might now be thought of as an age of illusion. But history is a record of illusions; and this was a noble, if too simple, one deposited by a great civilization.' Carr could not help admiring it; indeed he could remember being part of it. But he held culpable those who went on thinking and acting as though it had not disappeared. The task was to throw off these blinkers and to understand the twentieth century, something the British were, in his view, not well placed to do. This gave him a role, and writing his huge *History* was part of that role.

IV

To the end, Carr remained a critic of the insularity and nostalgia that he saw as pervading British culture. In the introduction to the last book published in his lifetime, *From Napoleon to Stalin*, a collection of his occasional essays principally from the *Times Literary Supplement*, he returned to his familiar theme of the contrast between the pre- and post-1914 worlds. As one who had grown up in the former (he was in his late eighties when he wrote this), he felt the magnitude of the change personally and always emphasized that there could be no return to the conditions of that earlier

age. And from this he sought to draw a moral for his countrymen: 'Indeed,
if we sought to enumerate the reasons why Britain, which in the last century
led the world economically and politically, now lags behind almost all the
other Western nations, we should have to accord a high place on the list to
the nostalgia for past glories which dominates—unconsciously, but none
the less profoundly—our national thought and attitudes.' The result is that
other countries try to grapple with the new world, but (here the first-person
plural slides from the authorial into the national) 'we face only the past.
The remedies we seek to apply belong to the past, and are irrelevant to the
present or the future.' The future figured much more largely in Carr's writing than in that of most historians.

One of the features of his Trevelyan lectures that had provoked a chorus
of criticism was precisely his insistence that the historian needs to have 'a
long-term vision over the past and over the future'. (This was what Labedz
was later mockingly to term his 'futurological stance'). But in one respect,
at least, the question of where one stood on the future was a matter of lively
controversy at the beginning of the 1960s, especially in Cambridge. In his
celebrated lecture on 'the two cultures', C. P. Snow had recently berated
'the literary intellectuals' for their cultural conservatism, their disdain for
the satisfaction of ordinary material wants, their self-indulgent pessimism.
By contrast, scientists, according to Snow, had 'the future in their bones'.
In his lectures, Carr signalled a certain affinity with Snow's position by
quoting the latter's remark that Rutherford 'like all scientists … had,
almost without thinking what it meant, the future in his bones', and went
on to say: 'Good historians, I suspect, whether they think about it or not,
have the future in their bones.' For Snow, this endorsement of the future
meant acceptance of technological advance, industrialization, and the consequent ability to feed the world's population and lengthen its life span.
Carr, too, broadly endorsed these trends, accenting the role of the planned
economy in delivering the benefits of industrial progress. Both identified 'the intellectuals' as the spokesmen for resistance to these beneficial
advances.

Once again, the question arises of where Carr placed himself in relation
to this category. By any ordinary measure, he obviously belonged among
'the literary intellectuals'. After all, his first book, now almost half a century
before, had been a biography of Dostoyevsky, one of the figures whom Snow
had singled out as exercising a particularly damaging influence over later
literary intellectuals. Thereafter, although he had been associated with academic institutions for the greater part of his later career, he remained essentially a private scholar, more akin to the tweed-jacketed man of letters than
to the scientist in his lab coat. So where, in the end, did Carr place himself?

Sometimes, it could be said, he placed himself in the Foreign Office, or at least in the chancelleries of the great powers; he came to the writing of history relatively late, and always retained some of the brisk instrumentalism of the career official. Sometimes, he placed himself in Printing House Square, unembarrassed at putting on the authority of the traditional journal of the Establishment. At other times, he seemed to place himself in Moscow, and at still other times he adopted the perspective of what came during the years he was writing to be called 'the Third World'. Increasingly, as far as these last two locations were concerned, he could be said to be placing himself in the future. But, in the final paradox of all, there was a sense in which Carr—the great scourge of all nostalgists, the unyielding champion of progress—placed himself in Victorian England. And he did so as a way of taking his distance from fashionable opinion, by which he meant above all opinion as expressed by the intellectuals. As he grew older, he grew more insistent that it was the intellectuals and not 'the man in the street'—still less the man or woman in the slums and the shanty towns, in the prairies and the paddy fields—who were responsible for the prevailing cultural pessimism and for declinism generally. And to Carr, preparing a never-completed new edition of *What is History?* shortly before his death, it was scarcely surprising that 'the seat of the most profound intellectual pessimism is to be found in Britain', for 'nowhere else is the contrast between nineteenth-century splendour and twentieth-century drabness, between nineteenth-century superiority and twentieth-century inferiority, so marked and so painful'. This pessimism he saw as a form of elitism, a yearning for lost privilege, articulated by intellectuals, maintaining that 'intellectuals, by definition, form an elite group'. But societies, he allowed, do tolerate exceptions to such groups:

For more than forty years I have carried the label of 'an intellectual'; and in recent years I have increasingly come to see myself, and to be seen, as an intellectual dissident. An explanation is ready to hand. I must be one of the very few intellectuals still writing who grew up, not in the high noon, but in the afterglow of the great Victorian age of faith and optimism, and it is difficult for me even today to think of a world in permanent and irretrievable decline.

Carr, as we have seen, cultivated the voice of unillusioned realism. But perhaps in most self-described 'realists', especially in those for whom this stance is one expression of belligerence, there is a streak of soured romanticism, or at least a tellingly insistent repudiation of Edens whose charms they half recognize. (In a letter, Carr recalled that 'Namier, whose rather crass egocentricity did not make him unperceptive, called me a Romantic— this at a time when I was generally regarded as a hardened cynic'.) In Carr's evocations of the 'splendour' and 'superiority' of the nineteenth century, at least as experienced by a member of the comfortable classes in Britain, it is hard not to hear a hint of sorrow, even of unappeased yearning. He often spoke with regret of what had been lost in August 1914, and among those losses, surely, was what still seemed to him a saner and more confident attitude towards the future. Perhaps Carr was able to 'have the future in his bones' precisely because his roots were so deep in the now distant past. He might not have been displeased to find himself described in such fittingly paradoxical terms.

13

Enduring Passion:

E. P. Thompson's Reputation

I

There is an inescapable indeterminacy about all questions of reputation where literary and intellectual figures are concerned. Membership of the jury is heterogeneous and potentially infinite; the various parts of a writer's œuvre or achievement may receive different ratings from different categories of reader; it is almost impossible to maintain a sharp distinction between questions of reputation and the neighbouring territories of celebrity and utility; and at any given moment judgement is almost inevitably contaminated by hearsay, selective recall, and cultural lag.

These caveats may have particular purchase in the case of E. P. Thompson, who died in August 1993 at the age of 69. Historian, critic, polemicist, activist, teacher—Thompson mattered, and still matters, intensely, to a wide range of people. Much more is involved than the simple question of how well or badly his specific historical hypotheses and reconstructions have worn. Thompson was a passionate, acerbic, extravagant writer who left few readers indifferent. Political loyalties and antipathies were always central to his reception. In addition, any attempted summation involves negotiating the treacherous border country between academic and non-academic writing, with the fantasies and animosities that are endemic to that troubled territory.

This essay was originally written in 2004 to inaugurate a series of essays in the *Times Literary Supplement* reassessing the reputations of literary and intellectual figures who had died in the 1990s.

In Thompson's case, all parties would have to recognize that his standing has declined pretty markedly since its peak, though whether it did so more in the decade before his death than in the decade since is a nice question. But at its height—say, between the mid-1960s and the late 1970s—that standing was quite extraordinary. In the two decades following the publication of *The Making of the English Working Class* in 1963, Thompson was more frequently cited (so the selective evidence summarized in the *Humanities and Social Science Citation Index* suggests) than any other historian. The preface to Thompson's book has been, according to one thought-provoking but ultimately unverifiable assertion, the most widely read preface since Marx's 1859 preface to *A Contribution to a Critique of Political Economy*, the classic epitome of the theory of 'historical materialism'. After Thompson's death, obituarists routinely referred to him as 'the greatest social historian of his generation'.

Obviously, his standing benefited from, as well as contributed to, the more general prominence of the intellectual Left in Britain in the 1960s and 1970s, and it has correspondingly suffered from the latter's decline. In 1980 Perry Anderson could declare: 'Edward Thompson is our finest socialist writer today—certainly in England, possibly in Europe. Readers of *The Making of the English Working Class*, or indeed *Whigs and Hunters*, will always remember these as major works of literature.' Given the sharpness of the exchanges, at times more fratricidal than fraternal, that Anderson and Thompson had been engaged in over the previous couple of decades, this was a generous tribute, though it also hinted at the limits of Thompson's achievement when viewed from Anderson's own strenuously theoretical perspective—he is praised as a 'socialist *writer*' and his books as 'major works of *literature*'.

From the end of the 1970s through to the mid-1980s, Thompson's vigorous polemicizing and public speaking against nuclear weapons, and his central role in promoting European Nuclear Disarmament (END) as the successor to CND, brought him an altogether different level of public attention. He was described (in another of those judgements that can never be subject to any kind of rigorous validation) as better known and more recognizable than any other intellectual in Britain in the four decades after 1945, with the possible exception of A. J. P. Taylor, also a historian who had been drawn into grass-roots political activity by opposition to nuclear weapons, but one who principally owed his wider fame to his performances on television.

In one of the most perceptive recent reassessments of Thompson, David Eastwood has spoken of *The Making of the English Working Class* as 'incontestably the single most influential work of English history of the post-war period'—'English history', note, not just 'social history'. That may well have been true for the years which it still made sense to describe as 'the post-war period', but now one has to begin to ask whether the book does remain, in any genuine sense, 'influential', or whether it has passed over into being one of those acknowledged classics which, however great their impact in their own time, come to be prized for their literary or imaginative qualities rather than serving as prompts to current research.

II

Any attempt to chart, even in the broadest terms, the contours of Thompson's posthumous reputation has to take account both of shifts in intellectual fashions within academic scholarship and of the seismic political changes of the last two decades. But it is no less important to recognize two defining features of Thompson himself that mean he could be seen as a somewhat archaic figure even during his lifetime. First, he was never really a professional academic historian; his seven years at the University of Warwick from the mid-1960s involved him in attempting, awkwardly and unsuccessfully, to put on that disguise, but he was essentially a freelance writer, active in adult education and in Left politics, a figure resistant to the kind of academic professionalization that became increasingly dominant in the decades after the Second World War and that has since swept almost everything before it. And secondly, his political and intellectual sensibility was formed in a milieu that had already largely disappeared by the time of his own greatest fame and that it now needs an act of historical imagination to recover. In some ways, Thompson always remained, it seems to me, a man of the 1940s.

Obviously, that was bound to be a formative period in purely biographical terms: it embraced his years as a student at Cambridge, on either side of his war service; his early membership of the Communist Party; and his first job as an Adult Education Tutor in the West Riding. But more than this, his enduring political and intellectual identity was grounded in the ethos (or at least one notable strand in the ethos) of these years, an ethos that experienced the war principally in terms of its mobilization of popular anti-Fascism in Europe and its nurturing of social solidarity and political idealism in Britain. More specifically still, Thompson's situation as a young left-wing intellectual and teacher working in the heartland of the mature, organized, industrial working class encouraged him (as it did many others like him in those years) to direct his efforts to the project that had been at the intellectual centre of this particular world for two or three generations: the attempt to explain, denounce, and seek to remedy the deforming impact

that the Industrial Revolution of the late eighteenth century was thought to
have had on English society.

Speaking informally in New York in 1985, Thompson reflected that
he (in company with fellow Marxist historians Christopher Hill and Eric
Hobsbawm, who were also present) was completing work begun '40 or
more years ago'. On that occasion he did not go on to specify the work or
the chronology any more exactly, but the implication that even the things he
wrote in the last decade of his life were workings-out of ideas first formed in
the mid-1940s seems right. The impelling urge behind Thompson's history
was surely that expressed most simply in his first major book, *William
Morris: Romantic to Revolutionary*, published in 1955. A revised version
of this work was published in 1977, in which the author had pruned the
luxuriant growth of digressions and polemics that he had come to feel (and
certainly been encouraged by readers and reviewers to feel) had encumbered
the first edition and made it too long, but the passionate and unguarded
nature of its informing inspiration remained undimmed. In direct, heartfelt language, he stated the belief that he shared with Morris and a long line
of his successors: 'The life of Victorian England was an intolerable life and
ought not to have been borne by human beings. The values of industrial
capitalism were vicious and beneath contempt, and made a mockery of the
past history of mankind.' This is an authentic expression of that sense of a
great, raw, wrong that was so widely shared in the milieu in which Thompson began his work. It bears witness to a sense of class grievance about the
introduction of a historically unprecedented level of exploitation, but goes
beyond that to encompass the moral condemnation of a whole civilization.
In his later work, Thompson became a little less free with such holistic
categories as 'the life of Victorian England' or 'the values of industrial
capitalism' (here equated, in effect), but the sense of fundamental moral
revulsion was abiding.

Thompson's early, forceful statement of this case also signalled his
enduring sense of affinity with its first proponents. 'The injury that
advanced industrial capitalism did, and that the market society did,
was to define human relations as primarily economic.' Marx attempted
to replace individualist economic man with collectivist economic man.
But, contended Thompson, 'the injury is in defining man as "economic"
at all. This kind of critique of industrial capitalism is found in Blake and
Wordsworth very explicitly and is still present in Morris.' These figures
remained his touchstones (his last, posthumously published, book was on
Blake), as they had been those of a long tradition of radical and working-
class critics of individualism and orthodox political economy right through
the nineteenth century and the first half of the twentieth.

The subtitle of the Morris book, *Romantic to Revolutionary*, also signalled the political direction in which Thompson strove to extend this tradition, seeing Morris's progression from his early medievalizing in the 1850s and 1860s, through 'Anti-Scrape' and the protection of ancient buildings, to the political campaigns of the Marxist Social Democratic Federation in the 1880s, as paradigmatic of the kind of growth to be looked for among critics of industrialism more generally. This emphasis was expressive of another enduring aspect of Thompson's sensibility—namely, his constant attempts to assemble, often from neglected or forgotten instances, evidence of the vitality and longevity of 'our tradition'. This use of the first-person plural was characteristic of his prose: its referent was in some cases hard to specify, but it usually had the effect of simultaneously celebrating, recruiting, and excluding.

Whether or not *The Making of the English Working Class* is the single most influential work of English history of the second half of the century, it is important, and sobering, to recall that it was not the product of a university History department. It was researched and written while Thompson was living in Halifax, working as an extra-mural tutor, engaging with manual workers, trade unionists, and political activists rather than with academic historians. We should also remember that it was completed when he was only 38. And it may be worth noting of the familiar trio of famous books by adult education tutors in this period that Richard Hoggart's *The Uses of Literacy* and Raymond Williams's *Culture and Society* were also completed when their authors were in their mid-to-late thirties (and, as in Thompson's case, these were not their first books, either); the conditions of work were evidently favourable for those with the will to take advantage of them.

The appearance of what will, presumably, always be thought of as his masterpiece transformed Thompson's reputation. In some quarters, the stature of *The Making of the English Working Class* was recognized immediately, including in a front-page review in the *TLS* that we now know to have been by his friend and fellow-member of the Communist Historians Group, Christopher Hill. Elsewhere, however, the book was subject to fierce attack, rather of the kind that had confronted J. L. and Barbara Hammond, in their classic early twentieth-century studies of the labouring poor, and the many others who had also been accused of subordinating historical judgement to political passion. In any event, the book's success led Thompson to be appointed as Director of the newly established Centre for the Study of Social History at the University of Warwick in 1965. He soon attracted a devoted band of collaborators and research students, committed to exploring what it was becoming fashionable to call 'history from below'.

These years also saw the publication of some of his most famous essays, especially 'Time, Work-Discipline, and Industrial Capitalism' (1967), one of his finest, and 'The Moral Economy of the English Crowd in the Eighteenth Century' (1971), which became the focus of another major historiographical debate. Both these pieces were first published in *Past and Present*, a journal that Thompson played an important part in transforming from a heavily *marxisant* journal of 'scientific history' in the early 1950s to the leading historical journal of the 1960s and 1970s, still principally addressing issues of large-scale social and economic change, but adventurous in both geographical and methodological range.

The chief historiographical fruit of his time at Warwick was his study of the workings of the Game Laws in the early eighteenth century, *Whigs and Hunters*, published in 1975 after he had resigned his university post. This work, too, stirred considerable controversy, not least for its seminal reflections on the Janus-faced nature of 'the rule of law', at once the instrument of governing-class repression and the great bulwark for the defence of popular rights. This was a topic where his history underwrote his cultural criticism in ways that emphasized the distance he had travelled from his earlier Communism. As he became more pessimistic in the late 1970s about the prospects for fundamental political and economic change, he came more and more to cherish existing legal rights as the least bad form of defence against the high-handed coerciveness of the all-seeing, all-managing modern state. In his spirited vindication of the institution of the jury, in the face of crass measures of legal 'reform', he could almost sound like an eighteenth-century Commonwealthman or a 'Wilkes and Liberty' pamphleteer, celebrating 'the right to be tried by one's peers' as a precious communal safeguard against the excesses of over-mighty rulers.

III

Thompson's tireless devotion to the cause of nuclear disarmament in the early 1980s entailed a considerable hiatus in his historical scholarship, and when he returned to his earlier themes towards the end of that decade some observers detected signs of failing powers (his health had begun to decline). In 1991 the republication of some of his earlier essays, along with some new and reworked material, in *Customs in Common* was not quite the major intellectual event his many admirers had been hoping for. This may partly have been because the best of these essays, such as 'Time, Work-Discipline, and Industrial Capitalism', had already had their impact. But it was also because this book was to have been the summation of a quarter of a century's thinking and reading about the nature of the world that the Industrial Revolution had allegedly destroyed, and although the new material was full of interest and characteristically rich in local detail, the looked-for general statement about the 'customary economy' of the eighteenth-century countryside did not really emerge.

Viewed in a longer perspective, Thompson can be seen in his later work to be bumping up against the problem that had also confronted the Hammonds and all those who had argued that the Industrial Revolution had introduced a wholly new form of society, one governed by economic imperatives in a way supposedly not true of its predecessor: how, in that case, was the working of seventeenth- and eighteenth-century English society to be understood? What was the place of 'the economic' and economic behaviour in the preindustrial order? Using the language of a long line of critics of industrialism in the nineteenth century, Thompson had represented his newly made working class as opposing 'the annunciation of Acquisitive Man', but that raised the question of how the emblematic figure displaced by this new beast should be characterized—perhaps as Communal or Customary Man? Struggling with this problem (even if not expressed in quite this form) in the introduction to *Customs in Common*, Thompson restated his fundamental conviction: 'The industrial revolution and the accompanying demographic revolution were the backgrounds to the greatest transformation in history, in revolutionizing "needs" and in destroying the authority of customary expectations.' This way of putting it risked making needs and customary expectations seem largely unchanging in the years before 'the great transformation'. Yet, on his own showing, needs were constantly expanding in the earlier period, and most of the customary rights whose operation Thompson analysed with such matchless command were being constantly adjusted to stay abreast of these changes, especially in response to the new encroachments of the seventeenth and early eighteenth centuries. The *idea* that custom possessed a quasi-legal authority and was rooted in ancient folk-ways may indeed have been more powerfully operative than in later periods, but Acquisitive Man seemed to have been abroad in the land for centuries past.

Although Thompson could be wonderfully attentive to the minute variations of economic circumstance, he was not always so discriminating when it came to economic thought, especially in the form of the 'bourgeois' political economy of the late eighteenth and early nineteenth centuries. He sometimes wrote as though the new world supposedly ushered in by the Industrial Revolution was bound to produce the ideological reflex of theoretical justification, and intellectual historians such as Donald Winch have recently pointed out how coarsely aggregative and approximate some of Thompson's references to 'Utilitarianism' and 'classical political economy' could be. In keeping with the tradition of romantic critique, Thompson tended to pillory the political economists as a gang of Gradgrinds, as though one could deduce from 'the logic of capitalism' what its apologists must, ultimately, have been saying, rather than looking more closely at a body of thought that was both sophisticated and various. As with the Hammonds' earlier version of this story (to which Thompson always gave proper and respectful acknowledgement), the drama of a 'great transformation' from a 'customary' to an 'acquisitive' economy encouraged a degree of exaggeration in depicting each side of the alleged contrast.

Of course, Thompson's account, unlike the Hammonds', was informed by his acceptance—albeit wary and ambivalent acceptance—of the historical-materialist analysis of the friction between the development of the forces of production and the pre-existing social relations of production. Quite how far, or in what sense, Thompson, especially the later Thompson, should be regarded as a 'Marxist historian' has been much debated. Notoriously, some of his fiercest polemics were directed at those, such as the editors of *New Left Review* in the mid-1960s or Louis Althusser and his English admirers a little later, whom Thompson saw as so carried away by the heady abstraction of modern Marxist theorizing that they lost all feel for the knotty individuality of particular historical instances. But this may chiefly signal how far he was from being any kind of theorist rather than how far he was from being any kind of Marxist. His rich armoury of styles as a controversialist—satire, mockery, hyperbole, literary allusion, and so on—allowed him to register criticisms without descending to what he felt were the arid abstractions of 'critique'. As Eastwood has shrewdly noted, much of Thompson's polemical writing displays 'that heavy humour—a kind of irony heavily worn', which may be not the least of his debts to Marx. On the broader question, a careful reappraisal by Michael Kenny published a few years ago concluded that Thompson 'never wholly abandoned the teleological view that collective self-consciousness would lead to a socialist society as the highest expression of human liberation'—though any such vestigial faith became hard to discern in the gloomy, sometimes apocalyptic, tone of his later political writings and of his only novel, *The Sykaos Papers*, published in 1988.

Attempting a different kind of characterization, Kenny also observed that Thompson stood for 'bloody-minded opposition to state wrongdoing, the elevation of moral principle in politics above more immediate calculations of advantage, and the celebration of a libertarian tradition of political self-activity beyond the state'. In these and other ways, Thompson's own political thinking exhibited a continuity with the demonization of 'Old Corruption' (or what Cobbett liked to call 'The Thing') by those early nineteenth-century radicals whom he resurrected. He assumed an intermittent but recurrent struggle between 'the secret state' and political dissent, stretching from the radical societies' conflicts with Pitt's spies in the 1790s to END's accusations of covert MI6 surveillance in the 1980s. More generally, his writing was energized by the tacit presence of a divide between Us and Them, where Us tended to include working men and women, the unlucky, the dispossessed, the struggling, plus dissenters, mavericks, and critics; and Them consisted, more shadowily, of power, capital, the State, the Establishment, the comfortable, the condescending.

There are, needless to say, moments of political conflict where this kind of sharp binarism is what is called for and where it provides the only stars we need to steer by, but at other times it can too easily oversimplify political choices and obscure the interlocking kinds of role and agency that ordinary political processes involve. After all, 'we' (and, for that matter, 'they') may be, by turns, members of more than one of these groups, and the categories don't stack neatly into two piles. This is also where a kind of sentimentalism may come in: it not only suggests that anyone with a generous heart will come down on the side of the dissenter and the underdog, but that this is always the primary, and usually a sufficient, criterion for affiliation. In an analysis of Thompson's prose published in 1990, Renato Rosaldo pointed to its dramatic, even Dickensian, qualities, which enlist the reader in 'Manichaean battles between virtue and vice' on 'a field of combat where the middle ground has been eroded'. In Thompson's best writing, the effects of this Manichaean tendency were kept in check by his vivid historical imagination and keen grasp of the operation of unintended consequences; some of those writing under his inspiration gave it rather freer rein.

More generally, 'struggle' was a central word in Thompson's historical lexicon. The extended wranglings about the theoretical basis of the dynamics of 'class formation' chronicled in *The Making of the English Working Class* may have obscured the extent to which that book represented class-consciousness as the outcome of an essentially *political* process. Thompson's account emphasized the context of political repression after 1789 and, correspondingly, the place of agitation and organization as a political response. Moreover, the book constantly returned to the question of what kinds of public spaces and associations encouraged genuinely independent and critical political thinking—what, in an older idiom, were the conditions conducive to the practice of citizenly virtue. This motif also runs through the later work, though it is not always so immediately visible. Writing about 'custom' can invite a kind of misty-eyed continuism, but Thompson was sharply alive to the ways in which many practices lauded as 'customs' represented the hard-won *political* achievements of previous generations. Many such 'customs' originated as defensive or conservative responses to attacks on existing freedoms by the invasive power of new forms of agricultural or commercial efficiency, backed by the might of a state that acted in the interests of the possessing classes. (It is salutary to remember how much Thompson, now thought of primarily as a social historian, actually focused on the state in both his historical and polemical writing.) Although his work, early and late, addressed questions of large-scale historical change, his patient handling of the fragmentary, inconvenient traces left by obscure, obstreperous individuals was one expression of his conviction that history is made by 'ever-baffled, ever-resurgent human agents'.

IV

Some of Thompson's most direct and heartfelt political polemics may now have less purchase simply because a world in which the intricacies of Marxist theorizing could command mainstream intellectual attention seems so distant, just as his assault not merely on the case for nuclear weapons but on the broader Cold War mentality is bound to appear less relevant after the events of 1989 and 1991. However, even deeper changes may have conspired to lend a somewhat dated air to his central historical preoccupation. The conviction that the changes brought in by the Industrial Revolution represented a great primal wrong, whose humanly deforming effects were all around us, was already beginning to lose its compelling power even in the 1960s and 1970s. The opportunities opened up by the cultural changes of those decades may have had something to do with this; the continued shrinkage of manufacturing industry and the related decline of trade unionism have certainly played a part, as has the greatly enhanced, if unevenly distributed, prosperity of the last half century. Even the deep and still bleeding gash that Thatcherism cut through so many of the patiently accumulated decencies and solidarities of British society did not really provoke a general return to any kind of Morrisian diagnosis of the 'mutilation' of English society brought about by industrial capitalism, and the wider appeal of any such diagnosis now seems ever more diminished in the face of what Perry Anderson has called 'the virtually uncontested consolidation, and universal diffusion, of neo-liberalism'.

At the risk of indulging a temperamental inclination to counter-suggestibility, I would argue that Thompson's example is in some ways more valuable now than in his heyday in the late 1960s and 1970s, especially since his achievement can now be seen in the round. Thirty years ago there may have been too exclusive a focus on his contribution to 'social history' and too involuted a concern with the distinctiveness of his position on 'class formation'. In the wider society, organized labour was still able to flex, even to abuse, its political and industrial muscle, and Thompson's work could be seen by its critics as encouraging an indulgent, sentimentalized Leftism that endowed bits of sub-Marxist vocabulary with coercive power. But now, a triumphalist corporate capitalism operating within a consumerist facsimile of democracy holds undisputed sway, while it is more often the detritus of a debased postmodernism that clogs intellectual discussion in universities and on the Left, and this new situation could be said to give an even greater timeliness to the example of Thompson, the Great Refuser, than he had in more favourable circumstances.

Rereading Thompson now, when some of the theoretical or historiographical controversies around his work cannot help but seem a little stale and unprofitable, what comes through with undiminished force is his intense realization, on the basis of fragmentary or indirect archival material, of both the hardship and the resilience of working people's lives in the past—and this not as a series of generalizations but as a joltingly immediate fact about particular lives in particular times and places. For Thompson, writing history involved an act of political imagination, so habitual as to be second nature, by which the daily pressures under which the poor lived, above all the pressures of economic exploitation and political harassment, were not buried by what he once called 'clumpish' terms, such as 'culture' and 'class', nor bathed in the rosy glow of the comfortable modern reader's nostalgia, but focused in the most mundane details about the extent of the wasteland on which the Warwickshire cottager could run his pig, or about the number of days on which Cornish tin-miners supplemented their income by pilchard fishing, or about the wording of the by-law protecting the Northamptonshire labourers' 'liberty to cut rushes at Xmas and not after Candlemas'. This was not the flaccid 'bringing the past alive' of middlebrow popular history, nor the sanitized 'heritage' of a tour of a country-house kitchen. It was a form of moral respect that took the trouble to itemize the precariousness of others' lives and to appreciate the kinds of courage and sheer endurance needed to sustain them.

If we take a longer view of his career, linking his last book, on Blake, back to his first, on Morris, Thompson's sustained engagement with literature comes more into focus, especially with literature as a form of moral imagination or moral criticism. The inter-relations between his 'politics' and his 'history' (to use the conventional categories for the moment), and between his work in those domains and his role as a freelance writer and activist, now properly take centre stage. Though academic specialization and inward-lookingness have increased in the interim, the limitations of placing him in terms of purely scholarly or academic categories have, not altogether paradoxically, become more visible. We are now better placed to see how Thompson the 'Marxist historian' was also Thompson the 'cultural critic', taking his place in a long line of English cultural critics from Blake and Cobbett through Ruskin and Morris and on to Tawney and Leavis.

Indeed, we can now see more clearly how applicable to his own case were the terms in which he wrote of his comrade-in-arms Raymond Williams, the leading celebrant of this 'culture and society tradition'. Reviewing Williams's *The Country and the City* in 1975, Thompson, while admiring the 'scholarly mind' that had written it, insisted: 'But the book is not a conventional work of scholarship, and whoever attempts to read it in this way will end up only in disagreements and irritation. It is the work of a moralist wearing a literary habit...His social history is the history of a moralist with a profound sense of the process of capitalism.' Thompson may have had a still more informed and more concrete sense of the process of capitalism, certainly of the process that produced capitalism, than Williams, and his everyday wardrobe led him to be placed in the company of historians more than of literary critics, but otherwise the cap fits. To say this is not to slight or minimize his continuing impact on the work of later academic historians, but it does, I think, suggest how some of the 'disagreements and irritation' that his work still generates might more readily coexist with respect and admiration. After all, the fact that 'a moralist with a profound sense of the process of capitalism' may seem a comparatively rare, even exotic, creature these days surely ought to enhance rather than diminish his continuing value.

14

Olympian Universalism:
Perry Anderson as Essayist

I

'It should be a matter of honour on the Left to write at least as well... as its adversaries.' Such a conviction, expressed with an almost antique downrightness of tone, is not common in contemporary writing, and neither, perhaps, is the confident division of the world into 'the Left' and 'its adversaries'. Nor, for that matter, has the sentiment generally been well regarded by much of the Left itself, which has often been wary of style and stylishness, suspecting such genteel notions of cloaking confusions and distractions that serve the interests of the established order. There is, therefore, something doubly bracing about encountering this sentence in the editorial that in 2000 launched a new series of *New Left Review*, a journal that has been at the forefront of sustained, engaged intellectual work on the Left since its inception in 1960, but one that in its early decades was scarcely a byword for good writing. This setting makes the choice of idiom all the more arresting: a 'matter of honour', no less! We are clearly in the presence of a bracingly distinctive voice, one not to be trifled with.

The voice in question is that of Perry Anderson, who has been intimately involved with the direction of *New Left Review* throughout most of the forty-five years of its existence and who has long been acknowledged as a formidable and accomplished intellectual figure in his own right— comparative historian, social theorist, political analyst. Traditionally, the chief obstacles to good writing on the Left have been located in a certain remorselessness of political and theoretical zeal, an unlovely union of over-abstraction and the doctrinaire exposition of a party line. Anderson himself

Perry Anderson, *Spectrum: From Right to Left in the World of Ideas* (Verso, 2005).

has never conceded this charge; good writing, in his view, can take various forms and should not be thought incompatible with rigorous theorizing or trenchant political judgement. But in that same editorial he identified a new threat: he remarked (in terms quoted in the Introduction, above) 'the widespread migration of intellectuals of the Left into institutions of higher learning' over recent years, and immediately registered a warning of the 'tares' this move has brought with it, above all 'standards of writing that would have left Marx or Morris speechless'. In *Spectrum*, his new collection of essays, Anderson is (in a passage also quoted in the Introduction above) equally unsparing in itemizing 'the baneful effects' of academia: 'peer-group fixation, index-of-citations mania, gratuitous apparatuses, pretentious jargons, guild conceit.'

Taking a deliberate, at times almost haughty, distance from these dis–figuring fashions, *Spectrum* reveals a constant responsiveness to matters of style. The conservative philosopher Michael Oakeshott is roundly denounced for various political and logical failings, but at his best, it is acknowledged, 'his writing...can rise to a lyric beauty'. The arguments of a book on the British constitution by the Tory political commentator, Ferdinand Mount, are vigorously dismantled, but not without registering this 'graceful', 'stylish' work's 'cool prose' and 'light touch'. Similarly, Anderson judges that the first part of *Interesting Times*, the autobiography of the British Marxist historian Eric Hobsbawm, is 'the finest piece of writing this famously accomplished stylist has ever produced', and he describes Hobsbawm's tetralogy of works on the making of the modern world from 1789 to 1991 as written in 'a style of remarkable clarity and energy, whose signature is the sudden bolt of metaphoric electricity across the even surface of cool, pungent argument' (thus displaying his own credentials in the matter as well).

Brooding on this recurrent feature of Anderson's recent writing, I recalled the adage 'writing well is the best revenge'. In so far as this applies in his case, one might say that it is 'revenge' on history. In the 1960s and 1970s, it was possible for Anderson and his collaborators to believe that history was on their side, that the proper union of intellectual labour and working-class militancy would help bring about the socialist supersession of capitalism. Marx provided the main theoretical framework, Trotsky much of the political inspiration; among more immediate seniors, Isaac Deutscher and Ernest Mandel were stars to steer by. Anderson's writing of those decades, much of it published in *New Left Review*, did not feel the need to make many concessions to those who were uninitiated theoretically or unsympathetic politically. The task was too urgent, the stakes too high, and in any case the 'bourgeois' media were too complicit with capitalism and its political outriders. Anderson wrote several brilliant pieces during these years (as well as two major works of comparative history, *Passages from Antiquity to Feudalism* and *Lineages of the Absolutist State*), but though their brilliance may be undimmed even at this distance, one cannot help noticing how the whiff of sectarianism, of laying down the 'correct' line, now hangs about some of these articles like stale cigarette smoke.

The 1980s and 1990s administered a series of painful shocks to the milieu to which Anderson's early writing had been addressed. He himself appears to have undergone something of a political or intellectual crisis in the mid-1980s, leading him not just to reassess the prospects for the Left in a world dominated by the neo-liberalism of rampant capitalism, but also, one may infer, to reconsider the function of his own writing. Displaying an enviable resilience and capacity for self-renewal, he has committed himself to the ideal of 'uncompromising realism', however politically discouraging the findings of such realism may be. Whether as a result of this refitting, or because of changes in the public sphere of Western societies—or for quite other, literary, personal, or material reasons—Anderson, always a powerful analyst and coruscating polemicist, has emerged in the past fifteen years or more as one of the leading intellectual essayists of our time, read and admired far beyond any sectarian confines. In 1992, Verso (which he had helped to found as the publishing arm of *New Left Review*) issued two collections of his essays: *English Questions* brought together several already celebrated longer articles on the 'deviant' character of British history and politics, viewed from within a particular European Marxist optic, while *Zone of Engagement* collected pieces mostly focused on recent and contemporary theorists and political commentators. Several of the essays in the latter volume, in particular, are models of serious intellectual appraisal: deeply informed, ranging, severe. There are few writers whose name on the cover of a periodical constitutes an irresistible incitement to find out what they have to say—on whatever the subject may be—but I know I am not alone in putting Anderson in that very select company.

II

Spectrum is a collection of fifteen essays, all but one of them previously published, the great majority in the *London Review of Books* or *New Left Review*. The contents are arranged in a progression across the political spectrum: from 'the Intransigent Right' of Michael Oakeshott, Leo Strauss, Carl Schmitt, and Friedrich von Hayek, through the reformist conservatism of Ferdinand Mount and the anti-communism of Timothy Garton Ash, to 'the Adjustable Centre' of John Rawls, Norberto Bobbio, and Jürgen Habermas, and on to 'the Vanquished Left' of E. P. Thompson, Robert Brenner, Sebastiano Timpanaro, and Eric Hobsbawm (plus two slightly more marginal pieces on Göran Therborn and Gabriel Garcia Marquez). Although Anderson is on record as regarding decolonization and the women's movement as the most significant developments in human emancipation in the second half of the twentieth century, his subjects in this collection, it will be evident, are all European or North American (Marquez aside) and all male.

Two further, less easily classifiable, pieces are included in an appendix. The first is a sympathetic assessment of the *London Review of Books* from its inception in 1979 up to 1996 (the piece first appeared as the introduction to an anthology from the journal published in that year). The other is a remarkable essay, arresting and haunting, on Anderson's father and the Chinese Maritime Customs Service for which he worked, one of the most improbable organizations thrown up by the uneven history of imperialism, largely staffed by well-educated Westerners but answerable to the Chinese government. This piece has some of the satisfactions of amateur family history, delving into Anderson's Anglo-Irish military background, but here bolstered by his habitual command of the forces, both proximate and distant, at work in shaping world events, and in places inflected by tones not usually associated with his writing—delicate, painterly, compassionate.

The chief impression left by the best essays in this volume is one of extraordinary intellectual power. The analysis of the theoretical and empirical claims made in the work of its subjects is both dazzling and unyielding: they are 'critiques' in the full sense of that term in its original German philosophical usage—immanent reconstructions of the logic of ideas, deductions of the intellectual and sociological conditions of their possibility, withering exposures of their inconsistencies and omissions. His range is proverbial: it hardly seems fair that one man could move with such ease through the history of so many periods and regions or through so many different kinds of writing. The word 'magisterial' is overworked, often a slack synonym for 'impressive', yet if one attends to its definition— 'having the bearing of a master, invested with authority'—then the aura of omnicompetent grandeur about Anderson's writing makes the term irresistible. That the contemporary Left should possess such a voice, one in which radical political aspirations are blotted neither by phoney populism nor by rebarbative academicism, is important and heartening. Anderson remains an inspiring example of thinking in the world about the world and for the world.

Yet to what readership, so much of the world having changed, does Anderson now address himself, and from what vantage point, so many of the old doctrinal certainties having shrivelled, does he now write? One of the phrases that has been used to identify the characteristic perspective of Anderson's recent work is 'Olympian universalism'. The noun is obviously apt: not only is Anderson a staunch adherent of the Enlightenment tradition of unfettered rational analysis, but he is a univeralist in the geographical as well as the philosophical sense, attending impartially to developments in all parts of the world, the least parochial of writers—apart, I feel bound to say, from his constant (and, in its way, parochial) dismissiveness of English culture as incorrigibly sterile and hidebound.

But 'Olympian', too, does capture something that may be becoming more and more characteristic of his writing voice. One index of this which may at first appear inconsequential, no more than an idiosyncratic indulgence, comes, when once focused on, to represent a systematic self-distancing from the popular and demotic, and that is Anderson's deliberate deployment of a recondite, but non-technical, vocabulary. Where else in contemporary writing is one likely to come across the following terms, culled almost at random from among these essays: magma, taxative, lustration, censitary, carmagnoles, scoria, galumphery, alembicated, exaptation, caducity, postilla, plus near archaisms such as 'contemn', 'glozing', and 'moiety', as well as 'neuralgic' (used to characterize an argument) and 'brigade' used as a verb (a particular favourite of Anderson's)? In addition, the extent to which his prose is sprinkled with words and phrases taken from other languages puts him in company with older grandees of European letters such as George Steiner (he hits the true Steinerian note in such sentences as: 'Leopardi is the last major European writer to be a direct interlocutor of Antiquity'). Even omitting the many French terms that can plausibly lay claim to a presence in current educated English, we encounter *état gratuit*, *salonfähig*, *glacis*, *cabotage*, *guerres en chaîne*, *signum rememorativum*, *déphasage*, *en toutes lettres*, *chasses gardées*, *décombres*, *in nuce*, *fin de non recevoir*, *plumpes Denken*, and many more. No one could accuse Anderson's writing of playing to the gallery. Instead, he moves with confidence among the choice spirits of European culture, past more than present, capable of seeming as distant as, say, Petrarch or Spinoza from the street-wise Net-heads who define contemporary popular styles.

Except, of course, when it comes to politics, and with Anderson it always does come to politics—or, rather, it always starts there. The primacy of the political in intellectual life is the uniting and insistent theme of these essays, and 'politics is always a *Kampfplatz*', as he (characteristically) put it in his *New Left Review* editorial. The limply academic 'site of struggle' would be a poor substitute for the German term here: Anderson has in mind a more direct clash, between two opposing sides. The informing impulse of his analyses is to reveal how there always are only two sides. On this matter he speaks admiringly of the contention by the conservative German political philosopher and Nazi jurist Carl Schmitt that the defining feature of politics is the division between 'friend' and 'foe'. This insistence lends a certain spatial simplicity to Anderson's charting of the intellectual field. On first inspection, various thinkers may appear to have multiple affiliations or be otherwise hard to classify politically, but one of the most familiar cadences of Anderson's prose is the sound of digging beyond these surface distractions. For example, Ferdinand Mount may seem to be sympathetic to a number of radical constitutional reforms, 'but the generous note struck on these pages must still find its place within the score as a whole'; similarly, Garton Ash's 'sincerity' in criticizing the Western record in the Balkans may be 'beyond question', but his promotion of the notion of 'Central Europe' needs to be unmasked as 'ideological', possessing 'a hard policy edge'. The centre always turns out to be uninhabitable ground in Anderson's polarizing political topography: the 'logic' (a favoured term) of the underlying affiliations will out. Even iconic Left-liberals such as Habermas or Bobbio 'ultimately' (another favoured term) reveal their true colours; a highly critical account of the two philosophers' responses to 'successive wars waged by the West' in the 1990s concludes: 'The political complexion of such positions is clear enough.' In these pieces, Anderson acts as a zealous Health and Safety inspector on behalf of the Left consumer, insisting that a range of interesting writing be labelled 'Dangerous: may contain liberalism'.

The other governing intellectual strategy of Anderson's writing is, these days, more implicit: it might, unsympathetically, be termed 'the tyranny of deep explanation'. In parodies of old-style Communist rhetoric, a place was always found for the phrase 'it is no accident, comrade, that...', where the contention in question would assert a common causality linking two improbably distant developments. Anderson could no more be charged with crude economic determinism than with crude anything else. But a disposition to explain 'consciousness' in terms of 'social being' (to invoke Marx's canonical formula) lingers. As in so much contemporary work in the humanities and social sciences, especially of a self-described 'radical' inclination, a particular cachet attaches to 'explaining' ideas or aesthetic creations as the expression of some set of social circumstances assumed to be more fundamental. When this strategy is conjoined with a thoroughgoing insistence on the underlying topography of the *Kampfplatz*, one always risks hitting a paranoid note or seeming to understand history in terms of conspiracy theory writ large. One does not have to be committed to a know-nothing nominalism to find some of these proposed connections implausibly tight, just as one does not have to be a political innocent to find some of the alleged mechanisms implausibly sinister. Certainly, there are times in reading Anderson when history can seem like 'no accident' waiting to happen.

III

This set of intellectual dispositions seems most likely to pay dividends when addressed to the work of figures who directly engaged in the ideological debate of their time, such as Schmitt or Hayek. Less promising material is provided by figures who stuck closely to their own disciplinary protocols, such as John Rawls. For the most part, Anderson provides a full and fair recension even of those theories he goes on to criticize, but I detect signs of impatience in his dealings with Rawls, perhaps akin to the impatience that characterized the younger Anderson's dismissive remarks about British philosophy of the 1950s and 1960s. What he terms Rawls's 'complete abstension' from commenting on current affairs is surely one source of this impatience; Anderson expects thinkers to act as public intellectuals, especially when their trade is political philosophy. But a knock-on effect of the tyranny of deep explanation may be at work, too. Thus, in his powerfully forensic recent piece just mentioned on the responses of Rawls, Habermas, and Bobbio to the international conflicts of the end of the twentieth century, Anderson looks to (a selective description of) early political experience to account for the character of their respective philosophical enterprises: 'Service in America's war to regain the Pacific; a boyhood in Nazi Germany; underground resistance against Italian Fascism. It would be surprising if three such distinct experiences were without trace in the work of those who went through them.' 'It would be surprising' sets off uncomfortable echoes of 'it is no accident'. But would it be so surprising? It is not, after all and *pace* Anderson's second sentence, the *distinctiveness* of the three experiences that makes them likely to leave this kind of trace: it would have to be, rather, that in each case the formative power of the experience was strong enough and relevant enough to affect the later work. The experiences in question came early in these figures' respective lives, before any of them had embarked on their defining adult activity. Moreover, not only are the experiences different, but the genres of subsequent work were different, too. One can readily see why, in Bobbio's case, his having been involved in the partisan resistance to Fascism might stand in an illuminating relation to his writings on postwar Italian politics. But Rawls was doing philosophy, and both the Kantian and analytic traditions that shaped his work gave that enterprise something of a formal or autotelic character. Anderson's tactics with Rawls, who comes in for some rough handling in this book, may occasionally appear to deny this enterprise its own internal imperatives.

Hardly surprisingly, Anderson's gift for entering into and imaginatively possessing work on widely differing topics is most winningly displayed in his dealings with figures whose writing he for the most part admires. The essay here on Robert Brenner's attempt to track the impact of new forms of mercantile capital on English seventeenth-century politics is a prize example, tirelessly analytical without ever being reductive. Yet even in these essays, a certain *hauteur* or sharpness of reprimand occasionally obtrudes. At one point, he teasingly reproaches Eric Hobsbawm for a weakness for honours and similar emblems of acceptance by the British Establishment, but then adds, as though in partial exculpation of the great man's foible: 'In Britain an inability to resist gewgaws is anyway as common among eminent scholars—historians of all stripes foremost among them—as once African agents of the slave trade.' At first reading, I did not properly register the offensiveness of this comparison. Is he really saying that the acceptance of knighthoods or (in Hobsbawm's case) the Companion of Honour by contemporary scholars displays a weakness that is on a par with that of those African intermediaries who sold their compatriots into a life of slavery, suffering, and early death? No, no, one protests, he is simply looking for a telling comparison in the matter of being unable to resist 'gewgaws', and the gullibility of African slavers in this matter was once a truism. The allusion is scarcely hobbled by political correctness, and may be the more vivid for that, yet still one wonders why Anderson's literary imagination proposed such a gratuitously slighting comparison.

The tonal lapse in this instance may, most charitably, be read as an expression of Anderson's own pride in a kind of outsiderdom, a prickly resistance to any kind of Establishment incorporation (a position not impaired by the half-time appointment at UCLA that he has held for some years). 'Uncompromising realism' involves standing out against more than one kind of compromise. When in the same essay he cites the older historian's astringent comments on contemporary liberal democracy as indicating 'how unassimilable Hobsbawm's work is to any comfortable consensus', he is bestowing his highest praise. When, by contrast, he comments, apropos Hobsbawm's tendency to find silver linings in his otherwise sombre account of the triumph of global capitalism, that 'a resistance that dispenses with consolations is always stronger than one which relies on them', he is pulling moral rank.

Anderson stands apart in another, more elusive, way, too. Although he is without question immersed in the effort to understand the contemporary world—restlessly ranging from China to Peru, searching for causality, registering variety—there is a sense in which he does so in the manner of the great intellectual figures of the nineteenth century. He is essentially a private scholar, not a professional academic; he is at ease in several languages and, by contemporary standards, unimaginably well read in the whole European intellectual and literary tradition; he charts both the evolution of civilizations and the spasms of the Zeitgeist with a mixture of command and intimacy; his majestic, long-paced essays would not have been out of place in *La Revue des deux mondes* or the *Edinburgh Review* in their prime; and whether in discerning the movement of mind in contemporary thought or the movement of capital in the world economy, he habitually operates with an intellectual ambition that is little short of Hegelian.

These qualities make him 'untimely', in Nietzsche's sense, for all that his reading and engagement with the world are strenuously *à la page* (as he might put it). And this is another way in which matters of tone and style start to become revealing indices of self-positioning. At one point in his recollections of his former comrade and antagonist E. P. Thompson, Anderson records that Thompson 'chaffed me for impudence about Swift'. The slight archaism is perfectly judged, hinting at the school prefect ticking off his fag; the idiom catches his sense of Thompson's seniority, a complicating ingredient in their famous (and famously fierce) exchanges several decades earlier. Something similar recurs in his winning essay on the eccentric Italian philologist, political theorist, and proof-reader Sebastiano Timpanaro, where Anderson rounds out his portrait by saying: 'As for questions of character, his categories retained an eighteenth-century ring: his most frequent term of dispraise was *mascalzone*—"scoundrel".' One senses the appeal of such a vocabulary to Anderson himself. In his appreciation of Thompson, he recounts an anecdote in which Thompson asked a mutual friend what Anderson was up to these days. The friend mentioned that the latter was writing a piece on conservative thinkers (reproduced as the first chapter of *Spectrum*), to which Thompson retorted: 'Yes, I know. Oakeshott was a scoundrel. Tell him to stiffen his tone.'

For all his pessimism about the course of recent history, Anderson has retained his conviction that scoundrels should not be allowed to get away without, at the very least, a good thrashing. This, too, he implies, should be a matter of honour on the Left, and so, in keeping with this aristocratic code, a number of those who have given offence are 'called out', challenged to a dialectical duel, theories at twenty paces. Anderson gives them both barrels; this collection resembles the reading room of the club, temporarily turned into a field hospital, the mortally wounded gasping in every armchair. Some of these unfortunates were fellow-stylists, and there are occasional moments in Anderson's prose that suggest he may be tempted to shoot in the air, honour satisfied. But then some inner ancestral voice barks at him with military-gentry gruffness: 'Stiffen yer tone, Anderson.' And by God, Sir, he has.

15

Hegel in Green Wellies:
Roger Scruton's England

I

Condition-of-England writing is the product of a perceived acceleration in the pace of social change. We owe the term to Carlyle, writing in the 1830s, when the 'Condition-of-England Question' largely turned upon the nature of the link between a new form of economic activity (then just coming to be termed 'industrialism'), one promising undreamed-of material abundance, and a newly visible squalor and degradation in the living conditions of the urban poor. There had, of course, been forms of writing in previous centuries that had attempted to take the temperature of the body politic and in so doing to register novelty or bemoan loss. But the first half of the nineteenth century was confronted by what it experienced as a wholly new form of civilization: writers such as Cobbett, Carlyle, Ruskin, and company were moved to try to take stock because the changes seemed so unprecedented and appeared to be threatening to eliminate a whole established way of life.

Since then, a long line of writers has attempted to emulate the first practitioners of this subgenre in a manner that has become increasingly self-conscious and prone to advertise its own literary affiliations. It is a style of writing that lays claim to a certain dignity: it aspires to rise above mere journalistic opportunism in order to delineate enduring characteristics. Where it once confidently spoke of 'national character', it now, less psychologistically but no less prescriptively, speaks of 'national identity'. And the very existence of this body of writing has latterly been adduced as

Roger Scruton, *England: An Elegy* (Chatto, 2000).
Kenneth Baker (ed.), *The Faber Book of Landscape Poetry* (Faber, 2000).

a constitutive element of the national distinctiveness it seeks to describe: it
has become almost fashionable to claim, when totting up the medals tally
in the cultural olympics, that one consequence of (or, in some versions,
compensation for) being 'the first industrial nation' is that England has the
proudest tradition of social criticism.

We might do well, however, not to be too complacent about the merits of
some of the writing that aspires to be recognized as part of this condition-
of-England genre. After all, various interests, not all of them benign, can be
served by representing the present as a sad decline from a healthier or more
agreeable past. Faced with some of the most sweeping indictments, we need
to remember that such snapshots can, of course, only ever be selective:
there can be no such thing as a comprehensive description of a whole way
of life. If such selective accounts are to rise above the level of dyspeptic
grumbling, therefore, they need to possess three features. They must, first,
work with an informed understanding of relevant conditions in earlier
periods. Second, they need to deploy an analytical frame that possesses
sufficient explanatory power to prevent the account of change from merely
latching on to eye-catching but epiphenomenal details. And, finally, they
must appeal, however implicitly, to a realistic conception of human flourishing that will enable some kind of balance sheet of loss and gain to be
drawn up. Condition-of-England writing may be personal in tone and light
in literary touch, but, if it is to substantiate its claim to be a form of social
criticism, it has to take these historical and (the word seems unavoidable)
ethical obligations seriously. Letters from 'Disgusted of Tunbridge Wells'
do not, by and large, meet these requirements.

Nor, in fact, do most of those book-length jeremiads that became increasingly common in the course of the twentieth century. The supposed critical
force of such tracts rested upon a somewhat misty idea of 'old England',
'the real England', or 'essential Englishness', an implicit standard of social
health against which the pathology of the present could be measured.
And ever since the origins of this tradition in the early nineteenth-century
conjunction of Romanticism and industrialism, 'England' has largely been
identified with the countryside. The rural is allowed to function as a privileged locus of value, and the rural is always figured as under threat; hence
the need for the jeremiad. Somehow it is never those who are pressing to
build another estate of Barrett starter homes on a 'greenfield site' who are
seen as the champions of essential Englishness. In its attempts to arrest
change so as to 'preserve' one historically contingent state of affairs, writing
in this vein cannot altogether disguise its interested and partisan nature. Its
purported analysis of trends in contemporary society all too often turns out
to be a cross between a polemic and a cry of pain; it expresses a powerful

desire to *stop* things. At the extreme, farmers blocking motorways with tractors can be seen as the condition-of-England tradition on the hoof.

II

Mr and Mrs Scruton farm near Malmesbury in Wiltshire, we are told, and Mr Scruton, like other farmers, thinks England is going down the pan. Indeed, he thinks it's dead (or says he does), and sees himself as pronouncing its 'memorial address'. He recognizes that his is 'not the first such oration', but offers two excuses for adding to the existing stock of such writing: 'First, that it is a personal tribute; second, that it is an attempt to understand, from a philosophical perspective, what we are now losing as our form of life decays.'

The claim, made more than once, that the book is not to be judged as a work of history, since it is merely 'a personal tribute to the civilisation that made me', is disingenuous. It is true that in this vein we are given a few tantalizing glimpses of the young Scruton, cycling off to visit old churches or being treated with imaginative generosity (and whisky) by a sympathetic teacher. The book as a whole, however, is insistently ideological rather than autobiographical: we are time and again told not so much how certain things came to possess personal significance for Scruton himself, as how they really were, what the character of English society actually has been, and how that character is now being lost.

The one revealing, but also in some ways disturbing, autobiographical element concerns Scruton's treatment of his father, to whom he returns or alludes several times. Jack Scruton was born into the lower ranks of the northern industrial working class: one of eight children, two of whom died in infancy, he grew up in the back streets of Ancoats, child of a Lawrentian marriage between a physical, drunken father and a mother with genteel aspirations. The support of his mother enabled Jack to win a scholarship to Manchester High School and eventually to qualify as a teacher, later moving to leafy Buckinghamshire, where young Roger grew up. But Scruton *père* nursed a vivid sense of the grievances of his class. He was not just what is now called Old Labour, he was Paleo-Labour: the country was in the grip of a ruling class whose comfortable way of life rested upon the exploitation of the workers.

Scruton *fils* treats his father's political views with smooth condescension: the fellow was simply consumed by resentment, a kind of rancour that his son, with the advantages of his 'philosophical perspective', can see no grounds for. We get an unpleasant instance of this loftiness in the course of Scruton's remarks about public schools. It would appear that these schools stood out, and produced so many of the leading figures in public life, simply because of their educational superiority. 'Still, it cannot be denied that the public schools had an upper-class image'—only an 'image', mind—'and for those who resent such things, this was sufficient to condemn them. My father was one of those who resent such things.' Scruton's father, we gather, detested such institutionalization of privilege: he wanted to see the abolition of the public schools and grammar schools that helped to perpetuate social divisions. That was the view, Scruton tells us, 'which I had imbibed, not with my mother's milk, but with my father's gall, which was distributed with equal abundance'. The conclusion is dismissive: 'By and large, therefore, when it came to education my father was against it.'

The casual cruelty of this would-be *bon mot* does not diminish with rereading. Consider: we are told that as a child Jack Scruton showed an early hunger for things of the mind; a more educated neighbour played a crucial encouraging role; school opened doors onto a wider world, and he in turn then spent his life as a teacher. It would not be surprising to learn that he was, in his own rancorous way, deeply proud of his exceptionally clever, scholarship-winning son. The general tone of condescension with which Scruton writes about his father is bad enough, but that he should put him down with this flip witticism about education, of all topics, seems particularly gratuitous.

More generally, this 'attempt to understand, from a philosophical perspective' looks remarkably like an attempt to 'understand' from a *Daily Mail* perspective. As a philosopher, Roger of Malmesbury might be expected to practise a more searching form of analysis than that shared by Squire Scruton and his fellow-farmers, but readers hoping for some profound treatment of questions of national identity will be disappointed. In fact, in dealing with the fundamental structure of English (or any other) society, Scruton pulls off the difficult achievement of making himself sound stupid. 'Class comes about because we divide people up.' So, if we could just stop that silly habit, it wouldn't matter that those who control great concentrations of wealth can systematically determine the life chances of the many who do not. It is, perhaps unsurprisingly, characteristic of Scruton's 'philosophical perspective' to regard talk of 'class conflict' as overdone—another expression, no doubt, of that groundless 'resentment'. English history, we are told, has, thankfully, been pretty free of it. 'Popular unrest was minimal in England' ('class conflict', you understand, takes place only if the 'popular' side starts it).

Even such events as the notorious 'Peterloo Massacre' of 1819 are not allowed to contradict this general truth: 'The panic at St Peter's Field, in which eleven people died, resulted more from clumsiness than malice.' It is revealing of the impoverished scheme of historical analysis that Scruton brings to such matters that the episode could only be regarded as demonstrating any regrettable 'class conflict' if the action of the authorities could be ascribed to 'malice'. That might not be the only way to think about the decision to use mounted yeomanry and hussars to charge an unarmed crowd containing many women and children, especially in the context of other evidence about the relations between social tension and state power during the years after Waterloo. In addition to the eleven dead, there were over 400 injured, of whom 161 had to be treated for sabre wounds. 'Clumsy' indeed.

But happy is the land where people know their place, 'and here we come to the essence of the English experience of class. It was not snobbery but a kind of decorum that motivated the English people to seek out their separate spheres of belonging.' Scruton, it seems, would have us believe that families clubbing together in the back streets of Ancoats to try to prevent more of their children from dying in infancy were more or less on a par with titled landowners paying their subs at White's or Brooks's, and that the two groups chose to keep apart out of a kind of innate tact. At such moments, all this sub-Waugh attitudinizing ceases to seem amiably harmless, and falls into place as part of a wider cultural tendency whose effect is to distract our attention from what 'the experience of class' is actually about. A similar grip on social realities is evident in his discussion of the 'ineffable charm' of the public schools (an Old Wycombist himself, from the Royal Grammar School, High Wycombe, he seems rather to hanker after this 'charm'). The 'cool, objective' social order of these schools, he tells us, 'was the perfect apprenticeship for English society, and the real reason why people educated in public schools could advance so quickly in the world outside'. It would be merely rancorous, I suppose, to wonder whether it didn't have something to do with the fact that their fathers owned most of the sodding 'world outside'.

In these ways, the book is full of reminders that Roger of Malmesbury is also Roger of Salisbury, having been the editor of the right-wing *Salisbury Review* since it started in 1982. And indeed, *England: An Elegy* is a veritable compendium of purple-faced Tory whingeing. Taxation is always 'punitive'; sport, 'once a rehearsal for imperial virtues, has become a battleground for hooligans'; and, more generally, 'the old courtesies and decencies are disappearing'. These days 'the English have the highest divorce rate in Europe, regard marriage as a bore, are blatantly promiscuous, and litter the country with their illegitimate, uncared-for and state-subsidised offspring' (perhaps the Countryside Alliance might put up notices saying 'Bastards destroy others' enjoyment; please take them home with you').

It is difficult to see quite how such sloppy, sensationalizing prejudice is the expression of 'a philosophical perspective', or quite how it belongs in a 'personal tribute'.

Inevitably, the real villains of the piece turn out to be 'the intellectuals', by which Scruton means that relatively small number of 'seditious bigots' who 'make the most noise', not 'the far greater number of less prominent, more modest and more worthy intellectuals who have become priests, civil servants, dons and schoolmasters, humbly accepting their place in the *status quo*'. Actually, he is rather equivocal about the noise-makers and whether they are of any importance by comparison to the forelock-tuggers. At one point he says they 'do most damage', but he also says they don't really matter: they are 'no more part of the national culture than the background crackle is part of a radio programme'. The more one ponders what this simile tells us about Scruton's conception of 'the national culture', the more alarming it becomes. There is no place for such critics: they are just not on the same wavelength.

Other areas of English life benefit equally by being considered from this 'philosophical perspective'. The constitution ought to be his home ground, a chance to combine Bagehotian shrewdness with Dimbleby-in-the-Abbey reverence. Instead, we get this sort of thing: 'The monarch is in a real sense the voice of history, and the very accidental way in which the office is acquired emphasizes the grounds of the monarch's legitimacy. ' Got that? The phrase 'the accident of birth' is clearly hovering in the wings of this sentence, though in the case of an hereditary monarchy one would have to say it's an accident waiting to happen. What one might generously call the 'argument' here is actually Hegel's in *The Philosophy of Right*, but there it genuinely does form part of 'a philosophical perspective'. Scruton, however, is Hegel in green wellies, a born-again Tory ideologue masquerading as a once-born countryman.

III

Just as there are hobby farmers so there are hobby historians, playing at understanding the past, but actually able to walk away from the problems whenever the going gets rough. There is unsteadiness bordering on evasiveness in the way in which this book oscillates between offering extended interpretations of the English past and disclaiming any intention to be writing history. One cannot take at face value such statements as 'I speak of England as I knew it, not as the country might appear to the historian', in part because so much of the book deals with centuries before Scruton was born. Moreover, his assertions about, say, the Middle Ages or the seventeenth century are bolstered by occasional, highly selective, footnote references to works by professional historians (although one of his main 'authorities' is G. M. Trevelyan's *English Social History*, which was published in 1944).

Over and over again, therefore, he wants to insist that his account of English history is *wie es eigentlich gewesen*. Do you doubt that the English country house really did 'dispens[e] kindness and hospitality' and 'provid[e] in wise measure for all its many dependants'? 'The papers of the Verney family are sufficient proof of the day-to-day reality.' At other points he acknowledges that a constant repackaging of 'the rural theme' in English culture has helped to prevent 'people from perceiving that the England of their dreams was no longer a reality'. But even if this 'rural idyll' is 'a myth, it is a widely accepted one', and 'since myths that are accepted become as influential as truths, it is a myth we ought to examine'. Myths may become as influential as truths, but that does not make them as true as truths.

As always with such unspecific narratives of 'decline', it is hard to pin down where exactly things went wrong. When was 'England' last fully alive, according to Scruton? There are moments when one wonders whether the rot didn't set in as long ago as the sixteenth and seventeenth centuries, as in his lament that, after the depredations of the two Cromwells, Thomas and Oliver, 'the great monuments of medieval England now lie ruined or mutilated in the landscape whose spirit they shared'. At other times, 'England' still seems to have been a lived reality when it formed and inspired the schoolboy Scruton. One of his most idiosyncratic choices of a date for the Fall is 1888, a year as symbolically important for this romantic Tory as 1688 was for his Jacobite predecessors. 1888, should you have forgotten, was the year of the Local Government Act that abolished the 'ancient' system of county and parish administration, replacing the wise personal touch of local notables by the mere machinery of elected boards and what have you. The spirit of locality was then further desecrated when 'addresses too were bureaucratised', as what had been 'a steady descent from shire to town to street to the plot of English earth so haloed' was replaced by '"postcodes" whose impenetrable symbolism effectively wiped away the sense of place, and reinforced the common perception that the English are really living nowhere'.

There is a real question here about how far Scruton himself, a former professor of philosophy at Birkbeck College, London, and author of several serious works in aesthetics and the history of philosophy, actually believes any of this. At one point he descants upon 'the English tradition of nonsense', by which he does not mean the higher blather about the virtues of hereditary peerages, but the writings of Lewis Carroll, Edward Lear, and others. Here he observes astutely that much of this writing was 'a way to spiritualize the world without *believing* anything'. One cannot help wondering whether this insight should be applied to Scruton himself. He speaks, often and insistently, of the loss of that 'enchantment' with which the English way of life used to be blessed. But a project of deliberate 're-enchantment' is bound to be rather artificial and calculated. And perhaps that is why one feels so often in reading this book that it is all a bit *voulu*.

A genuinely personal memoir by such a gifted writer would have been full of interest, just as a journey through some of the now fallen monuments of the world of his formative years could have been both poignant and attractive. But it seems that in Scruton the will to ideology is just too strong. And, as the heat rises within him and his denunciations become more and more sweeping, so he forfeits whatever sympathy we might have been willing to extend to his personal anguish. 'The global economy, the democratisation of taste, the sexual revolution, pop culture and television have worked to erase the sense of spiritual identity in every place where piety shored up the old forms of knowledge and local custom fortified the moral sense.' Ah, the sweet cadence of it all! 'Where local custom fortified the moral sense': how the elegant lines of the verbal drapery disguise the stark outline of a recipe for intolerance and persecution. And the relation of his own life to these changes is so disingenuous: no beneficiary he, we are meant to assume, of 'the democratisation of taste' and 'the sexual revolution', whereas in reality, of course, the complex social and cultural changes behind these labels have been among the main forces opening up the possibilities of life to every lower-middle-class grammar-school boy of the 1950s (and many others).

Many of these forces have been at work elsewhere, Scruton concedes, but the situation is worse in England because the English have wilfully inflicted the damage on themselves (hence the title of the last chapter, 'The Forbidding of England'). The text at this point takes such a mad turn that one can only wonder whether those who have welcomed the tonic effect of this book actually got to the end of it. 'Venerable customs and wise institutions are under threat or already abolished', including 'English weights and measures, English currency, local regiments, the Royal Tournament—every practice in which the spirit of England can still be discerned'. The Royal Tournament?! We may leave aside the inconvenient fact, not mentioned by Scruton, that this particular way of playing soldiers was invented only in the 1880s. But what would be absolutely gobsmacking were it not the expression of a 'philosophical perspective' is the claim that 'the spirit of England' has been mortally wounded because we no longer cultivate the 'wise' and 'venerable' tradition of firing dummy rockets from bazookas in Earl's Court.

Once he's galloping across open country, there's no stopping him. 'Any activity connected with the hierarchy and squirearchy of Old England is now likely to be persecuted or even criminalised: not only hunting and gentlemen's clubs, but uniforms, exclusive schools, old ceremonies, even the keeping of national customs and the display of the national flag.' I'm sorry that I seem to have missed the criminalization of 'exclusive schools', and even the most casual observer of English society might feel that the 'persecution' of uniforms and old ceremonies still had a little way to go (which is not to deny that, expressed in more exact and discriminating terms, there is an argument to be made against certain fashionable forms of populist *ressentiment*). But there is more: in the less 'exclusive' schools, they aren't learning any proper history any more—nothing about 'the heroism of a Royal Navy devoted to its sovereign and able through its fortitude to "rule the waves" '. I wish I could say, like Simon Hoggart, that I made that bit up. Actually, you couldn't make it up. The BBC, we are solemnly told, is 'now devoted to abolishing what remains of the national culture'. And it sends little green men into your living room, too.

Scruton is not mad, but he has been so maddened by the painfulness of the contrast between aspects of the world he actually lives in and the world he would have liked to live in that he can no longer bear to give the former any close, discriminating attention. One can always feel sympathy for the disappointed lover without feeling obliged to accept his account of the unique wickedness and duplicity of the now vilified love object (one kind of blindness may just be replacing another). The real question is: does any of this matter, or is it just the cod-philosophical equivalent of P. G. Wodehouse, an agreeable distraction from the unpleasing realities of contemporary life?

I think it does matter, partly because it helps to prevent people gaining a genuinely historical understanding of the relation of the present condition of their society to its past (and may therefore help to make them more receptive to alarmist or disingenuous prescriptions for dealing with the supposed maladies of that condition), and partly because it sells the life of the mind short. It is sometimes said, even by those who recognize that some of Scruton's views are batty, that his is nonetheless a refreshingly independent, unfashionable position, expressed with some flair and given a rigorous philosophical grounding. That may, or may not, once have been true, but it is certainly not true now. The fact is that 'philosophical Toryism' is the new *chic*. 'Stylish', donnish' conservatives are to the op-ed pages what celebrity chefs are to television. Scruton plays this part well, as willing to refer to Kant in the *Financial Times* as he is to tog himself out in hunting pink for the benefit of the cameras. But the claim to intellectual rigour is exaggerated: on the evidence of this book, at least, one would have to conclude that its author has now come to rest in some lay-by of the mind, where he no longer has to pursue strenuous argument and can instead sink back into the comfort of a few well-worn, familiar prejudices.

England: An Elegy ends by returning to 'my father's early lessons in discontent', albeit only in order to emphasize 'a feature that is seldom mentioned by the historians of radical thought, and unnoticed by our modern reformers'. Jack Scruton told his son he only had to look out of the window at 'the desecrated townscape of High Wycombe' to see that it was the owners of capital who were ultimately responsible for despoiling the country. Scruton Junior's rebellion against the values preached by his Labour-voting father has been long and public, and, as we have seen, he is still inclined to patronize him for his unyielding 'resentment'. But at this point he betrays an interestingly unsteady response to his father's lesson. His ostensible purpose in setting up this final vignette is to show that his father, too, was really animated by love of place, and so was really 'a patriot'. But in passing he reflects that perhaps his father was not 'wholly wrong' in identifying 'big business' as among the 'forces that were disenchanting England'. Scruton senior, it seems to me, was talking about something more structural than the 'disenchanting' of England, but even this half-recognition of something in his father's case means the book ends on a deeply incoherent note.

For, it has to be said that any properly serious endorsement of his father's view here would be fatal to the general scheme of Scruton's 'elegy'. In his discussion earlier in the book of changes in the City of London, Scruton gives the impression that capitalism was fine as long as the fund managers wore the old school tie and their word was their bond. But that England, too, has now disappeared and been replaced by 'the world of fast bucks, informal manners and cheerful offers of unmeant friendship; the world of takeovers, asset-stripping, insider trading and multinational capital'. This is, yet again, a rantingly undiscriminating list: it might not require a rancorous, knee-jerk radical to suggest that 'informal manners' and 'multinational capital' are not quite on a par as forces shaping the world. However, when in his final chapter Scruton is deploring the loss of those institutions that sustained local communities, such as 'the village shop', or when he cries out that 'England is becoming a no-man's land, an "elsewhere", managed by executives who visit the outposts only fleetingly, staying in multinational hotels on the edges of the floodlight wastelands', he seems to be hovering on the brink of recognizing that this may have something to do with 'the world of takeovers...and multinational capital'.

Were Scruton really to follow through on his father's insight and analyse contemporary society in its light, he would be establishing a genuine, rather than merely cosmetic, connection with his nineteenth-century predecessors as social critics. But it would, of course, make Scruton more a William Cobbett than an Edmund Burke, more a William Morris than an Evelyn Waugh. For the fact is that the unsleeping destructive energy of capital seeking to maximize its returns is not going to be tamed by a spot of huntin', shootin', and fishin'. It is not going to be tamed by a spot of Anglicanism, either, or any other prettied-up form of 're-enchantment'. It might, possibly, be tamed by a spot of Socialism. But in that case perhaps both Squire Scruton and Roger of Malmesbury could be a bit more generous in acknowledging that old Jack Scruton had a point after all.

IV

'Land' is, appropriately, the final word of Scruton's book, and its dual meaning, both *patria* and plot, has been readily exploited by those who seek to identify 'the country' with 'the countryside'. What is hymned here is not the blood-soaked soil of the French tradition of *notre terre, nos morts*, but more what one might call the National Trust model, a 'shared' past enshrined in places of beauty. (The National Trust itself, founded in 1895, still defines its purpose as being 'to preserve places of historic interest or natural beauty permanently for the nation to enjoy'.) This model encourages a conditioned response that tends to experience the historical as beautiful and the beautiful as historical, and both as displayed pre-eminently in landscape. The conjunction of verb and adverb in the National Trust statement expresses the informing sensibility (and, by implication, the corresponding anxiety): 'to preserve... permanently'. This is intended to reassure (to reassure donors, among others); change is equated with destruction, with loss, and so change is to be held at bay, for ever. Sentiment, including patriotic sentiment, can safely be attached to something that promises to escape transience. England is beauty, beauty England: 'that is all/Ye know on earth, and all ye need to know'.

Such is the power of this widely ramifying cultural pattern that a sentence like the following can easily slip by without anyone noticing: 'The spirit of a country is found in its history and its landscape.' But in fact the air ought immediately to be filled with the clamour of begged questions. Why should 'a country', whatever that is (is Northern Ireland a country? was Yugoslavia?), have a 'spirit'? What kinds of continuity does this suppose: did Mercia have the same 'spirit' as the West Midlands, has the 'spirit' of the domains of the Dukes of Burgundy been divided up between France,

Belgium, the Netherlands, and Luxembourg? Is everything that happened in a country's history an expression of its 'spirit', and, if not, then what criteria of selection are being brought to the interpretation of that 'history'? And why should one think that this elusive quality will be found in its 'landscape' rather than, say, its waste-disposal system?

The sentence in question comes from the introduction to Kenneth Baker's anthology of 'landscape poetry', and he does not pause to ponder its potential pitfalls. Indeed, there is much that Baker does not pause over, including, one must conclude, the scope and title of his anthology itself. It is not, of course, an anthology of just any 'landscape poetry', whatever that is: it is a collection of poems (and extracts from poems) in English that can be said to have some connection with particular parts of—well, of where? 'Britain and Ireland' seems the least misleading geographical expression, though in practice the concentration is heavily on England. Baker uses the first-person plural with a politician's readiness and speaks blithely of 'our country' throughout. Perhaps someone should send him a copy of Seamus Heaney's playful but just rebuke to earlier anthologists of 'British poetry'.

Baker's introduction is full of such cosy *obiter dicta*, which function as a kind of literary Ovaltine, soothing away the cares of the day and helping the mind to stop working. The fact that this volume seems to be aimed at the Christmas-present market should not obscure the ways in which it can be seen as the etiolated, genteel cousin of the once-proud tradition of 'condition-of-England' writing. 'Landscape poetry' embodies the Arcadian premiss, the world we have lost or are in the process of losing. This affiliation is evident in, for instance, Baker's observation that 'developers and industrialists' have had 'scant regard for the consequences of their actions', resulting in 'polluted rivers, slagheaps, pylons, urban villas taking the place of ancient forests, and concrete everywhere' (you see what I mean about dyspeptic grumbling). And he ends on the authentically minatory note: 'We are the losers now, but the greater losers are the generations yet to come.'

The sound of Kenneth Baker banging in his fence posts to keep out change is especially rich coming from a politician who held government office throughout the Thatcher years, including such positions as Minister for Information Technology at the Department of Trade and Industry and Secretary of State for the Environment. Similarly, I may have missed it but I have to say I don't recall that those who share Scruton's 'philosophical perspective' were in the forefront of opposition to those 'reforms' of the 1980s that ushered in the latest phase of 'liberalized' markets. And this, surely, is the disabling paradox of modern 'conservatism'—namely, that it wants simultaneously to liberate market forces and to lament the effects of market forces. Hence the deep structural dilemma of the modern Tory social critic: the forces that are destroying all that he loves are the forces he is ideologically committed to supporting. Unable to recognize let alone resolve the paradox, his only response is to pull on the wellies, to stuff a copy of Wordsworth into the pocket of his Barbour, to jump into the four-wheel drive, and to thank God that there are some things that even those blasted intellectuals can't spoil.

PART II

READING MATTERS

16

'The Great Age':
The Idealizing of Victorian Culture

I

When one reflects on all the bitterness that has been expended both in defending and attacking the Victorians, one cannot but regret that Queen Victoria was so long-lived. Had the great Victorians lived under three or four sovereigns, they would be judged on their own merits instead of being regarded as embodiments of an epoch which owes the illusion of its spiritual unity to the longevity of a single person.

Thus Hugh Kingsmill, quintessential bookman of the inter-war years, reflecting in 1932 on the changing reputation of the Victorians. By that date, three decades after the Queen's death on 22 January 1901, there had certainly been a good deal of both 'attacking and defending'. Not that critics of what was already referred to as 'Victorianism' had waited for the passing of the obstinately long-lived sovereign before weighing in against some of the alleged defects of British society during her reign. From Swinburne and Samuel Butler onwards, several late-nineteenth-century writers had inveighed against moralism and hypocrisy as characteristics displaying a natural affinity for the adjective 'Victorian'. But it was the immediate post-Victorian generation that had most famously breathed a long sigh of relief as the stays of respectability and prudery were released, and 'Victorian' became, in the first two decades or more of the twentieth century, a byword for stuffiness, pomposity, and (in a word put into circulation by an eminent 'Victorian') 'philistinism'. The canonical anecdote that has long served to symbolize the energies fuelling this reaction tells of Lytton Strachey,

This essay was originally written for an issue of the *Times Literary Supplement* marking the centenary of the end of 'the Victorian age' in January 2001.

on entering the drawing room of the emancipated Stephen sisters in 1908, pointing to a stain on Vanessa's dress and exclaiming 'Semen?' 'With that one word,' recorded Virginia hyperbolically, 'all barriers of reticence and reserve went down.'

Bloomsbury's adolescent desire to shock has received more than its share of subsequent attention, but by the time Strachey was making his literary name with *Eminent Victorians* in 1918 and his biography of the Queen herself in 1921, more serious reappraisals of the Victorian age were already under way, not all of them unsympathetic. Indeed, Kingsmill went on to observe that although 'by 1914 the prestige of the Victorians had sunk to its lowest level', in 'the ten years since Strachey's *Queen Victoria*, they have been celebrated with an ever-increasing respect and even tenderness'.

Representations of a previous era almost always serve several cultural functions simultaneously. In these terms, what one sees at work in the early and middle decades of the twentieth century in Britain is the dialectic between celebrations of the escape from Victorian*ism* and laments for the lost Eden of Victorian *culture*. The first part of this dialectic is extremely familiar, but its partial opposite may be rather less so. For what emerged in the inter-war period and then went on to colour a wide range of subsequent intellectual attitudes was a lament for the assumed structural conditions of Victorian cultural life, rather than for its specific intellectual and aesthetic content. At its heart was a nostalgia for a serious reading public.

In reflecting on the centenary of Queen Victoria's death, it would, presumably, be perfectly possible *not* to mention G. M. Young's *Victorian England: Portrait of an Age*, but such abstinence would surely be a little wilful. For that short book (barely more than a long essay), first published in 1936, probably did more than any other single work to disseminate a positive view of the period, once the heady exhilaration of Stracheyan debunking had died down. Young's book was in many respects a mannered, belletristic performance, evocative rather than analytical, addressed to a highly literate readership (the epigraph in ancient Greek remained, unattributed and untranslated, through all reprintings). But it had no rival as an introduction to the period until the publication in 1962 of Kitson Clark's *The Making of Victorian England*, a work that attempted to synthezise the research of the first generation of professional historians to address themselves systematically to Victorian sources (Young was a cultivated man, widely read in Victorian writings of all kinds, but he could hardly be said to have pursued 'research').

Not that Kitson Clark represented a radically different sensibility, as was made plain when, in a remarkable act of piety and (surely misplaced?) scholarly zeal, he issued an 'annotated edition' of Young's *tour de force*

in 1977, identifying (and tactfully correcting) Young's numerous buried
quotations and allusions, supplementing (and, scarcely less often, correcting) his selective, impressionistic account of men and events. The 'portrait',
as Young interpreted it—an extended, meditative, opinionated essay,
exuding familiarity with its subject rather than reporting new scholarly
findings—has long since ceased to figure among the approved academic
genres, but it perfectly suited Young's genial, somewhat post-prandial,
style. The original text had run to little more than 150 pages, but Kitson
Clark's digressive enthusiasm bulked this out to an 'edition' of 400 pages.

The influence of Young's book is, however, only part of my justification
for risking culpable predictability in focusing on a quotation from its
pages. For, it is the terms in which Young contrasted the Victorian age
with his own that now seem so revealing of the functions of an ideal of
Victorian culture in subsequent decades. 'As I see it,' he wrote with an
untroubled confidence our own age might, in its turn, feel inclined to envy,
'the function of the nineteenth century was to disengage the disinterested
intelligence, to release it from the entanglements of party and sect—one
might almost add of sex—and to set it operating over the whole range of
human life and circumstance'. Young applauded the way this 'disinterested
intelligence' had won many victories over 'ignorance or convention or
prejudice or greed' in the early and mid-Victorian decades, but he saw it as
having faltered thereafter, and he had no hesitation in identifying the main
culprit. 'Fundamentally, what failed in the late Victorian age, and its flash
Edwardian epilogue, was the Victorian public, once so alert, so masculine,
and so responsible.'

By the early years of the twentieth century, the rot had set in: 'the English
mind sank towards that easily excited, easily satisfied, state of barbarism
and childhood which press and politics for their own ends fostered, and on
which in turn they fed.' The terms in which he chose to generalize his case
are revealing of the implicit ideal: he described the present as characterized by 'the increase of routine and specialism on one side, the extension
of leisure and amusement on the other'. Both are contrasted with 'a serious
and liberal habit of mind'. Thus the period of, the late nineteenth and early
twentieth centuries is arraigned—'That time has left its scars and poison
with us'—but 'the great age' is still within reach, and Young concludes in
elegiac but minatory vein, calling his countrymen back to that age's ideal of
'the disinterested mind' before it becomes too late.

Indeed, Young himself represented a Victorian type that was starting
to acquire dodoesque status during his lifetime (born in 1882, he lived to
be 77). Greats at Oxford had been followed by a period as a Prize Fellow
of All Souls, and then a somewhat miscellaneous career as civil servant,

temporary diplomat, and man of letters. The very structure of his career was nostalgic, more closely resembling the plural public identities of his Victorian predecessors than the specialized activities of his increasingly professionalized contemporaries and successors. Few of the latter, after all, could have spoken so confidently of 'the function of the nineteenth century' nor so dismissively of the present having fallen into a 'state of barbarism and childhood'.

In drawing out the polemical bearing of his 'portrait', then, Young chose to emphasize the positive role of 'the Victorian public' and its subsequent decline in two equally undesirable directions—towards 'amusement' and 'specialism'. Looked at in this way, his book can be seen to take its place among those many laments about the 'disintegration of the reading public' that particularly flourished in (even if they were by no means confined to) the first few decades of the twentieth century. Any narrative of 'disintegration' requires the positing of an earlier 'wholeness', and one of the main functions served by reconstructions of Victorian culture in the first half of the twentieth century was to give historical location to the ideal of an 'integrated' culture, one not stratified between highbrow and lowbrow nor compartmentalized by 'specialism'.

But Young, it will be seen, did not entirely exonerate the Victorians themselves. His most intriguing criticism of where things started to go wrong in the later decades of the century concerned education (he had worked at the Board of Education when a civil servant). In one crucial respect, the public schools had failed. The education they offered, he acutely noted, was an education 'for an aristocracy rather than for a clerisy, and while an aristocracy can live a long while on its conventions, it is the business of a clerisy to keep all conventions under review, to maintain an informed and critical resistance against the propagandist, the advertiser, and all other agents of the mass-mind'. The public schools had instead come to give priority to a 'vaguely social, vaguely moral' conventional code.

The terms of this indictment are particularly revealing, since they illustrate from another angle that the feature of the early- and mid-Victorian period with which Young's affinities, nurtured by his classical education, were closest was that of an intellectual class that was at once critical yet culturally central. But his phrases here also seem uncannily similar to those employed in more familiar denunciations of the corruption of the times. For, the urgent need 'to maintain an informed and critical resistance against the propagandist, the advertiser, and all the other agents of the mass-mind' was a theme much dwelt upon by that strain of native *Kulturkritik* that flourished among 'educated' commentators on the rise of 'mass society' in the inter-war years. In particular, it was ceaselessly reiterated through the

1930s and beyond by F. R. Leavis and his fellow Scrutineers. The suave Toryism of the retired civil servant turned metropolitan man of letters may appear to have had little in common with the embattled provincial earnestness of the *Scrutiny* circle, but their common revulsion from features of contemporary 'popular culture' led them to look back to the mid-Victorian period with what was in some ways a similar nostalgia.

This nostalgia was most heavily invested in an ideal of the great Victorian reviews and their assumed public. From the earliest years of *Scrutiny*, which was launched in 1932, it was axiomatic that this public had now disappeared. For example, Denys Thompson, one of Leavis's closest associates, writing in the journal in 1935, could refer almost off-handedly to 'the disintegration of the reading public' as having been 'described elsewhere', and he confined himself to the unargued assertion that the great quarterlies in their heyday 'drew life from an educated, responsible and homogeneous public, to which they gave expression and coherence'. The rise of mass society undermined this, and 'the War destroyed the last vestiges of the nineteenth-century tradition in journalism, by increasing the demand for cheap stimuli, and supplying improved machines to meet it'. Thereafter (as I discuss more fully in the following essay), it became almost commonplace in literary circles to hark back to the world of the great Victorian reviews, an admiration not usually based on any deep familiarity with the crumbling bound volumes themselves, but one rooted in the need to be able to point to a previous state of health against which the ailments of the present could be charted.

II

It is always difficult to distinguish fact from fantasy in narratives of cultural decline, since tendentious selection and culpable exaggeration usually combine to misrepresent the nature and scale of actual changes, until all the delicate shadings of grey are crayoned over in deepest black. Many Victorian commentators had themselves lamented the loss of that 'commonwealth of readers' that the eighteenth-century men of letters were presumed to have been able to take for granted, and each generation embroiders this fantasy after its own pattern. Nonetheless, where the role of the press was concerned, there were some real changes that anxious cultural critics could point to. Here, the date which, for many early twentieth-century observers, symbolically marked the final passing of Victorian culture was not 22 January 1901 but 4 May 1896, the day that saw the launch of the *Daily Mail.* Indeed, it is hard to exaggerate the place of the Harmsworth press in the demonology of critics of 'mass culture'. Fact and phantasmagoria are particularly hard to disentangle here, since the success of the *Daily Mail* was actually quite a good index of the kinds of changes that so disturbed early twentieth-century cultural commentators.

It is important to recall that, prior to the launch of the *Mail*, there was no really popular national daily newspaper in Britain. There were, of course, the established morning dailies addressed to those comfortably-off, well-connected (predominantly but not exclusively male) readers who made up the governing and educated classes of mid-Victorian Britain. These staid publications carried verbatim reports of debates in parliament, often running to many pages, synopses of foreign and diplomatic news provided by the wire services, and in some cases financial news and price movements, all in similar-looking picture-free columns of closely set type. *The Times*, the undisputed eminence, may have catered well to the needs of the gentleman in his club in the 1860s and the *Telegraph* met some of the needs of the prosperous middle-class commuter in the 1870s, but they did not cater at all to the mass readership that was being created as a result of the Education Acts of the 1870s and 1880s, which were to make elementary education compulsory in Britain for the first time. Apart from their other defects, these solemn productions were too expensive: *The Times* cost an exorbitant threepence, and even the cheapest of them cost a penny. By 1895 the population of the United Kingdom had grown to about forty million, but it has been calculated that all the morning newspapers in the country taken together sold only a million copies.

The economic and technological preconditions for mass-circulation journalism had in fact been falling into place in the course of the nineteenth century. The spread of the railway network had transformed the process of getting the papers to readers anywhere in the country and had thus made truly national newspapers possible. The manufacture of paper had been revolutionized and cheapened with the introduction of wood pulp, and the invention of the mechanical linotype composing machines had enormously speeded up the business of printing a newspaper. The restrictive stamp duty had been lifted from newspapers in the middle of the century, further encouraging the growth of a vigorous and influential provincial press, but no national daily had arisen to take advantage of these conditions. One or two had been briefly tried but had failed. The diagnosis of the reasons for the failure in the late 1880s of one of them, called The *Morning*, was, as a contemporary put it, 'that it had a cheap look, and though the British public worships cheapness it abhors the appearance of cheapness'. By the middle of the 1890s, the sales of inexpensive popular novels and similar material showed that there was now a larger than ever reading public in existence, but, as Matthew Engel has pointed out in his excellent history of the popular press, *Tickle the Public*, no national morning newspaper existed that addressed the interests of more than a fraction of that public.

Alfred Harmsworth, setting up in business with his younger brother Harold, later to be Lord Rothermere and a newspaper proprietor in his own right, saw what would now be called a market niche, perhaps even a window of opportunity, and, after a great deal of canny advance publicity, they launched their new morning daily in May 1896. The *Daily Mail* was in several respects a new kind of newspaper. For one thing, it had news in it, as opposed to lengthy accounts of the regular public doings and sayings of those who had traditionally been considered the leaders of the country. Its reporters wired in vivid accounts of everyday dramas such as fires and murder trials. Any new paper needs luck, and the *Mail*'s early days happened to coincide with a particularly gruesome child murder case, always good for sales. Another novelty was that it cost only a halfpenny, and at the beginning of the twenty-first century we hardly need reminding how price-cutting can boost the sales of even quite poor newspapers. And, thirdly, it was written in a lively, colloquial style, concentrating on what would now be called 'human-interest' stories.

But more important still in some ways, Harmsworth had realized that what was wanted was a racy, newsy, genuinely popular paper that nonetheless retained the air of respectability. Though it seems almost unimaginable now, the *Daily Mail*, the harbinger of popular, even tabloid, journalism, was in appearance a broadsheet that followed the precedent of *The Times* and devoted its front page entirely to advertisements rather than news—and, even more surprisingly, it continued with this conservative practice right up until the Second World War. In other words, what Harmsworth got right was to produce a newspaper that was cheap, but without the appearance of cheapness.

The very success of the *Daily Mail* changed the nature of the press in Britain. There is no way of knowing quite how many copies it actually did sell at first, since audited sales figures were a thing of the future. It *claimed* almost 400,000, 'a world's record for a first number', as it immodestly but unreliably boasted in its second number. This was at a time when the *Telegraph*, the most successful of the older penny papers, claimed a maximum circulation of almost 300,000, and the more expensive and even more august *Times* only something around 50,000 copies (though it had many times that number of *readers*). Modern historians, ever sceptical of such claims, have concluded that the *Daily Mail* probably sold far fewer copies at first than it boasted, perhaps only half that number, but the circulation climbed steadily, reaching 400,000 in 1898 (and over twice that number on some of the more dramatic days of the Boer War), averaging around 700,000 in the years before the First World War, finally passing a million in the early 1920s.

Harmsworth, all the evidence makes clear, had a journalist's instincts, which means that respectable opinion branded him a ruthless sensationalist, but he was also the first figure to demonstrate the power, including political power, of the popular press. The support of his growing stable of newspapers, of which the *Mail* was the flagship, became an important concern of governments, especially Conservative governments promoting the policies of imperialism in general and the Boer War in particular. But, in a manner that has since become all too familiar, even ostensibly non-conservative governments could seem desperate to keep on good terms with him, and thus it was that he became Sir Alfred Harmsworth, then Lord Northcliffe, and finally in 1917 Viscount Northcliffe. He died in 1922, having declined into clinical insanity a couple of years previously; indeed, he thought he had been poisoned by Belgian ice cream and in his last days issued a briefly observed diktat that the paper should not cover Belgian news, perhaps the earliest example of British tabloid hostility to Brussels.

III

In the terms in which G. M. Young characterized the signs of decline, the *Mail* thus represented the corrosive power of mere 'amusement'. But what of that other unhealthy symptom, the increase in 'specialism'? Again, this complaint had been heard often enough long before Victoria's death; indeed, the modern generic sense of 'specialist' and 'specialization' is a nineteenth-century coinage. As an expression of cultural anxiety, complaints about excessive specialization ranged across a wide spectrum of occupations and pursuits, from politics to sport, but the contrast with mid-Victorian culture was deployed above all to point up the perils of intellectual specialization, especially as represented by the increasingly professionalized academic world. Once more, there were real changes here, but yet again they were often perceived in distorted or exaggerated form. It is true that from the 1870s onwards new universities had been set up in the great industrial cities of the North and the Midlands, and that new disciplines began to differentiate themselves there as well as at the older universities. More significant still, perhaps, were the beginnings of what was to become a well-defined, essentially endogenous, academic career structure, something that had not been available for those Victorian gentlemen-scholars and men of letters who, among their various identities, may for a while have been Fellows of Oxbridge colleges.

One feature of this development much lamented by early twentieth-century commentators was the supposed 'withdrawal' from the sphere of public debate that this more self-contained and inward-looking academic culture was supposed to have entailed. Here, the founding of discipline-based specialist journals, dividing up between them the kinds of concerns that had been treated side by side in the mid-Victorian periodicals, seemed in retrospect to have signalled fragmentation of another kind. Thus, the *Law Quarterly Review* had been started in 1884, the *English Historical Review* in 1886, the *Classical Review* in 1887, the *Economic Journal* in 1891, and so on. Symbolism of a different sort could be found in the establishment of the British Academy, an institution devoted to the pursuit of pure scholarship by experts in their respective fields, an institution deliberately placing itself at one remove from that 'impure' world of high-Victorian literary and political writing that was now coming to seem, when measured against the high ideals of *Wissenschaft*, largely peopled by amateurs and partisans. Here, too, chronology conspired to create a sense of two disjunctive epochs: the centenary of Queen Victoria's death is also the centenary of the meeting that led to the founding of the British Academy.

Cultural specialization of another kind was evident in the way in which the literary and artistic movements we have come to call 'Modernism' developed for the most part in self-conscious antagonism to, and calculated removal from, the forms and outlets that catered to popular middlebrow taste. Indeed, the whole vocabulary of the classification by 'brow', beginning with the importation from the United States of the terms 'highbrow' and 'lowbrow' in the course of the 1910s, was taken to be further evidence of new forms of commercial and aesthetic stratification. When contemporaries protested against the deliberate cultivation of 'difficulty' by Modernist writers in the 1920s, the sometimes explicit (and nearly always implicit) model of desirable relations between writer and public was provided by the assumed accessibility of the great Victorians and their deserved commercial success.

These perceptions were filtered through a range of contemporary anxieties, but a frequent element was a return to the Victorian 'sages' who, mocked or disregarded in the decades immediately following their deaths, could now be retrieved and admired for their polymathic range and level of cultivation. For example, the inter-war years saw a minor Arnoldian revival on these grounds. In the uneasily professionalizing world of the humanities in the first part of the twentieth century, one way to emphasize one's distance from (and superiority to) the diligent pedantry that was seen as the *déformation professionelle* of the zealous new professionals was to identify with the Victorian men of letters, and the picture of Victorian culture as one long, well-mannered, interdisciplinary seminar may still serve some related uses today.

Hugh Kingsmill was right to suggest that the mere accident of Victoria's longevity created the illusion of a unified period, and this was further reinforced by the fact that none of the succeeding periods acquired such a distinctive and long-lasting label. 'Edwardian', hitherto a technical term referring to medieval architecture during the reigns of the first three Edwards, did indeed become current, but 'Edwardian culture' has never established itself as an autonomous presence, remaining, in Young's terms, 'the flash epilogue' of the Victorian age. 'Georgian' has only really lasted in reference to a particular school of poetry, and those invocations in the early 1950s of 'the new Elizabethan age' now look as dated and contrived as yesterday's election manifesto. Nostalgia clings like ivy to anything that has been in place long enough, and the changing conditions of the literary and intellectual life in the twentieth century gave the increasingly remote Victorian age the allure of a time when serious people wrote about serious topics and were seriously listened to.

It is not difficult to see why this ideal should have figured, and continue to figure, so largely in reflections by those scholars, most notably historians and literary critics, who have aspired to play a more than specialist role in public debate. For it is surely endemic to the situation of the intellectual to believe that the conditions that make that role fully gratifying are only ever properly instantiated elsewhere (I have tried to set this case out at greater length in *Absent Minds*). For intellectuals in the twentieth century, and not just in Britain, that preferred elsewhere has usually been France. But the past is also an elsewhere, if not wholly another country, and the preferred past for the cultural critic in twentieth-century Britain, brooding on the unsatisfactoriness of his or her lot, has by and large been an (idealized) version of mid-Victorian public debate. Nor is this vein yet wholly exhausted. It will be surprising if, among the various stocktakings occasioned by the centenary of Victoria's death, there is not some evocation of the ideal of the 'great' Victorian culture-heroes (Ruskin, Mill, Arnold, and company), moving easily between genres, spanning disciplines which confine lesser mortals, undefensively addressing an informed, responsive readership. The Victorian man of letters, or at least that multiform character's 'best self', has enjoyed a vigorous afterlife as a convenient way to figure the desire, necessarily frustrated but necessarily recurrent, summarized in the notion of 'the general intellectual'. In these terms, the 'great age' is always already over while being never entirely beyond recall, still able to act as a regulative ideal in the present.

17

Always Dying:
The Ideal of the General Periodical

I

When the intellectual history of twentieth-century Britain comes to be written, a large place will have to be given to an entity whose ontological status has hovered uncertainly between that of a holy grail and a will o' the wisp, a necessity of life and a lost cause, a commodity and a mirage. To try to fix this entity with a single name immediately risks resolving these expressive uncertainties into a lowering chronicle of apparent failure; better, perhaps, to register the play of need and deferral by speaking not of the thing itself, but of the desire for the thing, the desire that has issued in the recurrent ambition to produce what is variously referred to as a 'general cultural periodical' or a 'review of ideas'. And no sooner are those terms, themselves merely approximations or stabs at definition, used than one has to acknowledge that the century has also been marked by repeated laments that 'the general reader'—or, in aggregate form, 'the educated reading public'—to whom such a review would be addressed has long since died out. One sure sign of the supposed extinction of this always-dying species is, we are often told, precisely the impossibility under present circumstances of realizing the ideal of the 'general' periodical.

As with so many forms of fantasizing and idealizing, the desire for a general cultural review has had an element of nostalgia built into it from the outset. In addition to the recurrence of the term 'general' and its cognates,

This essay was originally written for a special issue of the *Times Literary Supplement* marking the journal's centenary in January 2002.

the other clue indicating that we are on a single trail here is (as I suggested in the previous essay) the constant invocation of the heyday of the 'great Victorian reviews'. The collective imagining of what intellectual life in these reviews must have been like can also be read as a symptom of a partially blocked or unrealizable desire, a longing to have another life while still being recognizably oneself. As a result, much of the abundant periodical journalism of the twentieth century has been scarred by a sense of its own belatedness, of coming after the real thing, of feeling that the conditions essential for its own flourishing have always already disappeared.

The truth is, it turns out, that jeremiads about the decline of 'the reading public' are more or less coeval with the existence of that category itself. The twentieth century has had no monopoly on alarmist bulletins of this type: the Augustans deplored the corruption of the public by sentimentalism, the Romantics complained of its commercialisation, the Victorians bemoaned its taste for sensationalism, the Modernists mocked its descent into middle-browism, and every generation has solemnly claimed to witness its final disappearance. Once alerted to the way these laments are symptoms of thwarted desires rather than accurate historical descriptions, we can begin to take the measure of the recurrence of obituaries for the 'general review'.

This also helps us recognize what may be called the 'Cretan Liar' quality in many of these death notices: the disappearance of old-style literary journalism is generally being announced by an old-style literary journalist, most often in an old-style literary journal. A classic example of the genre appeared in the *Times Literary Supplement* itself in 1938 in three articles entitled 'Present Discontents', written, we now know (thanks to Derwent May's massively informative history, *Critical Times*), by Orlo Williams, prolific reviewer, one-time House of Commons clerk, and a mainstay of Eliot's *Criterion* circle. The articles reiterated the standard lament about the rise of 'mass' entertainment and the consequent decline of 'quality' periodicals in England, the country that was 'once the home, now the grave, of the great review'. The articles prompted John Middleton Murry, veteran literary journalist and passionate advocate of causes, good, bad, or lost, to write in claiming that the disappearance of many literary magazines and the changes in the newspapers meant 'the decline in the amount and quality of reviewing has been catastrophic since 1914', and, with the kind of hyperbole that recurs on this issue, that 'book reviewing is a vanished profession'.

Sometimes these laments are part of a more specifically conservative cultural polemic. In 1943, Charles Morgan, writing the centenary history of the house of Macmillan, looked back fondly to the Victorian heyday of *Macmillan's Magazine*, in whose pages 'the great critics' were to be found alongside 'the theologians, the preachers, the men of science, the historians, the Laureate, the young lions, the great story-tellers, and the good story-tellers'. He then embarked on a familiar threnody: the dusty files of the now defunct journal revealed 'a catholic prospect closed to us since we allowed Austin Harrison's *English Review* and Squire's *London Mercury* to perish. A magazine in this liberal tradition, seeing literature as a wisdom and a delight... is a civilised asset of which we have strangely deprived ourselves. *Macmillan's* is gone, *Cornhill* is gone, *Scribner's* is gone. We have specialised in this as in all else.' The vocabulary of 'wisdom' 'delight', and 'civilised' is the stock-in-trade of bufferish keening for the good old days, but a historically specific conjunction is expressing itself here. Morgan, long-time drama critic of *The Times* and a somewhat popular novelist (more popular in France than in Britain), was a freelance bookman of the old school. The *English Review* had had a brilliant flowering under its founding editor, Ford Madox Ford, in 1908–9; it had then been taken in a more conventional direction by Austin Harrison, before declining, between 1923 and its closure in 1937, into a stridently nationalist organ. The *London Mercury*, which ran from 1919 to 1939, was the vehicle for the rather beery back-slapping bonhomie and self-satisfied anti-modernism of Sir John Squire and his acolytes ('the Squirearchy'). Morgan was thus mourning some very particular kinds of loss here, and the persuasiveness of his case was not helped by his premature inclusion of the *Cornhill* in his necrology (it survived for another thirty years).

   Over half a century later, looking back on the changes he had seen during a long career as a broadsheet literary editor, Anthony Curtis remarked: 'I am often told by people who grew up in the period covered by this book that reviewing is in decline.' Perhaps it always has been. Yet some of the same observers have been forced to recognize that the terminal patient can be disconcertingly frisky. Curtis again: 'The end seemed to be nigh for the old-style cultural weekly for so long an essential part of English life, but in spite of the change in cultural habits, it has stubbornly refused to die.' However, it has not always proved easy to accommodate these evident signs of life to the received historical narrative. The *Manchester Guardian* commented on the appearance of the 100th issue of *Encounter* in 1962: 'When a British intellectual monthly sells close on thirty thousand copies something is happening which we thought had gone out with the decline of the great Victorian reviews.'

   As always with this kind of nostalgia, the search for an origin, a locus of authenticity, necessarily proves delusory. It was Walter Bagehot who had famously declared that no genre was more central to modern reading than 'the review-like essay and the essay-like review'. Writing in 1855 (in, of course, a review-like essay that barely mentioned the books that were its ostensible occasion), Bagehot saw the rise of this hybrid genre as a consequence of the increased pace of modern life. 'There is, as yet, no Act of Parliament compelling a *bona fide* traveller to read. If you wish him to read, you must make reading pleasant... The essay-like criticism of modern times is about the length which he likes.' In offering this characterization of modern times, Bagehot was, in a double sense, facing backwards. First, although he was writing in mid-century, he was celebrating 'the first Edinburgh Reviewers'—that is, the founders of that journal in the opening decade of the nineteenth century, figures already assuming the status of giants to whom the pygmies of one's own generation could never measure up. But, second, his whole characterization of 'modern literature', of which the reviews were a defining feature, was premised on a contrast with 'the old days of systematic arguments and regular discussion'. The faster pace of life (the train plays an explanatory as well as a figurative role in Bagehot's own essay) now meant that only 'short views' were wanted. Thus, already, during the supposed heyday of the genre, there is both nostalgia and a premonitory anxiety about 'dumbing-down'. Bagehot's observation has, in turn, been frequently cited by later commentators, envious of both his opportunities and his assurance, and it will no doubt continue to provoke various nostalgic reactions, including the fond recalling of a time when it was possible to read on trains.

Certainly, the received wisdom now suggests that the genre of periodical that Bagehot was both celebrating and adorning barely survived into the twentieth century. The recent volume of *The Cambridge History of Literary Criticism* devoted to this period (see Chapter 20 below) rehearses this view in authoritative tones:

The days of the sage who could write on any serious subject for a generally educated audience had, by 1900, virtually disappeared. But so too had his medium. The generalist periodicals, such as the *Edinburgh Review* and the *Cornhill Magazine*, which in the middle of the nineteenth century carried articles on a wide range of subjects from science and politics to fiction and geography, were in the process of being superseded as forums for intellectual debate by the advent of the specialised professional academic journal.

This passage is representative not just in tracing this particular trajectory of decline, but also in its casual exaggeration of the nature and quality of the Victorian reviews. The individual 'sage' was, after all, an extremely rare bird, and even he, though polymathic by later standards, did not in practice write on 'any' serious subject. The generalist periodicals had a wide range of contributors, most of whom naturally confined themselves to certain broad areas. And, of course, the periodicals themselves differed enormously: some did not carry much intellectual 'debate' because they were so narrowly sectarian, while others were not really noted for 'intellectual' debate so much as light fiction and sketches.

Nonetheless, this particular backward glance has now become almost obligatory. Writing in a more journalistic and up-beat vein in 1999, A. N. Wilson observed that 'one of the truly extraordinary things about the British scene towards the close of the twentieth century is that there is still so much comparatively serious literary journalism'. But he went on to qualify this with the now-standard comparison: 'Less so, perhaps, than in the great nineteenth-century days of the *Quarterly*, the *Fortnightly*, the *Westminster*, and the *Edinburgh Review*, but still an impressive amount.' The category 'literary journalism' here hospitably gathers in both any writing that appeared in periodicals and (what Wilson clearly has in mind in the rest of his essay) book reviewing and writing about 'imaginative literature'. But perhaps, on closer inspection, it is not so clear that there really is 'less' of either of these forms than in 'the great nineteenth-century days'. The 'cultural' supplements of the Saturday and Sunday broadsheets now fulfil at least some of the functions performed by Victorian periodicals such as the *Saturday Review*, and they carry more 'literary journalism' than was available in any comparable form in the nineteenth century.

But how, comes the predictable riposte, could the reviews of 'the great nineteenth-century days' ever be matched for seriousness or quality? Well, truth to tell, the standard in the Victorian periodicals themselves was hugely variable: old India hands publishing complacent reminiscences of their days in the hill stations, lady travellers penning dainty sketches of the colourful bustle in Mediterranean markets, public-school headmasters recycling their speech-day addresses on the modern boy's lack of 'character', rural deans bidding for preferment by denouncing insensitive pieces of church restoration. The familiar kinds of padding and dross were there, still recognizable for all the lack of glossy pictures and roaring headlines. Nor, as I have already suggested, were such reviews always fully 'general' in the required sense, since many had a marked political or religious identity with readership to match: in its heyday, the radical *Westminster* was rather less ecumenical than *New Left Review* is today.

Moreover, we should be careful not to exaggerate the commercial success or social reach of the most celebrated of the serious Victorian reviews. In the 1860s, perhaps the peak decade for this kind of publication, the *Quarterly* was selling about 8,000 copies, the *Edinburgh* around 7,000, the *Westminster* about 4,000, the *Fortnightly* between 2,500 and 3,000, and so on. Certainly, it is more important with this kind of publication than with almost any other to distinguish between circulation and readership: a copy of the *Edinburgh* placed in the reading room of the Reform

Club would have been looked at by many who did not personally subscribe. Still, the absolute figures were not high, especially when one recalls that the *Daily Telegraph*, aimed at the newly suburban clerical middle classes, reached a circulation of 300,000, while *Reynolds's Weekly*, a penny paper popular with the aspiring working class, sold over 200,000 copies. The one (often cited) rip-roaring commercial success among the periodicals that is often quoted is the *Cornhill*, launched in 1860 as one of the first of the new breed of monthly 'shilling magazines'. But here again we have to acknowledge, first, that this was for long periods a pretty middlebrow publication, carried by its serialized fiction, which was not always of the highest quality, and, second, that its success was short-lived: it is true that it enjoyed a circulation of about 80,000 during its first year (with Thackeray as editor), but by the end of the decade this had fallen to 18,000. By the time the proprietor gently relieved Leslie Stephen of the editorship in 1882, sales were down to 12,000 and the *Cornhill* had been running at a loss for some years.

In estimating the impact of such periodicals, we have also to remember the place these readerships occupied in the wider society. The social structure of Victorian Britain has been compared to a distorted pyramid with a huge base surmounted by a narrow, sharply-tapering apex. The governing and educated class was small—contemporary usage spoke of 'the upper ten thousand'—and the leading reviews could claim to reach much of it. The price of such publications recalls us to the economic realities underpinning their prominence, for they were, by modern standards, remarkably expensive. In the middle of the century the quarterlies were selling for six shillings an issue. Even if we simply apply one of the standard inflation-adjusted indices for converting to early twenty-first-century values, this gives a price of around £15 per issue. But that does not allow for the different distribution of income and household expenditure across social classes into which this particular consumer purchase fitted; if, therefore, we calculate the cost in terms of the proportion of the average weekly wage represented by such an outlay, we arrive at a price per issue at current values of over £50 (for comparison, *Granta*, the most substantial so-called periodical published today, sells at £10). Even the 'shilling monthlies' such as the *Macmillan's* and the *Cornhill*, regarded as scandalously cheap on their first appearance, would, by that reckoning, cost about £10 per issue today (for comparison again, the monthly *Prospect* currently [2002] costs £3.50 and the fortnightly *London Review of Books* £2.95).

Such prices also meant that contributors could be handsomely paid, thereby helping to reinforce a confident sense of status. The twentieth century has seen a particularly sharp decline here, especially when measured against a generally rising prosperity: the number of words that a freelance reviewer needed to write in the 1920s to earn more than the average manual wage had doubled by the 1960s, and has more than doubled again since (largely because average earnings have increased so markedly in the second half of the century). Each generation has interpreted these changes as signalling the final impossibility of maintaining 'the critical function' and so on, but they could instead be seen as marking a change in the relations between classes; the vast army of very cheap labour that existed right up to the Second World War allowed members of the middle class to sustain a 'professional' level of existence on really quite modest incomes. More broadly, much of the lament for the 'great days' of the Victorian periodicals is, like some other forms of cultural pessimism, a wish to belong to a dominant elite whose intellectual tastes could hold sway unchallenged by the cultural consequences of mass prosperity.

For the fact is that in simple numerical terms several twentieth-century periodicals, including some of the most serious, have measured up to their Victorian counterparts: the chief difference has been the diminished place they have occupied in a far more diverse public culture. The sales of *The Times* are one index of this kind of change: in the first decade of the century its circulation was under 50,000, yet its authority was paramount; by the 1950s it was selling over 200,000, and today [2002] sales exceed 700,000, but it is just one market-hungry broadsheet among others, no longer the house organ of the governing class. Similarly, the *New Statesman*, launched in 1913 with an initial sale of 3,000, soon exceeded any circulation a Victorian political weekly could dream of, touching 100,000 in the print-starved 1940s; in the mid-nineteenth century, the *Saturday Review* sold about 14,000 copies per week, Bagehot's *Economist* around 4,000, and the *Spectator* about 3,000. Among the type of periodicals discussed here, the *New Age* averaged 3,000 copies during its fifteen-year existence; *Horizon* peaked at 10,000 copies per issue, and was still selling 9,000 when it closed after ten years; *Encounter*'s sales fluctuated markedly, but reached 38,000 in the late 1960s, and both the *Times Literary Supplement* and the *London Review of Books* claim circulations of that order or above at the beginning of the twenty-first century. No sooner is another wreath placed on the tomb of the Unknown Reader, than thousands step forwards to fill the ranks and pledge themselves to read for England.

Indeed, the sheer abundance of 'general' or 'literary' periodicals in twentieth-century Britain is striking. The standard reference work on 'British Literary Magazines' lists 140 titles in the period 1914–84 alone, and that does not include many that enjoyed only very brief existences.

'Periodical', of course, is simply a librarian's term, blankly classificatory: like buds and debs, like cuckoos in clocks and cryptos in closets, it is just something that comes out from time to time. The term 'review' at least suggests something with a little more dignity, distinguished by its essentially reflective quality or its extended discursive form rather than by its mere periodicity. Several main types distinguish themselves. Some can be seen as driven primarily by political comment and analysis: there is a proud list of such journals, from the *New Statesman* and the *Spectator* onwards, often with a bookish 'back end' enjoying a partial autonomy from the rest of the paper. Some may be seen as primarily literature-driven, aspiring to publish new works by the best writers, or the best writers of a certain tendency: from the Edwardian *English Review* to the current *PNReview* there have been any number of once-famous journals of this type, few of them long-lived. Others may be seen as ideology-driven, principally serving as vehicles for a particular political, religious, or cultural perspective, albeit often falling into eclectic inclusiveness: the *Criterion*, *Encounter*, and *New Left Review* would come into this category. And still others are largely books-driven, using the device of the discursive review-essay to take the pulse of the contemporary intellectual scene: both the astringent *Calendar of Modern Letters* and the indulgent *London Mercury* employed variants of this format in the 1920s, as does the *Literary Review* today. Risking the narcissism of small differences, one might dare to say, using Bagehot's terms, that at present the *TLS* tends rather to carry the essay-like review whereas the *LRB* leans more towards the review-like essay.

   Most such journals tend to follow a familiar life cycle, albeit considerably more extended in some cases than others. A few, intuiting that the future holds only further decline, issue a defiant end-of-civilization-as-we-know-it jeremiad in the last number and abruptly cease publication (after which, as Cyril Connolly observed of the closing of *Horizon*'s office in 1949, 'only contributions continued to be delivered, like a suicide's milk'). Others, conscious of their dignity as bearers of once-proud names, linger. In attending to the new reviews that set the pace, however briefly, it is easy therefore to forget how many of the older generation were also still around. The *Edinburgh* closed only in 1929, the *Fortnightly* in 1954, the *Quarterly* in 1967, the *Cornhill* not until 1975. In France *La Revue des Deux Mondes*, founded in the 1830s in imitation of the *Edinburgh*, still tries to keep up appearances, as, in its diminished way, the *Contemporary* does in Britain. Dying before it is too late can be as hard for reviews as for people.

II

Responding to the cultural logic sketched above, the journals founded in the twentieth century signalled the little-changing scope of their cultural ambitions in their often-changing subtitles, from the *New Age*'s 'A Review of Politics, Literature, and Art', through to *Encounter*'s 'Literature, Arts, Politics'. *Prospect*, self-consciously aspiring to take *Encounter*'s place, was launched in 1995 under the banner 'Essays, Argument, Review', soon changed to the more conventional 'Politics, Essays, Argument'. The *New Age*'s inspirational editor, A. R. Orage, had a particular flair for filling this space, and in 1932 he founded and, for the two years before his death, edited the *New English Weekly* (1932–49), which again described itself as a 'Review of Public Affairs, Literature, and the Arts'; it was intended to promote broadly Christian social thinking, and more especially the Social Credit ideas of Major Douglas, but this association brought it the kind of literary triumph that is the stuff of editors' dreams, the first publication of three of Eliot's *Four Quartets*.

This same cultural logic has meant that such periodicals have, throughout the twentieth century but more urgently in the second half, been attempting to carve out a space between two large empires that constantly threaten to overrun and absorb them: on the one side, the news-led pressures of Journalism; on the other, the discipline-driven pressures of Specialism. As John Sturrock, a practitioner of this intermediate genre both as editor and as contributor, recently observed, the ideal essay in such a journal should probably 'strike academic readers as journalistic and journalistic readers as academic', and he identifies the rationale of this kind of review-essay as being to restore 'a measure of integrity to an intellectual world that is forever looking to fly apart into its various well-defended specialisms'. Another form of nostalgia may be at work here in the assumption of a lost wholeness of intellectual life, but certainly the commitment to a genre of writing that falls between these two poles recurs in editorial manifestos across the century.

It is surely a kind of confirmation of the power of this cultural logic that one finds it registering itself in almost exactly these terms in the mind of one of the most intelligent figures ever to edit such a journal. In 1925 T. S. Eliot had been editing the *Criterion* for three years when he published a short programmatic piece squarely entitled 'The Idea of a Literary Review'. He acknowledged from the outset that the whole question turned on 'the precise application of the term "literature" in such a periodical'. Among the matching 'pairs of errors into which a "literary review" may fall', he argued, is that of 'being either too general or too strictly "literary" '. He cautioned that the literary is 'alimented from non-literary sources' and that you kill literature if you try artificially to sever these connections. A literary review therefore has to take literature 'merely as the centre from which we move', and then fan out to include 'the interests of any intelligent person with literary tastes'.

But then comes an intriguing passage that has to be quoted in full:

> We will not include irrelevant information, subjects of technical and limited interest, or subjects of current political and economic controversy. We must include besides 'creative' work and literary criticism, any material which should be operative on general ideas—the results of contemporary work in history, archaeology, anthropology, even of the more technical sciences when those results are of such a nature to be valuable to the man of general culture and when they can be made intelligible to him.

This, all due allowance made for differences of idiom and situation, is the credo of the editor of the general or literary review throughout the century (the repetition of 'general' by this most precise of writers betrays the demands such a review must try to meet). Evidently, some specialized work succeeds better than others in being 'operative on general ideas'. And this reveals the true sense of 'literary' at work here: the literary is not limited in the way archaeology, anthropology, and so on are seen to be. The trade is all in one direction: the literary is the limitless lake fed by the tributaries that are the more specialized disciplines.

When in June 1928 the *Criterion* ended its brief experiment of appearing as a monthly and reverted to being a quarterly, Eliot again took stock of the journal's place and purpose.

> It is desirable to maintain our designation of a 'literary' review, because there is no other label which indicates so briefly the subjects to which this review is indifferent. The term serves to remind us that we are not concerned with matters of passing interest. We continue to publish the best fiction and the best verse that we can find, and to interest ourselves in... the formation and maintenance of standards... But this same critical attitude is extended to all the problems of contemporary civilisation. Historical and biographical studies will have a larger part, naturally; but the *Criterion* is concerned with everything that can be examined in a critical spirit.

The emphasis appears slightly different here: the journal's range seems to be defined by the second-order operation of examining issues 'in a critical spirit', and the Scylla of topical journalism now seems more threatening than the Charybdis of specialized scholarship. But in the immediately following sentences, Eliot soon starts to tack in the opposite direction again, insisting that 'the *Criterion* is certainly not a technical review; the problems with which it wishes to deal are those of interest, even of excitement, to the generally civilized, and intelligent, and more or less educated person'. There was an element of mere posturing here, and F. R. Leavis was close to the mark when he later complained that 'there was nothing more adequate behind the *Criterion* than the general idea of a great European review'. But perhaps that makes Eliot's efforts to spell out the implications of that 'general idea' all the more revealing. When he finally came to close the journal eleven years later, Eliot obliquely acknowledged the intractability of the issues he had been struggling with in these definitional pieces, conceding that its engagement in the 1930s with cultural, political, and religious issues had led 'to emphases which somewhat stretched the original framework of a literary review'.

If Eliot often seemed preoccupied with fending off the encroaching 'specialisms', Cyril Connolly knew from personal experience the nature of the threat posed by the other greedy neighbour, journalism. As we saw in Chapter 1, above, among his ambitions for *Horizon* was that it should 'help free writers from journalism by welcoming unpopular forms and by encouraging those contributions that can be reprinted'. A monthly review, he believed, could combat some of the evils of regular journalism 'by encouraging authors to write on subjects about which their feelings are deepest, by asking for thought and imagination instead of the overwhelming brightness by which so many of us are dazzled, and by affording them as much space as possible'. Again, it is a credo that the editor of any 'general review' would be bound to recognize. Connolly, it must be said, put his pages where his mouth was: he allotted over a third of one issue to an essay on an unpromising subject by a not particularly successful journalist and minor novelist, and *Horizon* has ever after had the credit of having published George Orwell's 'Boy's Weeklies', as well as his 'Politics and the English Language' and several other frequently reprinted pieces.

One of the most intriguing general reviews to consider in this context is *Encounter*, since its ulterior purpose (discussed in Chapter 7 above) might at first seem to have exempted it from the logic of the cultural space it was attempting to occupy. But not so. When the first number was being planned in September 1953, Michael Josselson, its Congress for Cultural Freedom handler, complained to the first editor, Irving Kristol, that the contents were not political enough. Kristol replied:

The magazine, obviously, should be a 'cultural' periodical—with politics taken, along with literature, art, philosophy, etc, as an intrinsic part of 'culture', as indeed it is. The ratio of specifically political to literary etc. articles will naturally vary from number to number. In the first number, politics is relatively subordinate, since we are claiming to capture the largest possible audience.

Kristol took for granted that 'the largest possible audience' did not live by politics alone, and that the journal's 'cultural' identity was crucial to its success. That was why Stephen Spender had been recruited to be co-editor alongside, first, Kristol, and then Melvin Lasky. And the strategy was, for a while, a success. Frances Stonor Saunders, whose *Who Paid the Piper?* uncovers the murky history of the journal's official backing, calculates that 'there were half a dozen regular *Encounter* writers in Wilson's new cabinet' in 1964. But as she also points out, it was the 'cultural side of the magazine' that gave it its standing in British intellectual life—or the part that Lasky referred to crisply as 'Elizabeth Bowen and all that crap'.

When *Encounter*, mortally wounded after the revelation of CIA funding in 1967, finally closed in 1990, one well-placed observer called it Britain's 'only memorable journal of ideas since the great quarterlies of the nineteenth century', dismissing the claims of rivals such as the *Criterion*, *Scrutiny*, or *Horizon* on the grounds that they were too purely 'literary'. But this, I have been suggesting, is precisely to overlook the extent to which such 'literary' journals have played the part of the 'journal of ideas', have shared a common cultural aspiration. And, of course, it depends whose 'memory' is in question whether one considers a whole host of others from the *New Age* to *New Left Review* as possible candidates (including, in at least some people's memories, *Marxism Today*). And, risking embarrassment, one might wonder whether the *London Review of Books* or, under recent editors, the *Times Literary Supplement* should not qualify for this description.

Although the university, as the home of academic specialism, has usually figured in the chronicles of doom as the upper millstone (with Fleet Street as the lower), an idealized conception of a university, transcending its own division into departments, could also be seen as an embodiment of 'the critical function' and hence as favourably placed to sponsor a review that could be informed but non-specialized. *Scrutiny* is probably the best-known journal of this type, and it is worth recalling that it carried articles not just on literature but on topics as diverse as town-planning and intelligence-testing. In some ways a more revealing example of the generalist but university-based periodical was the *Cambridge Journal*, which ran from 1947 to 1954. Edited for most of its existence by the conservative political philosopher Michael Oakeshott, this high-quality review saw itself as upholding a fairly traditional notion of 'culture' against the 'macadamizing' tendency of modern egalitarianism (the post-war vogue for planning and 'manpower training' provided the immediate provocation). Although largely written by dons, it was rightly described as 'a general intellectual review, not a specialist organ'. Something similar could be said of a periodical of the opposite political tendency, *Universities and Left Review*, which eventually mutated into *New Left Review*, and one can see versions of this ambition being pursued in journals which, if hardly household names, are still well clear of the kinds of obscure or technical publications from which head-lines are taken in 'Have I Got News For You'.

III

None of the publications mentioned so far was, in the strict sense of the term, a 'little review'. The true 'little review', it may be said, exists to serve the needs of writers more than of readers; in extreme cases, the number of subscribers barely exceeds the number of contributors. For the most part, 'little reviews' are defined not by circulation size but by the way in which they eschew the generalist ambitions discussed here in order to promote the programme of a sect or movement. But a special glamour attaches to lack of popularity, as though public neglect were the only guarantee of lit-erary or intellectual seriousness. As Jeremy Treglown recently observed, commenting on this mythology: 'To be any good, it seems, a magazine, like a Romantic poet, has to be of erratic appearance, insult the respected, and die young.'

Nonetheless, even some of the most celebrated of the mainstream literary reviews have combined admirably wide ambitions with pitifully narrow readerships. Arnold Rowntree, philanthropist and Liberal MP who rescued the *Athenaeum* in 1919 (as his uncle had subsidized the *Nation* a decade before), believed, rather grandly, that a modern periodical should be 'what the public square was to the Greeks' (one assumes he was not thinking of the personal ads). In terms of this analogy, it has to be acknowledged that, though 'general' in the relevant sense, the public in question has usually been a restricted one, and that for much of the century it was probably a rather socially exclusive one, too. Bruce Richmond, editor of the *Times Literary Supplement* during the first third of its life, was wont to say of certain new books: 'This would interest our people', a phrase Derwent May glosses as referring to 'a recognised, faithful band of *Lit Supp* readers and reviewers'. Some of Richmond's confidence surely derived from his immediate social experience: it has been calculated that 20 per cent of the reviewers he-employed were members of the Athenaeum. Even more strikingly, when in the 1920s Leonard Woolf was literary editor of the *Nation* and Desmond MacCarthy of *The New Statesman*, a very small stable of Bloomsburyish reviewers enjoyed frequent outings. The two men would often discuss their respective choice of reviewers, and the clammily incestuous character of the situation was well captured by the occasion when MacCarthy asked Woolf who his lead reviewers were to be in the *Nation* that week, and, when told that they were Bertrand Russell and Robert Graves, replied: 'Oh that's all right, my Bertie comes out next week.'

Of course, even readers at the heart of such circles could weary of the game. For example, Virginia Woolf (an inveterate reviewer herself, it must be said) confided to her diary in December 1923: 'Talked a great deal about *The Nation*. It seems to me like a drug. Everyone reads it and discusses it in and out and there's always a lot of gossip about each article or review—one is quite out of it if one hasn't seen it for some weeks as I generally haven't. But it really bores me stiff, all this talk about writing no one can possibly remember in a year's time or less.' Print-weariness is a familiar condition among the review-reading classes, and we have most of us experienced that oscillation of mood between the dismissiveness expressed in Woolf's 'writing no one can possibly remember in a year's time or less' and the enthusiasm represented by Connolly's 'contributions that can be reprinted'.

But it may be salutary to end by recalling the difference that the existence of journals of this type can make to the lives of individual writers and readers. Christopher Hitchens, one-time doyen of Left Laddism, spoke for writers on this matter in the acknowledgements to a recent collection of his previously published essays when he reflected what he owed to the editors of the kind of journal discussed here: ' "Editor", indeed, seems to me a paltry word for those who have encouraged me; conceived of topics and subjects that might engage or interest me; printed me; corrected or rescued me; and finally (in the sense of last but not least, rather than tardily) paid me.' To see how often some such acknowledgement might be called for (indeed, often has been made) in broadly similar terms by writers who, if they are lucky, are inevitably vassals of more than one lord, we have only to try to imagine what the roll-call of twentieth-century writing would look like without those books that were almost wholly made up of pieces that had first appeared in one or other of the general cultural periodicals, including (any list is bound to be eclectic and highly selective) *The Sacred Wood*, *The Common Reader*, *Abinger Harvest*, *The Liberal Imagination*, *Shooting an Elephant*, *The Common Pursuit*, *Rationalism in Politics*, *The Dyer's Hand*, and *Required Writing*, not to mention some powerful examples by living authors.

As for readers, we may be inclined to discount the conventional tributes paid by the predictable kind of witness, as when John Lehmann, recalling Desmond MacCarthy's *Life and Letters*, spoke of 'the excitement with which, nearly twenty-five years ago, I devoured the first number', or when John Betjeman wrote that 'the death of *Horizon* is like the death of a relation'. It may be easier to identify with the less fulsome, more worldly note struck by A. N. Wilson's short apologia for the trade: 'Of course we would rather read a well-turned review than a dull book.' But the last word should go to someone neither famous nor (primarily) a writer, a representative of the Unknown Reader, speaking up for the pleasure, the sheer sensuous enjoyment, surely felt at some time by all those who have held the current issue of one of these journals in their hands. At Christmas 1908, the young D. H. Lawrence showed a copy of the first issue of a new 'literary review' to the companion of his calf-love years, Jessie Chambers, who later recorded the excitement in the household:

The very look of it, with its fine blue cover and handsome black type, was satisfying. Father thoroughly appreciated it, and we decided to subscribe to it amongst us. I remember what a joy it was to get the solid, handsome journal from our local newsagent, and feel it was a link with the world of literature. The coming of the *English Review* into our lives was an event, one of the few really first-rate things that happen now and again in a lifetime.

18

Boomster and the Quack:
The Author as Celebrity

I

In the early twentieth century, literary pilgrims to Stratford-upon-Avon already knew a lot about the great writer they were there to honour. The author's house in Church St has rather come down in the world since then and is now an outstation of Birmingham University, but in its heyday it was home to a writer with some claim to be the most widely read, in English and in translation, across the world. Visitors already knew so much because Marie Corelli, the author in question, not only boasted the longest entry in *Who's Who*, but had enjoyed commercial success and international celebrity on a scale unprecedented in literary history.

Corelli occupied her Stratford home in a style commensurate with her sense of her artistic accomplishments. Her domestic regime was supported by a major-domo, two maids, a cook, a gardener, a houseman-cum-assistant gardener, and eventually a chauffeur. As Philip Waller remarks in his extraordinary compendium about turn-of-the-century literary life in Britain, 'Corelli's sense of grandeur was the inverse of her sense of the absurd'. He does not stint his illustration of the point:

A daily ritual was her progress round Stratford in a miniature phaeton, like Cinderella, pulled by two Shetland ponies ... complete with coachman perched on high behind ... Best of all, she was regularly piloted down the Avon in her own gondola, named *The Dream*. This vehicle was specially imported from Venice, complete with gondolier, until the Latin's quarrelsome inebriation compelled his replacement by her costumed gardener.

Philip Waller, *Writers, Readers, and Reputations: Literary Life in Britain 1870–1918* (Oxford University Press, 2006).

This extravagant nonsense was made possible by the fact that in the 1900s Corelli had an income of around £18,000 a year from sales of her novels alone (a figure not far short of a million pounds at early twenty-first century prices). Critical opinion then and now appears to be united in deeming her books pretty much pure tosh; even the heroically laborious Waller remarks wearily of one of them that 'it is a challenge to summarize this extraordinary tale's crackpot complexity'. In other words, the age of the best-seller had arrived.

If we then jump forward a few years, to 2 September 1914, we encounter another tableau of literary life in the period that is, in its way, no less striking than our Grub Street Cleopatra on her barge. As a junior member of the Cabinet with intellectual leanings, Charles Masterman had been charged with the task of doing something about producing effective propaganda for the Allied cause, especially in the neutral United States. He responded by convening in Whitehall a gathering of 'eminent authors', attended by the following: William Archer, J. M. Barrie, Arnold Bennett, A. C. Benson, Hugh Benson, Laurence Binyon, Robert Bridges, Hall Caine, G. K. Chesterton, Arthur Conan Doyle, John Galsworthy, Thomas Hardy, Maurice Hewlett, Anthony Hope, W. J. Locke, E. V. Lucas, J. W. Mackail, John Masefield, A. E. W. Mason, Gilbert Murray, Henry Newbolt, Owen Seaman, G. M. Trevelyan, H. G. Wells, and Israel Zangwill (Arthur Quiller-Couch and Rudyard Kipling could not come but sent messages of support). At first glance, this may seem to be the literary and intellectual establishment in its pomp. If one pursues these figures into reference works and biographies, one realizes that they could collectively boast a remarkable level of official recognition (or would come to do so before their deaths). Taking such future honours into account, the group included several knights, two Nobel Laureates, two Poet Laureates, three Regius Professors, two Masters of Cambridge colleges, as well as holders of the Order of Merit and other honours.

The bringing-together of such literary worthies may not seem the most obviously efficient way of producing usable official propaganda, but it is the miscellaneousness of the gathering that may now appear most striking. Not only did it embrace novelists, poets, essayists, critics, historians, scholars, and all-purpose men of letters, but it also spanned a wide range of literary levels, including representatives of the popular and middle-brow markets as well as the critically acclaimed, extending from the fastidious Hardy through several gradations to popular romancers such as Caine and Locke. (We may now be more primed than their contemporaries to observe that they were all men; Corelli was one of several prominent female authors not present.) No doubt social contacts and bureaucratic indiscriminateness played some part in determining the make-up of the gathering. Still, not only is it hard to imagine a twenty-first-century British government responding to a crisis in the credibility of its foreign policy by summoning leading novelists and poets to Whitehall; it is even harder to believe that any such crew would include both A. S. Byatt and Jilly Cooper or would place Jeffrey Archer alongside Geoffrey Hill.

How, if at all, are these two vignettes from the literary life of the period to be connected? Should we be wondering about the ways commercial changes in the world of publishing may have affected the standing of authors? Should we be thinking about the resilience of the older, capacious conception of 'literature' despite both the intellectual specialization and the market segmentation of the closing decades of the nineteenth century? Should the mingling of canonical names with figures now largely unknown (Hugh Benson? J. W. Mackail? A. E. W. Mason?) surprise us? The fact that *Writers, Readers, and Reputations* does not even pose, still less answer, these or comparable questions is part of what makes it a deeply puzzling production.

It is not easy to say what this book is about, other than by amplifying its subtitle. It is not held together by a single argument; indeed, there is practically no analysis of any kind in it. In Waller's own words, it 'conjures up aspects of literary life in late nineteenth- and early twentieth-century England'. One sense of 'conjure up' is 'to cause to appear to the fancy', and it may be that some such stirring of the historical imagination is indeed Waller's purpose, were he to avow anything so vulgar as a purpose. Individual paragraphs of his book are, on the whole, engagingly written, but the relation between them, let alone between the chapters, is often maddeningly opaque. The book contains some deft portraiture, several good stories, a mass of quotations, a few statistics (well, numbers), and an abundance of miscellaneous information, some of it all but buried in the small type of long discursive footnotes. But there is scarcely a breath of argument, no hint as to which elements might be most significant, complete silence on whether some things may have been the cause of others. Although the book's bibliography includes various items of secondary scholarship on the topics he treats, there is no explicit engagement with their claims, no sense of whether he is extending or revising historiographical orthodoxies.

In his preface, Waller maintains that his topic, once eccentric, has become fashionable: 'It is now enveloped as "Life Writing", characteristically sonorous jargon that signifies a new academic specialism (aka a professional job creation scheme), though it risks simultaneously throttling public interest.' Even leaving aside the sneer at fellow-scholars, this seems ill judged: 'life writing' is the label often now given to the study of various forms of biography and autobiography; it is not a term likely to be applied to Waller's sprawling description of the trades of writing and selling books. And as though to emphasize his distance from the jargon-ridden joylessness imputed to academic writing, he adds: 'This book is designed to entertain as well as inform.' It does indeed do both those things, at least for those with stamina. Waller writes attractively for the most part, and by now he may well know more about out-of-the-way aspects of largely forgotten literary figures from this period than anyone else alive. But if his declaration signals the ambition for this to succeed as a 'trade' book, then both author and publisher seem to have approached the task in a very peculiar way. Nearly 1,200 pages, many with a dense growth of footnotage covering the bottom third, and a price tag of £85 do not seem the most tempting bait with which to snare the elusive 'non-specialist reader'.

There is clearly something deliberate, even self-indulgent, about the digressive miscellaneousness of the whole enterprise, something again in which the publisher appears to have colluded with the author. All this is a great shame, because Waller has a wonderful subject, a vast fund of information, and a stylish way with an anecdote. Perhaps the most useful thing a reviewer can do is to try to signal some of the riches this huge volume contains, and, risking the author's disdain for such schematizing, make a few suggestions about their possible significance.

II

In so far as the information can be marshalled into supporting any kind of narrative, it tells an everyday story of capitalism in which established patterns of production and distribution at first resist and then are displaced by new market conditions. In the 1870s and 1880s, new fiction publishing was still dominated by the three-volume novel priced at 31s 6d. Only a tiny fraction of the population could afford such an expenditure (it represented the entire weekly income of many working-class families), but sales to individual purchasers were anyway not the chief support of the system. That came from the bulk purchases of the circulating libraries, above all Mudie's and to a lesser extent W. H. Smith's, for whom the three-volume format tripled their loan stock. The high prices suited established authors, whose earnings on moderate sales were correspondingly substantial, and the reliability of the libraries' purchases suited established publishers, who thereby risked less on each individual title. The system gave considerable power to the buyers for Mudie's and Smith's, who in turn feared offending or disappointing the taste of their largely conventional upper- and middle-class clientele. As usual with such rigged markets, the whole system was invisibly underpinned by shared social assumptions and common values. It would take newcomers, whether among authors, publishers, or readers, to buck the system, and it was the social changes of the closing decades of the century that gave such interlopers the necessary economic clout.

Briefly summarized, those changes included the following. There was a significant growth in the size of the reading public, especially once the effects of the Acts making elementary education compulsory began to come through in the 1890s and 1900s. Technological advances reduced the costs of production and distribution. A large international market became easier to access and more remunerative, especially after the US Copyright Act of 1891, which all but ended the 'pirate' American editions that had deprived British publishers and authors of income earlier in the century. The new profession of literary agent emerged to enable the most successful authors to take full advantage of these new opportunities. Cheaper one-volume reprints were taking an increasing market share. By the 1890s, the conditions were falling into place that enabled publishers to make a commercial success of heavily advertised new novels at lower prices with bigger print runs.

Waller does not really explore the causes of the demise of the old 'three voller', but as so often in cases where accumulated change in the forces of production produces a change in the social relations of production, the end, when it came, was sudden and complete. The symbolic moment came in 1894, when the newly established house of Heinemann published Hall Caine's *The Manxman* in one volume at 6s: it was a runaway best-seller, and the format became the industry standard almost overnight. In 1894 184 new titles were still published in the old format; by 1896 only 25 appeared in this form, and by 1897 this had shrunk to just 4 titles. Even more remarkably, the new price of 6s remained in place for new novels for (it would seem) the next fifty years.

For authors and publishers to make money out of this system, some new titles had to sell in much greater quantities than previously (cheap reprints had been selling in large numbers since at least the 1880s). The disparity between authors who achieved only modest if steady sales and those who produced one of the season's 'hits' now had even greater financial consequences. But this market logic was to some extent constrained when it came to the third party to the operation, the booksellers. Normally, the existence of a large market for an identical high-volume commodity from a single producer would be likely to lead to 'underselling', as the most powerful retail outlets use their financial muscle to undercut their smaller rivals. But the still gentlemanly world of publishing closed ranks against this logic and introduced the Net Book Agreement, which bound booksellers to sell at the published price. This was first introduced by the publisher Frederick Macmillan in 1890, and by 1899 it had become the official code for the whole trade. Once again, a partly implicit consensus of cultural values propped up this arrangement: books were not to be regarded as simply one commodity among others. This convention suited the interests of publishers and authors, both of whom were guaranteed set returns per volume sold, and perhaps helped protect small booksellers, but clearly acted as a restraint on the marketing tactics of the larger outlets. It was for long accepted wisdom that it operated to the benefit of the book-buyer, though in the more aggressively capitalist Britain of the last couple of decades of the twentieth century this assumption was increasingly challenged, and the NBA was finally abolished in 1997.

So, what were the consequences for 'literary life' of these accumulated changes? Can we say anything about the types of author who flourished or what the consequences of such success were for their standing and public role? Waller does not ask such questions, but he provides a mass of useful detail for anyone willing to chance their arm at providing answers.

A few star authors had, of course, enjoyed dizzying commercial success earlier in the century, none more so than Dickens. Indeed, he remained a top seller even posthumously, selling an estimated 4.24 million copies in the twelve years after his death in 1870. Tennyson, the comparable grandee in poetry, naturally made much more modest sums for most of his long writing lifetime, though by the final stages of his grand career he was earning £10,000 a year from his writings in all forms. But these two were recognized as being in a class of their own. In 1892 Walter Besant, founder of the Society of Authors, calculated that there were approximately a hundred novelists in Britain living by their writing, and only half of them ever earned £1,000 or more in a year. A little-known author might make only £50 to £100 from a novel.

The first part of this period saw some notable commercial successes among authors who also attained a certain literary standing. For example, in the late 1880s, following the publication of *Treasure Island*, *Kidnapped*, and *Dr Jekyll and Mr Hyde*, Robert Louis Stevenson earned £5,000 per year for a few years. But he was easily surpassed by Rider Haggard, 'perhaps the country's best-paid writer between 1887 and 1894, when his earnings exceeded £10,000 annually'. His income started to fall away thereafter, but later reissues continued to do well: '*She* (1887) had sold half a million copies in its first penny edition in 1903.' And, of course, book publication was not the only source of income for the writer: three-quarters of all periodical literature in the late nineteenth century was fiction, and serialization could be highly lucrative. Arthur Conan Doyle was another of the big names in the market in the 1890s, and the serialization of his Sherlock Holmes stories 'yielded him four times the income that they produced in book form'. The potential for high foreign earnings also increased markedly after the US Copyright Act: in 1892 Mrs Humphry Ward was one of the first beneficiaries, Macmillan paying the then-record sum of £7,000 for American rights to *David Grieve* in the (disappointed) hope of repeating the phenomenal success of her previous hit, *Robert Elsmere*.

After the ending of the three-voller in 1894, and still more with the expansion of the market in the 1900s, the possibilities for large earnings from fiction increased markedly. The currency of the term 'best-seller', an American import, dates from the early 1890s. Some of the most informative chapters in *Readers, Writers, and Reputations* are devoted to those figures to whom this new, vulgar label could properly be applied. Four such authors stand out. The first was Charles Garvice, whose popular romances were selling at almost a million copies a year worldwide in the late Edwardian period (or, as *The Times* obituary put it in 1920, in characteristically superior tones, he had 'a larger circulation than any other purveyor of fiction'—a phrase that kept him in his place among the milliners and grocers). Hall Caine, one of the participants in Masterman's 1914 gathering and an author with greater literary pretensions, claimed in 1908 to have earned more than any writer in history had ever done thus far. He was the author of *both* the candidates for the accolade of having been the first million-selling novel in Britain: the *ODNB* gives the prize to *The Christian* (1897), while John Sutherland, in his *Companion to Victorian Fiction*, bestows the title on *The Eternal City* (1901).

For sheer quantity of production, however, few could touch Nat Gould, who wrote some 130 novels, all set in the world of horse-racing. It has been estimated that by 1927 he had sold twenty-four million copies, which put him ahead of any of his pre-war rivals, partly because he retained his popularity into the inter-war years better than they did (helped by the fact that twenty-two of his novels were not published until after his death in 1919, the publishers having prudently stockpiled to keep the brand going). But for sustained high earnings combined with international celebrity, Corelli took the palm: according to Sutherland, the publication of *The Sorrows of Satan* in 1895 established her 'as the best-selling novelist of the English-speaking world'.

Authors who enjoyed the critical esteem of a cultivated readership never approached these earnings, certainly not across a period of years. Perhaps the figure who came nearest was Arnold Bennett, partly because of his simultaneous success as a novelist, playwright, and journalist, and partly because he employed the services of J. B. Pinker, one of the leading literary agents of the day. By 1913 he was earning £17,000 a year from all sources.

'He now bought a Queen Anne house in Essex, and a yacht—"just to show these rich chaps that a writer can make money too"'. Among authors who have since become canonical, Kipling may have been the most popular, having sold more than a million copies of his works in various genres by 1910. It would be difficult to say whether Corelli or Kipling was the greatest literary celebrity of the age internationally, but it was a meaningful comparison in a way it would not be between, say, Danielle Steele and Seamus Heaney.

The scale of best-sellerdom increased sharply after the end of the First World War. *The Sheikh*, by the hitherto little-known Mrs E. M. Hull, appeared in 1919 and soon sold over a million copies (the film version gave Valentino one of his best-remembered roles). This novel, Waller remarks, tapped into the large market for literature about the unsatisfied romantic longings of women, married and unmarried (Hull herself was married to a pig-farmer in Derbyshire). The contrasting fates of 'serious' and 'popular' literature became even more marked: 'For every reader of Henry James and D. H. Lawrence', observed the publisher Michael Joseph in 1925, 'there are a hundred readers of Nat Gould and Ethel M. Dell.' And if we look forward further into the inter-war period, the peaks of the popular market become higher still, especially as represented by the thrillers of Edgar Wallace: 'By 1928 it was reckoned that, excepting the Bible, a quarter of all books published and bought in England was a Wallace.'

Two further points about the supremacy of fiction in the period emerge from Waller's book. First, textbooks and religious works aside, sales of non-fiction works rarely reached the heights of the true best-sellers, though they were often steady earners over a longer period. Occasionally, a book such as John Morley's *Life of Gladstone* (three volumes, 1903) could enjoy frequent reprintings, as the shelves of second-hand bookshops still testify, but probably the greatest hit in this category came just after the end of Waller's period: H. G. Wells's *The Outline of History* (1920) 'amassed sales of 3 million and earned Wells more than all his other works combined'. And secondly, print was not yet challenged by any other medium, at least not until film took off as a commercial prospect in the last decade of the period. Waller includes some particularly interesting detail about the impact of early cinema, showing that it could actually benefit those popular authors whose work was adapted for the cinema (or who, more rarely, contributed original screenplays).

III

The question of the effect of these developments on the standing and public roles of authors is particularly complicated. At one level, a theme implicit throughout this long book is that of the tensions between commercial and cultural 'value'. This was obviously not a new theme, but the changes I have briefly summarized did give it a sharper edge and made writers, in particular, more self-conscious about their status. One index of a greater sensitivity to this tension was the recurrrence during this period of projects to establish some kind of literary 'Academy', usually accompanied by allusions to the standing of the Académie Française. At the heart of these sometimes comically misconceived proposals lay a desire for there to be an officially sanctioned source of authority in literary matters (and sometimes linguistic matters, too: the role of 'the Immortals' in France in regulating changes in the language was referred to rather wistfully on several occasions).

In 1892, Walter Besant canvassed opinion on the idea of the Society of Authors (founded in 1884 to 'protect the rights and further the interests of authors') coming to occupy a similar relation to writers as the Inns of Court did to barristers. In 1897 the *Academy* (by then a less austere periodical than its high Victorian incarnation) took the idea further by drawing up a list of forty founding members for such an academy (the magic number in the Académie Française). The journal may then rather have clouded the issue of finding a source of authority beyond the market by inviting readers to suggest further names. For once, Waller does not provide much detail here, but if we track down the lists drawn up by the *Academy* and its readers, we find they are instructive about the inclusiveness of the conception of 'literature' at stake, since many of those named had made their mark in fields of scholarship, such as history, philosophy, and philology, far removed from the narrower sense of 'literature' that was coming to be established as the dominant one in the course of the second half of the nineteenth century.

In 1902–3 the question was again raised in the *Author*, the journal of the Society of Authors, in terms that betrayed the underlying concern: 'The lower forces of literary productiveness are amply organised. The higher are without representation. There is no council at the head of literature to control or keep order, or by example to discountenance the indecencies of advertisement ... '. Again, responses were mixed, so the Society of Authors took the highly academic step of setting up a committee to explore the question, led by scholarly heavies such as James Bryce and J. G. Frazer, but nothing much came of it. In 1910 the Royal Society of Literature invited the Society of Authors to collaborate in selecting the Famous Forty for such a venture again: this fraternal initiative was rebuffed, so the RSL went ahead alone, and under the guidance of Edmund Gosse (whose presence was itself a sign that institutional standing and social respectability were likely to play a large part) it proposed thirty names initially. I wonder whether any modern reader, asked to nominate the thirty leading British authors alive in 1910, would include such names as S. H. Butcher, W. J. Courthorpe, Austin

Dobson, Maurice Hewlett, Alfred Lyall, J. W. Mackail, E. H. Pember, and A. W. Verrall, several of whom were impeccably well-connected scholars of classical or modern literature rather than what have come to be termed 'creative writers'. That this list was all male was not due simply to the fact that such lists at that time nearly always did turn out to be all male: there was also the problem that most of those drawing up the list simply could not bear the thought of the overbearing 'Ma Hump' (Mrs Humphry Ward) as a founding member but could see no plausible way to prefer any other woman writer above her.

The 1910 venture did struggle into a kind of being; a few peevish meetings were held and invitations extended to new recruits from the ranks of the eminent literati. Among those who resisted, H. G. Wells gave the most spirited response: 'This world of ours, I mean this world of creative and representative work we do, is I am convinced best anarchic. Better the wild rush of Boomster and the Quack than the cold politeness of the established thing.' The 'Academic Committee' of the RSL mouldered on into the inter-war years, but it was only ever an irrelevance. The 'higher forces' of literature had to get by as best they could in the irreverent company of Boomster and the Quack.

What, of course, most authors wanted were sales *and* standing: much of the activity recorded in this huge book expressed the recurring desire to obtain critical acclaim, social prestige, and cultural authority while at the same time collecting large royalties. The pull of what Wells called 'the established thing' was very strong: writers clambered over each other to join the right clubs and get invited to the right aristocratic salons. Exploring one's literary potential could not be allowed to imperil one's status as a gentleman. The absurd trappings of gentility so maladroitly adopted by Marie Corelli encouraged dismissals of her not just as a mediocre romancer but as irredeemably nouveau riche, too. By contrast, many of those most exercised about safeguarding the status of 'Literature' shared a world that was epitomized by the *Westminster Gazette*'s fortnightly competition, which ran for the two decades up to 1915 and which involved turning a piece of English poetry into Latin or Greek verse. The editor, J. A. Spender, 'was a former Balliol classicist; the competition was set by a Brasenose tutor, H. F. Fox; and it was most frequently won by the Warden of All Souls, F. W. Pember'.

One of the things that is surely striking about Masterman's 1914 gathering is how many of those present had pretty much achieved the heady aspiration of conjoining substantial sales with accepted status (even if the snobbish A. C. Benson, in recording the occasion in his diary, did disparage Bennett for 'looking every inch a cad'). Later critics, schooled by Modernism to value difficulty and the address to a minority audience, might scorn the likes of Sir James Barrie or Sir Henry Newbolt, but at the time such figures *were* both popular and respected, a combination that it became harder to sustain as the twentieth century wore on and as 'highbrow/lowbrow', 'popular/elite', 'serious/commerical', and similar dichotomies became more entrenched.

No doubt some readers will find in Waller's book ample confirmation of their unshakeable prejudice that things were better in the past (I rather wonder whether Waller himself might not be of this party), while others will no less confidently conclude that it bears out the wisdom of *plus ça change*. Certainly, an account of the book's main themes can be given that may seem uncannily familiar: publishers concentrating their efforts more and more on a few best-sellers; small bookshops being driven out of business; celebrity and personality replacing critical assessment; the increasing power of the popular media; the rise of the visual over the verbal; the stifling of literary pleasure by academic orthodoxies; reviews becoming little more than puffing and backscratching; the excesses of advertising; and so on. Let me therefore end with two vignettes that may lend themselves to divergent readings in terms of familiarity or remoteness.

In 1885, the publishing firm of Macmillan placed a letter in the press: 'We are requested by Lord Tennyson to inform his correspondents through *The Times* that he is wholly unable to answer the innumerable letters which he daily receives, nor can he undertake to return or criticise the manuscripts sent to him.' We seem closer here to the Court Circular than to the modern fanzine, though Macmillan's motives may have been somewhat mixed since they managed to slip in a little indirect advertising about how the problem had suddenly got much worse 'since the publication of his new volume of poems'. Commercial practices and Establishment rituals were entwined in a different way in the second vignette. 'In 1906 the *Daily Mail* had advertised the serialization of William Le Queux's *The Invasion of 1910* by a march of sandwich-men along Oxford Street wearing Prussian soldiers' uniforms and helmets. This led to questions in the House and a denunciation by the Home Secretary, who called the escapade "foolish and offensive".' Now, that really does conjure up a world we have lost: just imagine, a Home Secretary daring to criticize the *Daily Mail*.

19

Private Reading:
The Autodidact Public

I

You are about to be told a series of poignant love stories, each of them wholly distinctive and unprecedented, all of them enacting an ages-old pattern. A young man has an encounter with transforming joy. Whole new universes of experience are opened up to him, introducing him to scenes that he could not have anticipated and yet that offer the shock of recognition, a homecoming to somewhere he has never lived before. He has to overcome or evade parental disapproval and the half-jealous mockery of his peers. His love inspires him to write, in an effort to give undying shape to precious yet transient experience—sometimes to write poetry or some form of prose poem, more often to write a memoir, a record of his *histoire sentimentale*, beginning with his calf-love (or calf-bound love), perhaps going on to detail later conquests in Leporellan quantities, but always expressing gratitude that the arid desert of the workaday world has, for him, become an oasis of luxuriant foliage, heady scents, and inexhaustible abundance.

Reading may not make the world go round but it can make it go away, for a while. If one's actual world is dirty, poor, oppressive, and unfair, then that may be no small service. Books do furnish a mind, and in a form that the bailiffs cannot repossess. If we could recover the reading activity of past generations, we would be in touch with a level of experience that was at once intimate and formative, on a par with, even part of, the history of love. But reading is, for the most part (at least in recent centuries), a private activity, something that people do when they are not doing the things that may earn them a place, if only a statistical place, in the attempts

Jonathan Rose, *The Intellectual Life of the British Working Classes* (Yale University Press, 2001).

of subsequent generations to re-create the past. What can we know of all those quiet hours that have left so little direct trace in the historical record? The literary tradition yields some evidence for select members of the well-connected, articulate, document-preserving classes, but what of the little-recorded majority of the population? In Britain, the first industrial nation, the 'working classes' (pragmatically defined) made up more than 70 per cent of the population until at least the middle of the twentieth century. How much could we ever know about the practice of this form of solitary vice on such a mass scale? Can there be a proper history of working-class reading?

Jonathan Rose believes that there can, and after 500 pages, 24 tables, and over 1,600 footnotes one begins to think that he may have a point. His introduction (and still more the publisher's blurb) makes much of the book's 'innovative research techniques'—the need to shift attention from text to reader, from elite readers to working-class readers, and so on. Such work has not been exactly unheard of in the last decade or so, but Rose demonstrates how much can be learned about this particular dark continent by the energetic and resourceful combing of some relatively familiar, and some less familiar, types of evidence. The sources upon which he relies most heavily, and from which the love-stories are quoted to such good effect, are the various kinds of autobiography and memoir written by those from working-class or other modest backgrounds—people who had usually received very little formal schooling, at least until the middle years of the twentieth century. But he also makes good use of library records, educational archives, oral histories, and Mass Observation and early social surveys.

The book is ambitious in scope, but even so it does not really measure up to its title. Its actual subject is not 'the intellectual life of the British working classes', but 'the reading habits of the autodidact tradition within the British industrial working class from the early nineteenth century to the mid twentieth'. It is still a big and underexplored subject, and the results of Rose's enterprising research make fascinating reading. But his attempts to arrive at large historical generalizations run aground on the awkward, indeed insuperable, difficulty that the working-class autobiographers upon whose testimony he so largely relies were, by the very fact of their writings, exceptional. He proposes to 'enter the minds of ordinary readers in history', but the readers who testify so eloquently in his pages thereby reveal themselves to be far from ordinary. At times he acknowledges this, and tries to get round it by supplementing their testimony with other forms of evidence. But the fact remains that what we mostly have here is anecdotal evidence, drawn from those who had a particular fondness for telling this kind of anecdote about themselves later in their lives.

No doubt experts in the burgeoning field of 'the history of the book' will want to take issue with Rose on this and similar grounds, but for a range of other readers his work will provide an invaluable compendium of information enlivened by a series of often very moving individual stories—weavers propping books up on their looms, miners disputing the merits of their favourite poets while digging coal deep underground, office boys reading far into the night to sustain themselves through the tedium of another day in the counting-house. We hear of extraordinary feats of omnivorous reading that would surely merit a place in some literary equivalent of *Wisden* ('the largest number of multi-volume histories read by a Lancashire cotton-spinner . . .'). And on a few occasions we stumble upon episodes that seem more at home in the *Alice* books or even Monty Python, such as this account of a group of London police constables between the wars:

They clubbed together to buy used BBC classical records from a Shaftesbury Avenue shop. They circulated among themselves copies of the *New Statesman* and a collective season ticket to the Promenade Concerts at Queen's Hall. They read Proust and Spengler, Macaulay and Gibbon, Tom Paine and Cobbett, Hume and Herbert Spencer. They never missed a Harold Laski public lecture. They went in a solid phalanx to hear Shaw, Belloc, and Chesterton debate at Kingsway Hall. And they formed an archaeological group to look for relics of Norman and Roman London whenever they happened to have freshly excavated building sites on their beats.

Policemen don't only look younger these days: they read less Proust, too.

Thus far I have colluded with Rose's tendency to concentrate on male readers, but he does make some efforts to illuminate that even darker recess, the history of working-class women's reading. Lacking endorsement by the public culture, less encouraged by family and workmates, often more isolated and more burdened, rarely invited to publish later accounts of a rise from obscurity, women tell many fewer tales of love in these pages than men do. But just occasionally, especially when the chronicles of the poor and unknown intersect with the life stories of the rich and famous, Rose strikes pure gold. Catherine McMullen was the daughter of a washerwoman who had been in the workhouse. A chance reference in a popular romance led her to make her first visit to a public library in order to see for herself what the book referred to was like. Improbably, she was entranced by *The Letters of Lord Chesterfield to his Son*, and this, in turn, 'launched her into a lifetime course of reading, beginning with Chaucer in Middle English, moving on to Erasmus, Donne, *The Decline and Fall of the Roman Empire*, and even *Finnegans Wake*'. In this case, the visit to the local library was repaid with interest: under the name of Catherine Cookson she went on to write more than ninety novels, and 'at one point she was responsible for one third of all the books loaned by Britain's public libraries'.

II

The Intellectual Life of the British Working Classes is an important and, in some ways, impressive work, but its very profusion makes it a difficult book to summarize. Although there is a broad progression from the end of the eighteenth century to the middle of the twentieth, it is really a loosely knit series of individual studies on topics ranging from 'cultural literacy in the classic slum' to the popularity of Bunteresque school stories even among those who could never dream of setting foot inside an actual Greyfriars. Nevertheless, three broad themes can be identified, though Rose does not isolate them as such: the cultural conservatism of the autodidact tradition; the emancipating power of great literature, whatever its ideological colouring; and, somewhat undercutting this, the sheer uncontrollability of readers' responses.

The cultural conservatism of autodidact literary taste through the nineteenth and well into the twentieth century is abundantly illustrated here. Once certain authors acquired 'classic' status, they were not easily displaced. The names of Defoe, Swift, Scott, Dickens, Hardy figure in almost every story of a life transformed by reading, along with those of the major poets (Milton, Wordsworth, Tennyson), dramatists (none matched Shakespeare and Shaw in popularity), discursive prose writers (Carlyle and Ruskin stand revealed in all their glory as the constant companions of the earnest seeker after light), and the great unclassifiable, John Bunyan. The composition of this canon changed somewhat over this period as new names established themselves, though working-class reading always lagged a literary generation or two behind. (One has to remember, of course, that penurious readers, picking up their books cheaply from second-hand stalls and the like, could rarely afford the new literature of the day.) But it is the durability of particular names, and still more of particular books, that emerges most strikingly, as well as the fact that the canon, at least as recognized by readers with little formal education, petrified in the Edwardian era, with no serious, as opposed to 'popular', later writer earning a place alongside the immortals. This increasing datedness of the autodidact canon could become a handicap in its own right: we have already encountered (in Chapter 2 above) the young V. S. Pritchett lamenting, as he dreamed of entering literary bohemia on the eve of the Modernist 1920s, that 'all my tastes were conventionally Victorian...I seemed irredeemably backward and lower class and the cry of the autodidact and snob broke out in me in agony "Shall I never catch up?" '

On some matters, Rose's findings allow us to be more specific still. For much of the nineteenth century, the three books most commonly found even in homes having no other books were the Bible, *Pilgrim's Progress*, and, somewhat less predictably, *Robinson Crusoe*. This trinity was progressively supplemented, though never entirely displaced, by later novelists, but as Rose records, 'only one other author ever matched the steady and overwhelming popularity of Defoe and Bunyan', namely Dickens, and here it tended to be the earlier, lighter, novels, such as *Pickwick*, *Nicholas Nickleby*, *Christmas Carol*, and *Oliver Twist*, rather than the darker, more complex works of the later 1850s and 1860s. Both the reading public and the supply of reading matter expanded dramatically in the later nineteenth century, fuelled partly by the Education Acts of the 1870s and 1880s, partly by improvements in technology and distribution. But Rose's evidence suggests that although these developments did somewhat extend the range of working-class reading, they had an even more marked impact in increasing the numbers of readers for already established classics.

Here the greatest single engine of diffusion was the Everyman Library, launched in 1906. The publisher J. M. Dent was himself a product of the autodidact tradition, and he hit upon a winning formula (later exploited on an even grander scale by Penguin): large print runs, low prices, handsome design, classic authors. The last of these was the key to the prestige of the Everyman series: Rose describes Dent's literary tastes as 'naive, old-fashioned, petit bourgeois, and blindly worshipful', but he was shrewdly advised by his general editor, Ernest Rhys, another self-made man of letters, and between them they correctly judged the deferential seriousness of their potential market. Rose, understandably, finds it impressive that 'Dent was willing to invest in so many lengthy and intimidating classics: George Grote's *History of Greece* in twelve volumes, Hakluyt's *Voyages* in eight, J. A. Froude's *History of England* in ten, fifteen volumes of Balzac, and six of Ibsen'. No less impressive were the stamina and catholicity of the implied Everyman reader, and the viability of such publishing ventures speaks of a hunger for reading that was Asiatic in scale.

This appetite was stimulated by what it fed on, and this connects to Rose's second recurrent theme: the emancipating power of great literature, whatever its ideological colouring. The testimony of actual readers on this point was unanimous: the more serious and ambitious the book, the more it opened worlds, expanded horizons, stirred imaginations. Many working-class autobiographers were emphatic that they had been encouraged in their political radicalism more by the rich panorama of life opened to them in Shakespeare or Milton or Macaulay than by reading approved 'left-wing' authors. Robert Blatchford's Socialist newspaper *The Clarion* was truer to working-class experience here than Fabian pamphlets were. As Rose puts it: 'Blatchford realized that [the Labour Party's] doctrinal texts were nothing less than the whole canon of classic literature.'

In these terms, Rose's discussion of the Workers' Education Association and Ruskin College in (but not of) Oxford engages with another long-running debate in working-class history: did such institutions serve to stifle proletarian radicalism by 'buying off' its leaders, seducing them with the delights of bourgeois culture and the means to self-advancement at the expense of efforts to right the collective wrongs of their class? Rose tackles this question at its most obvious level, by showing that there was no single ideological bias to the material studied in such settings, that the working-class students themselves wanted the best of traditional culture, not a selection of politically congenial texts, that WEA and Ruskin tutors were often to the left of their students, and so on. However, the subtler point here surely is that while in many cases such reading may well have nurtured a healthy political radicalism, it stimulated several other powerful responses as well, with the psychological if not strictly logical consequence that the more the world came to seem a rich, complicated and wonderful place, the harder it was to channel all one's energies towards the practical tasks of radical politics.

That the WEA and similar ventures did indeed transform lives is well attested, and in this case by women scarcely less often than by men. The testimonies here are among the most moving in the book: 'I did not know the joy of living until I was enabled to understand the problems of life ... Even if it had made economic conditions more difficult for me, I think I would not regret the time given it. It has made life so much more interesting ... This is happiness.' Rose is quick to press his case: 'Far from doping the workers by imposing middle class cultural hegemony, Ruskin College and the WEA did precisely the opposite: they made their students happier but less content.' The true sources of working-class radicalism, he insists (he does quite a lot of insisting), were to be found in such experiences, not in the heavy tomes of socialist theorists.

Going further, Rose argues, in one of his several echoes of Orwell, that nothing put people off Marxism more than meeting a few Marxists. Championing his 'ordinary readers', he delights in what he takes to be their indifference to ideological purity. 'The primary motive of autodidacts had always been intellectual freedom.' This perhaps understates the incidence of working-class readers who were driven to master difficult works of economics and social analysis by a deep desire to understand the causes of, and possible remedies for, the great historical injustice suffered by their class, though in mitigation it may be said that this category of readers has already received considerable scholarly attention, not least in the more celebratory accounts of 'the labour movement'.

Rose's third theme is the sheer uncontrollability of readers' responses, the many ways in which different readers may take from books things that their authors, or censorious later historians, may well not have expected. He is always eager to insist (more insisting) that theoretically sophisticated accounts of 'social control' and 'cultural hegemony' are constantly undercut by the maverick unpredictability of readers who didn't know that they were supposed to be being indoctrinated with bourgeois, patriarchalist, racist values, and who simply read the books quite differently. Actual readers can fail to bear out cherished generalizations in other ways, too. Paul Fussell and others have made us all familiar with the common soldiers who demonstrated the cultural sway of literary Englishness by reading Palgrave's *Golden Treasury* in the trenches during the First World War, but Rose also unearths the Glasgow wood-carver James Murray, who responded to the horrors around him by carrying a different volume of poetry in his kitbag—Goethe, in the original.

Reading could be uncontrollable in other ways, too: female readers read books for boys without adopting 'masculinist' values; religious readers read secular books without finding their faith threatened; radical readers found inspiration for their radicalism in the authoritarian Carlyle, and so on. Rose has a particularly good chapter on how school stories and books for boys did not necessarily inculcate an imperialist and racist perspective in their readers: boys (and girls) screened out whole dimensions of such stories, reading in a narrative-devouring way, finding (as one reader playfully recorded) that 'the interestfulness was terrific'. And that reader did not need to be lectured to about the pernicious social consequences of making Hurree Jamset Ram Singh such a thin caricature: thin caricature is a staple of many forms of comedy, and it would be rash, as well as patronizing, to assume that readers cannot recognize and discount for that.

The three themes I have identified help bring a kind of coherence to this otherwise rather sprawling book, but they certainly do not exhaust its interest. For example, in reading, as in some other matters, a special romance seems to attach itself in retrospect to the culture of the Welsh mining communities. In this case, 'intellectual life' does seem the right category, as issues of philosophy, politics, and literature were debated while underground as well as in more conventional settings. The tradition of self-improvement was strong and the appetite for ideas could be keen. Wil John Edwards (b. 1888) recalled the education he began to receive once he had left school: 'Guidance in the choice of good books came to me deep down in the pit, in the darkness and dark dust of a narrow tunnel more than a thousand feet below the earth's surface.' On one shift he listened

to an informed literary-critical discussion of the merits of Meredith over
Kipling: 'That evening he tried to borrow Meredith's *Love in a Valley*
from the Miners' Library, only to find twelve names on the waiting list for
a single copy.' (One cannot help wondering whether the author's mislead-
ingly Welsh-sounding name and topographically apt title didn't produce a
few disappointed borrowers.)

Miners' institutes were funded by a levy upon wages, supplemented
after 1920 by the Miners' Welfare Fund, which helped to finance various
benefits, including the libraries. For Rose, the particular interest of the
surviving records of these libraries lies in the fact that they were administered by the miners themselves; the acquisitions and patterns of borrowing
reflected the tastes of the readers rather than the do-gooding intentions
of local middle-class worthies. These libraries flourished in the pre-1914
heyday of the industry, and by 1934 there were more than a hundred of
them in the Welsh coalfields, with an average stock of about 3,000 volumes.
But the savage levels of unemployment between the wars hit these libraries hard: by the late 1930s many of them had bought no new books in the
past decade. Thereafter, they fell into decline, as rival sources of recreation
increased and as the proud tradition of the 'miner intellectual' dried up. By
the 1950s and 1960s, most of those with any intellectual ambition sought
other routes of self-advancement, while even the less ambitious tried to
make sure their sons didn't have to go down the pit.

Only three usable registers of these libraries survive, and they tell
interestingly complicated stories of eclectic reading habits. Shakespeare
and the major poets had their place, and the Victorian and Edwardian
classic novels did not fare badly, but in the years after 1914 they were
increasingly outnumbered by popular fiction and romances; books on
economics and politics, for all the reputation of the Red Rhondda, figured
little. Representative of the taste for a traditional kind of romantic fiction
was Mrs Henry Wood's *East Lynne*, first published in 1861, which had sold
close to a million copies by 1909. On Rose's analysis, Mrs Henry Wood was
the fourth most frequently stocked novelist in the miners' libraries, behind
only Dickens, Scott, and Rider Haggard. He is, as always, quick to point the
moral: 'Any historian of working-class culture in early twentieth-century
Britain must deal with this inescapable fact: the readers of Marx and Lenin
were infinitesimal compared with the fans of Mrs Henry Wood.'

In practice, the moral his evidence suggests is how vulnerable all generalizations on this subject are. There was enormous variation in reading
habits even among neighbouring communities, and of course the surviving
records tell only a very small part of the story. It looks as though Joyce,
Woolf, and company made no impact on the traditional canon in the first

half of the twentieth century, at least as far as places such as Treharris and Cwmamam were concerned. But who knows: as Rose engagingly concedes, 'perhaps across the valley, they were reading *Mrs Dalloway*'.

III

The question of whether working-class readers in Britain more generally were reading *Mrs Dalloway*, or any of the other classics of Modernism, is one Rose returns to at greater length in his penultimate chapter. His argument here is reminiscent of John Carey's *The Intellectuals and the Masses* (the echoes of Orwell and Carey accurately suggest the occasionally intrusive plain-manishness of Rose's literary persona, as in his table-thumping endorsement of 'the only true test of literary greatness—borrowing from the public library'). Rose seems to regard Modernism as a snobbish conspiracy to preserve the rarity value of literature by making it difficult, but, as other literary and cultural historians have amply demonstrated, the impact of Modernism on the structure of an already changing market was complex. An important part of the story here must also be the way in which social changes from the 1940s onwards, including the spread of secondary educa-tion, eroded the foundations of the traditional autodidact culture before it had a chance to adjust to the literary innovation of recent generations.

Rose's hostility to Modernism (part, perhaps, of his more general distaste for intellectuals, literary theorists, and postmodernists, categories he at times comes close to equating) shapes his account of the early twentieth century. Attempting to disarm Lord Salisbury's sneer at the 'new journal-ism' of the 1890s onwards that it was 'written by office boys for office boys', Rose tries to rescue an 'office-boy intelligentsia', represented (unrep-resentatively) by such figures as Neville Cardus, later music (and cricket) correspondent for the *Manchester Guardian*, and Richard Church, pro-lific author and subsequently poetry editor for Dent. This leads him into a fierce attack on E. M. Forster for his supposedly condescending portrait of Leonard Bast in *Howards End*. Rose quotes one of Cardus's fond retro-spective accounts of the rich intellectual and artistic life he and his fel-low clerks lived in early twentieth-century Manchester, and then, flushed with belligerent righteousness, asks: 'Why isn't there a scene like that in *Howards End*?' But this is more street-corner oratory than literary criti-cism; one might as well ask why the novel contains no portrait of a deeply cultivated businessman or a creatively fulfilled intellectual. Some of the autodidacts whom Rose champions were, as he repeatedly makes clear, better readers than this, intuitively acknowledging the imagination's right to roam.

Rose hits an elegiac note in his last chapter: 'The old classics-educated autodidacts have disappeared with the factories that employed them.' But that may be to allow synecdoche to stand in for explanation: there seems no reason why the substitution of, say, call centres for production lines should of itself produce such a change. If this book does describe a tradition that has come to an end, that may lead us to look again at what it was a tradition *of* and to ask what, if anything, has replaced it in 'the intellectual life of the British working class'. Of course, no so-called 'autodidact' was ever literally, *self*-educated: this book is also a history of the necessary sustaining social processes behind the heroic feats of individual self-improvement. But there have certainly been fundamental changes in those processes in the last half century or so: contemporary working-class readers generally have had more formal schooling than their predecessors; they have access to vastly more sources of information and entertainment; and they tend to be far less imbued with an ethic of cultural deference. We live in a less 'didactic' society, auto- or otherwise, and the proportion of 'classics-educated' people at any social level may be becoming vanishingly small. Changes of other kinds are signalled by the shock of remoteness one feels at finding a 1920s-educated woman recalling that 'the teaching profession was greatly admired by all the people I knew'.

So, in this age of 'access', Jude would not have had to scrawl on the walls of Christminster: he would already have been the target of an 'initiative' aimed at 'mature students from disadvantaged backgrounds'. If the 'mute, inglorious Miltons' are taking Creative Writing courses and the 'village Hampdens' are doing part-time law degrees, the meaning of 'autodidact' would have to be stretched to accommodate them. Nonetheless, there remain other forms of 'exclusion' than those dreamed of in Whitehall, and less material forms of 'aspiration' than those now given official benediction. However we reconfigure our descriptions of social structure, there will always be those who, in Richard Hoggart's phrase, quoted by Rose, 'are still looking for larger meanings'. But we can't tell where they might find them, if they do. Somewhere, out there, someone is at this moment picking up a book. They may be about to change their life for ever, or they may be about to escape from it for a while. The book may be one of the hundreds that are mentioned in these information-rich pages, or it may be one of the millions that are not. Who knows: perhaps in another valley someone is even reading *Mrs Dalloway*.

20

The Completest Mode:
The Literary Critic as Hero

∼

I

'No other literary tradition...attributes so much importance to the role of the critic as the English today'. That was how it seemed, at least to one observer, writing in the mid-1950s, a period frequently dubbed 'the age of criticism'. Referring back to that period, Bernard Bergonzi later remarked: 'For a few years, there was a climate in both England and America in which literary criticism could make claims for intellectual centrality.' Taking a somewhat less sympathetic view of the process that had led up to this situation, Francis Mulhern was scornful of literary criticism's ambition in the middle decades of the century to establish itself 'as the privileged arbiter of social thought'.

'The role of the critic', 'intellectual centrality', 'the privileged arbiter of social thought': these phrases point to different concerns and different idioms, but they each register the impact of what was a remarkable historical development. For earlier, at the end of the nineteenth and the beginning of the twentieth centuries, critics had by and large been thought of as figures whose wide reading and cultivated sensibility entitled them to be heard with respect on the merits of particular books rather than as the great pro-consuls of far-flung intellectual empires. Pater might put the fingertips of his prose together and murmur about 'life' and 'experience', Wilde might perversely hold up the critic as the true artist, but for the most part criticism meant the Gosses and Symonses and Saintsburys enthusing about this author or pointing to neglected felicities in that. Certainly, there was no widespread

A. Walton Litz, Louis Menand, and Lawrence Rainey (eds), *The Cambridge History of Literary Criticism*, vii. *Modernism and the New Criticism* (Cambridge University Press, 2000).

assumption that the rather subjective and strictly ancillary activity in which they were engaged should be understood as any form of political theory or moral philosophy teaching by example.

But, by the 1950s, the imperial role of criticism had become almost commonplace. 'English' paraded its claims to be considered a kind of presiding discipline in the increasingly specialized universities, and the literary critic figured as the very model of the modern general intellectual. 'A real literary interest', declared F. R. Leavis, one of the most noted imperialists, 'is an interest in man, society, and civilization, and its boundaries cannot be drawn'. How did this happen? What conception of 'criticism' informed this expansive *Weltpolitik*? And how should we, criticism having been stripped of its imperial pretensions, now draw up the balance sheet?

The long-awaited volume of the *Cambridge History of Literary Criticism* dealing with Modernism and the New Criticism offers to provide at least some of the answers. Its twenty chapters, written by a distinguished team of (largely American) contributors, cover most of the peaks and a few of the valleys of Anglo-American criticism between, approximately, 1910 and 1960. The majority of the chapters are on individual figures, but there are also a number of thematic chapters on such topics as 'criticism and the academy', 'criticism and fiction', and so on. If even its 500 pages leave the changing fortune of the literary critic during this period still somewhat underexplained, this may be partly due to the fact that such large-scale shifts in social practice and perception cannot be accounted for purely in terms of developments within criticism itself—the contributions of educational, cultural, and social historians would need to be called upon—but it also has to do with the tricky question of what exactly a history of literary criticism should be a history *of.*

II

T. S. Eliot famously said that in criticism the only method is to be intelligent. The history of attempts to be intelligent about books (including, in the more comprehensive versions, the many unsuccessful attempts) would be a mammoth, uncompilable history indeed. Reviews in newspapers may be literary criticism, as may introductions to paperback reprints, as may footnotes in school editions; writing a poem or novel may itself be a form of literary criticism, as indeed may conversations over dinner about the most recent book one has read. But that, of course, is not what we now expect from a work of this title, no that is not it at all: the word has got around that literary criticism is an academic subject, and so its history, like histories of sociology or physics, will be largely a history of Precursors and Founding Parents.

So, for at least a couple of generations now, such histories have comprised two main strands. On the one hand, they survey the literary opinions, both general and particular, of a long procession of figures who have usually distinguished themselves as creative writers as well as critics—a procession that, in the English case, rounds up the usual suspects between, say, Sidney and Dryden and, say, Arnold and Eliot. And, on the other hand, they include accounts of a wide range of philosophers and aesthetic theorists: the procession here tends to be longer and more international, sometimes even starting with Plato and Aristotle, and usually including Kant and Croce and similar heavyweights. Histories of literary criticism have, therefore, become principally histories of *ideas about literature* rather than histories of the activity of noticing things in particular works. The unignorable monument here is René Wellek's multi-volume *History of Modern Criticism*, an exercise in the history of ideas in the grand European manner tempered by dashes of New Critical austerity.

The even larger Cambridge history—this is the sixth of the projected nine volumes to appear—belongs, broadly speaking, to this capacious genre, but the identity of the present volume reflects a more specific notion: indeed, that the volume even exists as a separate volume at all is due to the success of the central story its chapters have to tell. The previous volumes in this series are all defined chronologically, but this one shares the coverage of its period with another, still to be completed, on 'historical, philosophical, and psychological perspectives'. That volume, too, will be part of a 'history of literary criticism', though the slightly weaselly term 'perspectives' suggests something of a collection of residual hybrids.

But the present volume is, at least in principle, about 'criticism' *pur sang*, an activity that has come to be understood, largely as a result of the writings discussed within it, as centrally involving a close engagement with the verbal texture of particular works of 'imaginative literature', an essentially inter-pretative or explicative activity, as opposed to a whole range of other ways of talking about books—biographical, historical, philological, theoretical, and so on. It is this notion of 'criticism', at once pure and imperial, that was seen as promising (or threatening) to occupy a position of 'cultural cen-trality' and, more bizarrely still, to become 'the privileged arbiter of social thought'. The history of literary criticism in this period has, therefore, to be partly the usual account of views about literature, but partly an account of how one distinctive way of reading and reporting on one's reading installed itself as the defining activity of both an academic subject and a cultural practice. It has, in other words, to be above all the story of how 'criticism' came to be such a Big Deal.

Whatever view one takes of the level of historical explanation required by such an enquiry, there will surely be general agreement that a, perhaps even *the*, key figure in the story is T. S. Eliot. But the story does not really have a readily intelligible narrative line. Once upon a time, a young American graduate student in philosophy came to England, and after a while quite a lot of academics in Britain and America thought that they were doing criticism in a wholly new, and newly serious, way. It is still hard to give the story much more coherence than that. We are so used to thinking of Eliot as the root and inspiration of New Critical and formalist 'approaches' (as we pedagogically say) that it can be a salutary shock to place one of Eliot's essays next to a standard piece of later academic *haute explication*. For example, although Eliot quoted pointedly, there is actually rather little of what came to be recognized as 'close reading'; its place is taken, on the whole, by lapidary *obiter dicta* and the opportunistic reviewer's pose of omniscience. Similarly, it is Article One of the New Critical doxa that literary judgements are judgements of *form* and do not depend upon agreement or disagreement with the *content* of a work; yet Eliot can frequently be found asserting just the opposite (as well, characteristically, as the opposite of the opposite, too). If we throw in the facts that he was mostly scornful of university departments of English and that he never wrote anything extended or programmatic about the 'method' of criticism (there may be some truth in his epigram that 'the only method is to be intelligent' but it is hardly the blueprint for a graduate programme), then it becomes more puzzling still quite how it was that Eliot, or at least Eliot's name, came to preside over the great 'Industrial Revolution in criticism'.

The editors of this volume of the Cambridge history make a stab at accounting for Eliot's role by describing him as 'the first non-academic critic who sounds like an academic critic'. There is something to this: his early essays on the Elizabethans and Metaphysicals, in particular, combine a severity of tone and a show of historical learning that did seem far from the belle-lettristic latitudes allowed conventionally to the lay reviewer. He did also repeatedly insist that literature be treated as literature and not as something else (biography, ethics, religion), even though he later went back on some of his more stringently purist remarks. All this suited a discipline struggling to establish that it had a distinctive subject matter and enough rigour to justify its place in the university. But clearly the answer to the puzzle, if it is admitted to be something of a puzzle, must also be looked for in places other than Eliot's teasing critical essays themselves.

In the first chapter in the volume, which is also one of the best, Louis Menand makes a brave and thoughtful attempt to arrive at some balance sheet of these essays, without imputing to them more weight and consistency than they actually possessed. Menand rightly observes that Eliot was 'a controversialist': 'His strongest suit as a critic was not originality or argumentative power, but scepticism. He could sustain ... an attitude of seeing through everything.' 'An attitude of seeing through everything' is an apt characterization of Eliot's critical voice in his early journalism, though I'm not sure that this is scepticism exactly: it manifestly prided itself too much on its unillusioned state, and was always threatening to degenerate into a pose of seen-it-all nihilism. But this leads Menand into an excellent discussion of what he calls 'the great riddle' of Eliot's criticism—namely, 'the proper place of ideology, or belief, in literary appreciation and critical judgement'. He concludes that despite some of Eliot's well-known later pronouncements about the primacy of belief or even 'orthodoxy', he actually kept his practical literary criticism oddly independent of his larger religious and political commitments. Not to have done so would have been to risk lapsing into 'romanticism'. 'In reacting against what he took to be one of the principal errors of modern thought, Eliot produced a criticism that could be understood as presenting a highly disciplined theory of poetry and critical method.' The discussion may perhaps understate the extent to which the authority of Eliot's criticism came to depend on the increasingly high standing of his poetry, but Menand's chapter is an excellent introduction to the early critical writings of the young American who adapted European ideas to champion a form of English Modernism.

The historical problem, then, becomes to understand how in the next generation certain critics, themselves fairly diverse, took inspiration from selected features of Eliot's occasional writings and generated from them both a more systematic critical and pedagogic practice, and a programmatic account of the nature of literature and the role of criticism in relation to it. Three key notions may be singled out here. The first was the elaboration of the grounds for the alleged distinctiveness of the work of literature (what John Crowe Ransom liked to refer to as 'the special ontology of the poem'), an aesthetic object not to be confused with arrangements of words of other kinds, such as scientific propositions or ethical imperatives. Here, Eliot's repeated strictures on not confusing literature with other things could be taken as founding statements. The second, which could be presented as a consequence of the insistence on the autonomy of the work of literature, was the disenfranchisement of the author as the privileged authority on the meaning of what he or she had written. As W. K. Wimsatt later put it: 'Critical enquiries are not settled by consulting the oracle.' In this way, anti-intentionalism in interpretation and the elevation of the role of the critic went together. The third notion, even more important and perhaps even more opaque, is the idea that the 'great' or 'fully achieved' literary work (one of the costs of working at such a high critical temperature all the time is that less good writing, and lesser genres generally, tend to be ignored or dismissed) somehow embodies, holds together, or reconciles the maximum complexity or, in a favoured word, 'tension'. Short lyric poems are, for obvious reasons, the preferred candidates here, but the talk of embodying complexity in form and the consequent prizing of irony, paradox, and multiple meanings was in principle extendable to other, larger (though not usually baggier) forms. It is this latter notion, I would argue, that proved to be vital in enabling criticism to lay claim to a broader cultural role.

Something of a developmental line is signalled by phrases associated with three important characters in the story. First, I. A. Richards: 'Poetry is the completest mode of utterance'; second, R. P. Blackmur: 'Form is a way of thinking'; and, third, Cleanth Brooks: in contrast to 'practical and scientific discourse', the critic's task is to take 'the more inclusive view'. The movement that these slogans (barely more than ideograms) may be taken to chart is, in very rough terms, from a claim about the power of literature, to a focus on form as the means of that power, to an identification of the critic as transferentially possessing a cognate power on account of a uniquely disciplined and receptive engagement with form. One outcome of embracing this sequence is to be provided with a recipe for the critic as generalist: among the contending idioms in which to perform the role of intellectual, criticism becomes 'the completest mode'.

The most illuminating analysis to date of the implicit social function of these claims seems to me that provided by John Guillory in his book *Cultural Capital*, published in 1993. Guillory argues that what he calls 'the ideological efficacy of the New Criticism' resided not in the politically and culturally conservative *views* of the individual critics, but in their promotion of the idea of 'complex form' as itself adversarial to the dominant instrumental culture. The formal unity that is a fully realized work of literature (so the critical *patois* of the day tended to put it) functions to reproach the partial and the mechanical, and thus to trump the merely propositional language characteristic of both liberal utilitarianism and science. Exploiting the cultural capital of 'difficulty', made newly powerful by Modernism, the New Critics could also fend off some of the perceived challenges of 'middlebrow' culture. As Guillory points out, everything that was ring-fenced within the elevated category of 'literature' was thereby presumed to possess this distinctive kind of wholeness: criticism then became less a matter of discriminating better from worse, and more a process of identifying and displaying the mechanisms by which all genuinely 'literary' works embody this transcendent formal power.

This analysis opens up a rather different perspective from that favoured in some of the more celebrated recent accounts of the 'rise of English'. The emphasis in these accounts, reflecting their roots in the work of the British New Left, has been upon seeing the expansion of the teaching of literature as an attempt to reconcile class antagonism—or, more sinisterly, to mask class conflict—by representing a particular selection of vernacular literature as an expression of 'our common humanity'. The other merits or defects of this emphasis aside, it has never seemed to offer a very illuminating way of understanding the function of New Critical pedagogy in the United States, or, more generally, of accounting for the enlarged conception of the literary critic as social critic.

Focusing on the issues clustering around form-as-wholeness is also a helpful way of thinking about the actual social criticism of the leading figures in this history. They expressed, as has long been recognized, a variety of anxieties about the impact of 'mass society', and the voice of literary criticism lent itself more readily to laments for something lost than to confident or cheerful anticipations of the future. A subsequently neglected motif, however, was their search for an antidote to what Blackmur called the 'fragmented and specialised knowledge' characteristic of modern societies (some of the newer academic disciplines, he growled, were little more than 'malicious techniques'). At issue here was the intellectual's characteristic search for a 'generalist' perspective, a transcending of specialization, ultimately a critique of the instrumentalist reasoning of everyday life in what Leavis infelicitously termed a 'technologico-Benthamite civilization'. Other idioms, such as philosophy, now merely replicated the disabling scientism of industrial society; only criticism, it was claimed, promised to bring the full lived unity of human response and judgement into play in a disciplined way.

Indeed, one could push this whole line of enquiry further still and speculate on the structural resemblances between, on the one hand, Eliot's implied ideal of 'the associated sensibility' or Richards's 'synasthaesia of conflicting impulses', and, on the other, the Southern Agrarians' idea of 'the South' or Leavis's of 'the organic community'. They are all prized as forms of wholeness, the opposite of the partial, the fragmented, the specialized, the instrumental. Thus understood, even the most intricate New Critical teasing out of the play of ambiguity and paradox in long-familiar poems encodes a cultural argument. 'The well-wrought urn', 'the verbal icon' and the rest function as allegories of the overcoming of dividedness, all the more effective (and perhaps all the more ideological) for being immune to the kind of merely empirical counter-evidence that can always be cited against any historically located model. Treated in this way, 'literature' functions as a kind of conservative utopianism voided of actual social content. Small wonder the critic, the figure uniquely well placed not just to identify but in some (still rather obscure) sense to 're-enact' the kind of unity found in the literary work, could pose as the most completely equipped cultural critic.

Perhaps it is appropriate that the chapters in this volume that do most to deepen our understanding of this development are those that are most accomplished *critically* (Menand's already praised chapter belongs in this company). That the task of trying to do justice to the off-hand humanity and spiky brilliance of Empson was assigned to Michael Wood was clearly a happy choice; that he is the only contributor who undertakes two chapters (he also takes the measure of Blackmur) starts to look like Divine Providence. If anyone could be said to make good the large promissory notes written on behalf of criticism as the play of 'unspecialized intelligence', it would be Empson, especially perhaps the Empson of *Some Versions of Pastoral* and parts of *The Structure of Complex Words*. Wood brilliantly conveys the flavour of these idiosyncratic works; his own tone is sympathetic yet decisive, which of course suits his subject, and he is one of the few professor-critics one could trust to stand up to Empson, in every sense, without any grating fuss or flannel.

Virtues of a different but complementary kind are displayed by Michael Bell's tough-minded assessment of Leavis, whom he splendidly rescues from the shallow textbook travesties, without ever losing sight of his several impossible sides. Bell is especially good on the part played in Leavis's later works by the idea of language as the 'enactment' of experience, and he indirectly makes out a good case for seeing much of the writing about Leavis as a prime illustration of the mistake, identified in general terms in Wallace Martin's chapter, made by those 'readers who infer that an anti-theoretical position must be anti-philosophical'. By contrast to these masterly and illuminating chapters, the first generation of New Critics—the so-called Southern Agrarians, John Crowe Ransom, Allen Tate, and Robert Penn Warren—receive rather disappointingly schematic treatment, and the late Donald Davie gives a strong impression of a grumpy man in a grumpy mood in his brief, intensely judgemental, account of Yvor Winters.

In their introduction, the editors rightly insist that there were other dimensions to Modernist criticism apart from those that second-generation New Critics retrospectively singled out as key parts of the genealogy of modern academic criticism. Several chapters make an effort to broaden or diversify the story accordingly, though it has to be said that, despite containing much that is of interest in other ways, the case for seeing many of these writers as outstanding or undervalued *critics* remains unproven, and the manner of the treatment of them may reflect this. The chapters on

Gertrude Stein and Wyndham Lewis, for example, are essentially useful contributions to intellectual history, providing well-documented synopses of their careers. Similarly, the historically rich chapter on Yeats concentrates, quite justifiably, on the nationalist theme, his hopes of using literature to create what Lucy McDiarmid aptly terms a 'Celtic Byzantium', rather than on his criticism as such (which perhaps Yeats himself did not value that highly: 'One has to give something of oneself to the devil that one may live. I have given my criticism.') And the chapter on 'the Harlem Renaissance' is understandably preoccupied with the appeasing of yet other gods: Zora Neale Hurston, concludes Michael North, 'was not really a literary critic at all' but concerned rather with 'the verbal culture of the race'.

The one chapter on a Modernist writer that does go some way towards sketching a style of criticism that can be seen as offering some kind of alternative to the orthodox Eliot-to-New-Criticism narrative while also being of compelling interest in its own right is Maria DiBattista's spirited portrait of Virginia Woolf. Taking her clue from her subject, DiBattista places the emphasis on Woolf as a 'reader' rather than a 'critic', noting how often in her critical essays Woolf herself stages 'the scene of reading'. 'Her best essays nimbly juggle the throng of contradictory but dependably fertile suggestions the mind tosses up while reading until it settles, in the pensive aftermath of reading, upon a final, lingering impression.' 'The pensive aftermath of reading' is a nice epitome of what Woolf's deceptively informal criticism is like, and 'a final lingering impression' strikes a seductively different note from the locked-and-barred definiteness, the disagree-on-peril-of-ideological-damnation aggression, of the 'readings' announced by so much later academic criticism. The very range and promiscuousness of Woolf's reading struck a non-academic, perhaps even anti-academic, note; only such an unshackled reader, remarks DiBattista, 'could understand the pleasures of bad books without being obliged to attribute to them imaginary merits'. The contrast between 'pleasures' and 'merits' says a lot.

III

The three editors of, and the great majority of the contributors to, this volume are Americans, and its balance and much of its tone of the volume reflect this dominance. Two long chapters, approaching 25,000 words each—Morris Dickstein's on 'The Critic and Society, 1900–1950' (which was, one might say, 'pre-printed' in a collection of his essays as long ago as 1992), and Wallace Martin's on 'Criticism and the Academy'—are followed by a very brief chapter entitled 'The British "Man of Letters" and the Rise of the Professional', implying (as is indeed the case) that the geographically 'unmarked' chapters had been heavily American in focus. Although the undergrowth of reviewing and journalistic criticism in the United States is explored in Dickstein's chapter in particular, this level of everyday critical activity in Britain gets very short shrift. There is only passing attention to substantial critical presences in the period such as A. R. Orage or John Middleton Murry, none at all to *The Calendar of Modern Letters* or *Horizon*, or to early Auden, or to any lesser Bloomsberries such as Desmond MacCarthy, and so on. Obviously, any such synthetic volume will have its debatable omissions: in the present case they are certainly not grave and are worth remarking simply to indicate that, in so far as undeclared criteria of selection may have been at work, they point, perhaps understandably, towards a concentration on what will fly in American college classrooms.

This is, of course, a reminder of where the big battalions are stationed these days, and that in turn provokes a concluding thought about the social or cultural preconditions for the flourishing of 'criticism' as Empson and Blackmur and company practised it. The informal conversational register of the best of such criticism, the easy assumption of a shared literary culture, the undefensive absorption in the task in hand—such character-istics point to the way in which a lot could be taken for granted. It was not just the bow-tie-and-tweed-jacket Anglophilia of Ivy League English departments in the heyday of the New Criticism, but a broader cultural confidence (which was, *pace* later parodies of it, perfectly compatible with genuine political radicalism in individual cases).

Referring to Leavis's well-known impact in the sixth forms of grammar schools between the 1940s and 1970s, Michael Bell shrewdly observes how 'Leavis was of his time, one in which the older hierarchical assumptions of social leadership overlapped with a new openness as to who might perform this function'. This point might be extended to help account for the broader cultural position of criticism. The exchange that Leavis famously suggested as emblematic of the collaborative nature of criticism was where a judge-ment is initially offered in the form 'This is so, isn't it?', anticipating the response 'Yes, but . . .', followed by an attempt to resolve disagreement by pointing to particulars.

But this can also be seen as the transcription into critical (and pedagogical) practice of the social moment Bell describes. In principle, it is open to anyone to proffer the 'Yes, but . . .' response, but the broader terms of the exchange are to be taken as given. To object that a quite different form of discourse about a differently defined subject matter is needed would be to disrupt the 'collaboration', as would the still more political insistence on the right to initiate the exchange rather than merely respond to it. Theory, one might elliptically say, is what happens when social change prevents certain starting points from being taken for granted. Presumably, some readers will plunder this volume to document the horrors of life in the bad old days, just as others will cradle it as an evocation of a lost Eden. It is capacious enough to meet both needs. It also provides some wonderful instances of what, in propitious circumstances, being 'intelligent' about literature can be like.

21

From Deference to Diversity:
'Culture' in Britain 1945–2000

I

In 1954 the Independent Television Authority was established to oversee the new commercial channel that was to bring an end to the BBC's monopoly. The Postmaster-General, Lord de la Warr, needed to appoint a chairman for the new board, so he rang up that quintessential arts mandarin, Sir Kenneth (later Lord) Clark, and offered him the job. Clark's later account is rich, in more senses than one:

Why did Buck de la Warr invite me? I can only suppose that my name had respectable associations, and he thought that it might allay criticism in what might be called Athenaeum circles. In this he was mistaken. Their odium was not allayed, but was focused on me, and when, soon after my appointment was announced, I entered the dining room of the Athenaeum (as a guest) I was booed.

It is a wonderful vignette, deeply revealing of the state of Establishment culture at the time. Clark's feigned puzzlement was intended to strike a properly insouciant note, though in fact it borders on the pathological: one might indeed 'suppose' that the name of the recently appointed Chairman of the Arts Council, and former Director of the National Gallery, had 'respectable associations'. There is also the strenuously casual signal of social intimacy: 'Buck' was known to hoi polloi as William Herbrand Sackville, the 10th Earl de la Warr. And how appropriate that it should take place in that traditional citadel of the administrative and intellectual elite, the Athenaeum Club (though Clark is careful to indicate that he was not a *member*).

This essay is a revised version of a series of articles written in 2000 to introduce a new *Guardian* supplement on 'the state of the culture'.

But what an astonishing moment it really was, an utterly scandalous display of disapproval in such a subdued setting: whatever could have possessed the assembled judges, bishops, dons, civil servants, and others to boo one of their own? The reason was outrage that money-making should be allowed to invade a cultural domain, albeit a 'popular' one. 'Independent' television, after all, was a euphemism: it was commercial. In other words (not that the disapproving diners needed words), wide boys from the business world were being allowed to pollute the airwaves in search of profits: a later, more Americanized, idiom would surely have labelled the minister 'Quick Buck' de la Warr.

The episode is also significant precisely because the medium in question was television, the greatest single transformer of cultural life since 1945. And the transformation took place with remarkable speed. In 1946 there were only 15,000 TV licences, mostly in London; by 1956 there were over five million, and pretty much the whole country could receive transmissions; by 1960 this had doubled to ten million, and by 1969 nine out of ten households had a television. (The greatest casualty, of course, was cinema: the peak of film-going had been reached in 1946, representing an average of almost one visit a week for every member of the population over 15; by 1962 cinema attendance had dropped to less than a quarter of its peak figure.)

Clark himself did not possess a television at the time, nor, it is a pretty safe bet, did many of those who voiced their disapproval in the Athenaeum dining room. In its early days, it was understood that television was a medium principally watched by the lower orders: television, Noel Coward explained with camp magnificence, 'is for appearing on, not watching'. The various regulatory authorities were examples of the common pattern from this period whereby the tastes of one class were policed by the members of another. But the potential of TV quickly became clear. Indeed, Clark himself was to become one of its great beneficiaries, especially as the presenter in 1969–70 of a thirteen-part series simply called *Civilisation* (on the BBC, of course). 'Civilization' here largely meant the high art of Western Europe, and Clark made clear that he thought culture in the present was going to the dogs (though, in common with those country landowners whom he came to ape, Clark was very fond of dogs, especially one called Plato, 'a noble character, but not very clever'.) The barbarians were now well inside the gates in cultural terms, and as Clark crisply put it, 'popular taste is bad taste, as any honest man with experience will agree'.

Clark's manner of social grandeur was part of his authority in this role. The final moments of the programme were shot in his 'study' at Saltwood castle; it was not exactly cramped, having once been the Archbishop of Canterbury's Hall of Audience. But all was not quite as it seemed. Some years later, Clark's scarcely less celebrated son, Alan, was notoriously to mock the pretensions of an arriviste like Michael Heseltine by describing him as the kind of feller 'who has to buy his own furniture'. But actually Clark senior was the kind of person who has to buy his own castle. Saltwood in Kent was far from being the ancestral home: Clark bought it in the 1950s from a Mrs Levi Lawson, 'an American lady of unknown origin'. Still, it all helped make Clark visibly a toff, and toffs were the ones who knew about 'culture'.

In measuring the distance travelled in Britain's cultural journey over the last half century or so, perhaps no change has been more important than the loosening of the connection between social status and cultural authority. There are, necessarily, elites who exercise disproportionate power in most areas of social and cultural life, but there are now a far greater variety of such elites than fifty years ago, and, crucially, they are much less likely to overlap, still less to form a series of concentric circles. Concomitantly, the notion of a single hierarchy of cultural forms now has to coexist with a much more pluralist acceptance of a diversity of more or less equally legitimate cultural activities. At the beginning of the twenty-first century, even the tired old distinction between 'high' and 'low' culture (which after all tacitly presumes such a single hierarchy even when challenging it) no longer works. For many people under 30 at the beginning of the twenty-first century, the ministry responsible for the most significant part of their cultural life has been the Ministry of Sound.

This expansionist narrative partly rests, of course, on a shift in the sense of 'culture' itself. As Stuart Hall, doyen of that form of sociology plus street cred that has become known as 'cultural studies', influentially put it:

Culture not as a body of work, or particular media, or even as a set of ideal standards and rules, but rather as lived experience, the consciousness of a whole society; that peculiar order, pattern, configuration of valued experience, expressed now in imaginative art of the highest order, now in the most popular and proverbial of forms, in gesture and language, in myth and ideology, in modes of communication and in forms of social relationship and organisation.

No single historical explanation accounts for this shift in the understanding of 'culture', but it does need to be connected to some very large-scale changes in British society over this period. And the main story to be told here is one of increased prosperity and increased democratization, entailing a corresponding decline, not in material inequality itself (which is in some respects even sharper than ever), but in deference and acceptance of traditional forms of authority.

In the middle of the twentieth century, Britain was, numerically speaking, still overwhelmingly working class: that class, broadly defined, accounted for approximately 72 per cent of the population (the middle class made up roughly 28 per cent and the upper class a mere 0.05 per cent). And it was a highly class-*conscious* society, with class identities recognizable at a glance and strong patterns of deference (not unmixed with resentment, of course) governing relations between classes. Half a century later, inequality and exploitation may be no less pervasive in British society, but an enormous rise in general prosperity and an accompanying change in social attitudes mean that this rigid pyramid, with its huge base and tiny apex, no longer corresponds to the lived experience of daily life in the tangible, all-pervading way it once did. Forelock-tugging has declined even more sharply than ferret-keeping. The rich, it is now felt (to adapt Hemingway's famous remark), are no different from us: they just have more money.

The seeds of this change were sown in the 1940s themselves, a decade that saw the working class register substantial gains in their standard of living and their political influence. The Second World War had the greatest impact here, rescuing large swathes of the population from the long night of un- or underemployment and disturbing many of the assumptions of service and subordination on which pre-war social relations had been based. (As Ross McKibbin has pointed out, between 1939 and 1941 'the number of private domestic servants declined by nearly two-thirds and was never to recover'.) The radicalizing experience of the Second World War, the confidence and bargaining power that full employment gave to the working class, and the consequent electoral triumph in 1945 challenged the established social order in several ways, though it is important to remember just how little *cultural* radicalism there was among Labour's leaders (apparently Attlee 'suffered acutely if the port was circulated the wrong way at his dinner table').

Nonetheless, the *social* changes consequent upon increased prosperity were highly visible in the ensuing decades. From the mid-1950s there was a widespread preoccupation, shared by politicians and social scientists alike, with two related but distinct developments. The first was the rise of what was called the 'affluent worker'. By contrast to pre-war poverty and unemployment, a long period from the late 1940s of full employment and rising real wages meant that the average manual worker and his family (as the social units tended to be defined) were enjoying a much higher level of prosperity than ever before (for example, between 1951 and 1963 prices rose by 45 per cent, but wages rose by 72 per cent). Wages in particularly flourishing sectors, such as the car industry, now started to exceed the salaries of some traditionally middle-class occupations. The second change is what was called 'the embourgeoisement of the working class'. This was not just a matter of increased prosperity, but a fundamental change of identity.

It involved losing or repudiating the old self-consciously separate, fatalistic, working-class stance, and adopting broadly middle-class attitudes and ways of life, including saving and the pursuit of upward social mobility, as well as the development of more individualistic and self-interested political allegiances.

Contributing to this blurring of class identities at all levels, the decades of post-war prosperity brought vast new markets into existence, and the technological innovations that responded to these markets introduced a greater diversity of cultural media. The development of commercial television after 1954 is an obvious example; the multiplication of radio stations, at first in the form of 'pirates', is another. And the phenomenon of the 'pop star', the new celebrities of the 1950s and 1960s, would have been impossible without widespread ownership of record players. But this same development simultaneously made classical music vastly more available than it had ever been: one cultural form's gain was not necessarily another's loss.

What records were to music, the paperback was to books, leading to what one might call the Penguinification of British reading in the 1950s and 1960s. The ways in which the icons of traditional upper-class culture and the expressions of new consumer power coexisted are especially striking here. Paperback publishing had been in its infancy in the 1940s, but in the course of the 1950s the whole commercial exploitation of the medium was transformed (the expansion of secondary education after 1944 played a part in this). The curve of Penguin's success provided a dramatic index of this cultural transformation: from selling a few hundred thousand copies in total, its sales rocketed to the point where in 1959 alone it sold twelve million paperbacks. But the 1960s saw an even more extraordinary expansion, and by 1968 its annual sales had risen to twenty-nine million. It is interesting to note which titles were the greatest beneficiaries of this huge expansion: how many readers, I wonder, would correctly identify which four Penguin titles had by the late 1960s each sold over a million copies (or, to borrow from another medium, look away now if you don't want to know the answer and would rather guess for yourselves).

The best-selling Penguin of all, which had by then sold over three and a half million copies in eight years, was Lawrence's *Lady Chatterley's Lover*. The publicity impact of the trial in 1960 does not need to be spelled out. And the three other titles were Homer's *Odyssey* (perhaps the *Brief History of Time* of its day where good intentions were concerned), Orwell's *Animal Farm* (this was the Cold War, after all), and—wait for it—John Braine's *Room at the Top*. Pan Books was the other paperback publishing giant at the time, and its number-one seller during this period, which also topped a million copies, was Alan Sillitoe's *Saturday Night and Sunday Morning*.

The novels by Sillitoe and Braine might be seen as the literary expression of, respectively, the 'affluent worker' and the 'embourgeoisement' theses.

But before reading too much into these figures, we need to recognize that these large sales were the fruits of new marketing strategies that skilfully exploited the potential links between different media. The success of *Room at the Top* illustrates this trend. It appeared as a hardback, with accompanying newspaper serialization, in 1957; it was published as a paperback in 1959, and in the same year, crucially, it appeared as a film. The film was obviously enormously influential on the sales of the book, and it followed the increasingly common pattern whereby stills from the film were used on the cover of the book (thereby, among other things, imprinting on the reader one particular image of the character or scene represented). But this was not the end of the commercial chain: a sequel called *Life at the Top* was published in 1962, which itself then appeared both in paperback and as a film, and then later in the 1960s there appeared a television series called 'Man at the Top'. Not surprisingly, the paperback sales of Braine's original novel were boosted by each of these subsequent developments, and by 1970 it was in its nineteenth printing. And there was a similar pattern with Sillitoe's *Saturday Night and Sunday Morning*, which was made into a very successful film starring Albert Finney, who still stares out at us from the cover of the current paperback version.

The traditional possessors of cultural prestige did not, to put it mildly, welcome these developments. Somerset Maugham had a word to describe the new wave of irreverent, 'redbrick' (though actually Oxford-educated) novelists such as Kingsley Amis and John Wain, and the word was 'scum'. Actually, Amis himself was soon to be numbered among those who denounced the increasing democratization of social and cultural life: his slogan 'more means worse' (referring to the expansion of education) formed part of a swelling threnody on the theme of the decline of cultural 'standards'. The cultural life of almost any period can be represented as a conflict between the Old Farts and the Young Turks, but much of the special energy of that complex phenomenon known as 'the Sixties' derived from the fact that the Young Turks realized that recent social changes meant that they no longer had to wait their turn: they could take over the place immediately.

One can speak of a 'decline of deference' during this period in more metaphorical senses, also. Critics of the expanding cultural forms complained of 'Americanization', as the great engine of capitalism exploited new markets, but this can also be seen in terms of a diminished deference towards Europe as the traditional home of inherited culture. Increased national self-assertion in other parts of the British Isles could be seen as loss of deference towards the internalized values of Englishness. Even the

beginnings of so-called second-wave feminism could be understood in terms
of a repudiation of deference towards men (with clubs, in the Pall Mall sense
of the word, offering one of the most salient symbols of the overlap of class
power and gender power). In the spaces thus opened up for groups, most
notably ethnic groups, to assert their demands for recognition and dignity,
public respect for distinctive forms of cultural self-expression has partly
functioned as compensation for lack of political and economic power.

But the disorienting speed of such social and technological change generates nostalgia, not only among those who have actually lost more than they
have gained, and nostalgia can sometimes seem to have been the dominant
ethos of British culture since the 1970s. Or, rather, here one should say
'English', for there has been a particularly intimate connection between
nostalgia and ideas of Englishness. Anachronism is, for many, constitutive
of English distinctiveness: the concept of England as a modern society is
for them an unthinkable thought. Evelyn Waugh, John Betjeman, and a
host of costume-drama producers have fed this appetite for self-definition
through loss. At its core is the self-indulgence involved in revelling in the
sublimity of the defeat of the stylish and the graceful by the harsh realities
of the functional, the effective, the modern. This equation of the beautiful
with the past and of the functional with the modern has been a recurrent
motif of English sensibility in the past half century; it has perhaps blighted
discussion of architecture above all. All the dangers of essentializing are in
play—is 'England' medieval churches any more than it is supermarkets?—
and it reveals the difficulties in ever successfully associating an essence with
the present.

The result is the psychological or cultural mechanism by which sheer
pastness confers a charm, the frisson of irrecoverability, the pleasures of
longing. Things not in themselves particularly beautiful—things considered the height of new, functional vulgarity when they first appeared—
come to seem the quintessence of a more lovable age. Think how this has
happened to nineteenth-century terraced houses, or to 1930s cinemas, or
to 1950s railways, and so on. And, of course, art itself prolongs the life of
past artefacts and thereby adds to their appeal: how much more essentially
English the station buffet in *Brief Encounter* now seems than does the
AMT coffee stall in a contemporary 'Travel Centre'. By the same token,
culture is regarded as something that happens elsewhere, and in England
the elsewhere of choice for many people is the past.

As a result of these complex, dislocating changes, so much contemporary
cultural debate consists in trying to pick one's way between, on the one hand,
an embattled nostalgia issuing in ill-directed cries of 'dumbing down', and,
on the other, a kind of knee-jerk cultural correctness that locates virtue

exclusively in whatever can be claimed to have been previously neglected, marginalized, or, best of all, suppressed. In this situation, bewilderment and indifference disguise themselves as relativism and tolerance. But abstaining from making cultural judgements of value is not necessarily the best way to show respect for other people's differences: that can be simply to hand control over all our lives to the unsleeping drive of capital to maximize its returns. People are making judgements of value about what other people should want all the time: it is just that now they work in advertising and sales. Meanwhile, economic and technological change press remorselessly on, simultaneously empowering and disempowering. The upbeat response is to urge those who have something to say about it to set up their own blog; more jaundiced observers note that those whose employers have brutally 'downsized' are left with ample time for such e-chat.

We are by and large very pleased with ourselves about the distance we have travelled from a world dominated by the values of the Athenaeum dining room c.1954, and to express our self-satisfaction we rush to damn all that we suspect still belongs to that world by calling it 'elitist'. The elites represented there have indeed lost much of their prestige, but the elites gathered in boardrooms have thereby only increased *their* power. The complacent and intolerant attitudes on many issues of those who took their social and cultural superiority for granted half a century ago may indeed be part of a world well lost, but those muted boos were not altogether wrong in identifying the force that would transform British culture beyond the powers of even the Kenneth Clarks of this world to regulate it.

II

'I do not believe it is yet realised what an important thing has happened. State patronage of the arts has crept in. It has happened in a very English, informal unostentatious way—half-baked. A semi-independent body is provided with modest funds.' With these words, John Maynard Keynes informed listeners to the BBC in July 1945 of the creation of the Arts Council. It was only a matter of weeks since Germany had surrendered; the war against Japan was still going on; London and many other British cities were covered in rubble. But Keynes wanted the country to know that those who cared about such things were taking steps to ensure that the brave new post-war world would not only have new social and economic policies, but something hitherto unheard of in British history: a cultural policy.

However, the tensions that were to dog the Arts Council throughout its history were evident in the very terms of Keynes's celebratory remarks. 'By provision of concert halls, modern libraries, theatres and suitable centres,' he went on, 'we desire to assure our people full access to the great heritage of culture in this nation.' 'Access' was to be in competition with 'excellence'; culture was at once lodged in the past as 'heritage' but also located in creative and participatory activities in the present. And aims were mixed in other ways, too: Keynes spoke of the need 'to make London a great artistic metropolis', but also pledged the new body to 'let every part of Merry England be merry in its own way' (the Grand Opera plus Morris Dancers view of 'culture'). The only really unequivocal statement was the cry from the heart that Keynes interjected in the middle of his broadcast (and that no official spokesperson for the arts would dare to utter these days): 'Death to Hollywood'.

The history of the Arts Council is important not just because it became the main funding body for the arts, but because it functioned as a kind of microcosm of the relation between politics and culture in Britain in the second half of the twentieth century. At first, the 'culture' it fostered largely corresponded to the traditional tastes of the cultivated elite; then, in the 1960s and 1970s, it attempted to do right by various forms of 'popular' culture (a revealing category, particularly when contrasted with unpopular culture); finally, in the 1980s and 1990s, it fell in with the prevailing economism of public discourse, treating culture as one of the 'leisure industries' that contributed to the GNP—or, as the Thatcher-appointed Arts Council Chairman William Rees-Mogg put it in 1985: 'The arts are to British tourism what the sun is to Spain.'

These developments were conditioned by social attitudes towards culture that had deep historical roots. Summarizing ruthlessly, one might say that the dominant tradition in Britain had been an uneasy mixture of indifference, suspicion, and the largely unreflective perpetuation of the tastes of the traditional upper class. It has often been argued, most influentially by Matthew Arnold in the mid-nineteenth century, that the pervasive impact of Protestantism, especially in its Puritan form, and the power of the commercial middle class in the world's first industrial nation combined to produce a suspicion of or resistance to culture that deserved to be called 'philistine'. But Britain's traditional elites, too, contributed to this uneasy relationship. The court and the metropolis were less the focus of upper-class cultural life than in some other European countries; the landed classes tended rather to be provincial in their attachments and rural in their pursuits.

It is true, of course, that historically most of the 'high-art' forms were dependent upon the patronage of the wealthy classes, but in Britain even these were (and perhaps still are) primarily pursued as conventional elements in an established social season, where a visit to the opera at Covent Garden might be seen in much the same light as a cricket match at Lords or the regatta at Henley. This in turn helped to fortify popular hostility to these art forms, and although the labour movement's high regard for education has left its monuments in the statute book in the form of public provision of schools and libraries, the arts have attracted only limited attention from the chief reforming governments of the past century.

Seen against this historical backdrop, the long absence (until recently) in Britain of any kind of 'Ministry of Culture' is hardly surprising. In place of a 'cultural policy', Britain has had a miscellaneous collection of cultural institutions with different statuses and varying degrees of public support whose operation has depended upon the shared values, social contacts, and tacit agreements among leading members of the social and professional elites. Anything more explicit or systematic threatened to grate on those British sensibilities that detected a totalitarian resonance even to the phrase 'Ministry of Culture'. As Lord Goodman, the then Chairman of the Arts Council, drily remarked in the 1960s: 'One of the most precious freedoms of the British is freedom from culture.'

Prior to the Second World War, the only 'national' provision of culture took the form of the central government's responsibility for certain major museums and art galleries. Even these tended to have originated in acts of private patronage (the National Gallery was founded by a gift to the nation, after all), and they were almost all actually administered by their own board of Trustees or Governors. More common than public provision was private initiative, even where this dealt with a matter of 'national' concern: the National Trust, for example, was privately established in 1895, primarily to preserve 'places of historic interest and natural beauty'. (It is noticeable that there has long been greater readiness in Britain to spend money to conserve 'nature' than to foster 'culture': part of the utility of 'heritage' is that it cunningly embraces both.) The British Broadcasting Corporation, established in 1926, was regarded from the outset as fulfilling a public function, though its Charter as a self-governing corporation was designed to ensure that broadcasting in Britain did not simply become a vehicle for official opinion.

The first steps towards public provision for 'the arts' were effectively prompted by a concern for the morale of the civilian population during the Second World War. (The exigencies of war have provided the occasion for the most substantial extension of the powers of the state in Britain in the twentieth century.) The Council for the Encouragement of Music and the Arts was set up in 1940; it was initially intended both to assist people to perform music and drama for themselves and to make the work of professional performers more widely accessible, though the latter aim soon predominated. In 1945 the warm glow of victory led many wartime expedients to be looked upon with favour, and all political parties concurred in transforming CEMA into 'The Arts Council', whose objects (as stated in the Royal Charter it was eventually granted in 1967) are: 'To develop and improve the knowledge, understanding, and practice of the arts; to increase the accessibility of the arts to the public throughout Great Britain; to advise and cooperate with Departments of Government, local authorities, and other bodies on any matters concerned, whether directly or indirectly, with the foregoing objects.' In the ensuing decades some small amount of state aid was extended directly to several other organizations, such as the British Film Institute (which actually pre-dated the war) or the Crafts Council, but generally speaking the Arts Council became the main institutional means for channelling public funds to support the arts.

The establishment of the Arts Council may have represented a significant extension of the *range* of activities receiving public support, but the *means* adopted conformed to an established British pattern. The guiding principle remained that of 'arm's length' administration—that is, a system where public funds were not disbursed directly by a government department, as in most other European states, but were allocated to intermediate bodies that were charged with fulfilling certain public obligations, usually phrased in very general terms, and then left free to disburse the funds as they saw fit. The Arts Council thus took its place alongside those other 'Committees of the Great and the Good' that were alleged to run so much of the public life of the country—the Governors of the BBC, the Trustees of the National Gallery or the British Museum, the Directors of the Royal Opera House, the members of the University Grants Committee, the Board of the National Trust, and so on.

As far as Westminster and Whitehall were concerned, both the level of political attention given to the arts and the size of the sums involved remained negligible for at least the first two decades after 1945. But then in 1965 the Labour government signalled its intention of pushing the topic up the political agenda by appointing a junior minister with special responsibility for the arts (Jennie Lee, a forceful politician in her own right and the widow of Aneurin Bevan, one of Labour's most charismatic figures and the effective founder of the National Health Service). In practice, subsequent governments, especially Conservative ones, tended to resist any expansion of the power and prestige of this office: the Arts portfolio was shuffled around various ministries, never commanding a ministry of its own, and so the minister concerned was in a correspondingly weak position when negotiating with the Treasury for an increase in its spending powers. Until 1992, the Arts Minister headed the Office of Arts and Libraries; it was a junior post that did not bring membership of the Cabinet.

Inevitably in the later decades of the century, with the heightened political profile of conservation and 'heritage' issues, with the increased political clout of the 'tourist industry', and with the alleged economic benefits of a thriving 'arts sector', numerous issues that might in other countries be classified as the responsibility of the Ministry of Culture came, in piecemeal and unsystematic fashion, under the supervision and sometimes the control of government. But administratively these responsibilities remained dispersed until very recently. Thus, the Foreign Office oversaw the work of the British Council, the body whose task is to disseminate British culture abroad. The Department of the Environment was responsible for various historic buildings and other sites of national interest. The Home Office had overall responsibility for radio and television, though the cinema fell under the Department of Trade and Industry, while the Office of Arts and Libraries was administratively in the charge of the Lord President of the Council, having previously been under the Department of Education and Science. Some may see in this a wise Burkean system of internal checks and balances in which no one department has a monopoly of 'cultural policy'; others may see it as a characteristic muddle, tolerated only because the British have traditionally not taken 'culture' seriously enough to merit the formulation of effective procedures and policies for its support. Or, as one senior official wonderfully remarked in 1996: 'It is not part of our culture to think in terms of a cultural policy.'

From its beginnings, the Arts Council was subject to criticism from various quarters, especially on the grounds of its being too 'elitist' and taking too narrow a view of its functions. Certainly, in its early years the Council appeared to adopt a rather restricted conception of 'the arts' that gave primacy to the traditionally high-status genres of opera, ballet, drama, and classical music. State support for drama, in particular, expanded enormously during this period. Between 1958 and 1970, fifteen theatres were built around the country, all at least partly financed from public sources. The Royal Shakespeare Company was turned from a minor, ailing private venture into a flourishing, two-centre national company largely through Arts Council funding. The National Theatre opened in 1963, and Denys Lasdun's South Bank complex, built to house it, was one of the outstanding monuments of the alliance between the high arts and state funding.

But there were also mounting misgivings about the way in which the Council operated, and critics on both the Left and the Right of the political spectrum urged that its freedom be curtailed (generally urged by the Right) or its constitution be altered (generally urged by the Left). Neither the process of appointment to the main Council and its panels nor the funding decisions they took were open to any kind of democratic control: much appeared to depend upon the close social links between members of the metropolitan elite. In this vein, it has been suggested that the reason why the independence of bodies like the Arts Council involved no great tension with successive governments until the 1980s was that the members of such bodies so deeply shared the attitudes and values of the traditional political class (or, as Sir John Colville, former private secretary to Prime Ministers, put it, with culpable blandness: 'the Treasury Knights, being cultivated men, felt a sympathy for the arts').

In the 1960s and 1970s, as part of wider social changes, the Council came under pressure to take a more democratic or popular view of the cultural activities that should be funded. To a limited extent the Council did extend the range of its clients, though one of the main consequences is that it came under further criticism from Tory backbenchers who complained that public money was being used to support 'indecent', 'subversive', or simply 'mediocre' artistic activities (Tory backbenchers have a tendency to conflate these three categories). In fact, it is clear that for some time now the Arts Council has uncomfortably juggled various not always consistent criteria in making its decisions. In the mid-1980s, under Rees-Mogg, it thumpingly declared its commitment to 'excellence' (as opposed to attempting to further other desirable social goals), but taken narrowly this was always bound to conflict with the council's duty, as laid down in its charter, 'to increase the accessibility of the arts to the public throughout Great Britain'. The relative autonomy accorded to the Regional Arts Councils further complicated the picture, since they (especially Greater London Arts, which inherited some of the social concerns of the abolished Greater London Council) tended to look more favourably on a variety of 'community' or participatory activities than had the parent council.

Although the big cultural satrapies such as Covent Garden, ENO, the National Theatre, and the RSC were always its major clients, the overwhelming bulk of the support provided by the council was in smaller grants to a huge variety of organizations—dance companies, local theatres, individual writers, poetry magazines, crafts associations, and so on. And here 'high' and 'low' increasingly mingled side by side, with grants to 'early music' bodies such as the Monteverdi Choir matched by others to 'African Caribbean or South Asian' music organizations, such as the National Steelband Music Company.

In the course of the 1980s, the Thatcher governments exercised one obvious kind of influence by their reductions in the real value of the arts budget, but they also exercised a more insidious influence by manipulating the system of appointments to the relevant public bodies along simple partisan lines. Thus, for example, in 1980, shortly after the Tories had taken power, the self-made businessman (and major donor to the Tory party) Alastair McAlpine was nominated for membership of the Arts Council. There was immediate protest, since not only did McAlpine have no obvious qualifications or experience in the arts world, but he had already noisily expressed his opposition to *any* public subsidy to the arts. The protest was overridden by the Arts Minister's revelation that 'this nomination comes from a very high source'; McAlpine had been one of Mrs Thatcher's closest supporters and a fervent advocate of 'free-market' policies.

Then in 1982 Richard Hoggart, a literary and cultural critic with a distinguished career in education (and a man of moderate *Guardian*-reading left-wing views) who had for some years served very effectively as Vice-Chairman of the Arts Council, was abruptly dismissed. This was contrary to established practice and against the stated wishes of the Chairman and the rest of the council. When pressed, the (Tory) Arts Minister confessed it was because 'Number 10 doesn't like him'. Rees-Mogg was appointed as Chairman the following year. When Roy Shaw, the long-serving Secretary-General of the Arts council (its senior administrative officer), retired later the same year, he wrote an article for the council's *Bulletin* regretting this increasing politicization of appointments. Rees-Mogg attempted to prevent the publication of the article, which only led to its receiving vastly greater publicity by its appearance in the *Observer*. (It was also Rees-Mogg who made the decision, since reversed, to cut all subsidy to literature on the grounds that it was perfectly capable of financing itself in the market place.)

The official view in the closing decades of the century was that any short-falls in public provision would soon be made up by private sponsorship, but the problems with this assumption have become increasingly clear. Expenditure on sponsorship is part of the normal commercial accounting of businesses, not a charitable activity. It is another form of advertising, and thus introduces its own demands, whether in the form of opera programmes printed in the colours of a well-known cigarette company or, more worry-ingly, of pressures towards 'safe' and uncontroversial events ('nothing to frighten the directors' wives'). Moreover, sponsorship is only for a limited term, and likely to be cancelled abruptly as commercial self-interest dictates; it is therefore dangerous for any cultural organization to build income from such sources into its regular budgetary expectations, and there is not much sign that such sponsorship has helped to address the *long-term* needs of the chronically underfunded arts organizations.

The one new ministry set up by John Major after his election victory in 1992 was 'the Department of National Heritage', embracing tourism, sport, and the arts. The title aptly reflected the Prime Minister's sepia-tinted views: village greens and country houses are part of the nation's 'heritage', experimental theatre and minimalist art are not. In practice, what really transformed the relation of government to the arts were the huge yields from the new national lottery. The capital infrastructure of culture became heavily dependent on what Adam Smith famously described as 'a tax on ignorance'; regular funding channelled through the Arts Council was now only part of the story. After Labour's victory in 1997, the word 'culture' finally crept into the title of a department of state without too many Orwellian or Koestlerian bogeys being roused. The department of 'Culture, Media, and Sport' embraced an even more heterogeneous remit than its predecessor, continuing to reflect deep confusion about the distinctive nature and value of art. In so far as there is an organizing principle it is economic: these activities are grouped together as a category of 'optional' consumer choices, they are 'leisure industries'. By the end of the twentieth century, costume dramas had become the emblematic 'product', milking heritage to help the export drive. 'Death to Hollywood' has mutated into 'long live Merchant Ivory'.

Broadly speaking, therefore, what has happened is that one, largely extraneous and inherited, form of confidence has been eroded without yet being replaced by another that would allow discriminations of quality to be persuasively made on intrinsic rather than merely instrumental grounds. We are now encouraged to think of works of art not as expressing some of the deepest probings of the human condition, but as leisure products whose 'rebranding' will contribute to 'national competitiveness'. All the while this is the prevailing official ethos, we had perhaps better hope that the familiar lack of a 'cultural policy' in Britain continues, thereby at least allowing a little genuine creative expression to be fostered in the cracks.

22

Well Connected:
Biography and Intellectual Elites

I

There is an irresolvable tension between the individualistic form of biography and the kind of analytical, sociological framework that is required to illuminate the historical situation and cultural role of elites. The task of narrating the trajectory of the single life is bound to be somewhat at odds with that of displaying the mechanisms through which a class or other grouping maintains, exercises, and reproduces its social power. This tension assumes a particular form in the case of those who may be thought of as belonging to literary and intellectual elites, where the achievements of the figure who is the subject of biography are bound to appear tangibly individual, the expression of apparently autonomous creative energies, while the enabling effect of belonging to certain advantaged groups is usually more implicit or resistant to demonstration than in the case of conventional social and economic elites whose power and influence are so highly visible. Of course, the language of 'elites' is one kind of abstraction, suggesting clear and fixed identities for their members, whereas the reality of actual lives is messier and multiple. Literary and intellectual figures usually belong to several overlapping categories that may, for some purposes, be regarded as 'elite', but that in practice need to be discriminated—birth or family connection; the economic advantages of class; a shared educational background at high-prestige institutions; a common level of publicly recognized achievement; circles of acquaintance, friendship, and mutual support; and so on. (I leave aside the pejorative force that much

Nicola Lacey, *A Life of H. L. A. Hart: The Nightmare and the Noble Dream* (Oxford University Press, 2004).
Olivier Todd, *Malraux: A Life*, translated from the French by Joseph West (Knopf, 2005).

contemporary usage builds into the terms 'elite' and 'elitist'; for historical purposes, the term 'elite' is surely a neutral sociological category, expressing neither approval nor disapproval of the distinctiveness thus identified.)

Several of the essays in Part I of this book have, in passing, drawn attention to the limitations of the genre of literary or intellectual biography as conventionally practised at the beginning of the twenty-first century, especially in Britain, where, as has often been observed (complacently or quizzically), the genre of biography appears to enjoy a status and commercial success unmatched elsewhere in Europe. As a genre, it is largely a creature of 'trade' (rather than 'academic') publishing, though there are notable exceptions or crossovers. Trade publishing is an unambiguously commercial activity, and its executives and editors believe that the demands of the market translate into several implacable imperatives where literary biography is concerned: the biography must, above all, be 'readable', must stick closely to a detailed chronological narrative, must imaginatively give access to the interiority of the subject's life, must have as much detail as possible about 'relationships' and the subject's sexual life, must recount details of 'everyday' life, must draw heavily on letters and diaries, must mine the subject's published work for biographical material, must largely eschew overt engagement with the work of historians and other scholars of the period in question, must be long, and so on. There have in recent years been some notable exceptions that adapted this bland and rather unenquiring recipe to purposes that are rather more analytical, historical, tough-minded, or experimental in form. I have discussed one of these admirable exceptions in Chapter 6—Bernard Crick's *Orwell*—but other examples are Ray Monk's *Wittgenstein*, Hermione Lee's *Virginia Woolf*, Roy Foster's *Yeats*, and John Haffenden's *Empson*. Several of the chapters in Part I above address themselves to biographies that, though they may be rather more conventional in style than the outstandingly impressive works I have just mentioned, are nonetheless excellent in their own terms and genuinely illuminating about their subjects. But the tensions I have identified are present even in them: what it was about, say, the literary milieu in which these figures moved or the intellectual discipline in which they worked that inspired, enabled, and partly constituted their own ostensibly autonomous achievements remains difficult to analyse within the bounds of the unbroken narrative of the single life.

In less distinguished versions of the genre, of course, there is not even any attempt to address these matters, and there is at present an additional reason why any such searching analysis is often discouraged. In its most conventional guise, biography participates indirectly in the nostalgia boom. Reading about the details of the everyday lives of exceptional people,

people who by background or achievement lived exceptionally comfortable and well-connected lives, evidently has some of the same attractions as costume dramas and country-house kitchens. Biography can easily collude with snobbery, allowing the contemporary reader to keep company with, even to identify with, an altogether wealthier, more famous, and more colourful crowd from the past than actual life yields in the present. This must partly account for the thousands and thousands of pages that read as though written by a conscientious but sadly unstimulated voyeur: 'He had lunch with Vanessa and Clive; Roger and Lytton were there, disputing fiercely about mushrooms. In the evening he dined with Maynard and Lydia; she wore her fox stole throughout the evening, he spoke at length about German reparations. The next day he went down to Sussex . . .'.

I initially described the tension between biography and more analytical approaches as 'irresolvable', but that may seem too defeatist: each has its own conventions and constraints, but both are, ideally, necessary fully to recapture the quiddity of the literary and intellectual life of the past. A relatively simple distinction that seems to me helpful here is that between, on the one hand, a focus on the life and character of a particular individual, and, on the other, a full-scale biography. The former is often indispensable, yet without bringing with it the disadvantages of the latter (including irrelevant detail and sheer length). We often want to understand where something comes in the curve of a life, but it may be that in such cases the biographical essay, essentially an intellectual portrait, will suffice, will indeed be practically of greater use. Of course, such an essay or portrait may well rest on the detailed findings of the fully-paid-up, no-archive-left-unvisited biographer. I like to think that one of the functions of essays such as those in Part I of this book may be to give non-specialist readers (who might be unlikely to make the large investment of time and effort required to get through some of these massive tomes) a sense of the shape and significance of a particular writer or thinker's career and to connect these to a more analytical or critical account of the individual's work than is usually provided by the biographer.

I have placed this chapter in the second rather than the first part of the book because it attempts to focus attention on these more general questions (which are also present, in various guises, in the immediately preceding and succeeding chapters). I have grouped together the discussion of two individuals who indisputably belonged, through one route or other, to powerful elites, and I try to illustrate something of the variety of contemporary biographical approaches to the role of such an advantageous position in their subject's lives. (On grounds of nationality, Malraux, like Edmund Wilson in Part 1, may seem something of an interloper, but his membership of the ferociously elite category of French literary intellectuals

refracts my theme in a revealing way.) It will be clear that I have some
misgivings about how this theme is handled or avoided in most biographies, but even Nicola Lacey's life of the legal philosopher H. L. A. Hart, which
seems to me an exceptionally intelligent and rigorous attempt to bring her
subject's life and work together, cannot quite encompass, within the form
of a biography, what it was about Oxford 'ordinary language' philosophy in
the mid-twentieth century that gave it such cultural power. And that there
is something intriguing and germane about the question of elites in this
case is surely suggested by a tantalizing detail noted in her biography: when
Hart was involved in delicate negotiations on behalf of MI5 during the
Second World War to enable that agency and MI6 to share secret information,
three of the officials in MI6 with whom he had closest dealings were Hugh
Trevor-Roper, Gilbert Ryle, and Stuart Hampshire.

                                    II

In 1945, Herbert Hart was a 38-year-old London barrister who had spent
the previous six years largely working in military intelligence. What could
be more obvious, then, than that he should be thought the perfect candidate
for a full-time teaching position at Oxford in philosophy, a subject with
which he had had no sustained connection since it formed part (though only
part) of his undergraduate degree sixteen years earlier? Similarly, in 1952
Hart was a 45-year-old philosophy tutor who had by that point published
only three essays and two book reviews. Self-evidently, he was the ideal
man to elect to Oxford's Professorship of Jurisprudence.

By the standards prevailing at the beginning of the twenty-first century,
these two appointments are bound to seem scandalous, perhaps even
barely intelligible. Yet they launched the academic career of the man
whose work had perhaps a greater impact on the philosophy of law in
the English-speaking world in the twentieth century than that of any
other, more conventionally qualified, figure: Hart's *The Concept of Law*,
published nine years after taking up the chair, has been described as simply
'the most important book about law to have been written' in that century.
In themselves, the circumstances of these two appointments already hint
at why a biography of this hugely influential figure might have much to
offer. But they also suggest why a purely biographical focus will struggle to
account adequately for this striking trajectory. For we are dealing here with
a prize example of an academic class at the apogee of its intellectual confidence and social standing, a case that cries out for exploration in historical
and collective terms. That, however, would be to undertake the kind of
analytical and comparative enquiry that can be only lightly touched upon

in a biography ambitious to enjoy a publishing success beyond the confines
of a specialist readership.

Academics are, for the most part, very unpromising subjects for
biographies, especially biographies partly aimed at this wider audience.
The uneventful solitude that generated the work by which they made
their mark yields little narratable material, and in many cases the
significance of the work can be fully appreciated only by a small group of
fellow-specialists. These defects as subjects for biography can, it is true, be
partially offset by other characteristics not unknown among this species:
a rich and well-documented sexual life, preferably with people already
familiar to readers for other reasons; a prominent role in public life and
debate beyond the confines of their discipline; a penchant for writing, and
keeping, self-revealing letters or diaries. Hart scarcely displayed the first
of these, though his limitations in this respect are more than made up for
by the enthusiastic sexual bohemianism of his energetic and colourful
wife, the historian Jenifer Hart. The second, a public role, he had only to
a limited degree, most notably in relation to law reform in the 1950s and
1960s; in general he was not outspoken and did not regularly contribute
to non-specialist publications. But the third characteristic he certainly did
have: Lacey's biography relies heavily on his funny, self-ironizing letters
and especially on the many searching, lacerating examinations of his own
character and work that survive in his papers.

Quite successful biographies of several of Hart's contemporaries as academics have been published in recent years, and they turn out to have a
further characteristic in common. Figures such as A. J. Ayer, Isaiah Berlin,
A. L. Rowse, and A. J. P. Taylor (all born within two or three years of Hart)
differed intellectually, politically, personally, but they were all identified
to a greater or lesser extent with Oxford, and Oxford's standing in the
national culture during the middle decades of the twentieth century was a
crucial element in their reputation among a broader public. They belonged
to what is sometimes called 'the golden age of the dons', part of a generation
that may be said to have brought a pre-war social confidence to post-war
opportunities for addressing wider publics, through radio and television as
well as through paperbacks and Sunday papers. Although Hart addressed
these publics rather less than did his leading contemporaries, he was at the
centre of this milieu (even if not, as Lacey shows, always quite at ease in it);
he was an 'Oxford philosopher' at a time when that was widely regarded
as constituting a kind of gold standard in intellectual life. Moreover, he
applied his superlative analytic abilities to the law; jurisprudence can, of
course, be as impenetrable to the outsider as any other academic specialism, but the issues with which the law deals are issues of general interest

and acknowledged public and political importance, so Hart's work was assumed to be of some general consequence even when it was in practice quite technical. He is a curious case of a figure who attracted the kind of attention devoted to what is now coming to be called 'the public intellectual' even though he played that role to only a limited extent in his lifetime.

Hart was born in 1907 into a comfortably-off Jewish family in the genteel end of the rag trade in then-fashionable Harrogate. A spell at a public school was intended to ease the young man's assimilation into the upper reaches of English society (Hart hated the hearty athleticism), but a move to Bradford Grammar School proved more congenial as well as more stimulating intellectually. From there he won a scholarship to New College, Oxford, which opened the doors to a wider world: his brilliance was recognized by his teachers and contemporaries, and he came to know several of the members of the still small elite that was to occupy the leading positions in national life in the ensuing decades. Moreover, after his London years and an interesting war, Oxford was to be not just his home for most of his long life (he died in 1992), but also the defining mark of his social identity and the enabling setting for his work.

In the 1930s Hart appeared on the surface to be a fairly conventional young barrister, dining his way to preferment and participating in the traditional activities of the English upper classes ('just off to murder animals' was his somewhat less than conventional announcement of his hunting activities). But his inner life was both richer and more tortured than appearances suggested, and his life as a whole became still richer, though also more tortured, from the late 1930s as a result of his relationship with, and then marriage to, the socially unconventional and politically radical Jenifer Williams, who had just come higher in the Civil Service entry examinations than any woman had ever done previously. Jenifer's radicalism included a period as a member of the Communist Party, and later the couple were to endure some anguish as the result of a media-stoked fuss over whether she had worked for Soviet intelligence and whether during the war her high-ranking husband had known of her activities. Lacey's careful account demonstrates how little substance there was to the charge, though Jenifer's characteristically incautious dealings with the press did not help. And, of course, there was some general plausibility to the concern, especially when one remembers that, as Lacey nicely puts it: 'In the period before the war, Soviet intelligence had more British graduates working for it than did MI5 and MI6 combined.'

Hart had a good war. His evident abilities found a satisfying outlet in organizing the information derived from MI5's counter-espionage activities; he was so highly thought of by his colleagues that he became the crucial link between MI5 and MI6, eventually enabling the former to have access to the top secret information yielded by Bletchley Park's decoding of the German ULTRA signals. It says much about the way the British academic elite was used in the Second World War, as well as about the interlocking of their post-war careers, that (as mentioned above) the three figures with whom Hart worked most closely in trying to bring about more fruitful forms of coopera-tion between MI5 and MI6 should all have been young Oxford academics who, like Hart himself, were to go on to be professors or heads of house.

After his return to Oxford, Hart became a core member of the group who practised what was coming to be termed 'ordinary-language philosophy', the pursuit of philosophical enlightenment through the almost obsessively close attention to the distinctions embodied in (highly educated) everyday speech, an activity carried on in its purest, and subsequently most legendary, form at the Saturday morning gatherings that took place in the rooms of the acknowledged leader of the group, J. L. Austin (it seems to have been taken for granted that these men—they were all men—were free to devote Saturday morning to philosophical argument, rather than, say, trips to Sainsbury's). Philosophy of this kind was the subject done by the very clever boys, and they were confident that it was a more rigorous and worthwhile subject than many of those practised by their putatively less clever colleagues. When Hart was elected to the Chair of Jurispru-dence (partly as a result of machinations by Austin himself), he was congratulated by Austin in revealing terms: 'It is splendid to see the empire of philosophy annex another province in this way—not to mention the good you're going to do them.' Yet this great success was simultaneously an acknowledgement of a kind of defeat, for, like his close friend Isaiah Berlin at about the same time, Hart was recognizing that he was never going to be an absolutely first-rate philosopher, in which case (they both seem to have decided) it was better to apply one's philosophical abilities in a field where they could make some real difference than to be an also-ran in what they and their circle never doubted was Top Subject. Hart's later, charac-teristically self-mocking, assessment of the result of this move was that 'the philosophers thought I was a marvellous lawyer and the lawyers thought I was a marvellous philosopher'.

The transformation that Hart wrought in jurisprudence as a result of this particular piece of intellectual imperialism is now the stuff of text-book histories. The law is in some ways ideal terrain for ordinary-language philosophy: cases constitute a vast library of conceptual distinctions using the everyday language of causation and responsibility, and Hart's first book, *Causation in the Law* (written jointly with his Oxford colleague A. M. Honoré), showed just what could be done using the techniques of

Austinian analysis. But his masterpiece, *The Concept of Law*, published in 1961, was altogether more ambitious, since it attempted to work out the defining characteristics of the very notion of 'law', especially what made a legal system different from either a moral code or a set of authoritative commands. Hart's answer to this question has been at the centre of subsequent jurisprudence, and Lacey gives an admirably lucid account of the positions taken both by his leading critics, such as Ronald Dworkin, and by Hart himself in his later responses to criticism. To the outsider, it is the sheer ambition of *The Concept of Law* that is so impressive: from its opening pages, one registers the calm assurance in its prose that, although the history of thinking about this subject is largely a history of muddle, a sufficiently careful and patient examination of fundamental notions will allow the daunting variety of empirical examples of legal systems to be successfully encompassed in a conceptual analysis that is clear, coherent, and persuasive. For all the clarity and crisp decisiveness of Hart's writing, his book can be hard going for any but specialist readers, though this has not unduly limited its impact: Lacey reports the surely astonishing fact that it has sold over 150,000 copies and still continues to sell, over forty years after its first publication, several thousand each year.

The other book by Hart that also still has a remarkably flourishing existence is *Law, Liberty, and Morality*, a slim volume containing three lectures he gave at Stanford in 1962. Here he argued against the view—a view that had a distinguished intellectual genealogy and that had recently been reasserted by the conservative judge Patrick Devlin—that the criminal law should attempt to enforce society's moral code. Hart argued passionately for the separation of law and morality, especially in the area of sexuality; his support, here and elsewhere, for the decriminalization of homosexuality was to be influential on law reform in the 1960s. These lectures evince a deep temperamental liberalism (the Mill of *On Liberty* is hailed as a fellow-spirit), and this is one of the areas where the biographical evidence about his own life and the account of his jurisprudential work are brought into fruitful contact. Unlike some advocates of toleration (including perhaps Mill himself), Hart really does seem to have been admirably tolerant in his own life, a quality that was repeatedly put to the test in his marriage even more than in most marriages. At the same time he shared that somewhat moralistic asceticism that marked this whole high-thinking but rather plain-living 'intellectual aristocracy', a social formation that was notably more indulgent towards adultery than towards laziness, far more forgiving of various forms of nonconformity than of any form of vulgarity.

Thereafter, though Hart wrote some important new papers and restatements of his earlier positions, he did not publish any other major books;

perhaps the most important project of his later years was his general
editorship of the massive (and still-ongoing) edition of the works of Jeremy
Bentham, long one of his intellectual heroes. Indeed, with the unsparing
honesty in self-examination that comes to seem wholly typical of him, he
decided in 1968 to retire early from his chair (at age 61) precisely because
he felt he had no further original contribution to make. By this point he had
become, almost despite himself, a member of the Great and Good, and so
was called upon for various forms of public service; he also agreed, with
much misgiving, to become the Principal of Brasenose College in Oxford.
Becoming the head of a college is one of the most curious forms of distinction
in the Oxbridge world, a largely social and administrative role that might
be thought to reverse the prerogative of the harlot and confer responsibility
without power. Hart's habitual liberalism and easy informality saw him
through a turbulent period in the life of universities without undue mishap.

He was also an international academic superstar in the period that, thanks
in part to post-war prosperity and jet travel, saw the first real flourishing of that
species. He was particularly fêted in the United States, in whose universities
he discovered that, reversing the Oxford order, law outranked philosophy in
glamour and prestige. When Hart visited Israel in 1964, he was advertised
as lecturing on 'Contemporary British Philosophy and Jewish Prudence'. It
would have been a wonderfully revealing subject on which to have heard him.
A certain reticence about his Jewishness could be seen as a form of prudence,
and it would have been intriguing to learn whether he thought there was
any intrinsic, rather than biographically contingent, connection between
this characteristic and the nature of the intellectually bold but sociologically
constrained (and in some ways typically English) analytical philosophy at
which he excelled. But alas, the announced title had resulted from the locally
plausible garbling of his actual, and more conventional, topic.

Lacey tells her story well, with some lengthy intermissions to brief the
reader on the main positions in the jurisprudential controversies in which
Hart was involved. There is occasionally a slight grinding of the gears as
she attempts to cater for different types of audience, learned and lay, British
and American, and a few of the slips seem surprising in an author so alert
to the social and cultural context of Hart's life (for example, misdating
the affair of the Oxford honorary degree for Thatcher to 1987 rather than
1985, or referring to the Third Programme of the 1950s as 'Radio 3'). Lacey
received full cooperation and encouragement from Jenifer Hart (who died
only in March 2005, after the book's publication); being on the receiving
end of the widow's might can be a decidedly mixed blessing for a biographer, and some readers may feel that this book is a little too indulgent
to Jenifer, perhaps too indulgent to indiscretion generally, but Lacey's

primary purpose is to exhibit and illuminate the character of a man whom she clearly admired, and in this the biography succeeds handsomely.

The drawing of larger conclusions from her subject's life is, understandably, not part of her purpose. To my mind, the most significant general thought one may take away from the narrative is the empowering effect of an academic culture that was socially secure, politically liberal, and intellectually confident. As an individual, Hart himself, as Lacey shows in some detail, was wracked by anxiety, depression, and inner conflict. But he was sufficiently brilliant to gain acceptance from the small group who set the pace in the subject that had the highest prestige in the university that took its pre-eminence for granted in a society that had an immense accumulation of self-confidence. Many values and assumptions were so deeply shared in that academic culture, and so readily accepted and deferred to by the wider society, that they never really needed to be articulated, let alone justified. Hart possessed his full share of the analytical philosopher's urge to strip any topic down to its conceptual building blocks and then to reassemble it in a tidier form, but he was not constrained by any inhibiting self-doubt about the value of this kind of philosophy or the significance of the conclusions that he and his immediate colleagues came to. The important thing was to be very clever about important questions: it was taken for granted that the relevant parts of the world would be interested in the outcome and not disposed to be too tiresome about what constituted either cleverness or importance. After all, only the slow-witted would linger over propositions that were (in a favoured idiom of the tribe) 'manifestly false'. Seeing things in the form of 'propositions', and then conducting a stiff philosophy tutorial on their clarity and coherence, could indeed dispose of a lot of fuzzy thinking, though it was perhaps less well adapted to doing justice to matters of deep human experience that could not without loss be formulated in a series of neat 'propositions'.

No contemporary reader can fail to be aware that it has since become fashionable to emphasize the weaknesses of any kind of socially confident, largely male, ethnically homogeneous ruling caste, and much effort now goes into sociologizing the conditions of possibility of such elites and probing the coercive power of what is left unsaid and unacknowledged in their supposedly transparent activities. The estranging labour of such criticism is obviously necessary and valuable in many cases, but in our rush to democratic self-congratulation we should not lose sight of the ways in which a certain mix of intellectual assurance, secure status, and relaxed agreement on fundamentals can prove fertile ground for thinking of the highest quality. This confidence, and an associated puzzlement that anyone could take a serious interest in propositions that were said, in another crisp piece of the local patois, to be 'either trivial or false', actually made that world's political and social liberalism all the stronger. Hart and his circle obviously appreciated that there were a lot of people out there who held passionately to a whole slate of illiberal prejudices and convictions, but since they could themselves see 'no good reason' for upholding these beliefs they were not going to be easily derailed from the task of making more enlightened ideas prevail. Much good came from this confidence, an alliance of theory and practice that was most winningly represented in the 1960s by Hart as legal philosopher and Roy Jenkins as Home Secretary. The social assurance of this milieu was, it is now needless to say, a two-edged sword, but, if one was in a position to share it, then it was immensely empowering, sometimes precisely because it was simultaneously blinkering. Lacey's biography does not really explore this academic culture in these terms, but it does provide some marvellous material that could be put at the service of a more analytical and less biographical account.

This is in some ways a brave book that deserves its success. British literary culture is still extremely indulgent to biography as a genre, and the level of attention and controversy that Lacey's book has already attracted, well beyond the confines of academic legal philosophy, shows what can be done by a determined and worldly biographer even with ostensibly unpromising clay. Lacey provides a sympathetic and emotionally imaginative narrative of Hart's life and a well-informed, thoughtful account of his work. Throughout, she attempts to link these two things, always a tricky enterprise that risks falling into various forms of biographical reductionism as well as being hampered in other ways by the individualistic focus that the genre demands. After reading this book, I am persuaded that Hart's inner conflicts are germane to an understanding of his *career*, but I am left feeling that they may be of only limited relevance to characterizing his *thought*. That thinking, the activity that Hart was so supremely good at, is inherently historical and dependent upon a world of social practices and cultural assumptions that inevitably exceed the biographer's remit. It is no criticism of Lacey's excellent book to reflect that Hart himself would have been among the first to acknowledge the ways in which thinking well about law needs, like law itself, to be understood as a social practice.

III

André Malraux incarnated a certain ideal of 'the French intellectual'. A writer of international renown, he distinguished himself as a man of action before going on to become an eye-catching politician. But above all else, Malraux was a world-class fantasist. Having invented himself, he then constantly reinvented a past commensurate with the stature he imagined himself to have attained. General de Gaulle said that by having Malraux at his right hand he was thereby 'shielded from the commonplace'. That was indeed Malraux's speciality. What he represented—politically, artistically, humanly—was transcendence of the mundane. He regarded his first duty to himself to be that of escaping from the petty. The nouns in his life all had to have capital letters. The great novel or epic that his career always strove to become needed to be freed from the entangling minutiae of history so that he could take his place in History. Malraux was on intimate terms with Mankind; his diary was filled with dates with Posterity. The day-to-day was tiresome, the Eternal was exhilarating. One did not belong among pygmies.

Malraux gave himself airs so that others could more easily recognize his greatness. He never answered the telephone himself, even at home; it was not consistent with his dignity. 'Nobody disturbs General de Gaulle' on the telephone, he commented, justifying his affectation by placing himself in the only company he thought appropriate. The relationship with de Gaulle is the key to the second half of Malraux's life. After the Liberation of France in 1944, Malraux supported de Gaulle against the Communists in the struggle to become the legitimate representatives of post-Vichy France. Thereafter, it suited de Gaulle to have the unconditional allegiance of a leading writer and intellectual who was also an accredited hero; Malraux gave de Gaulle a certain cultural legitimacy just as de Gaulle gave Malraux a certain political protection.

In turn, Malraux provides a clue to understanding what outsiders often find so baffling about the behaviour of the French state. Occupying lead roles in the theatre of appearances, both de Gaulle and Malraux were more exercised by the need to cut a fine, and wholly French, figure than by the obligation to pursue the least bad course of action. The ambition was partly individual, but it was also historical and collective, a tradition of conceiving politics more in terms of *la gloire* than of GNP. Moreover, it is a recurring vanity in French leaders to want to be thought of as writers as well as statesmen: one aims to shape History but also to shape the history books. Malraux encouraged de Gaulle to think that he was penning the national epic; de Gaulle encouraged Malraux to believe that he was an actor on the world stage. In either case, one does not fulfil one's tryst with Destiny by scrabbling about among the footnotes. One embodies one's Country, one expresses one's Century, one illumines the Human Condition. De Gaulle and Malraux recognized the grandeur of France in each other.

A life passed in this elevated register is not likely to emerge unscathed from that most mundane and unforgiving of forms, the carefully researched, coolly appraising biography. Olivier Todd's lively account, now translated as *Malraux: A Life*, is not primarily distinguished by its coolness, but his research in the biographical sources and his knowledge of the period are more than enough to show up the fabrications out of which the myth of Malraux was woven. Yet even the unvarnished facts read like an amalgam of famous fictional characters—out of Victor Hugo by Ernest Hemingway, with a dash of Graham Greene (for several years Malraux was a whisky minister to match Greene's whisky priest).

Born in 1901 into a struggling lower-middle-class family, Malraux did not follow the *cursus* of the classic French intellectual. He did not even finish his secondary schooling, let alone receive any higher education (though later in life he mostly got away with the claim that he had taken a degree from the École des Langues Orientales in Paris). Having dabbled in the second-hand book trade and become a minor reviewer, he was still in his early twenties when he was arrested for looting temples in Cambodia; suitably buffed up, this episode became the foundation for his later reputation as an expert on Eastern art. He briefly edited an anti-colonial newspaper in French Indochina, before returning to make a literary career in Paris, a strategy that paid off handsomely when his second novel, *La Condition humaine*, won the *Prix Goncourt* in 1933. One of the things that most strikes the non-French reader of this biography is the extraordinary prestige accorded to writers in France during this period: their utterances, however vacuous or pernicious, were guaranteed respectful attention. Winning the Goncourt at the age of 32 was a success from which Malraux's career never recovered.

From the Cambodian escapade onwards, the heart of the Malraux myth lay in the ideal of the Writer as Man of Action. The Spanish Civil War provided the perfect stage. Without ever joining the Communist Party, Malraux was committed to the anti-Fascist cause, and he gave practical expression to this allegiance by 'commanding' a volunteer air squadron on the Republican side. (It is true that he did largely procure and organize the aircraft, but in fact he never flew them himself.) In reality, the terrain of his greatest triumphs was that of publicity. He ensured good press coverage of 'the Malraux squadron'; rumour had it that his fetching uniform was specially made by Lanvin. At the same time, the Spanish experience fed his imagination, providing the setting both for his novel *L'Espoir*, published in 1937, and for a film he made in 1938, *Sierra de Teruel*. Malraux was becoming a twentieth-century Renaissance Man; it seemed there was nothing he could not do—or, at least, nothing he could not get away with.

Even in a life largely made up of murky episodes, Malraux's role in the Second World War is where the relation between myth and reality are at their murkiest. In the years immediately following the end of the war, Malraux made much of how he had been in the Resistance from an early date, acting as 'regional commander' in south-west France, arrested by the Germans and wounded while making a brave escape. For these exploits, he was decorated by both the French and British governments. In fact, these claims were nearly all untrue. After the French defeat in 1940, Malraux lived peacefully in southern France, refusing to join the Resistance, right up until March 1944, only a few weeks before the Allied landings in Normandy. He then characteristically set himself up as 'area coordinator', though no Resistance forces corresponded to the units he claimed to be 'coordinating'. On the strength of this invented standing, and an ability to cut a fine figure in beret and fatigues, he assumed command of a Free French brigade that fought the Germans in eastern France in late 1944. 'Colonel Malraux' had never been commissioned and had never received more than basic training, but he proved himself a brave and inspiring leader of his raggle-taggle soldiers, albeit relying on subordinates to look after the nuts and bolts of the operations.

By the end of the war, Malraux had made the personal and political choice that was largely to determine the rest of his life. He became de Gaulle's indispensable man. He was rewarded with a post in the General's first post-war government; only now can one properly appreciate the irony that this incorrigible fantasist was put in charge of 'information'. Meanwhile, his literary standing continued to grow. In 1947 he was only the second living author (Gide had been the first) to be honoured with a *Pléiade* edition of his works; for the next couple of decades there was a constant rumour that he was about to be awarded the Nobel Prize for Literature (on several occasions he turned down election to the Académie Française, believing he should save himself for the higher, more fitting, honour).

When in 1958 de Gaulle founded the Fifth Republic and became its first President, he created a new Ministry of Culture: this provided Malraux with the ideal stage for his theatrical talents (though he, characteristically, had hoped for something grander still). He stayed in office until de Gaulle's final resignation ten years later, an extraordinary length of tenure for a minister in the unstable world of post-war French politics. Malraux was de Gaulle's cultural *force de frappe*: his mere presence helped the French government to face down potentially damaging critics. Malraux, needless to say, still yearned for the glamour of front-line action. When in 1961 right-wing generals briefly threatened an uprising against de Gaulle's policy of granting independence to Algeria, the 60-year-old Minister of Culture declared himself ready to command a tank unit against them; his officials had to look away. For a period in the mid-1960s, Malraux was sometimes too drunk to conduct the daily business of his ministry—but, then, the daily anything was never his forte.

His strength as a politician lay in making the large public gesture. He gloried in being the man who 'took the Mona Lisa to Washington' (against the unanimous advice of the Louvre's curators). He committed substantial sums of public money to the cleaning and restoration of Paris's monuments and façades (though it had been begun by others before him). He established *Maisons de la culture* in French provincial towns. But, as any B-list celebrity instinctively knows, what really counts is who you are photographed with. Just as he had met Trotsky before the war, now he met Mao (a much mythologized and embroidered event) and Nehru, and Kennedy, and Nixon. Nor did he neglect his literary reputation. When his hard-to-classify *Antimémoires* came out in 1967, its success (it sold 200,000 copies in three weeks) surprised everyone except the author. As he informed his daughter at the time: 'I am the only writer who counts.' A sign of another kind of standing was the fact that he had a dish named after him at Lasserre, his favourite, and very expensive, Parisian restaurant (*pigeon André Malraux*; Todd includes the recipe), thereby achieving at least one kind of immortality to match Chateaubriand's. For some years before his death in 1976 he was, as Todd nicely puts it, 'drugged with honour and respect'. He had long been intoxicated with a sense of his own importance; his remarkable achievement was to persuade so many others to share that sense.

'Lie' is a rough word. Todd has occasion to use it more than once of Malraux, and with reason, but there is a sense in which it reduces him unduly. To term Malraux's high-handed doctorings of the historical record 'lies' is to domesticate them, to reinsert them in the fabric of the everyday. To Malraux, they were expressions of an essential, supra-mundane truth. As with certain religious thinkers, his mind roved beyond the borders of the knowable with an easy majesty. Unclarities and inconsistencies showed only that one was a true explorer of the universe of the imagination; tidying up the loose ends would at least provide some employment for the pygmies.

One danger of living one's life entirely in the major key is that bathos and humiliation can never be far away. But in Malraux's case it also meant that he could rise to the state occasions of human experience more readily than any of the earth-bound plodders, and there are times when only the elevated will do. He had, it must be said, a marvellous capacity to inspire, whether addressing troops facing a high risk of death or recalling the claims on the living of some moral giant now dead. Wrapped against the cold, his voice cracking and echoing in the badly connected microphones, Malraux gave the eulogy for the German-executed Resistance leader, Jean Moulin, on the occasion of the transfer of the latter's ashes to the Panthéon in 1964.

It remains a haunting performance. The oratory is more than dated: it has a Racinian, even Roman, cadence to it. It is excessive, and thereby right for an occasion when mere accuracy of fact and characterization would have been thinly inadequate.

Todd's biography has a certain racy charm, but the reader should be warned that it is written in the present tense throughout: in English, this comes across as a striving for dramatic immediacy, something that, across several hundred pages, is bound to grate. There is also a good deal of reconstructed dialogue, quite a few asides to the reader, and some maddening descents into the style of tabloid journalism. This, for example, is how Todd narrates the moment when Malraux learns that his lover, Louise de Vilmorin, is simultaneously having an affair with another man: 'Why should Malraux have it all? Some kind soul tells him about the Vilmorin–Sieburg affair. Free love? No thanks, and not with me: Malraux breaks it off. Three women to run away from... Travel is a cure for women. Sometimes.' Malraux's own prose could be oracular, gnomic, and mannered, but it never, ever, sounded like a series of captions to a photo-spread in *Paris Match*.

The final tragedy of the life of this compelling, extravagant, flawed man—a tragedy he would have felt more keenly than almost anyone with whom he shared 'his' century—was that there was no André Malraux on hand to pronounce the *éloge* when, in 1996, twenty years after his death, he was accorded the ultimate accolade of having his ashes transferred to the Panthéon. He was installed in the temple of France's *grands hommes*, among those few peers whose company he had long craved, to the accompaniment of tired clichés spoken by that most banal of Gaullist machine politicians, Jacques Chirac. At the last, Malraux had fallen among mere mortals, a giant carried on the shoulders of pygmies. Sometimes, History can be the cruellest mistress of all.

23

National Lives:
The Oxford Dictionary of National Biography

I

Let me begin with a few unusual admissions. First, I haven't read all the work under 'review'; indeed, I haven't read most of it. Second, I wrote some of it. Third, some of the bits not written by me were written by my close friends and colleagues. In the light of these incriminating facts, you may be less than wholly astonished to learn that I think the *Oxford Dictionary of National Biography* (hereafter the *ODNB*) is a quite magnificent achievement. But, just to dispose of one possible ground for suspecting the motives behind my enthusiasm, I should also say that I didn't get a review copy.

This last fact is probably fortunate given that I live in quite a small house, but it does mean that I have been consulting the *ODNB* in the way most users presumably will, taking down the reassuringly solid volumes in the familiar Oxford blue and gold livery from the shelves of my university library's reading room or sitting at my desk calling up the online version (to the joys of which I shall return). A dictionary is, first and foremost, a practical resource; its usability when subjected to a variety of everyday scholarly demands must be the chief test of its worth. But a work on this scale is bound also to be seen as much more than a reference tool: as, by turns, a statement of national identity, an occasion for communal pride, a showcase for contemporary historical scholarship, a piece of swagger publishing, and, less directly, a kind of stay against oblivion, a giant memorial slab designed to stir thoughts on fame and obscurity, on mortality and immortality.

H. C. G. Matthew and Brian Harrison (eds), *The Oxford Dictionary of National Biography*, 60 vols (Oxford University Press, 2004).

And then (let's be honest) there's the respectable nerdiness of it all. Leslie Stephen, founding editor in the 1880s of the original Dictionary of National Biography (hereafter *DNB*), hoped that work would turn out to be one of the 'most amusing' of books. This remark may have to be interpreted in the light of the fact that Stephen's own preferred form of 'amusement' involved hanging by his fingertips from a ledge on the Matterhorn in the middle of a blizzard, but it is true that an abundance of pleasure, of a certain kind, is to be had from the sixty volumes assembled by his successors. As ways of simultaneously wasting one's time while increasing one's knowledge, they leave skinny tomes such as *Wisden* or *Whitaker's Almanac* standing.

Since its carefully orchestrated launch at the end of September 2004, this extraordinary publication has hardly lacked for attention ('the greatest book ever' according to the *Daily Mail*), and by now many readers may be weary of hearing about the sixty-two million words, the 10,000 contributors, the 587 miles of sewing thread, the four tons of glue, the entries on the earliest known importer of garden gnomes or the eighteenth-century woman who claimed to have given birth to seventeen rabbits, and so on. Stephen expressed characteristic anxiety as the moment approached when his first volumes would 'come before the infernal body of reviewers' (the original *DNB* marched through the alphabet at a rate of four volumes per year rather than being published simultaneously as a complete set), and at a later point, when he guessed the authorship of a forthcoming review in the *Quarterly Review*, he anticipated the worst from someone 'who always pays us a big compliment or two and then nags at us all through the article'. The publication of the *ODNB* has been the occasion for many 'big compliments' and rather little nagging, though there are already a few signs that the sport of pointing out errors may help to fill the vacuum left by the banning of fox-hunting. Well-meaning friends and colleagues have rushed to provide me with examples of errors, but since every visit to shelf or screen has left me in a state of head-shaking amazement at the quantity of exact information packed into its pages, I feel no inclination to 'nag'. Moreover, the *ODNB*, exploiting the resources of electronic publication, will henceforth be a continuing operation, so corrections should be sent direct to Oxford for incorporation into the forthcoming updatings (the first of which is already online). What it may be appropriate to do here, apart from applauding and giving thanks, is to reflect on the assumptions implicit in the inclusions and exclusions, the style and content of the entries, and the general strategy of the enterprise, and to consider in what ways, if any, these may be thought to differ from those informing the original *DNB*.

II

The project of undertaking a national biographical dictionary was first announced at Christmas 1882, and already by March 1885 Stephen was mock-moaning to Edmund Gosse: 'I have made more enemies in these two years than in ten years of editing the *Cornhill*. One man signed himself the other day "your justly incensed enemy"—because I had not asked him to write articles already assigned to others and he is not an extreme example of the antiquarian.' As copy started to arrive, Stephen wailed over 'the insane verbosity of the average writer', and he cut some contributions by over half. One assumes that in the 1880s conversation in the smoking room of the Athenaeum was considerably taken up by the venting of comparative grievances about the injuries contributors' prose had suffered at Stephen's hand. One enemy he certainly made was Alexander Balloch Grosart DD, who was invited to contribute several entries for the first volumes, principally on seventeenth-century divines. As early as October 1883, Stephen was complaining that he had 'had my usual letter of abuse from that old fool Grosart', but things took an altogether more serious turn when it was discovered, very late in the day, that Grosart had not only reproduced, without acknowledgement, entries he had already published in the *Encyclopaedia Britannica*, but had actually resorted to inventing some of his sources as well. This discovery entailed much revision and checking of entries, delaying the publication of the first volumes. Stephen, always given to lamentation and gnashing of teeth, feared the whole project would be shipwrecked by this 'clerical scoundrel' ('his D.Dship gives an extra flavour to my execrations', noted the firmly anti-clerical Stephen), but with the help of his indefatigable assistant, and eventual successor, Sidney Lee, the ship was put back on an even keel. Curiously, although the Grosart debacle, fully documented in John Bicknell's edition of Stephen's letters, is briefly mentioned in Alan Bell's exemplary entry on Stephen in the *ODNB*, these misdemeanours make no appearance in Arthur Sherbo's entry on Grosart himself.

Thereafter, the *DNB* maintained its announced schedule most impressively, reaching the end of the alphabet with the four volumes published in 1900, and completing the enterprise with three supplementary volumes in 1901 that were designed to remedy obvious omissions (as well as providing the opportunity to include the recently deceased queen). The achievement was hailed as bearing out the familiar truths of national character. The dictionary had been undertaken by the publisher George Smith as a piece of private enterprise, with no official or institutional backing, and it had been brought to completion in record time by a very small staff. Less fortunate nations, in whom the spirit of liberty and the energy of 'character' had been suppressed by centuries of tyranny and regulation, may have committed public funds to corresponding enterprises, but their progress had been slower and the outcomes less glorious. 'Our British lexicographers', declared the *Athenaeum* in 1900, 'have had the satisfaction of administering a handsome beating to their most formidable competitors, the Germans.' Our dictionary had 'trotted the distance' in little more than half the time it had taken the initiative-lacking Teutons 'to waddle through the alphabet'.

The *ODNB* has operated with a far larger and better qualified team of research editors than Stephen and Lee ever had at their command, and one assumes that any contemporary Grosarts were picked up early on (though there may continue to be minor alarums, such as the recent spat over the entry for Patrick O'Brian). Nonetheless, a not dissimilar kind of sleep-disturbing responsibility fell on its editor, and the project was fortunate to find the ideal man for the job in the Oxford historian Colin Matthew, who had demonstrated his capacity for the task in his monumental edition of the Gladstone diaries. Matthew became the founding editor of the *ODNB* in 1992, and much of the credit for both the conception and the early stages of execution of the work clearly belongs to him. The labour and anxiety of the original *DNB* so told on Stephen's health that he had to be more or less bullied into resigning the editorship with the dictionary only half completed (though he continued to contribute entries to the end). We shall presumably never know whether the burdens of the post contributed to Matthew's sudden death in 1999 at the age of 58, but the structure he created proved its durability at this crisis, and when another Oxford historian, Brian Harrison, was appointed as editor in 2000, he was still able to bring the whole enormous project to completion on the very date that Matthew had laid down eleven years before. It is tempting to think of Matthew and Harrison as the Stephen and Lee of the *ODNB*, though Harrison, his task completed, has now stepped down and handed the oversight of the continuing life of the dictionary to a third Oxford-based historian, Lawrence Goldman. An incidental but peculiarly fitting consequence of Matthew's early death was that he thereby qualified for inclusion himself, an entry done quite beautifully by his friend and colleague Ross McKibbin.

The explanation for Matthew's inclusion should also answer the question that may be forming in the minds of the more self-important readers who are assuming that this compilation is something like an extended *Who's Who*. Putting it at its simplest, if you are reading this you are not in the *ODNB*. Candidates for inclusion must have died by 31 December 2000. Those anxious about their posthumous status need not despair, however: henceforth the new editorial team will be sitting in more or less constant session, acting like a collective St Peter to decide who should be admitted through the electronic pearly gates of the regularly updated version.

So what *are* the criteria for inclusion, aside from being dead? These have been stated in slightly different terms at different stages in the progress of this project, but the most inclusive brief formula is that subjects must have 'in some way influenced national life'. Flocks of begged questions immediately descend like gulls in a trawler's wake, since what individual has not 'in some way' 'influenced' the 'life' of the society in which they lived? On the broadest construal, this would issue in a kind of comprehensive prosopography of everyone who had ever lived in a given territory (and of a good many who lived outside it as well). In practice, the *ODNB* has interpreted this criterion in a relaxed and pragmatic way: the emphasis on 'national' life is not just a stab at delimiting the geographical spread but has also been taken to mean that a candidate must in some way have come to the notice of a wider world beyond their own immediate circle. The upshot is a gathering that extends far beyond just 'the Great and Good', 'the Establishment', or 'the nation's heroes', as is suggested by the much-cited cases of Sir Charles Isham (1819–1903, 'rural improver and gardener') and Mary Toft (1703–63, 'the rabbit-breeder').

The *ODNB*'s greater inclusiveness is one of the ways it differs not just from its predecessor but also from *Who's Who*, often regarded in the twentieth century as the antechamber to the *DNB*. In that curious publication, archaic categories such as pedigree and social rank still apply, alongside office, achievement, and, erratically, celebrity; in a world where it is very hard to say who is who any more, its listings evince a nostalgia for a time when viscounts outranked baronets, and when cooks and dressmakers knew their place (that is, not at the top of the best-seller lists). The *ODNB* is in several ways more democratic: mere rank (at least in the modern period, and below a certain level) won't get you in, but committing a murder that makes you a 'household name' will (indeed, simply being the victim of the murder will do it as well in some cases).

Broadly speaking, one can distinguish seven main sociological layers of *ODNB* subjects. First, there's the retrospective 'burial in the Abbey' layer: monarchs, statesmen, prelates, and the like. Next, there's the 'land and glory' crowd: owning a lot of acres or killing a lot of foreigners have ever been among the most reliable passports to distinction in British life. Then there's the 'Athenaeum Club of the ages': judges, authors, civil servants, scientists, professors, and their ilk. Next comes the 'Institute of Directors across the centuries': the controllers of capital and the boss class generally. After that there's the '*Hello!* in history' gang: the celebrated, the notorious, the newly rich, the eternally shameless. Then we have the 'historical oddities' category: the very old, the very weird, the very unlikely. And finally, there's the 'would have been invited to the Buckingham Palace garden party' category: the local notables, the top nurses, the holders of gongs, and so on. We don't seem quite to get down to the historical equivalents of deserving lollipop ladies and organizers of the local scout troop, but one imagines the editorial committee greeting each new suggestion with a collective 'Respect!'

One way to see implicit hierarchies at work among these groups is to consider the length of the various entries, since these were laid down by the editorial team and represented an attempt to secure broad parity of treatment for individuals of broadly comparable 'importance'. It is mildly paradoxical that a figure about whose life we know very little emerges by this measure as the undisputed Top British Person: William Shakespeare (1564–1616, 'playwright and poet') is allotted more than 30,000 words, a length achieved only by devoting a large proportion of them to various aspects of his literary after-life—about which, of course, we know a good deal more. The usual suspects are close on his heels—Elizabeth I (1533–1603, 'queen of England and Ireland'), Cromwell (1599–1658, 'Lord Protector of England, Scotland, and Ireland'), Wellington (1769–1852, 'army officer and prime minister'), Victoria (1819–1901, 'queen of the United Kingdom of Great Britain and Ireland, and Empress of India'), Churchill (1874–1965, 'prime minister'), and so on. So far, so conventional, though none of this comes close to the monstrous exercise in sycophancy represented by the decision to include in the original *DNB* an entry of no fewer than 93,000 words on Queen Victoria. That entry was written by Lee himself, and, as the historian A. F. Pollard drily noted, it 'ran to double the length of Shakespeare, though in her case bibliographical detail was as scanty as biographical was in Shakespeare's'.

Not many figures, it should be said, qualify for treatment at anything like this length. Brian Harrison's informative introduction to the dictionary tells us that the average size of entries is 1,087 words. Since the tariff for even middle-ranking literary and intellectual figures (the areas where my interests have largely dictated my use of the dictionary) seems to start at around 3,000 words, and since most of the people the reasonably well-educated reader would have heard of in any sphere receive more than this, that average underlines just how inclusive the *ODNB* actually is. It is worth adding that one further way to qualify for inclusion in the *ODNB* was to have been in the old *DNB*. One of the most controversial early editorial decisions was to retain every subject from the *DNB*, even though one or two of them turn out never to have existed. In some cases, entries in the old *DNB* have merely been revised, but in the majority of cases entirely new entries have been commissioned. Given the constituency that responded most enthusiastically to Stephen's request for suggestions in the 1880s, this decision has also had the result of including disproportionate numbers of minor clergymen, perhaps the scout-troop leaders of their day.

III

A lot of fuss has been made about how the *ODNB* defines (or fails to define) 'the nation', but commentary soon gets mired in the intractable problems of defining such an entity in the case of the inhabitants of this particular north-west European archipelago over more than two millennia. From the point of view of the purists, the rot sets in early in this respect. Those of sardonic disposition may be pleased to find that the national history begins with a hoax: the chronologically earliest 'figure' is Piltdown Man (*supp. fl.* 4 million BC, 'archaeological hoax'). Then comes Leir or Lear (*supp. fl. c.*820 BC, 'king of Britain'), followed by several other equally doubtful types whose inclusion prompts the thought that although subjects absolutely must be dead to merit inclusion, there is no equally stringent requirement about having lived in the first place; even some very dodgy figures such as 'Friar Tuck' (*fl.* 15th cent, 'legendary outlaw') get in. The chronologically earliest subject who indisputably existed is Pytheas (*fl.* 4th century BC, 'explorer'), a Greek who wrote the first known account of 'Britain', and he is followed by Julius Caesar (100–44 BC, 'politician, author, and military commander'), one of the first to have thought it was time Britain joined the larger European community.

While it is easy to see the merits of taking a fairly relaxed and inclusive view on the nationality question for the earliest periods, a degree of arbitrariness is bound to become more obvious the nearer one gets to the present. Hitler and Stalin 'influenced the nation's life' more than most in the twentieth century: the idea of their inclusion immediately strikes us as perverse, but would it really possess any greater logic if Hitler had, say, visited his troops at their Kent bridgehead in 1940? The porousness of the 'nation' as a category is most tellingly exhibited in the case of American subjects. Oxford University Press has been understandably keen to enhance the appeal of the dictionary in the United States; the inclusion of over 700 inhabitants of the American colonies before 1776 is obviously one cunning but defensible way to do this. But how thereafter are the discriminations to be made, given that relations remained so close for so long? Presumably, we have Thomas Jefferson (1743–1826, 'revolutionary politician and president of the United States') but not Dwight D. Eisenhower because the former was born in what was still at the time a British colony, though the latter spent more time in this country and arguably had a greater effect on its fate. Rather different considerations must have lain behind the inclusion of the nineteenth-century evangelist preachers Dwight Moody and Ira Sankey: though they were born, lived, and died in the United States, their revivalist meetings were hugely popular during their visits to Britain in the 1870s and 1880s, leading David Bebbington to make the startling claim in the course of his entry on them that 'Moody and Sankey probably represent the chief cultural influence of the United States on Britain during the nineteenth century'. Of course, if one really took seriously the criterion about having 'in some way influenced the nation's life', this would require the inclusion not only of Henry Ford and Walt Disney, but also of the CEOs of most big American corporations in the past century. This is one of the several ways in which one runs up against the limitations, for the purposes of historical understanding, of taking individual lives and 'the nation' as organizing units: the *forces* 'influencing the nation's life' are only intermittently half-visible in narratives of the lives of individuals who mostly happened to live mostly here. Even a hypothetical 'Dictionary of Global Biography' would not take one very far in trying to understand the processes summed up as 'globalization'.

If 'the nation's' history, as represented here, begins with a hoax, it ends with a whimper, but a whimper of a particularly frightened, appalling kind. It is true that the last entry, in terms of date of death, is Sir Jack Jacob (1908–2000, 'barrister and jurist'), who died on 26 December 2000, but the last to be born are, soberingly, Stephen Adrian Lawrence (1974–93, 'murder victim') and James Patrick Bulger (1990–3, 'murder victim'). And so ends the twentieth century.

Turning from subjects to contributors, the roll-call is undeniably impressive; surely no other project could come near to matching the success of the *ODNB* in commanding the labour of so many busy (and in many cases distinguished) people. Historians naturally predominate, and we get the grandmasters of the trade, such as Patrick Collinson on Elizabeth I, Michael Howard on Sir John Hackett, Eric Hobsbawm on Karl Marx (well, he lived here for thirty years, after all, and undeniably 'influenced the nation's life'). Also impressive is how frequently those who have already written the authoritative intellectual biography have been persuaded to contribute an epitome here—such as Roy Foster on W.B. Yeats or Ray Monk on Bertrand Russell—and some of our leading literary scholars have similarly undertaken to wax biographical about their favourite critical subjects, such as Christopher Ricks on Tennyson or Marilyn Butler on Jane Austen. There are one or two notable absences among those leading historians who have written principally on British topics—nothing from Linda

Colley or Quentin Skinner, for example—and some of the best-known contemporary exponents of biography have not contributed—no Peter Ackroyd, no Hermione Lee, no Victoria Glendinning, though there are three entries by Claire Tomalin, including Katherine Mansfield and Ellen Ternan, and four by Michael Holroyd, including Augustus John. Given the (exaggerated) claims made for the dictionary as 'the panorama of the national past', it is also worth remarking that there is nothing by those currently celebrated as the leading presenters of the nation's history, such as Simon Schama or David Starkey (the payments for contributions, it should be said, were meagre).

One cannot help wondering about the combination of self-restraint and sly wit that led Sir Keith Thomas, chairman of the dictionary's supervisory committee from inception to completion and himself one of the leading historians of his generation, to confine himself to a single entry, that on the figure known simply as Old Parr (d. 1635, 'supposed centenarian'). In my ignorance, I thought at first that this might have been the one joke entry all such reference works are said to contain, but if so it is an old joke, in every sense: Old Parr is in the original *DNB*. Thomas itemizes Parr's claims on the national attention—a bachelor till he was 80, he did penance for adultery when 105, married for the second time at 122, and died at 152—before scrupulously recording that they 'lacked documentary support'.

It would appear that Thomas, who at the time of the project's inception combined the key roles of President of the British Academy and Chairman of Oxford University Press's finance committee (as well as its Delegate for history), deserves much of the credit for persuading the project's three parent institutions—the university, the Academy, and the Press—to collaborate on the project. The financial commitment alone would surely have frightened off most publishers. In the historical account of the making of the *ODNB* given in Harrison's introduction, we are told that in 1993 the Delegates of Oxford University Press approved the final version of the proposal for the new dictionary, agreeing to undertake it 'as a service to scholarship in no expectation of a commercial return'. We are also told that OUP's total investment will have amounted to something over £22 million.

The quirky inclusiveness signalled by the presence of Old Parr in both versions of the dictionary is worth remembering as one concentrates on the differences between them. Stephen included some relatively obscure and even shady individuals, but Sidney Lee, and still more the editors of the supplementary volumes across the twentieth century, tended to favour those who wore well-cut suits and tightly knotted ties. Other exclusions aside, this contributed to the striking underrepresentation of women in the original dictionary and its supplements, satirically underscored by the well-known lament of Virginia Woolf (Stephen's daughter) in *Three Guineas* that 'it is much to be regretted that no lives of maids... are to be found' in the *DNB*. In the sixty-three volumes published by 1901, only about 4 per cent of subjects overall were female, and even the most recent supplementary volume (on the first half of the 1980s) managed only to increase this proportion to 12 per cent. Overall, the *ODNB* contains three times as many women as its predecessor, and for the twentieth century the proportion rises to (or still fails to rise above) 18 per cent.

Some of the other differences between the *ODNB* and its predecessor leap to the eye, not least as a result of the decision to include approximately 10,000 portraits and other likenesses; in addition to its main accomplishments, the *ODNB* now claims to be the largest collection of British portraiture ever published. Scarcely less visible on the page are the much fuller citations of sources, the very extensive listings of surviving archival deposits, and the provision, where available, of details of 'wealth at death'; against this, bibliographies of a subject's writings are no longer included. The accuracy and comprehensiveness of these features are the outcome of a major programme of co-operation with other national bodies, such as the National Portrait Gallery, the National Archives, and the General Registry Office.

As all this suggests, the most fundamental contrast between the two dictionaries lies in the hugely greater manifest presence of professional scholarly expertise in the *ODNB*. The original *DNB* was something of a belts and braces undertaking, where Stephen thought of himself as training up the kinds of contributor he needed. Even by 1906 when F. W. Maitland was writing his biography of Stephen (who had died two years earlier), he could reflect how much easier it would be to get such a scholarly enterprise going at that date than it had been for Stephen a couple of decades earlier, so marked had been the growth and professionalization of historical study in the interval, as represented by the founding of the *English Historical Review* and the expansion of the numbers studying history at the universities. Needless to say, the processes of professionalization and specialization have only accelerated in the century since Maitland's comment. It is true that an impressive volume of writing for the *ODNB* has still been done by the editors and a smallish number of in-house researchers: in addition to revising 631 entries, Matthew himself wrote 147 new articles, including those on leading politicians such as Balfour, Asquith, and, of course, Gladstone, as well as taking on Victoria (as co-author) and Edward VII. There have also been several largely unsung heroes and heroines among the in-house researchers, such as Anita McConnell, who wrote or revised almost 600 entries, chiefly on inventors and lesser scientists. Nonetheless, it is indisputable that the *ODNB* is far more an assemblage of the work of experts than its predecessor was, reflecting the mushrooming of specialized scholarship in the last century. The contrast is made most tellingly by two remarkable facts: first, that where the *ODNB* has some 10,000 contributors, the *DNB* had 647; and second, that more than half of the latter was written by just thirty-four people.

The correlative shift in our expectations can be illustrated by considering Stephen's own contributions. It is not so much the absolute number that is significant, though we must remember that his 378 ('I am surprised to find that I did so much in the way of articles') all had to be written from scratch, requiring in many cases considerable original research; it is, rather, the astonishing range of big names whom he felt competent to take on. Stephen wrote the entries for practically all the major literary and intellectual figures between the mid-seventeenth and mid-nineteenth centuries: Milton, Hobbes, Dryden, Locke, Addison, Pope, Hume, Johnson, Gibbon, Smith, Scott, Austen, Wordsworth, Coleridge, Malthus, Carlyle, Dickens, Macaulay, Mill, George Eliot, and more. The passing of the heroic age of biographical dictionary-making is nowhere more clearly signalled than in the fact that in the *ODNB* the entries for these twenty names have required twenty different contributors, all of them affiliated to academic institutions.

The tonal shift between the entries for these figures in the two volumes is particularly striking. Stephen's prose is full of tangy appraisals and bracing judgements. His preferred terms of admiration reflect the Victorian preoccupation with 'character', inflected perhaps by his own post-Carlylean endorsement of strenuousness as the essential ingredient of moral heroism. There's a fair bit of 'manliness' about in Stephen's entries, not a term that finds much favour in modern scholarly writing. And although he excelled at compressing a lot of information into the factual part of his narratives, there was also some splendidly uninhibited literary criticism in his concluding assessments, of that worldly, conversational, *Cornhill* kind he and his contemporary readers had long savoured (for example, on Macaulay: 'Nobody can hit a haystack with more certainty'). Stephen could place his own sardonic stamp on what were in some cases widely shared late-Victorian literary tastes. He did not, for example, consider Jane Austen a novelist of the first rank: he disposed of her in a meagre four columns, while taking his distance from ardent Janeites in other ways too ('I never knew a person thoroughly deaf to humour who did not worship Miss Austen'). Shifts in critical reputation as well as the progress of scholarly research on Austen's life are reflected in the *ODNB*'s deeply historical treatment of her as a challenging and intellectually serious writer, as well as in the fact that the entry is fourteen times longer than its brisk predecessor.

Stephen thought much more highly of George Eliot, on whom he wrote the volume in the unselfconsciously named 'English Men of Letters' series, but, like many of her first readers, he had a particular weakness for the affectionate evocation of simple country folk in her early works, such as *Adam Bede*, and he rather regretted the later expansion of her literary ambitions: 'The later books, in which the didactic impulse is strongest, suffer in comparison with the earlier, where it is latent.' And, although he did acknowledge the 'extraordinary power' of *Middlemarch*, he still lamented that 'the singular charm of the first period is wanting'. The taste of more recent generations (if not, perhaps, the absolutely most recent critical vocabulary) is evident in the *ODNB*'s praise for Eliot's 'study of provincial life' as 'astonishingly fully realized'. Actually, Rosemary Ashton is a little nearer to Stephen in manner than some of her more cautiously academic fellow-contributors, writing, for example, that 'Marian's was a difficult life, but a brave and extremely interesting one'. Of course, Stephen would have preferred to let his fingers slip off that Matterhorn ledge rather than refer to George Eliot as 'Marian', and that is not the only change in social mores illustrated in her entry. When one looks up 'George Eliot' in the *ODNB*, one is sent to the entry for 'Evans, Marian'; in the *DNB* one was directed to 'Cross, Mary Ann or Marian', her married name at the time of her death.

Other social as well as historiographical changes can be encapsulated in what the *ODNB* terms the 'statement of occupation or historical significance' that follows a subject's name and dates. For example, in the *DNB* Adam Smith appeared simply as 'political economist', the identity under which he had become so toweringly important for the Victorians; in the *ODNB* he is given as 'moral philosopher and political economist', reflecting the way the scholarship of recent decades has restored the eighteenth-century intellectual framework within which *The Wealth of Nations* was conceived. Other alterations in the primary descriptions reflect other kinds of recent development, if not always so happily. In the *DNB*, John Stuart Mill was simply styled 'philosopher', the label most often applied to him during his lifetime; in the *ODNB* he becomes 'philosopher, economist, and advocate of women's rights', which may be more informative, but which may also risk importing one slightly anachronistic term ('economics' and 'economist' did not become established usage until just after his death) as well as one disproportionate characterization—he was a forceful advocate of equality generally, not just in relation to gender. But, by and large, the categories used in the *ODNB*, like the substantive entries themselves, do not seem likely to date as quickly as many of those in the old *DNB*, in part because of the sheer variety of scholarly perspectives that find representation here.

IV

It is surely impossible to know whether, as some reviewers have claimed, this is the last work of reference on this scale that will ever be published in what the jargon of the computer age forces us to call 'hard copy', but it is surely the first to exploit the potential of electronic publication on so vast and imaginative a scale. Quite apart from identifying individuals by name and a variety of ancillary details (date of birth, place of burial, religious affiliation, and so on), the entire text of the *ODNB* is searchable in several different ways, while supplementary windows will yield lists of monarchs, officer-holders, and such like. As with all kinds of electronic catalogue, one occasionally draws a mysterious blank and is left uncertain whether the failing is the software's or one's own; looking up by family name under the helpful group entries produced some particularly baffling defeats, but on the whole even I could outwit the program's occasional obtuseness. So extensive are the possibilities opened up by the online version for accessing and organizing the hoard of information contained in the dictionary that one can easily overlook the fact that it also, almost incidentally, provides access to the complete text of the original *DNB* as well (though this does not seem to be searchable and downloadable in the ways in which the main text is). All this allows for 'amusement' far beyond what even the twinkly Stephen could have anticipated. Here is the report of an afternoon spent in the company of the *ODNB*'s powerful search engine.

Since this is a dictionary of those who have in some sense made a name for themselves, I begin by tapping in 'egotist'. This produces only ten results, which seems a touch on the low side when we remember that we are talking about some 50,000, largely famous, people. Similarly, 'insufferable bore' turns up only once and that in a quotation. Perhaps I need another term to try to flush out some of the common elements in these successful lives, so I try 'careerist'. This throws up thirty-six results, but, quite apart from the indirect or negative form of many of its appearances, nearly all the rest refer to clerics and minor state officials in the early modern period; careerism, you may be pleased (and surprised) to learn, seems to have more or less disappeared from British society after the eighteenth century. Maybe I should try an indisputably modern type: what about 'ruthless businessman'? Even this produces only three results, two of them comparative or indeterminate in application, while the third describes Sir Titus Salt (1803–76, 'textile manufacturer and politician') as 'an outstanding, occasionally ruthless, businessman', where the second adjective is presumably intended to qualify rather than intensify the first.

I don't feel that so far I am getting to the heart of British society; clearly, I need to think of other qualities that may have distinguished the nation's worthies. I try 'religious bigot': this produces four results, two negative ('zealous but no religious bigot...') and two, in entries by different contributors about other subjects, that, remarkably, refer to the same person. The man who would have been James III, 'the Old Pretender' (1688–1766, 'Jacobite claimant to the thrones of England, Scotland, and Ireland'), thus emerges as the one agreed religious bigot in our history (I reflect that this has long been an officially Protestant country). Is it perhaps that our history has been marked by greater disinterestedness or nobility of motive than I am assuming? I tap in 'love of liberty', but this produces only fifteen hits, mostly in quotations. This leads me to try 'a true Englishman', a phrase, it turns out, that is entirely confined to quotations, part of a vocabulary of appraisal no longer current. Then I try 'the good of others'. This throws up six results, in most of which the phrase is used in some indirect or allusive way, though they do include Steven Bilsland (1892–1970, 'banker and Scottish business leader'): 'He was a caring capitalist, who felt responsible for promoting the good of others.' It hadn't occurred to me to search under 'caring capitalist' (can't think why not), so I try that. Alas, only one result: the saintly Bilsland.

Perhaps I need to think a bit harder about the kinds of people who are *writing* the entries and in what terms they would be likely to characterize their forebears, so I try 'distinguished scholar'. Yes, this is more like it— forty-six hits—though most of them are not so distinguished that I had ever heard of them. In that case, what about 'inspiring teacher'? Bingo, ninety-three candidates. Now we're getting close to home, so for some reason it occurs to me to try 'high-handed editor', but no results; ditto for 'autocratic editor' (well, jolly glad to know we haven't had any of those in our national life, at least not among the dead). Even 'brilliant editor' produces only two hits, though these turn out to be grist to my mill because one is to Rachel Beer, *née* Sassoon (1858–1927, 'newspaper proprietor and editor') who was 'not considered a brilliant editor', and the other is to James Thomas Harris (1856?–1931), who is listed—not pleonastically, I hasten to add—as 'journalist and rogue'. In the same innocent spirit I try 'amusing reviewer', which produces no entries at all; the search engine must be temporarily on the blink.

Anyone who has done global electronic searches for frequently used words or phrases in a piece of their own prose will recognize that this procedure is almost bound to be humbling. In one of his periodic newsletters in the months leading up to publication, Harrison noted that the entries for the supplementary volumes that were produced decade by decade across the twentieth century to cover people who had died since the completion of the *DNB* in 1901 tended to be by contributors who had known their subjects personally and who, perhaps as a result, leaned towards piety. Continuing the bracing tone set by Colin Matthew, Harrison declared: 'The familiar supplement phrases—"much loved by all who knew him", "did not suffer fools gladly"—will not now suffice.' Well, it turns out that they suffice more often than you might expect in the *ODNB*. It is true that 'loved by all who knew him' produces only two results (both Scots, as it happens; various explanations suggest themselves), but 'suffer fools gladly' yields a cornucopia of seventy-one hits. This formula is used only in the negative (no one, it seems, is ever distinguished by a positive capacity to suffer fools gladly), so here, perhaps, we are getting nearer to some of those missing egotists, as in the entry for Dame Mary Colvin (1907–88, 'army officer'), described as 'a formidable figure and forceful personality who did not suffer fools gladly'. Ah yes, 'forceful personality', that has the ring of official euphemism about it, let's try that: eighty-one results, a disproportionate number of them to women—has it, I suddenly wonder, been a recognized social code for 'domineering old bat'? But this phrase does at last produce the kind of representative figure one might expect to force his way onto the national stage. 'Even his admirers admitted that he had serious personality defects', we are told of Ernest Abraham Hart (1835–98, 'medical journalist'): 'He had a forceful personality, being ambitious, opinionated, egotistical, self-confident, and inclined to intolerance'—all of which, plainly, sets him apart from the other subjects in this compendium. 'No flowers' had been Stephen's gruff instruction to the first generation of contributors; clearly, standards haven't slipped in that respect.

Since this is still predominantly a compendium about men written by men, the right searches ought to yield some illumination about favoured male self-descriptions. Surprisingly, only seventeen of our national heroes were 'all-round sportsmen', and only two had 'dashing good looks', but 'attractive to women' throws up a fascinating medley of attitudes among its twenty-seven results. Some concentrate on the physical, such as the entry for Edwin Booth (1833–93, 'actor')—'with dark eyes, long dark hair, romantic good looks, and a warm musical voice, Booth was attractive to women'—and some do not, such as that on Marcus Cunliffe (1922–90, 'Americanist'), who is described as 'generous, relaxed, charming, urbane, vivacious, witty, playful, and attractive to women' (such an eight-barrelled eulogy surely risks attracting a bit of envy and resentment from other men). Others excite more sympathy, such as Thomas Jones (1870–1955, 'civil servant and benefactor'), whose agreeable qualities 'made him particularly attractive to women, especially after his wife's death'; one immediately

senses a whole squadron of those female 'forceful personalities' steam-
ing over the horizon. A bracing female perspective peeps through in the
entry on Fanny Kemble (1809–93, 'actress and author'), which refers to her
unhappy marriage to Pierce Butler (a cad's name if ever I heard one): 'He
was clever and handsome—or at least very attractive to women', which
suggests burnt fingers veering towards cynicism on someone's part. Perhaps
most intriguing of all is Sir Edwin Landseer (1802–1873, 'animal painter'),
described as 'especially attractive to women'; initially I had assumed that
'animal' referred to the objects he painted, but now I start to wonder.

Naturally, with all these alpha-males around, things soon get competi-
tive, so even within the space of a couple of letters we find not only that
Landseer was 'especially attractive to women', but that Lloyd George
was 'immensely', Krishna Menon 'devastatingly', and a character in a
G. A. Lawrence novel 'irresistibly' so. At first I had hoped that a scientific
analysis of these posthumous personal ads would enable me to crack one
of the mysteries of the universe, but all I learn is that it may help to be
either quite short or quite tall or somewhere in between, to have either blue
eyes or dark eyes, to be a good talker though also a good listener, to be
witty but sensitive, courteous yet forceful, and, possibly, to be 'luxuriantly
whiskered'.

Perhaps not surprisingly, 'attractive to men' throws up only seven
references, two of them to men (in both cases 'attractive to men and
women alike', so adding to the score for the previous search really), and
one—surprising to me, at least—to Florence Nightingale (1820–1910,
'reformer of Army Medical Services and of nursing organization'). From
that entry I also learn that the Lady with the Lamp was 'a good mimic',
which is not what I recalled from Lytton Strachey, though in the entry
for Strachey (1880–1932, 'biographer and literary reviewer') I learn that
he thought the *DNB* 'one of the most useful works ever written'. From
the same entry, by S. P. Rosenbaum, I also learn that Freud thought more
highly of *Eminent Victorians than* of *Queen Victoria*. That's Sigmund
Freud (1856–1939, 'founder of psychoanalysis'), whose rather surprising
inclusion is presumably due to his having lived the last year of his long life
in London. For some reason, that leads me to check whether it is true that
Thomas Batty (*c*.1832–1903, 'animal trainer and circus proprietor') died in
a lunatic asylum; wonderfully, he did. Batty was apparently the first man to
train an elephant to stand on its head... no, wait, this has got to stop.

A final confession: when I said earlier that I wrote 'some' of this work I
was exaggerating wildly. I now calculate that I wrote approximately 0.025
per cent of it, or even slightly less as one of my entries (on R. G. Colling-
wood) was written jointly with the late Bernard Williams. At the time, I

grumbled as much as everyone else about the labour involved in checking such details as place of burial and mother's maiden name for the subjects for whom I was responsible, tasks that were no doubt even more demanding if one was writing the entries on any of the sixty-three John Smiths. But now, as I leaf through the beautifully produced, clearly laid-out volumes, as I reflect on the incalculable quantity of painstaking, disinterested labour they represent, and as I think of generations to come making use of this vast consolidation of scholarly accuracy for purposes of their own that may be barely imaginable to us now, I find myself experiencing a rare, and wholly unironic, feeling that mixes pride and humility with a dash of wonder. I assume that some premonition of such a feeling must have been what helped persuade so many busy people to write for it in the first place.

In the guidance notes that all contributors were sent, we were exhorted (the Gladstonian prose was presumably Matthew's own) that 'the preparation of the *New DNB*', as it was then being called, 'puts a generation on its mettle. Let that generation show itself liberal, firm, and just.' I recall that, at the time, this elevated register made me feel a little uneasy, but now it is coming to seem entirely fitting, in line with the stature of the undertaking. Of course, the sheer volume of hype surrounding the launch of the *ODNB* is bound to provoke the counter-suggestible to fits of scepticism, but as one settles down to using it on a regular basis, it becomes apparent that the scale and the quality of the achievement cannot be gainsaid, and thus that a generation *has*, in some sense, risen to a daunting challenge. And what cannot be celebrated enough are what might be called, in Nietzschean vein, the project's 'untimely' qualities. Whether or not it proves to be the last work of reference ever to be published on this scale, it most certainly flies in the face of the logic governing contemporary commercial publishing. It is a stupendous benefaction *pro bono publico* on the part of Oxford University Press above all, but also of Oxford University and the British Academy. That it should have been conceived and launched during the sour, bottom-lining years of gutter Toryism, and brought to completion at the very time when a notionally Labour government is bent on subjecting even more of our collective life to 'market principles', is a historical irony that can at least remind us that the political and social processes shaping public life in Britain are still far from uniform.

Similarly, the whole splendid enterprise is a slap in the face to that conception of an academic career which our masters have largely succeeded in imposing on British universities. That so many have been willing to expend so much labour for an impersonal, collaborative cause is profoundly cheering, for you may be sure that contributing to the *ODNB* is the route neither to academic star status for oneself nor to a high Research Assessment

Exercise ranking for one's department. Instead, such work requires and encourages proportion rather than exaggeration, information rather than provocation, accuracy rather than speculation, self-effacement rather than self-promotion. And it will last and be used long after the leading members of this generation have met the one unnegotiable criterion for inclusion in future updatings. In deeply unpropitious times, the *Oxford Dictionary of National Biography* has refreshed and fortified our sense of what can still be meant by the collective endeavour of 'scholarship'.

24

HiEdBiz:
Universities and their Publics

I

We see a higher education sector which meets the needs of the economy in terms of trained people, research and technology transfer. At the same time it needs to enable all suitably qualified individuals to develop their potential both intellectually and personally, and to provide the necessary storehouse of expertise in science and technology, and the arts and humanities which defines our civilisation and culture.

It is hardly surprising that universities in Britain are badly demoralized. Even those statements that are clearly intended to be upbeat affirmations of their importance have a way of making you feel slightly ill. It is not simply the fact that no single institution could successfully achieve all the aims crammed into this unlovely paragraph, taken from the introductory chapter to the government's White Paper, *The Future of Higher Education*, published in Spring 2003. It is also the thought of that room in Whitehall where these collages are assembled. As the findings from the latest survey of focus groups come in, an official cuts out all those things that earned a positive rating and then glues them together in a straight line. When a respectable number of terms have been accumulated in this way, he or she puts a dot at the end and calls it a sentence.

There are two sentences in the paragraph quoted above. The first, which is clear enough though not a thing of beauty, says that the main aim of universities is to turn out people and ideas capable of making money. The second, which is neither clear nor beautiful, says there are a lot of other points that it's traditional to mention in this connection, and that they're

This essay was written late in 2003 when the proposals outlined in the White Paper of that year (*The Future of Higher Education*) were before Parliament; I have not attempted to update it.

all good things too, in their way, and that the official with the glue pot has been having a busy day, and that we've lost track of the subject of the verb in the last line, and that it may be time now for another full stop.

It should be acknowledged that it is not easy to characterize what universities are and what they now do, and so not easy to lay down a 'vision' of what they might do in the future. That is partly because of the intrinsic difficulty of talking about intellectual activity in terms that are both general and useful, partly because the 'higher education sector' embraces a diverse range of institutions each of which is something of a palimpsest of successive social and educational ideals. But it is also and above all because the populist language that tends to dominate so much discussion in contemporary market democracies is not well adapted to justifying public expenditure in other than economic or utilitarian terms, and it is principally as a form of expenditure—and a problematic or resented one at that—that universities now attract political and media attention.

The result is that even, or perhaps especially, within universities, opinion tends to congregate around two almost equally unappealing extremes. On the one hand, there is the mournful idiom of cultural declinism: 'standards' are falling, 'philistinism' is rampant, 'autonomy' has been lost, and even the barbarians are going to the dogs. And on the other, there is the upbeat idiom of brave new worldism: 'challenges' and 'opportunities' abound, 'partnerships with industry' beckon, 'accountability' rules, and we're all 'investing in the future' like billy-oh. As with larger questions of social and cultural change, it can be difficult to escape the magnetic pull of these extremes, difficult to get the measure of the changes that have been taking place without either falling into the absurdity of suggesting that everything would be all right if we could just go back to universities as they were *c.* 1953, or the equal absurdity of proposing that more ruthless cost-cutting and more aggressive marketing could soon have HiEdBizUK PLC showing healthy profits for shareholders.

Attempts have been made, principally among those more sympathetic to the first rather than the second of these extremes, to arrive at a defining statement of the 'idea' of the university, an up-to-date version of John Henry Newman's Victorian classic *The Idea of a University*. But for all their many merits, such ventures are bound to fail in the sense that 'higher education' currently embraces such a diversity of types of institution fulfilling such a variety of functions that they cannot be gathered under the umbrella of a single 'idea', even if one believed in the general value of searching for such Coleridgean essences. Hardly surprisingly, no deathless prose has been written on 'The Idea of the Tertiary Education Sector'. The truth is that the different justifications currently offered for universities, even those ineptly soldered together in the paragraph from the White Paper quoted above, are a series of residues from earlier stages of social and educational development. Over and over again, as Sheldon Rothblatt, one of the foremost historians of British universities, pointed out some years ago, we meet attempts to define an ideal of university education 'by joining principles and values that at bottom have different historical origins and acutely different cultural meanings and purposes'.

This is certainly the case with the numerous ahistorical pronouncements one currently encounters about what defines a 'real' university or about what a 'proper' university education ought to be, and so on. On closer inspection, these pre-emptive definitions usually turn out to rest on a few selectively recalled details about the way some British universities functioned in the 1950s and 1960s, abstracted from the conditions that sustained them. Similarly, in current discussions about university funding, and especially about student support, it is often assumed that the system now undergoing such radical overhaul has been in place time out of mind. In fact, it was only at some point in the decade after 1945 that the state started to provide even half of the income of any British university, and it was only after the report of the Anderson committee in 1960 that a national system of mandatory grants for students was put in place. It is also worth remembering that when the Thatcher government's *Kulturkampf* against universities began in 1981, nearly half of Britain's forty-six degree-granting institutions had not been in existence as universities two decades earlier. From one point of view, the 1980s and 1990s look like the decades during which successive governments attempted to reduce the historic standing of universities and dismantle their traditional funding structure; but, taking another historical perspective, it is the 1960s and 1970s that can be made to appear exceptional, the first and last decades in which Britain tried to sustain a substantial but still rigorously selective, wholly state-funded system of high-quality, undergraduate-centred universities.

II

It is tempting, partly in order just to tease the hapless Charles Clarke, to suggest that no sensible thinking about universities can be done without going back to their medieval origins, but for present purposes the quick tour of the historical horizon need not begin any further back than the second half of the nineteenth century, the Palaeolithic Age of so many British cultural institutions. It was in the mid- and late-Victorian period that two developments took place that were to determine university development in Britain for almost a hundred years. First, the colleges of Oxford and Cambridge, which had long functioned as a cross between finishing schools for the sons of the landed classes and seminaries for the Anglican church, were reformed. The public-school ideal of character formation took hold; 'modern' subjects, such as history, languages, and science, were introduced; a new self-consciousness developed about educating the governing and administrative class of the future; and the sense of the universities' place in the national culture grew. Secondly, in the 1870s and 1880s new universities were established in the great cities that had grown up as a result of industrialization, such as Birmingham, Manchester, Leeds, and Liverpool. Initially, these colleges were the result of local initiatives and aimed at meeting local needs: they were not afraid to teach practical subjects such as 'commerce' alongside the traditional curriculum; many of their students lived at home. A different 'idea' of the university was required to take account of them.

Thus, by the beginning of the twentieth century there were already at least three different kinds of institution among British universities, quite leaving aside the various medical schools, teacher-training colleges, and numerous ecclesiastical, voluntary, and professional institutions. There was the Oxbridge model: residential, tutorial, character forming. There was the Scottish/London model: metropolitan, professorial, meritocratic. And there was the 'civic' model ('Redbrick' was a later twentieth-century coinage): local, practical, aspirational.

At this point the state played hardly any direct role in financing universities; they were either autonomous foundations with their own endowments, or the result of local initiative and funding, or dependent on students' fees (or, usually, some combination of these). Only in 1919 was a body established to distribute the small grant-in-aid that governments had begun to make to some institutions; called the University Grants Committee, this was essentially a device for protecting the autonomy of universities by allowing a small group mostly made up of senior academics to act as an intermediary body to advise the government on the needs of universities and then to distribute such sums as the Treasury should allocate for the purpose. These were not large: in the 1930s the annual recurrent grant was around £2 million; post-war expansion, especially from the late 1950s onwards, saw this rise to £61 million by 1962. As late as 1956 the total allocated to universities via the UGC for capital projects (as opposed to recurrent expenditure) was only £3.8 million; by 1963 this had shot up to £30 million.

Although different national systems of higher education each have their own distinctive characteristics, scholarship and science are inherently international enterprises, and so no one system can be understood wholly in isolation from the others. For most of the nineteenth century, the German universities were the pace-setters; they were hugely influential in the United States, both intellectually and organizationally, and they constituted a source of rivalrous curiosity in France, particularly after the defeat of 1871, but they had considerable impact in Britain, too, not least in standing for an ideal of *wissenschaftlich* 'research' that came to be grafted onto the native traditions of teaching and scholarship. In the first two-thirds of the twentieth century, British universities provided a model frequently emulated elsewhere in the world, partly just for imperial reasons, partly on account of their perceived success in combining social and intellectual activity. But it is clear that for some time now the real powerhouses of the international university world have been in the United States, principally in the great centres of postgraduate and advanced scientific research, and many of the proposals (and some of the policies) of recent years have been aimed at trying to make British universities more closely resemble their American counterparts, or at least some imagined version of them.

But from the early years of the twentieth century a dialectic was already at work that was to become one of the dominant forces in the development of higher education in Britain, a dialectic that was at least partly powered by snobbery: the newer and different types of institution increasingly shed their distinctiveness and more and more conformed to the culturally dominant model. Thus, the civic universities progressively lost their local and practical character: they built more and more residences for students from other parts of the country; the traditional hierarchy of subjects reasserted itself; playing fields came to be regarded as essential to a university education, a historically curious association that still looks quaintly Anglo-Saxon when viewed from Berlin or Paris. And this is a pattern that has since been repeated with other relative newcomers such as, in the 1940s and 1950s, the former local colleges that granted external London degrees, or in the 1960s and 1970s with the Colleges of Advanced Technology, or again in the 1980s and 1990s with the Polytechnics. The pull has always been towards being a national rather than a local institution; towards offering a full spectrum of subjects; towards offering postgraduate as well as undergraduate degrees; towards supporting research as well as teaching; and towards having the autonomy and prestige traditionally associated with (though in recent years fast being lost by) the older universities.

Even so, universities expanded slowly in the first few decades of the twentieth century in Britain; on the eve of the Second World War, fewer than 2 per cent of the population passed through them; they were not, for the most part, objects of media attention; and many of the recently founded civic institutions were very small and somewhat fragile. Since 1945, however, change has been increasingly dramatic. Three main forces have been at work, and not just in Britain, though the process has taken a distinctive form here. The first is the explosion in student numbers; the second is the vast expansion of scientific research; and the third is political ideology.

The statistics showing the growth in numbers are eloquent enough. In 1939 there were about 50,000 students at the 21 universities in Britain (all such figures are disputable; even now matters of definition dog the attempt to produce agreed statistics). Post-war expansion saw this figure more than double to 113,000 by 1961. Thereafter, the rate of expansion accelerated sharply. Many people, including those who hold forth about universities, still think that the new 'plate-glass' universities of the 1960s were set up as the outcome of the famous 'Robbins Report', but simple chronology indicates how far from the truth this is. It was in the late 1950s that the UGC took the decision to found what became the seven 'new' universities, and the first of them, Sussex, opened its doors in 1961; the Robbins Committee did not report until 1963. Two years later, Anthony Crosland, the then Secretary of State for Education, enunciated what became known as 'the binary principle', according to which two different but parallel types of higher education were to be developed: the traditional kind in universities and a more vocationally oriented, community-responsive kind in the polytechnics. By 1980 there were around 300,000 students in some 44 universities, with ever-higher targets being set for each year's intake, but the reclassification of the former polytechnics as universities in 1992 almost doubled the number of those classed as 'university students', and since then relentless financial pressure to take more students has driven the total up to more than 1,750,000 studying at (depending, as always, on one's classification) some 115 universities. These totals mask particularly striking increases in the numbers of post-graduate students and those studying part-time at whatever level; in the last three decades the number of postgraduates has gone from around 60,000 to almost 380,000, while part-time students, rare at university level in the past, now account for over 600,000 of the total. (They also mask the gigantic educational enfranchisement of women that has taken place in the course of the last fifty years to the point where female students are now slightly in the majority.) Almost inevitably, staff–student ratios and unit costs per student have plunged dramatically.

During the same period, universities have been transformed to the point where they are now principally centres of scientific and technological research and, increasingly, of vocational and professional training. In the 1930s, half the students at British universities were in the arts faculties; more strikingly still, at Oxford and Cambridge the proportion studying in arts faculties were 80 per cent and 70 per cent respectively. Now, those studying pure 'humanities' subjects (classification problems again) account for only some 18 per cent of undergraduates and 12 per cent of postgraduates in British universities. But the really significant change concerns expenditure, above all expenditure on research rather than teaching: the huge growth in the costs of 'big science' and the extraordinary expansion of the scope of the biological sciences mean that the science budget has now soared into the billions, dwarfing the amounts spent on the humanities and social sciences. Inevitably, funding systems will be designed to fit the activities involving the most money. Public funding of higher education is now hugely concentrated on supporting science, medicine, and technology, and these departments account for an overwhelmingly large proportion of any individual university's operating budget. It is hardly surprising that so many of the characteristics of the funding system under which universities now operate, from the reliance on winning large grants from commercial and charitable sponsors to the categories of the Research Assessment Exercises, should reflect the economic clout of the sciences.

These first two changes have been cumulative, only partly deliberate, and often barely noticed as they were taking place. But the impact of political ideology, especially when viewed from within universities, has been dramatic, programmatic, and controversial. Up until the late 1970s, universities expanded on the back of what might be called the 'welfare-state model of cultural diffusion'. As with the arts, the traditional form of some cultural good was to be extended to more and more people by means of state support. 'Culture' was seen as an antidote to or refuge from the grubby pressures of economic life, and universities were expected to be beacons of culture. This model had its paternalist side—the mandarins knew what was worth having more of whether people clamoured for it or not—and also its hidden subsidies to the middle class, who were overwhelmingly the chief recipients of the cultural goods that were partly paid for by the large proportion of the population that did not directly benefit from them. But it also had deep roots in British social attitudes, and although the shocks sustained by the British economy in the late 1960s and 1970s entailed various forms of retrenchment in university funding, they left the assumptions governing this model more or less intact.

Thereafter, four dates marked successive stages of a calculated assault by Tory governments on institutions that they perceived as expensive, self-absorbed, arrogant, and liberal. 1981 saw a savage reduction in university funding in a move that appeared almost deliberately to undermine rational planning and damage morale. Across the whole system, the reduction was of the order of 11 per cent, in some places it was much higher—several universities, including one or two of the most highly regarded, suffered sudden funding cuts of around 20 per cent, and the

University of Salford (one of the former Colleges of Advanced Technology so smiled upon in the Harold Wilson/C. P. Snow years) saw its budget cut by over 40 per cent. The second key date was 1986, which saw the first of the Research Assessment Exercises, the brainchild of the then Chairman of the UGC, Sir Peter Swinnerton-Dyer. This was an attempt to measure the quality of the research carried on in different departments; the resulting ranking would determine the amount of the 'research' element in the block grant going to any given university. This was the beginning of the all-devouring audit culture that has since so signally contributed to making universities less efficient places in which to think and teach. The third date was 1988, the year of the 'Great Education Act', which, among other things, changed the legal status of academic tenure and abolished the UGC, putting in its place funding bodies empowered to give direct effect to successive government policies largely by making funds dependent upon compliance in carrying out various reforms or in meeting specific targets. And the fourth was 1992, when legislation was enacted to allow the former polytechnics to become universities, thereby pretty much doubling their number overnight and further depriving them of any status accruing from exclusivity or historic association. By and large, universities offered remarkably little resistance to these changes, bending the knee whenever their funding masters passed by.

Since then, the political pressures have been unrelenting. In recent years, the total sum spent by the government on universities has increased somewhat, usually for strictly earmarked purposes and tied to continuing 'reform', but the direction of change has remained constant. The two most frequently reiterated goals of official policy are now, first, to make universities more responsive to the needs of the economy and more like commercial companies in governance (although in the business world the wisdom of strictly top-down, chief executive models has increasingly been questioned); and second, to expand numbers and achieve a 'truly democratic inclusiveness'. So in the long march that has seen universities function as seminaries, finishing schools, government staff colleges, depositories of culture, nurseries of citizenship, and centres of scientific research, the next step would seem to be to turn them into PLCs.

III

Faced with these developments, it is no good simply saying that universities are autonomous bodies and what goes on inside them is no business of the state's. That idea would have seemed pretty odd at most times and places in the history of universities, whether in Renaissance England or eighteenth-century Germany or, for that matter, contemporary France. It is true that Britain had a long tradition of leaving various functions to be performed by independent, local, and voluntary bodies, which then become suspicious of or resistant to state 'intervention'. But even the colleges of Oxford and Cambridge, prime examples of this style of legally autonomous corporation, were investigated and eventually reformed by successive Royal Commissions in the middle and late nineteenth century; they were forced to make proper use of endowments and to direct the education they offered towards what were seen at the time as national needs (particularly for the training of an administrative class). And wherever the state has become the piper, tunes have been called. The UGC was a cunning device that deferred the full consequences of this logic until the later decades of the twentieth century, but it has long been apparent that universities cannot have it both ways: if they want generous financial support from the government of the day, then they have to accept becoming answerable to that government and its conception of what the electorate will bear.

But universities are a problem for governments, and they are an especial problem for populist governments in market democracies. The only two forms of justification that such governments can assume will be accepted by their electorates are, first, the benefits of 'research', especially the medical, technological, and economic benefits; and, second, manpower planning, the training of future employees in a particular economy. A third function, the preservation, cultivation, and transmission of a cultural tradition, cuts some ice if it is understood to be confined to a small number of outstanding institutions, somewhat analogous to the case for national galleries and museums. A fourth justification, one that has had considerable purchase in the United States and, in a different idiom, in France, concerns socialization in civic values, but that has never played very well in Britain, partly because the implicit nature of the political and social ideals allegedly governing British life have not, to most people, seemed to need explicit formulation and inculcation. That complacent view has been considerably shaken in recent years, and official recognition of the needs of an increasingly heterogeneous population suggests this justification will become more and more prominent in the future.

Of course, as I suggested earlier, these various justifications do not simply differ among themselves; in some forms they can be in active contradiction with each other. Thus, from the nineteenth century onwards, the research ideal has obviously been at odds with that of character formation: the narrowness of focus required by the former precludes the breadth and diversity conducive to the latter. Similarly, the currently fashionable emphasis on enabling people to develop their potential is equally at odds with the no less fashionable emphasis on fostering economic competitiveness: what if the potential that people find they have to develop is to become unsaleably esoteric poets? It is still common to hear it said, notably by those who see themselves as resisting most of the changes that have taken place in British universities in the past couple of decades, that the animating idea of a university is the unfettered pursuit of truth. This is a better one-phrase credo than many, but it doesn't really seem to encompass the professional training and validation of nurses, surveyors, civil engineers, and so on, let alone the eager exploitation of 'technology transfer'.

Throughout their long history, universities have been selective institutions: at different times selective by religious, vocational, or political criteria, nearly always selective in terms of social class, and in the course of the twentieth century increasingly selective by intellectual aptitude. The surface egalitarianism of market democracies is uneasy with claims about the differential capacities of individuals and still more with ideas about intrinsic differences of worth between activities. The ideology of consumer choice is that all wants are in principle equal: the only acceptable indication of value is consumer demand. Anything else smacks of 'elitism', the paternalist attempt by some to dictate to others what they ought to want. The idea that some things are intrinsically more valuable than others and that they can be seriously cultivated only by those with the relevant aptitudes raises hackles.

That is particularly the case when there is any suspicion that the selection in question has been influenced by traditional forms of privilege. To bring out what is at issue here, it is interesting to consider, by contrast, the nearly complete absence of anxieties about 'elitism' where the upper rungs of major sports are concerned. There is widespread acceptance of the principle of utterly ruthless selection by ability, both at the level of sports academies and youth squads, and at the level of top teams competing internationally, as well as acceptance that those who succeed at these levels should have the best facilities and back-up that money can buy, including, in some cases, taxpayers' money. One obvious precondition for this public support is the perception that neither social class nor, increasingly, ethnic origin constitute any kind of barrier to success in these sports. When there have remained misgivings on this score, as with cricket until very recently and perhaps still with Rugby Union, charges of 'elitism' quickly come into play. It is also essential that the sports should have wide popular appeal and be at least in part financed by a paying public, who in turn expect high standards of performance. Individuals from ordinary backgrounds who excel at activities for which there is widespread popular enthusiasm are not automatically suspected of being 'superior'. Universities do not enjoy these advantages.

So, the fundamental conundrum facing those attempting to justify public support for universities is this: much of what goes on in them is, by its very nature, likely to be regarded as both 'useless' and 'elitist'—that is to say, it is hard to justify in terms either of its direct contribution to economic prosperity or of its direct contribution to 'social inclusiveness'. But rather than currying favour by pretending that these are in fact the chief purposes of universities, their defenders might do better openly to acknowledge the non-utilitarian nature of much intellectual enquiry while at the same time drawing attention to the common fallacies and misconceived categories that hamper discussion of the issue. As a start, one might want to insist, first, that intellectual activity can, for the most part, be judged but not measured; second, that although a number of so-called skills may be a by-product of a university education, they are certainly not its defining purpose; and third, universities bear only superficial and largely misleading resemblances to commercial companies. If such measures of mental hygiene were combined with a basic grasp of the history and diversity of higher-education provision in this country, it would at least provide a better starting point for discussion than the present *mélange* of media stereotypes, commercial analogies, and political tendentiousness.

IV

This, however, may be a particularly important moment to try. Parliament is about to debate the proposals set out in the White Paper, and it is already obvious that the legislation that ensues will have far-reaching consequences. This is why the muddled thinking and slack, prefabricated prose of *The Future of Higher Education* are both depressing and alarming. One must, of course, be realistic about the genre to which this document belongs. It is a functional production, doubtless the work of many hands; it is not a philosophical meditation on its subject nor does it aim at literary distinction. Nonetheless, some White Papers have in the past constituted major statements about an area of our common life, and one would expect the phrasing of such an important document to reflect the fact that it has been worked on intensively by some of the best minds among politicians, civil servants, policy advisers, and so on. The alarming thought is that it may indeed reflect that process. In this respect, the whole bullet-point-riddled assemblage is an index of the difficulty that the public language of a contemporary market democracy has with social goods that can neither be quantified nor satisfactorily distributed by means of a market mechanism.

It's hard to know where to start. The issue on which the present government has its knickers most completely in a twist is 'access', and, not surprisingly, there is a whole chapter in the White Paper devoted to 'Fair Access'. Every year a large part of the media coverage of universities concerns this issue, too, with vacuous stories about some school pupil from a working-class background who is rejected by snobby Oxbridge despite getting outstanding A-levels. The general implication of these stories is that, in an otherwise fair and open society, elitist universities continue to favour the offspring of the traditionally privileged.

So, to restore a little sanity to this issue, let's begin with the following, rather striking, fact. In Britain, entrance to a university is almost the only widely desired social good that cannot be straightforwardly bought. Money can buy you a better house than other people; money can buy you better health care; money can even buy you a better school education for your children. In each of these cases it is a simple cash transaction. Our society apparently feels no shame about any of this: advertisements in the national media spell out in the starkest terms the advantages your child will get, including the improved exam results, if you can afford the high school fees. But money cannot directly buy you a better university place for your child, or indeed a place at all (apart from at the private University of Buckingham, whose recruitment pattern confirms that it has not become the institution of choice for most British students). Of course, as in any strongly class-divided society, advantages are self-perpetuating: statistically, children of the wealthy stand a much better chance of going to university than do children of the poor (interestingly, children of the well-educated stand a better chance still). But the facts are the very reverse of the picture painted by silly-season newspaper headlines: money can buy you pretty much everything except love and university entrance.

The whole question of 'access', therefore, needs to start from somewhere else. It is absurd to think that universities can unilaterally correct for the effects of a class-divided society. Of course, the figures showing how much greater are the chances of children of the professional classes going to university than children of manual workers reveal a scandalous situation. But the scandal is not about university admissions; it is about the effect of social class in determining life chances; the corresponding figures about, say, mortality are a much worse scandal.

As with so many other matters in contemporary public debate, serious thinking about class has been displaced by shallow sloganeering about 'elitism'. One of the reasons the admission-season stories can be worked up in the way that they are is because the individual cases can be made to seem to turn on adventitious matters like accent or manners. Anything that smacks of favouring what were the contingent accoutrements of the dominant class in an earlier period are 'outmoded', 'archaic', 'elitist' (the stories are usually accompanied by Bridesheady images of supposed Oxbridge types in dinner jackets and punts). The outrage is that a working-class girl from, say, Essex or Tyneside is being 'excluded' or even 'denied her rights'. Clubby upper-class men are cloning themselves, admitting chaps who 'fit in', and so on.

Now, it goes without saying that the judgements of university admissions tutors are fallible, but, as an account of systematic bias currently at work in the process, this fantasy doesn't stand up to a moment's scrutiny. One wonders whether the journalists who write these stories have ever met any contemporary admissions tutors or considered their, often far from privileged, social backgrounds—or even noticed the fact that a lot of them are not male. And one also has to ask what the academics' motives are supposed to be for selecting less able Hooray Henrys to have to teach for the next three years. For the most part, university teachers have a much more real and informed interest in the intellectual 'potential' of those whom they are to teach than do the mouthy hordes of journalists and politicians over-quick to scent scandal. The majority of these stories are in any case based on the misleading premiss that very good A-level results will guarantee applicants entry to the university of their choice, when in fact top universities could often fill their places many times over with applicants who have such results, so that other factors, including judgements about intellectual autonomy and suitability for the course, legitimately come into play. The willingness of leading members of the government to sound off about the shameful 'elitism' they insist must have informed such judgements shows only how quick they are to attack what they think will be soft targets with populist appeal. This is the other face of 'modernization': we need to sweep away 'privilege' in the form of the trappings of status, but we allow the market to entrench the real differentials of class more deeply than ever.

In these circumstances, it would take an exceptionally clear-headed and brave official document on higher education not to succumb to making cheap shots about 'access', and it will already be clear how far this White Paper is from displaying those qualities. Of course, some of what it says about 'opportunity' and 'potential' and so on is unexceptionable enough, and to its credit it does acknowledge that the story starts much further back, with matters of family background and early schooling. But it never seems to grasp the full significance of this acknowledgement nor to understand how, in consequence, participation rates for different social groups are only marginally affected by variations in universities' admissions practices. This obtuseness is particularly evident when the White Paper observes, almost in passing: 'It is worth noting that students from lower socio-economic groups who do achieve good A-levels are as likely to go on to university as young people from betteroff backgrounds.' The sentence isn't sufficiently precise in its phrasing really to do the work that it promises—do the young people from better-off backgrounds have the *same* results, do they go to the *same* universities?—but it surely makes clear enough that the problem is not to do with university admissions in themselves. Nonetheless, the White Paper pushes on in the only way it knows how: by setting 'benchmarks' for each institution to achieve in recruiting from 'low participation groups', and then setting 'improvement targets for year-on-year progress'. And what if admissions officers find that not enough schoolchildren with 'potential' apply from the right postcodes (or whatever other rough marker of 'disadvantage' is used)? Tough: they'll fail to meet their 'targets', and their institutions' funding will suffer accordingly. It seems possible that the early stages of consultation have led the government to drop or modify the idea of an 'Access Regulator' who would check that individual universities were meeting their access 'contract', and would deny them the right to charge higher fees if they weren't. But the fundamental confusion remains.

A still deeper confusion is at work in the signs of the off-the-cuff manpower planning that informs this document. Its premiss, as we have seen, is that higher education needs 'to enable all suitably qualified individuals to develop their potential'. But how many people is this, and how can we know? You may well think it is impossible to answer that question, and you'd be right. But the government knows. Or at least it knows, apparently, that by 2010 50 per cent of the age cohort in this country will have the potential to develop themselves intellectually and personally in higher education. The absurdity of this marriage of high principle and random guesswork becomes more glaring a few pages later when we are told in successive bullet points that

> our vision is of a sector which:
>
> * offers the opportunity of higher education to all those who have the potential to benefit
> * is expanding towards 50 per cent participation for young people 18–30 years from all social backgrounds.

There is clearly a case for trying to extend the Geneva Convention to outlaw the dumb-dumb bullet point as a particularly inhumane form of intellectual warfare. The obvious fact is that the '50 per cent in higher education' was an opportunist soundbite, a figure chosen for its electoral appeal not as the expression of some deep analysis of the population's intellectual potential, still less of an understanding of the nature of university education. Most of that expansion, entirely reasonably, will not take place in traditional university courses anyway. Much of it will be in directly vocational and employment-directed forms of training, and some may happen within a proposed two-year 'foundation degree'. These are good and necessary things for the state to help to provide, but there is no rational way to determine how many people, short of the entire population, should benefit from them.

A similar incoherence is evident in the chapter ominously entitled 'Teaching and Learning—Delivering Excellence', which speaks of 'all' students having the right to choose the 'best' places. 'All students are entitled to high quality teaching' and to the information that will enable them to choose where to study. Publishing information about teaching quality will, through the operation of consumer choice, 'drive up quality'. Students need this information in order, as the White Paper unashamedly puts it, 'to become intelligent customers of an increasingly diverse provision' (Cardinal Newman, thou shou'dst be living at this hour!). But if teaching in some places is better than in others, then, logically, not 'all' students can have access to it. Ah, but 'student choice will increasingly work to drive up quality', so before long everywhere will be 'best'. Standards will be 'high and continually improved'. What do they think they mean by 'continually improved'? This is advertisers' pap, but teaching isn't soap powder. What kind of 'right' to choose the best place is being exercised when everywhere is, in this performance-indicator sense, 'best'? And should we all simply acquiesce in the blithe assumption about consumer choice 'driving up standards'—as it has done in the case of, say, TV programmes or the railways?

Ironically, the White Paper itself illustrates the logical problem here in its comments on 'measuring student achievement'. It worries about the 'increasing numbers of first and upper-second class degrees' and wants to look at alternative methods of measuring student achievement. But this is exactly the problem inherent in all attempts to combine measurement (rather than judgement) with targets, benchmarks, league tables, and all the other paraphernalia of market simulation. You devise some system that supposedly measures achievement in quantitative terms and you allocate rewards on the basis of these scores; you decree that more of the players (universities, schools, individuals) have to exceed a certain score; then, when they inevitably do so, you cry that the currency has been debased and you have to start again from somewhere else.

But the prize for bare-faced inanity goes, perhaps predictably, to the White Paper's comment on the Research Assessment Exercise that has been carried out every five years since its introduction in 1986. It proclaims that the RAE 'has undoubtedly led to an overall increase in quality over the last 15 years'. Rarely can the Fallacy of the Self-Fulfilling Measurement System have been better illustrated. More departments receive higher ratings now than in 1986 when the system was instituted: ergo, quality has gone up. This corresponds to the period assessed by RAEs: ergo, it is the existence of the RAEs that has 'led to' this 'increase in quality'. In reality, it is hard to see how anyone could *know* whether there had been some general 'increase in quality' in the research and scholarship carried on across all subjects in all British universities during this period. What can be said is that the RAE is a crude form of measurement that is used to distribute funds to universities: its indisputable effect has been to encourage academics to publish more, and more quickly. It is not obvious, let alone indisputable, that this situation has been conducive to any 'increase in quality'.

There are moments, it has to be said, when one starts to wonder whether the officials at the Department for Education and Skills aren't indulging in their own little joke. For example, as part of the policy of encouraging excellence in teaching (can there be a kind of policy that doesn't do this?), a few university departments will be designated 'Centres of Teaching Excellence' and given all kinds of goodies. But then (don't laugh), in order to recognize those departments that come close, but not quite close enough, to this standard, the Higher Education Funding Council 'will also offer a "commended" status'. This will 'make it clear to prospective students that they can expect a particularly high standard of teaching on their course.' We have now entered the world of hotel and restaurant guides: some departments will have signs next to the entrance saying 'HEFCE commended', while prospective students will decide whether they will be content with 'plain regional teaching' (one mortar board), or would prefer 'high-quality teaching in its category' (two mortar boards), or perhaps even stretch to 'exceptional teaching of international quality' (three mortar boards). Suicides among heads of departments who are stripped of one of the coveted mortar boards cannot be ruled out.

One of the most predictable places where pseudo-market guff comes in is the issue of 'rewards' for academics (as if they had just found lost treasure or an escaped criminal). HEFCE has already been on to this, we are told, with its insistence that certain elements of the annual grant are tied to institutions having in place 'human resources strategies' that, above all, 'reward good performance': 'This process has successfully kick-started the modernisation of human resource management in higher education.' 'Modernisation' is, of course, trademark NewLabourSpeak, here combined with the language of the personnel departments of commercial companies. What it essentially means is that, given a number of people doing roughly the same job, a way has to be found to pay some of them less than others. Otherwise, given the assumptions of market democracy, no one will have sufficient reason to try to do their best: they will do this only if they can see that it could earn them more money than their colleagues. 'Modern' here means using the market model. Result: endless procedures involving specious attempts to measure effort or effectiveness that have the net effect of being divisive and demoralizing. On this point it is worth recalling the moral confidence of what one historian has described as 'one of the great state papers of this century', the Robbins Report of 1963: 'We believe any such disparity between the incomes and prospects of persons doing similar work in different universities, which are all in receipt of public funds, to be unjust; and we consider its effects to be harmful.'

How remote that seems from the idiom of management consultancy in which these matters are discussed now. 'Comparing US and UK academic salaries, it is striking that the difference in average salary scales is far smaller than the difference in salaries at the top end for the best researchers. This raises questions about whether our institutions are using salaries to the best possible effect in recruiting and retaining excellent researchers.' Does it? Or does it suggest that Fat Cat Syndrome is not yet as out of hand in British as in some American universities? It is another of the misplaced market assumptions of our time that giving a lot of money to a few individuals at the top of an institution is what best contributes to the overall performance of that institution. In fact, in many activities morale, commitment, cooperation, and a sense of solidarity are far more precious, and they tend to be fostered by a system that uses only modestly differentiated pay scales.

More generally, the language of the White Paper repeatedly reveals that the only terms in which the government believes the electorate can be conned into supporting universities are those of economic gain. The madness that follows from this is most starkly evident in, yet again, the discussion of 'participation rates'. It is worth observing that, as historians of education have constantly demonstrated, all measures of participation in higher education are controversial and depend upon contested definitions; hence the pitfalls in drawing conclusions from what may not be properly comparable data. For example, according to OECD figures, Poland has a 62 per cent net entry rate for first degree or equivalent education, whereas Germany has only 30 per cent, which doubtless accounts for the fabled superiority in economic performance of Poland over Germany... But let's accept for the moment that in Britain the rate has gone up from something like 6–8 per cent of the age cohort at the beginning of the 1960s to something like 43–44 per cent today. The White Paper is keen to disarm possible criticisms of this trend, and so it goes on: 'Despite the rise in numbers participating in higher education, the average salary premium has not declined over time and remains the highest in the OECD. It is not the case that "more means worse".' So that's what Kingsley Amis and the Black Paper critics were really on about: letting in hoi polloi might endanger earnings differentials. The crassness of the thinking here hardly needs comment: it's all right for you to be allowed to go to university—as long as it still leads to your earning more than certain other people.

But notice, too, the picture of society that is implied in this unlovely argument. When only 6 per cent of the age cohort went to universities, they went on to earn on average (let us say) twice what the members of the remaining 94 per cent earned. Now 43 per cent of the age cohort go to university and each of them also earns twice what members of the remaining 57 per cent do. What this actually points to is a marked, though still limited, diffusion of prosperity and a radically changing social and occupational structure. Thus, it is entirely possible, given the social and economic changes of the past fifty years, that the same 43 per cent would be earning twice as much as their less fortunate brethren even if universities didn't exist. Still, there is a glimpse here of one possible criterion this government may be working with to decide at what level to cap 'participation' in higher education: there have to be enough people outside to look down on in order to make the whole business of becoming a graduate worthwhile.

The question of whether these higher salaries are actually the result of their recipients having had a university education also exposes the fatuity of the rhetoric of 'potential' and 'fairness'. Let us, first of all, attend honestly to the facts of who gets a higher education. Overwhelmingly, it is the children of the professional and middle classes, who come from homes which give them cultural and linguistic advantages from an early age, which help them to succeed at school, which develop their educational and career aspirations, and so on. In formal terms, those who go to universities are on the whole those who, largely for these kinds of reason, then get the best results in the school-leaving examination system. Now let's suppose there were no such institutions as universities, and everybody went straight into work at age 18 or 19. Who would be likely to be earning, on average, salaries twice those of their contemporaries? Exactly the same people as do so now. Charging universities with 'elitism' because they are largely powerless to dent this structure of systematic injustice is a particularly telling indication of the extent to which this government has come to endorse a version of the familiar American combination of market individualism plus the rhetoric of 'equal respect' plus the fail-safe of litigation.

In other ways, too, the world as imagined by this White Paper is a world of educational Darwinism. Higher education in this country is locked in mortal combat with its 'competitors' elsewhere; only the 'strongest' departments deserve proper research funding; universities 'compete' for the 'best researchers'; institutions that fail to 'price' their courses appropriately for their 'market' will be eliminated, and so on. The document urges us to wise up to these realities: 'Our competitors are looking to sell higher education overseas, into the markets we have traditionally seen as ours.' This may indeed reflect the practice of some universities, but may there not be a distinction between 'attracting good students from overseas' and 'selling higher education' in those 'markets'? And might that distinction not rest on the difference between deepening international links in a common transnational intellectual enquiry, on the one hand, and making a profit, on the other?

Indeed, in what relevant sense *are* other countries 'our competitors' where intellectual activities are concerned? This bit of market language has become so pervasive that we hardly notice it any more. What chiefly lies behind it is an assumption about who reaps the economic benefits of applied science. But it is not clear that this is any kind of zero-sum game: the benefits brought by the widespread use of any particular form of technology across a wide range of societies far outweigh any notional benefit to the country in which a certain stage or application of the relevant science was first developed. And anyway, applied technology is not the whole or even the greater part of what universities do—at least, not yet. There may be *rivalry* between different national groups of scholars as between individuals, but not in any meaningful sense *competition*. British archaeologists are enriched not impoverished if one of their colleagues from another country unearths a key bit of the jigsaw of an ancient civilization.

But then scholarship of this kind, scholarship in the humanities that may be undertaken by individuals but that relies upon and contributes to cumulative intellectual enquiry that transcends boundaries between nations as well as between generations and that has no direct economic utility, scarcely figures in the White Paper, so preoccupied is it with science seen as a source of technological applications. About a third of the way into the chapter on 'Research Excellence—Building on our Strengths' there is one numbered paragraph that consists only of a single short sentence. Its combination of intellectual flaccidity and lazy off-handedness is at once breathtaking and depressing. In its entirety it reads: '2.10: Some of these points are equally valid for the arts and humanities as for science and technology.'

V

In political terms, the two hottest potatoes among the government's proposals concern fees and their payment by students. The plan is, first, to allow universities to choose whether or not to introduce 'top-up fees', up to a limit presently set at £3,000, over and above the existing system-wide fees. The assumption seems to be that the leading universities, confident that they would still attract the best students, would choose to charge the additional fees, while less-well-placed institutions might opt to 'compete on price' by not doing so. The second element in the proposal is then to 'charge' these fees to the students concerned, though not as upfront payments but as a form of tax levied on their subsequent earnings. These two proposals are presented as part of a single package, but they could in fact be de-coupled. Requiring students to contribute individually to the costs of their university education does not entail the divisive and inadequate notion of 'top-up fees': it could perfectly well be combined with the abolition of 'fees', which are anyway a partly symbolic notation for a contract that is made directly between universities and the government, replacing them with a simple increase in direct funding. Under the proposed 'Graduate Contribution Scheme', which is clearly preferable to the present regime of upfront fees, the state would in time recoup much of this outlay without introducing a financially-distorted 'market' among universities and courses.

According to the proposed scheme, once graduates start to earn beyond a given limit (£15,000 is suggested for the first year of the scheme), a small amount is deducted from their earnings through the tax system up to a point where they are considered to have 'repaid' a contribution to the costs of the education that they were publicly subsidized to undertake at the time. But the justification given for this measure runs together two different principles: that of students paying 'the cost of the course', and that of students paying in some proportion to their later earnings. Although in some cases (for example, medicine) these might point in the same direction, they certainly will not do so in general, and it ought to be clear that the second is a more acceptable basis than the first. Students should not have to pay individually for education: that is a public good whose costs one generation of the community defrays for the next. But in so far as prospective higher earnings are either a motive to undertake higher education or a consequence of it, then there is an argument for saying that students should contribute in proportion to the benefit gained (though the actual proposal is for a flat-rate, not a graduated, tax). But the idea of students paying the 'cost of the course' is one of the places where the whole commercial language of students as customers making price-sensitive purchases is so misleading.

Any calculation of the 'cost' of a university 'course' is pretty notional anyway. So much goes on at a university that is not specific to any particular course that it's next to impossible to work out the real 'costs' spent on each student (as opposed to some arbitrary percentage of existing departmental budgets and so on). And in any event the 'cost of the course' principle has potentially pernicious consequences: no one with a vocation to do so should be deterred from studying medicine because the fees are higher, any more than someone should unenthusiastically enrol for a philosophy degree because it's cheap. Ever since 'Blunkett's botch' in 1998, when the then Secretary of State for Education, in the face of expert advice to the contrary, opted to introduce fees, payable by students in advance, and to phase out maintenance grants, the government has been struggling, and failing, to combine the aims of widening 'access', forcing students to make a higher direct contribution to the costs of their education, and providing universities with adequate yet politically acceptable levels of funding. A suitably long-term form of the 'Graduate Contribution Scheme' would be one of the least damaging ways to achieve these goals; 'top-up fees' one of the most damaging.

Although the White Paper contains some proposals that may be welcomed, it is hard to see the panicky bravado evident in so much of its language ultimately helping to do anything but further demoralize universities in this country. That is not to say that we should be trying to go back to some status quo ante, even if there were any agreement on when, exactly, that was. But it would be a good start to acknowledge that the diverse activities now carried on in institutions called 'universities' may require to be justified in diverse ways. In principle, this should be done in a way that makes clear that 'different' does not mean 'inferior', but in practice cultural attitudes may be too deeply entrenched. Just as a kind of snobbery helped to sink the idea of the polytechnics in the end, so snobbery, and the anxieties snobbery expresses, may be the biggest obstacle to trying once again to differentiate types of institution in terms of their respective functions. It would also help if proper acknowledgement were made of the fact that the social patterns legible in the statistics about who goes to university are largely determined by forces beyond universities' own admissions practices. It may be that the outdated perceptions about universities that fuel public suspicion about admissions will diminish as we approach the point where half the adult population comes to experience higher education at first hand (though that experience may, of course, foster other resentments). In that case, provided that a broadly satisfactory system of funding is put in place (a large and perhaps optimistic assumption), then it seems possible that, while there will no doubt always be individuals who feel they have been unjustly rejected by a university of their choice, there will be less political mileage to be made out of such cases in the name of 'access'.

What is more doubtful is whether any government will have the political courage to declare a university education a social good the costs of which each generation helps to bear for its successors. This would involve acknowledging the limits of justifications couched exclusively in terms of increased economic prosperity. And, perhaps more difficult still, it would involve accepting that there are some kinds of intellectual enquiry that are goods in themselves, that need to be pursued at the highest level, and that will necessarily continue to require a considerable amount of public support. These may now form a relatively minor part of the activities carried on in universities, and it is much easier, using economic and utilitarian arguments, to justify the other activities; but they remain indispensable. Amid the uncertainties currently facing universities, the only certain thing is that these are all problems that will be exacerbated rather than solved by placing them in the lap of a deity called 'the market'.

ACKNOWLEDGEMENTS

As I indicated in the Introduction, earlier versions of the great majority of these essays have already been published in some form. Nine of them appeared in the *Times Literary Supplement* and nine in the *London Review of Books*; three draw on pieces that previously appeared in different guise in *The Nation*, *The Guardian*, and *Modern Law Review* (while three are here published for the first time). I am grateful to all these publications for permission to reuse material.

Any author of periodical essays owes a particular debt to his editors, not just for the initial commission, but also for that peculiar mixture of faith, forbearance, and firmness that the role requires. I feel myself to have been exceptionally lucky in this respect, and I offer heartfelt thanks to the editors of the *London Review of Books*, especially Paul Laity and Mary-Kay Wilmers, and of the *Times Literary Supplement*, especially Alan Jenkins, Ferdinand Mount, and Peter Stothard, for their encouragement, their high standards, and their (mostly) tactful editing.

I also owe thanks to Christopher Wheeler and Matthew Cotton at Oxford University Press for easing the way at every stage; to Russ Hargrave for practical assistance; and above all to those friends who read the typescript—John Burrow, Peter Clarke, Angela Leighton, Ruth Morse, Helen Small, John Thompson, and Donald Winch. In many cases, these friends have now had more than one opportunity to try to improve my thinking and my prose in these essays, and so the burden of blame for the remaining shortcomings is correspondingly heavier.

REFERENCES

~

In the interests of brevity, this list includes only works actually referred to or quoted in the text; it is not intended as a list of 'sources' nor as a guide to further reading on the topics discussed.

Chapter 1

Cyril Connolly, *Enemies of Promise* (Routledge, 1938).
—— *The Unquiet Grave*, by 'Palinurus' (Hamish Hamilton, 1944).
—— *The Condemned Playground: Essays 1927–1944* ([1945], preface by Philip Larkin, Hogarth, 1985).
—— *Evening Colonnade* (Bruce and Watson, 1973).
Jeremy Lewis, *Cyril Connolly: A Life* ([1997], Pimlico, 1998).
Michael Shelden, *Friends of Promise: Cyril Connolly and the World of 'Horizon'* (Hamish Hamilton, 1989).

Chapter 2

V. S. Pritchett, *Mr Beluncle* (Chatto, 1951).
—— *A Cab at the Door: An Autobiography: Early Years* (Chatto, 1968).
—— *Midnight Oil* (Chatto, 1971).
—— *Collected Stories* (Chatto, 1982).
—— *A Man of Letters: Selected Essays* (Chatto, 1985).
—— *The Complete Essays* (Chatto, 1991).

Chapter 3

Aldous Huxley, *Music at Night and Other Essays* (Chatto, 1931).
—— *Brave New World* (Chatto, 1932).
—— *Ends and Means: An Enquiry into the Nature of Ideals and into the Methods Employed for their Realization* (Chatto, 1938).
Sybille Bedford, *Aldous Huxley: A Biography*, 2 vols (Macmillan, 1973–4).
Julian Huxley (ed.), *Aldous Huxley, 1894–1963: A Memorial Volume* (Chatto, 1966).

Chapter 4

Rebecca West, *The Young Rebecca: Writings of Rebecca West 1911–1917*, selected and introduced by Jane Marcus (Macmillan, 1982).
—— *The Strange Necessity: Essays and Reviews* (Cape, 1928).
—— 'What is Mr T. S. Eliot's Authority as a Critic?' *(1932)*, in Bonnie Kime Scott (ed.), *The Gender of Modernism: A Critical Anthology* (Indiana University Press, 1990).
Victoria Glendinning, *Rebecca West: A Life* (Weidenfeld and Nicolson, 1987).
Carl Rollyson, *Rebecca West: A Saga of the Century* (Hodder, 1995).
Harold Orel, *The Literary Achievement of Rebecca West* (Macmillan, 1986).
Frank Swinnerton, *The Georgian Literary Scene* (Heinemann, 1935).
Virginia Woolf, 'Mr Bennett and Mrs Brown' (1924), and 'Modern Fiction' (1925), in *The Essays of Virginia Woolf*, (ed.) Andrew McNeillie, 6 vols (Hogarth Press, 1986–).

Chapter 5

Edmund Wilson, *Axel's Castle: A Study in the Imaginative Literature of 1870–1930* ([1931], Fontana, 1961).
—— *The Triple Thinkers: Twelve Essays on Literary Subjects* (Humphrey Milford, 1938).
—— *To the Finland Station: A Study in the Writing and Acting of History* (Secker & Warburg, 1940).
—— *The Wound and the Bow: Seven Studies in Literature* (Allen and Unwin, 1941).
—— *Classics and Commercials: A Literary Chronicle of the Forties* (Farrar, Straus and Giroux, 1950).
—— *The Shores of Light: A Literary Chronicle of the Twenties and Thirties* (Allen and Unwin, 1952).
—— *Patriotic Gore: Studies in the Literature of the American Civil War* (Deutsch, 1962).
—— *Upstate: Records and Recollections of Upper New York* (Macmillan, 1972).
Lewis M. Dabney (ed.), *Edmund Wilson: Centennial Reflections* (Princeton University Press, 1997).
Janet Groth, *Edmund Wilson: A Critic for our Time* (Ohio University Press, 1989).
Stanley Hyman, *The Armed Vision: A Study in the Methods of Modern Literary Criticism* ([1948], Knopf, 1952).
Russell Jacoby, *The Last Intellectuals: American Culture in the Age of Academe* ([1987], Basic Books, 2000).
Jeffrey Meyers, *Edmund Wilson: A Biography* (Houghton Mifflin, 1995).
Lionel Trilling, *A Gathering of Fugitives* (Secker & Warburg, 1957).

Chapter 6

The Complete Works of George Orwell, (ed.) Peter Davison, 20 vols. (Secker & Warburg, 1986–98).
Bernard Crick, *George Orwell: A Life* (Secker & Warburg, 1980).

John Rodden, *The Politics of Literary Reputation: The Making and Claiming of 'St George' Orwell* (Oxford University Press, 1989).

Peter Davison, *George Orwell: A Literary Life* (Macmillan, 1996).

Jeffrey Meyers, *Orwell: Wintry Conscience of a Generation* (Norton, 2000).

Michael Shelden, *Orwell: The Authorized Biography* (Heinemann, 1991).

Chapter 7

Stephen Spender, *Poems* (Faber, 1933).

—— *World within World: The Autobiography of Stephen Spender* (Hamish Hamilton, 1951).

—— 'The English Intellectuals and the World of Today', *Twentieth Century*, 149 (June 1951).

—— *Journals 1939–1983*, (ed.) John Goldsmith (Faber, 1985).

Stephen Dorril, *MI6: Fifty Years of Special Operations* (Fourth Estate, 2000).

Frank Kermode, *Not Entitled: A Memoir* (HarperCollins, 1996).

F. R. Leavis, 'This Poetical Renascence', *Scrutiny*, 2 (1933).

—— 'Keynes, Spender and Currency Values', *Scrutiny*, 18 (1951).

Frances Stonor Saunders, *Who Paid the Piper? The CIA and the Cultural Cold War* (Granta, 1999).

Chapter 8

William Empson, *Seven Types of Ambiguity* (Chatto, 1930).

—— *Some Versions of Pastoral* (Chatto, 1935).

—— *The Structure of Complex Words* (Chatto, 1951).

—— *Milton's God* (Chatto, 1961).

—— *Argufying: Essays on Literature and Culture*, (ed.) John Haffenden (Hogarth, 1988).

John Haffenden, *William Empson* , i. *Among the Mandarins* (Oxford University Press, 2005).

Roger Sale, *Modern Heroism: Essays on D. H. Lawrence, William Empson, and J. R. R. Tolkein* (California University Press, 1973).

Chapter 9

A. L. Rowse, *Politics and the Younger Generation* (Faber, 1931).

—— *Mr Keynes and the Labour Movement* (Macmillan, 1936).

—— *Tudor Cornwall; Portrait of a Society* (Cape, 1941).

—— *A Cornish Childhood* (Cape, 1942).

—— *The Spirit of English History* (Longman, 1943).

—— *The England of Elizabeth* (Macmillan, 1950).

—— *The Early Churchills, an English Family* (Harper, 1955).

Richard Ollard, *A Man of Contradictions: A Life of A. L. Rowse* (Allen Lane, 1999).

Chapter 10

Arthur Bryant, *King Charles II* (Longman, 1931).

Arthur Bryant, *Unfinished Victory* (Macmillan, 1940).
—— *English Saga (1840–1940)* (Collins, 1940).
—— *The Years of Endurance, 1793–1802* (Collins, 1942).
—— *Years of Victory, 1802–1812* (Collins, 1944).
—— *The Age of Elegance, 1812–1822* (Collins, 1950).
—— *The Story of England: Makers of the Realm* (Collins, 1953).
Peter Mandler, *History and National Life* (Profile, 2002).
Andrew Roberts, *Eminent Churchillians* (Weidenfeld and Nicolson, 1994).
Julia Stapleton, *Political Intellectuals and Public Identities in Britain since 1850* (Manchester University Press, 2001).
Pamela Street, *Arthur Bryant: Portrait of an Historian* (Collins, 1979).

Chapter 11

Herbert Butterfield, *The Whig Interpretation of History* (Bell, 1931).
—— 'History and the Marxian Method', *Scrutiny*, 1 (1932).
—— *The Englishman and his History* (Cambridge University Press, 1944).
—— *The Origins of Modern Science, 1300–1800* (Bell, 1949).
—— *Christianity and History* (Bell, 1949).
—— *Man on his Past: The Study of the History of Historical Scholarship* (Cambridge University Press, 1955).
E. H. Carr, *What is History?* ([1961], Pelican, 1964).

Chapter 12

E. H. Carr, *The Twenty Years' Crisis 1919–1939: An Introduction to the Study of International Relations* (Macmillan, 1939).
Michael Cox (ed.), *E.H. Carr: A Critical Appraisal* (Palgrave, 2000).
Jonathan Haslam, *The Vices of Integrity: E. H. Carr 1892–1982* (Verso, 1999).
Jack Hayward, Brian Barry, and Archie Brown (eds), *The British Study of Politics in the Twentieth Century* (Oxford University Press, 1999).
Derwent May, *Critical Times: The History of the Times Literary Supplement* (HarperCollins, 2001).

Chapter 13

E. P. Thompson, *William Morris: Romantic to Revolutionary* (Lawrence & Wishart, 1955 [2nd edn, 1977]).
—— *The Making of the English Working Class* (Gollancz, 1963).
—— 'A Nice Place to Visit', *New York Review of Books* (1975), reprinted in *Making History: Writings on History and Culture* (New Press, 1994).
—— *Whigs and Hunters: The Origin of the Black Act* (Allen Lane, 1975).
—— *Customs in Common* (Merlin Press, 1991).
Perry Anderson, *Arguments within English Marxism* (New Left Books, 1980).
David Eastwood, 'History, Politics and Reputation: E. P. Thompson Reconsidered', *History*, 85 (2000).

Michael Kenny, 'Edward Palmer (E. P.) Thompson', *Political Quarterly*, 70 (1999).

Bryan Palmer, *E. P. Thompson: Objections and Oppositions* (Verso, 1994).

Renato Rosaldo, 'Celebrating Thompson's Heroes: Social Analysis in History and Anthropology', in Harvey J. Kaye and Keith McClelland (eds), *E. P. Thompson: Critical Perspectives* (Polity, 1990).

Donald Winch, 'Gradgrind and Jerusalem', in Stefan Collini, Richard Whatmore, and Brian Young (eds), *Economy, Polity, and Society: British Intellectual History 1750–1950* (Cambridge University Press, 2000).

Chapter 14

Perry Anderson, *English Questions* (Verso, 1992).

—— *A Zone of Engagement* (Verso, 1992).

—— 'Renewals', *New Left Review*, NS 1 (Jan.–Feb. 2000).

Gregory Elliott, *Perry Anderson: The Merciless Laboratory of History* (University of Minnesota Press, 1998).

Chapter 15

Roger Scruton, *The Meaning of Conservatism* (Macmillan, 1980).

—— *On Hunting* (Yellow Jersey, 1999).

Thomas Carlyle, *Chartism* (Fraser, 1839).

The Salisbury Group, *The Salisbury Review* (1984–).

Chapter 16

Matthew Engel, *Tickle the Public: One Hundred Years of the Popular Press* (Gollancz, 1996).

Hugh Kingsmill, '1932 and the Victorians', *English Review* (1932).

Lytton Strachey, *Eminent Victorians* (Chatto, 1918).

—— *Queen Victoria* (Chatto, 1921).

Denys Thompson, 'Hundred Years of the Higher Journalism', *Scrutiny*, 4 (1935).

G. Kitson Clark, *The Making of Victorian England* (Methuen, 1962).

G. M. Young, *Victorian England: Portrait of an Age* [1936], annotated edition, (ed.) G. Kitson Clark (Oxford University Press, 1977).

Chapter 17

Kate Campbell (ed.), *Journalism, Literature, and Modernity: From Hazlitt to Modernism* (Edinburgh University Press, 2000).

Anthony Curtis, *Lit Ed: On Reviewing and Reviewers* (Carcanet, 1998).

Stephen Glover (ed.), *Secrets of the Press: Journalists on Journalism* (Allen Lane, 1999).

Christopher Hitchens, *Unacknowledged Legislators: Writers in the Public Sphere* (Verso, 2000).

Eric Homberger, 'Ford's *English Review*: Englishness and its Discontents', *Agenda*, 27 (1989).

Jeremy Lewis, *Cyril Connolly: A Life* (Pimlico, 1998).

A. Walton Litz, Louis Menand, and Lawrence Rainey (eds), *The Cambridge History of Literary Criticism*, vii (Cambridge University Press, 2000).

Derwent May, *Critical Times: The History of the Times Literary Supplement* (HarperCollins, 2001).

Frances Stonor Saunders, *Who Paid the Piper? The CIA and the Cultural Cold War* (Granta, 1999).

John Sturrock, *The Word from Paris* (Verso, 1998).

Jeremy Treglown and Bridget Bennett (eds), *Grub Street and the Ivory Tower: Literary Journalism and Literary Scholarship from Fielding to the Internet* (Oxford University Press, 1998).

Chapter 18

Anon., 'An Academy of Letters', *Academy* (Nov.–Dec. 1897).

Joseph McAleer, *Popular Reading and Publishing in Britain 1914–1950* (Oxford University Press, 1992).

John Sutherland, *Longman Companion to Victorian Fiction* (Longman, 1988).

Chapter 19

Richard Altick, *The English Common Reader 1800–1900* ([1957], 2nd edn, Ohio State University Press, 1998).

John Carey, *The Intellectuals and the Masses: Pride and Prejudice Among the Literary Intelligentsia, 1880–1939* (Faber, 1992).

Chapter 20

Bernard Bergonzi, *Exploding English: Criticism, Theory, Culture* (Oxford University Press, 1991).

Morris Dickstein, *Double Agent: The Critic and Society* (Oxford University Press, 1992).

John Guillory, *Cultural Capital: The Problem of Literary Canon Formation* (University of Chicago Press, 1993).

Francis Mulhern, *The Moment of 'Scrutiny'* (New Left Books, 1979).

George Watson, *The Literary Critics: A Study of English Descriptive Criticism* (Chatto, 1962).

Rene Welleck, *History of Modern Criticism 1750–1950*, 8 vols (Yale University Press, 1966–93).

Chapter 21

Kenneth Clark, *The Other Half: A Self Portrait* (Murray, 1977).

Stefan Collini, 'Du financement public de la culture en Grande Bretagne: Sage pluralisme ou tradition de negligence?', *Le Débat*, 70 (1992).

Stuart Hall (ed.), *Culture, Media, Language: Working Papers in Cultural Studies, 1972–9* (Hutchinson, 1980).

Robert Hewison, *Culture and Consensus: England, Art and Politics since 1940* (Methuen, 1995).
Richard Hoggart, *An Imagined Life: Life and Times 1959–1991* (Chatto, 1992).
John Maynard Keynes, 'The Arts Council: Its Policy and Hopes', *Listener*, 34 (July 1945).
Ross McKibbin, *Classes and Cultures: England 1918–1951* (Oxford University Press, 1998).

Chapter 22

Ray Monk, *Ludwig Wittgenstein: The Duty of Genius* (Cape, 1990).
Hermione Lee, *Virginia Woolf* (Chatto, 1996).
Roy Foster, *W. B. Yeats: A Life*, 2 vols (Oxford University Press, 1997–2003).
John Haffenden, *William Empson*, 2 vols (Oxford University Press, 2005–6).
H. L. A. Hart, *The Concept of Law* (Oxford University Press, 1961).
—— *Law, Liberty and Morality* (Oxford University Press, 1963).
—— and Tony Honoré, *Causation in the Law* (Oxford University Press, 1959).
André Malraux, *La Condition humaine* (Gallimard, 1933).
—— *Antimémoires* (Gallimard, 1967).

Chapter 23

John W. Bicknell (ed.), *Selected Letters of Leslie Stephen*, 2 vols (Macmillan, 1996).
F. W. Maitland, *Life and Letters of Leslie Stephen* (Duckworth, 1906).
H. C. G. Matthew, *Leslie Stephen and the Dictionary of National Biography* (Cambridge University Press, 1997).
Leslie Stephen and Sidney Lee (eds), *The Dictionary of National Biography*, 63 vols (Smith, Elder, 1885–1900).
Virginia Woolf, *Three Guineas* (Harcourt, Brace, 1938).
Who's Who 2004 (A.C. Black, 2004).

Chapter 24

John Carswell, *Government and the Universities in Britain: Programme and Performance 1960–1980* (Cambridge University Press, 1985).
Sheldon Rothblatt, *Tradition and Change in English Liberal Education: An Essay in History and Culture* (Faber, 1976).
Universities UK, *Higher Education in Facts and Figures* (HMSO, 2002).

INDEX

~

life writing 238–9
  see also autobiographies; biographies
literary criticism 5, 257–67
  academic 59
  collaborative nature of 266
  Connolly 10
  Empson 102–3, 107–8
  history of 258–9
  preconditions 266
  West 48–51
  Wilson 65
literary journalism 12, 63, 225
literary life *see* writing life
literary periodicals 61, 229–30, 232;
  see also periodicals
Literary Review 228
literature
  classic 251
  emancipating power of 250, 251–2
  New Criticism 262
  status of 244, 245
  teaching of 263
'littérateur' 13
little reviews 233
Litz, Walton A. et al (eds), *The
  Cambridge History of Literary
  Criticism* 257
Living Novel, The (Pritchett) 28
Locke, W.J. 237
London Mercury 223, 228
London Review of Books 157, 166,
  189, 190, 226, 227
London School of Economics
  (LSE) 111
Longmans (publisher) 125
Love in a Valley (Meredith) 254
lowbrow 214, 219, 246
Lowell, Robert 105
Lucas, E.V. 237
Lucky Jim (Amis) 89
Lyall, Alfred 245

McAlpine, Alastair 281
Macaulay, Rose 4
Macaulay, T.B. 120–1, 135, 139, 140, 249
MacCarthy, Desmond 11, 233, 234, 266
McCarthy, Mary 66, 69
Macchiavelli, Niccolo 167
McConnell, Anita 308
McDiarmid, Lucy 265

McEwan, Ian 31
Machado de Assis 31
McGovern, George 68
McIntire, C.T., *Herbert Butterfield:
  Historian as Dissenter* 138,
  143–4
Mackail, J.W. 237, 245
McKibbin, Ross 271, 302
Maclean, Alan 53
Macmillan (publisher) 222, 241, 242,
  246
Macmillan's Magazine 222
McMullen, Catherine (Catherine
  Cookson) 249
MacNeice, Louis 90
Madge, Charles 99, 103
Maitland, F.W. 308
Major, John 281–2
Makers of the Realm (Bryant) 128–9
*Making of the English Working
  Class, The* (Thompson) 176–7,
  179, 183
Making of Victorian England, The
  (Kitson Clark) 212
Malraux: A Life (Todd) 283, 295, 298
Malraux, André 285, 293–8
  Antimémoires 297
  Condition humaine, La 295
  and de Gaulle 294, 296–7
  L'Espoir 295
  and the Resistance 296
Man of Contradictions, A
  (Ollard) 109, 117
man of letters
  historian as 121
  last of 1, 6, 11, 12
  nineteenth century 1, 220
  Pritchett 27–9
  readership 121
  Rowse 111
  USA 29
  West ('woman of letters') 43, 57
  Wilson 58, 61
  Young 214
Man of Letters, A (Pritchett) 27–8
*Man on his Past: The Study of the
  History of Historical Scholarship*
  (Butterfield) 148
Manchester Guardian 223
Mandel, Ernest 188